THE CHREIA
IN ANCIENT RHETORIC

Volume I. The *Progymnasmata*

Society of Biblical Literature

TEXTS AND TRANSLATIONS
GRAECO-ROMAN RELIGION SERIES

edited by
Hans Dieter Betz
Edward N. O'Neil

Texts and Translations 27
Graeco-Roman Religion Series 9

THE CHREIA IN ANCIENT RHETORIC
Volume I. The Progymnasmata

THE CHREIA IN ANCIENT RHETORIC

Volume I. The *Progymnasmata*

by
Ronald F. Hock
and
Edward N. O'Neil

Scholars Press
Atlanta, Georgia

THE CHREIA
IN
ANCIENT RHETORIC

Volume I. The *Progymnasmata*

by
Ronald F. Hock
and
Edward N. O'Neil

© 1986
The Society of Biblical Literature

Library of Congress Cataloging-in-Publication Data
Main entry under title:

The Chreia in ancient rhetoric.

(Graeco-Roman religion series ; 9) (Texts and translations ; 27)
Bibliography: v. 1, p.
Includes index.
Contents: v. 1. The progymnasmata.
1. Chreiai. 2. Chreiai—Translations into English. 3. Classical literaure—Translations into English. 4. English literture—Translations from classical languages. 5. Classical wit and humor. 6. Rhetoric, Ancient. I. Hock, Ronald F., 1944— II. O'Neil, Edward N. III. Series. IV. Series: Texts and translations ; no. 27.
PA3469.C48C5 1985   888'.002'08   85-142002
ISBN 0—89130—846—6 (v. 1 : alk. paper)
ISBN 0—89130—847—4 (pbk. v. 1 : alk. paper)

Printed in the United States of America
on acid-free paper

CONTENTS

CONTRIBUTORS

EDWARD N. O'NEIL, Professor of Classics, University of Southern California. Director of Chreia Project at the Institute for Antiquity and Christianity, Claremont. Co-editor of Volume I.

RONALD F. HOCK, Associate Professor of Religion, University of Southern California. Co-editor of Volume I.

BURTON L. MACK, Professor of Religion, School of Theology at Claremont, Institute for Antiquity and Christianity.

LESTER L. GRABBE, Lecturer in Old Testament, University of Hull (England).

JAMES R. BUTTS, Assistant Professor, Department of Religious Studies, Le Moyne College.

PREFACE

᾿Ισοκράτης τῆς παιδείας τὴν ῥίζαν
πικρὰν ἔφη γλυκεῖς δὲ τοὺς καρπούς.

Isocrates said that education's root
is bitter, its fruit sweet.

Chreia 43

This project has indeed been an education for the members of the "Hellenistic Texts Seminar," the successor to the Corpus Hellenisticum at the Institute for Antiquity and Christianity. It took root, however, in an entirely different field from the one in which it has grown.

Our study of the chreia began in the spring of 1979 while we were reading various compositions by and about Cynics. As we read, we kept encountering the little vignettes called chreiai, and we soon realized that we did not know enough about this form to understand its role in the compositions.

A look at the secondary literature failed to satisfy our curiosity or to inform us sufficiently. We found that many people had discussed the chreia, but very few had ever taken the trouble to read the texts of the rhetoricians who had formulated the rules. Many of the discussions which we found were shallow, mis-informed and contradictory.

Disappointed with the secondary material, the group put aside the Cynics and turned to the Greek rhetoricians them-selves: Theon, Hermogenes, Aphthonius, Nicolaus, Doxapatres, Libanius and others. Here, too, we found problems. We soon realized that little work had been done on these texts in the last hundred years or so, that in particular no satisfactory translation existed for any of the authors, much less any real commentary. Furthermore, the books themselves are scarce, and only people who have access to a large library can find copies of all the texts.

As a result of these conditions we formed a plan. We would collect all the discussions of the chreia, make a translation and provide the Greek or Latin text to accompany it. Then we would add a few notes and comments to assist in understanding the passages. Even in the initial stages of our work, it became apparent that we were dealing with more material than a single volume could hold. Further analysis showed that the selections fall into three natural groups and that each group is large enough to fill at least one volume.

Consequently, the present volume contains only the selections of rhetoricians whose primary purpose is to define and classify the chreia. Most of these passages stand as chapters in *Progymnasmata*, and we have simply lifted them out of their context. The second volume will have the selections which demonstrate how one should manipulate the chreia. Two basic exercises appear here: the ἐργασία and the κλίσις. The third volume will contain the various scholia and commentaries on the passages which appear in the first volume.

This, then, is the basic pattern of the three volumes, but we have added other features designed to provide additional information wherever we consider them necessary and useful to others.

A word about the division of responsibility in the volume. Although each chapter is attributed to one or two individuals, the project has been a team effort. In the early stages, every chapter profited from the careful criticism of the whole group, and in that process many problems were solved. In the final stages, the co-editors have reworked all the material, revising wherever the need arose. For any shortcomings that remain they alone are responsible.

As always, of course, the evenings which we have spent in the Boardroom of the Institute have been enjoyable and rewarding. For such pleasant surroundings we express our gratitude to all the members of the Institute and in particular to Professor James M. Robinson, its Director. Without his friendly counsel our labors might never have borne fruit.

Lastly, but most importantly, all the contributors to this volume—and especially the co-editors—here pay homage to their long-suffering wives who have spent many lonely hours while their husbands labored in fellowship to produce this volume. So, to B. J., Charlotte, Carol, Elizabeth and Jane, thanks. Take heart! Only two more volumes to go — on this project!

ABBREVIATIONS

ARW	*Archiv für Religionswissenschaft*
BAGD	W. Bauer, W. F. Arndt, F. W. Gingrich, and F. Danker (eds.), *A Greek-English Lexicon of the New Testament and Other Early Christian Literature.* Chicago: University of Chicago, 1979.
BICS	*Bulletin of the Institute of Classical Studies*
BJRL	*Bulletin of the John Rylands Library*
Bonner, *Education in Ancient Rome*	S. F. Bonner, *Education in Ancient Rome from the elder Cato to the younger Pliny.* Berkeley: University of California, 1977.
BZ	*Byzantinische Zeitschrift*
CAH	*Cambridge Ancient History*
Christ-Schmid-Stählin, *Geschichte der griechischen Literatur*	W. v. Christ-W. Schmid-O. Stählin, *Geschichte der griechischen Literatur* (Handbuch der Altertumswissenschaft; Vol. 2, part 1; 6th ed.; Munich: Beck, 1924)
CJ	*Classical Journal*
CPh	*Classical Philology*
CR	*Classical Review*
CSM	*Colonial Society of Massachusetts*
G & R	*Greece & Rome*
GRBS	*Greek, Roman and Byzantine Studies*
Hunger, *Die hochsprachliche profane Literatur*	Hunger, *Die hochsprachliche profane Literatur der Byzantiner* (Handbuch der Altertumswissenschaft; 2 vols.; Munich: Beck, 1978)
JHS	*Journal of Hellenic Studies*
Kennedy, *Art of Rhetoric*	G. Kennedy, *The Art of Rhetoric in the Roman World.* Princeton: Princeton University, 1972

Kennedy, *Greek Rhetoric*

G. Kennedy, *Greek Rhetoric under Christian Emperors.* Princeton: Princeton University, 1983

Kennedy, *Rhetoric ... from Ancient to Modern Times*

G. Kennedy, *Classical Rhetoric and Its Christian and Secular Tradition from Ancient to Modern Times.* Chapel Hill: University of North Carolina, 1980

Kustas, *Studies in Byzantine Rhetoric*

G. Kustas, *Studies in Byzantine Rhetoric* (Analecta Vlatadon 17; Thessaloniki: Patriarchal Institute for Patristic Studies, 1973)

LSJ

H. G. Liddell, R. Scott, and H. S. Jones, *A Greek-English Lexicon.* Oxford: Clarendon, 1968 (with Supplement by E. A. Barber *et al.*)

Pack[2]

R. A. Pack, *The Greek and Latin Literary Texts from Greco-Roman Egypt.* 2nd ed.; Ann Arbor: University of Michigan, 1965

PhW

Philologische Wochenschrift

QJS

Quarterly Journal of Speech

RE

A. Pauly and G. Wissowa *et al., Paulys Realencyclopädie der classischen Altertumswissenschaft.* Stuttgart, 1884–

Reichel, *Quaestiones Progymnasmaticae*

G. Reichel, *Quaestiones Progymnasmaticae.* Diss. Leipzig, 1909

RhM

Rheinisches Museum

Schanz-Hosius-Krüger, *Geschichte der römischen Literatur*

M. Schanz, C. Hosius and G. Krüger, *Geschichte der römischen Literatur bis zum Gesetzgebungswerk des Kaisers Justinian.* (Handbuch der klassischen Altertumswissenschaft; Vol. 4, pt. 2; Munich: Beck, 1920)

SM

Speech Monographs

SO

Symbolae Osloensis

TAPA

Transactions of the American Philological Association

Viator

Viator, Medieval and Renaissance Studies

ZPE   *Zeitschrift für Papyrologie und Epigraphik*

GENERAL INTRODUCTION
TO VOLUME I

by

RONALD F. HOCK

I

The chreia (Greek: χρεία, Latin: *chria*) existed as a literary form[1] long before it became a subject for rhetorical analysis and instruction in those beginners' textbooks on composition, or *Progymnasmata*, whose chapters on the chreia form the principal texts collected in this volume. Consequently, before discussing this rhetorical treatment of the chreia it is necessary to look briefly at the chreia as a phenomenon in its own right. We will look at the origin and popularity of the chreia and then at the ways the chreia was transmitted and preserved. Throughout this discussion we will quote numerous chreiai, not only to illustrate the various aspects of the phenomenon but also to familiarize ourselves with the form.

Origin and Popularity of the Chreia. At one time scholars looked to the Cynics, and specifically to the disciple of Crates, Metrocles, as the originator of the chreia, or at least of books that were collections of chreiai.[2] Others have rightly rejected this view, since the data point back at least a century to the Socratic circle.[3] For example, Plato includes a chreia attributed to Sophocles,[4] and Diogenes Laertius credits Aristippus with having written whole books of chreiai.[5]

But while we can no longer be so certain about the origin of the chreia, there can be no doubt of its popularity, which began almost immediately and continued down to the end of antiquity and beyond. The chreia was always especially popular with philosophers, who used this form to capture and preserve the characteristic teaching and behavior of their most worthy representatives. And among philosophers pride of place belongs to the Cynic Diogenes of Sinope. In Diogenes Laertius' day, probably the early third century A.D., the chreiai attributed to Diogenes were beyond cataloguing,[6] and even today the extant chreiai may number, according to one estimate, perhaps a thousand.[7] Indeed, what people today most typically know about Diogenes is preserved in a chreia:

> Diogenes lit his lamp in broad daylight and went
> about, saying: "I am looking for (an honest) man."[8]

Diogenes, or Cynics generally, were, however, not the only
ones to be immortalized by chreiai. In fact, Diogenes Laertius
recites chreiai attributed to philosophers across the philosophical spectrum—Ionians and Italians, pre-Socratics and
later philosophers, major figures and, on occasion, minor ones.

Moreover, a sampling of these chreiai will serve to indicate
some of the specific uses philosophers made of the chreia
and to introduce us to the form. Thus, for example, chreiai
are sometimes based on an incident in a philosopher's life:

> Bias was once sailing with impious men. When the
> ship was caught in a storm and those men were
> calling on the gods, he said: "Hush, lest they
> realize that you are sailing in this ship!"[9]

> Diogenes, on once seeing a boy drinking with his
> hands, threw away the cup from his begging-
> bag and said: "A boy has vanquished me in living
> simply."[10]

At other times chreiai depict philosophers in typical
situations, such as chiding students, attacking vices, responding to critics, debating with one another, and reflecting
on the philosophical life.

> Zeno, on seeing a student's young slave bruised
> from a severe beating, said to his student: "I
> see the traces of your anger."[11]

> Anacharsis said that the market-place is a place
> for men to deceive and cheat one another.[12]

> Aristippus, on being censured for living
> extravagantly, said: "If this were bad, it would
> not take place during the festivals of the
> gods."[13]

> When Plato defined man as a two-footed, featherless creature and was highly esteemed, Diogenes plucked a rooster, carried it into the school, and said: "This is Plato's man!"[14]

> Diogenes, on being asked what he had gained from philosophy, said: "If nothing else, then at least I have prepared myself for every eventuality."[15]

In general, however, chreiai celebrate a philosopher's wit, or at least his quick-wittedness. Diogenes, for example, was known as never being at a loss for an apt statement in any situation.[16] Diogenes' skill at repartee may have been exceptional but still one that he shared with many other philosophers.[17] Two examples will suffice:

> Diogenes, on being asked why people give to beggars but not to philosophers, said: "Because they suppose they might become lame and blind but they never suppose they might take up philosophy."[18]

> Antisthenes, when someone over wine said, "Sing!" responded: "And you, you play the flute for me."[19]

Chreiai were popular among more people than simply philosophers. For example, other kinds of intellectuals, such as sophists and literary figures, have chreiai attributed to them. Again, a few examples:

> Isocrates used to say: "Teachers ought to receive large fees from their students —from the gifted because they learn much and from the dull because they are much trouble."[20]

> Polemo (the sophist), on seeing a gladiator sweating profusely and dreading the fight for his life, said: "You agonize, as if you were about to declaim."[21]

Menander, on being asked what distinguishes
Sophocles and Euripides from one another, said:
"Sophocles causes men to enjoy themselves, but
Euripides makes his audience sullen."[22]

Aesop, on being asked by someone how a great
upheaval could occur among men, said: "If those
who have died should arise and demand back what
belonged to them."[23]

While philosophers and intellectuals generally understandably dominate the chreia tradition, they certainly do
not monopolize it. Chreiai are attributed to a wide variety
of people, including kings (especially Alexander the Great),
generals, courtesans, and parasites, as these chreiai
illustrate:

Alexander, on being asked what kind of king
seemed to be the best, said: "The one who keeps
his friends with gifts and who makes friends of
his enemies through benefactions."[24]

Epameinondas (the general) used to say that
death in war is the most honorable.[25]

Gnathaena (the courtesan), when some youths
while drinking had come to blows over her, said
to the one who had been worsted: "Cheer up,
boy! The prize involved in this contest is not
a wreath, but money."[26]

Bithys, the parasite of King Lysimachus, when
Lysimachus threw a wooden scorpion in his cloak,
was terrified and jumped up. Then, on realizing
what had happened, he said: "I, too, will scare
you, King. Give me a talent!"[27]

The popularity of the chreia, finally, is shown not only by the variety of persons to whom chreiai are attributed, but also by the numbers of people who knew chreiai and by the numbers of chreiai that are used by various authors. Thus Dio Chrysostom remarks that everybody could recite chreiai about Diogenes,[28] and thousands of chreiai can be found in the writings of, say, Plutarch, Quintilian, Aulus Gellius, Lucian, Diogenes Laertius, Aelian, Philostratus, and Stobaeus. This is not to say that chreiai are ubiquitous in ancient literature; they are rare in Epictetus and Dio Chrysostom and even missing altogether in others, such as Pausanias. Still, there can be no doubt that throughout the period under consideration the chreia was a widely known and important literary form.

Transmission and Preservation of the Chreia. The fact that Diogenes Laertius, as we noted above, could not catalogue all the chreiai attributed to Diogenes, even though Diogenes had lived many centuries earlier, raises the question of how chreiai were transmitted and preserved. Doubtlessly, transmission was frequently oral, but preservation, over centuries, ultimately depended on chreiai being written down. Consequently, our discussion focuses on the written transmission of chreiai.

Two examples of oral transmission will suffice. On the one hand, Diogenes Laertius reports that the hedonist Arcesilaus, when rebuked for living openly with two courtesans, responded to his critics by reciting chreiai of Aristippus;[29] surely one of them was the following:

Aristippus the Cyrenaic, on being reproached because he was often in the company of the Corinthian courtesan Lais, said: "I keep her, not she me."[30]

On the other hand, Plutarch refers to the sayings of virtuous women, which Eurydice as a young woman regularly received while staying in his household.[31]

Plutarch is also helpful in tracking down the conventions of putting chreiai down in writing, at least on an informal basis. He refers to his own practice[32] and to that of others[33] of making personal collections of chreiai. Seneca, although he condemns the practice, nevertheless is another witness to it.[34]

But these personal collections are already largely a literary activity, the chreiai being gathered from various literary sources. Thus, the prior question is: where did a Plutarch or a Seneca look when making their collections? Neither one is specific at this point, but Menander of Laodicea, a rhetorician writing in the fourth century A.D., recommends Βίοι ("Lives")—and Plutarch's *Lives* at that![35] That *Lives*, and not just Plutarch's, were a fruitful source for those seeking chreiai is confirmed by Diogenes Laertius and Athenaeus, two writers who make extensive use of chreiai. They frequently cite various *Lives* as the source of their chreiai.[36]

But a perusal of their writings also shows that other genres frequently served as sources for chreiai—for example, Διαδοχαί ("Successions")[37] and Ἀπομνημονεύματα ("Reminiscences").[38] Deserving special attention, however, are the published collections of chreiai, called *Chreiai*. Diogenes Laertius quotes most frequently from the collection of Hecato. This collection provided Diogenes Laertius with chreiai attributed to Antisthenes, Diogenes, Metrocles, Zeno, and Cleanthes.[39] Moreover, Diogenes Laertius cites at least once from the similar collections of Metrocles, Zeno, and perhaps Ariston.[40] Finally, Diogenes Laertius seems to know of still other published chreiai, though presumably only indirectly, such as from lists of writings that he had of various philosophers. At any rate, the *Chreiai* in this category include those of Aristippus, Demetrius of Phalerum, Diogenes, Persaeus, and Cleanthes.[41] And to this considerable list of

Chreiai we can also add the use Athenaeus made of the *Chreiai* of Machon[42] and the use Stobaeus made of the similar collections by Dio Chrysostom[43] and Aristotle.[44]

Such, then, is the broader historical context of the chreia. The chreia, originating probably in the Socratic circle, was an exceedingly popular form for expressing the wit and wisdom of philosophers and, to a lesser extent, of sophists, kings, generals, and courtesans. Oral transmission was one way that chreiai survived the centuries, but preservation was more assured if chreiai were written down, either in informal personal collections for later use or in formal compositions like "Lives," "Reminiscences," and *Chreiai*. What remains is to consider the chreia in the more narrow historical context of ancient education.

II

A papyrus scrap from Oxyrhynchus introduces us to the chreia in an educational context. The papyrus, insofar as the preserved portions permit us to say, seems to have been a schoolboy's rhetorical catechism, containing various questions and answers about the chreia.[45] The questions begin, appropriately enough, with "What is a chreia?" The answer to this question—that the chreia is a concise and praiseworthy reminiscence about some character—is then clarified by further questions, such as why the word "reminiscence" is used, why the attribution to some "character" is essential, and why the form is called by the name "chreia." The answers to these questions will be given in due course, but for now the significance of this papyrus lies in a more general observation. The questions and answers of this papyrus merely summarize and simplify discussions of the chreia that are found in the *Progymnasmata*.[46]

In other words, if we want to learn more about the chreia than did this schoolboy, we need to look where this papyrus points. We need to familiarize ourselves with the *Progymnasmata* and especially with what they have to say about the chreia. Accordingly, after some introductory remarks

about the *Progymnasmata*—their origins and history, their
contents and function—we will investigate more closely their
discussions of the chreia.

Origins and History of the Progymnasmata. As was the
case with the chreia itself, the origins of the textbooks
that came to be called *Progymnasmata* are obscure.[47] The
earliest surviving textbook is that of Aelius Theon of
Alexandria, who most likely wrote sometime between the middle
of the first century A.D. and the beginning of the second.[48]
But Theon was not the first to write such a textbook, as
is clear from his own statements[49] and as is confirmed by
the remarks of his contemporary, the orator Quintilian. The
latter's survey of the early stages of rhetorical education
not only refers to specific exercises contained in these
textbooks[50] but also reveals that practices in teaching some
of them varied between the Greek East and Rome.[51] Quintilian
thus shows that these textbooks were already a standard
part of the educational curriculum of the early Empire.

Fewer and less precise statements from Suetonius push
these textbooks back to the first century B.C.,[52] an era
we would know more about if Cicero had not refused to speak
about the preliminary stages of rhetorical education.[53] Still,
there are hints in Cicero's writings, although the clearest
evidence of this period is in the anonymous *Rhetorica ad
Herennium*, which contains an elaboration of a maxim.[54] But
then the evidence ends, except for the ambiguous and
perhaps questionable occurrence of the word προγύμνασμα in
the much earlier *Rhetorica ad Alexandrum.*[55] Thus, a late
Hellenistic dating seems a likely, if vague, period for the
origins of these textbooks.[56]

How closely Theon's textbook follows his predecessors'
in form and content is hard to say,[57] but we should not
imagine the first examples to be as complex and self-
conscious as Theon's textbook, especially if they arose, as
seems plausible, out of lectures for students.[58]

We need to use less imagination, however, with the
subsequent history of these textbooks, although the

evidence is always frustratingly incomplete. Thus one Byzantine writer claims that many rhetors wrote these textbooks,[59] but only four (including Theon's) survive. Still, other data, such as notices in the *Suda* and quotations in later writers, tend to support this claim.

At any rate, the second century witnessed the publication of at least three more of these textbooks: two from the middle third of the century by Paulus of Tyre[60] and by Minucianus of Athens[61] and one from the last third of the century by Hermogenes of Tarsus.[62] Only Hermogenes' textbook has survived.[63]

The fourth century, however, represents the flowering of this genre. Three examples survive merely as titles in the *Suda:* those by epiphanius of Petra,[64] Onasimus of Cypris (or Sparta),[65] and Ulpian of Emessa.[66] But a fragment from the textbook of Sirikius of Neapolis survives,[67] as do numerous and lengthy fragments from that of the mid-century Sopater.[68] And surviving intact is the late fourth century textbook of Aphthonius of Antioch.[69]

Rounding out this review of rhetors who wrote these textbooks are two from the fifth century: Syrianus, who refers twice to his while commenting on the rhetorical writings of Hermogenes,[70] and Nicolaus of Myra, whose textbook has survived largely intact.[71]

One reason why so few of these textbooks survived—and the preceding review makes no claims to completeness[72]—is that Aphthonius' eventually became the unrivalled standard, achieving, as it were, virtual canonical status among Byzantine rhetoricians. But the story of Aphthonius' supremacy—how it was assured in the late fifth or early sixth century when this textbook was included in the *Corpus Hermogenianum*, the standard rhetorical books of Byzantine education; how it was extended to the Latin West during the fourteenth or fifteenth century; and how it lasted well into the seventeenth century, both in Europe and even in the American colonies—this story is best reserved until later.[73]

For now it is sufficient to draw attention to two lesser

aspects of the history of these textbooks. The first concerns their title. Scholars are in the habit of calling these textbooks *Progymnasmata*, thereby simply following the practice of the *Suda* and the reading of most MSS of the textbooks. Nevertheless, a closer inspection of the texts themselves reveals a more complex phenomenon than hitherto suspected.[74] The title *Progymnasmata*, as we will see, did not become standard until the time of Aphthonius at the end of the fourth century.

To be sure, Theon himself already uses the word προγύμνασμα, although only once and then not in a technical sense. He uses the word only to avoid confusing the encomium, one of the exercises in his textbook, with the encomiastic speech. When compared with such a speech, the encomium is indeed, he acknowledges, a preliminary exercise, a *progymnasma*.[75]

But when referring to his textbook exercises without any such comparison in mind, Theon does not use this term. For example, he refers to the chreia as an exercise, a γυμνασία[76] and similarly when speaking of the other exercises in his textbook, although he prefers γύμνασμα to γυμνασία twelve out of fifteen times. Thus Theon speaks generally of "the sequence of the exercises (γυμνάσματα)"[77] or specifically of, say, "the exercise (γύμνασμα) of comparison."[78] Clearly, for Theon γύμνασμα (or γυμνασία) is the technical term.

The same situation is reflected a century or so later when we can check the usage of Hermogenes. When referring to the exercises in his textbook on four occasions, he uses γύμνασμα each time.[79]

The evidence for the years between Hermogenes and Aphthonius is sparse. Still, one fragment of Sopater contains προγύμνασμα.[80] But Sopater is only a younger contemporary of Aphthonius, and hence his usage says little about when the shift from γύμνασμα to προγύμνασμα began, only that Aphthonius is not alone responsible for it. In any case, Aphthonius frequently and unambiguously uses προγύμνασμα as a technical term for the exercises in his textbook. For example, when speaking of the exercise "refutation" (ἀνασκευή) he says: "This preliminary exercise (προγύμνασμα) imparts by itself every strength of the orator's art."[81] Elsewhere he refers to all the exercises as προγυμνάσματα.[82]

In the fifth century Nicolaus continues this usage;[83] thus by the beginning of the sixth when Priscian translates Hermogenes' textbook into Latin he not surprisingly renders γύμνασμα by *praeexercitamina*.[84] Accordingly, it is understandable why in the succeeding centuries the *Suda* and copyists give all these textbooks—even Theon's and Hermogenes'—the title *Progymnasmata*.[85]

And yet, even at this late date the use of the word προγύμνασμα, while clearly dominant, is not universal. Commentators on Aphthonius still alternate between γύμνασμα and προγύμνασμα when referring to an exercise,[86] and a few MSS of Aphthonius' textbook have Γυμνάσματα as the title.[87] Indeed, his commentators repeatedly say that Προγύμνασματα, not Γυμνάσματα, is the proper title of the textbook.[88] In one sense these commentators are merely carrying out their responsibility to discuss any book in terms of "the rationale for the title,"[89] but their preference for Προγυμνάσματα over Γυμνάσματα may also reflect a fluidity of tradition regarding the title.

Therefore, while the traditional title of *Progymnasmata* for the textbooks of Theon and his followers has ancient sanction, a perusal of the evidence shows that this sanction is neither as ancient nor as unanimous as scholars suggest. In fact, the use of the title *Progymnasmata* for the textbooks of Theon and Hermogenes at least seems clearly anachronistic. Perhaps, these textbooks were known simply as *Gymnasmata*, as seems to be the case with Doxapatres' copy of Hermogenes' textbook.[90] In any case, *Progymnasmata* is probably not fully appropriate as a title until the time of Aphthonius when the exercises themselves begin to be called *progymnasmata*.

The reason for this change in terminology, seemingly so slight, may stem from a change, or at least a narrowing, of function for these textbooks. And although we will discuss the function of the *Progymnasmata* more fully below, it is necessary to anticipate that discussion here in order to conclude the discussion of the title.

The change is evident already in the quotation, made above, of Aphthonius in which the word προγύμνασμα occurs. The exercise of refutation, we recall, is a *preliminary* exercise in the sense that it imparts every strength of the orator's art.[91] This reference to oratory is significant. For while Theon regarded the exercises of his textbook as helpful to a variety of professions,[92] Aphthonius mentions only rhetoric. Indeed, in the fifth century Nicolaus conceives the purpose of his textbook just as narrowly, but more explicitly; his exercises are *progymnasmata* because they prepare youths to write speeches: "Some exercises train us with a view to the judicial speech, others to the advisory speech, and others to the third, or panegyric, speech. In addition, some exercises teach the function of the introduction, others that of the statement of the facts, others that of the arguments . . . , and others that of the epilogue."[93]

By the end of the fifth or beginning of the sixth century the textbook of Aphthonius is used to introduce the advanced rhetorical writings of Hermogenes, so that by the tenth century the *Suda* describes Aphthonius, understandably if also anachronistically, as having written his *Progymnasmata* for the rhetorical writings of Hermogenes.[94] And in the eleventh century Doxapatres explains the title *Progymnasmata* with this strictly rhetorical function in mind:

> [Aphthonius' textbook] is entitled *Progymnasmata* and not *Gymnasmata* because, strictly speaking, declamations on fictitious public subjects are called *gymnasmata* since by means of them we train ourselves for speeches on actual subjects. Therefore, since declamations on fictitious

subjects are called *gymnasmata*, the exercises
of Aphthonius are with good reason called
progymnasmata since they come before those
gymnasmata.[95]

In other words, the centuries-long shift in terminology
from γύμνασμα to προγύμνασμα for exercises like those on the
chreia seems to be the result of the role—increasingly
exclusive, but always subordinate—that these exercises
played in the training of an orator.

And yet, for all that has been said about the development
in terminology, it is probably impossible and perhaps
unnecessary to change scholarly habits regarding the title
of these textbooks. Consequently, throughout this book the
name *Progymnasmata* appears, even for Theon's and
Hermogenes' textbooks. For if we were to try to avoid
anachronism when speaking of these textbooks, we would no
doubt introduce intolerable circumlocution and confusion.

The second aspect of the history of the *Progymnasmata*
that requires our attention does not concern the textbooks
themselves, but rather the considerable secondary tradition
which they generated. This tradition is of two kinds. On the
one hand, various rhetors, following the lead of Aphthonius,
wrote model compositions for each exercise.[96] With respect
to the chreia the composition is the ἐργασία ("elaboration")
or, as it is sometimes called, διαίρεσις ("division").[97] Either way,
the composition consists of working out the meaning and truth
of a saying or action in a chreia by means of a set list
of topics, usually eight in all.

Besides Aphthonius' model elaboration of Chreia 43,[98]
various other examples are extant, such as the four which
are attributed to Libanius,[99] the four attributed to
Nicolaus,[100] and the four included by Doxapatres in his
commentary on Aphthonius.[101] These and other[102] elaborations
illustrate in detail the brief and usually formal comments in
the *Progymnasmata* themselves and hence will be dealt with
in our second volume, along with some examples of a more
grammatical exercise with the chreia, the κλίσις, or declension

of a chreia through the various cases (nominative, genitive, etc.) and numbers (singular, plural, even dual).[103]

The secondary tradition generated by the *Progymnasmata* includes, on the other hand, extensive reflection on the textbook of Aphthonius, including commentary and scholia as well as more general *prolegomena* on the nature and role of the *Progymnasmata* as a whole.[104] The ninth century commentary of John of Sardis[105] and that from the mid-eleventh century by John Doxapatres[106] are especially important, not merely in the sense that they provide helpful clarification of Aphthonius, but also because they incorporate earlier commentaries or even other *Progymnasmata* that would otherwise be completely lost. For example, Doxapatres quotes extensively from the tenth century commentary of John Geometres,[107] whereas John of Sardis quotes frequently from the *Progymnasmata* of Sopater[108] and the scholia preserve most of the *Progymnasmata* of Nicolaus.[109] In our third volume we will take up their respective sections on Aphthonius' chreia chapter.

To sum up: The history of the *Progymnasmata* was remarkably long, with its origins extending back into the Hellenistic period and its demise not occurring until well into the modern period. That history was also rich. It includes the writing of numerous *Progymnasmata*, but preeminently that by Aphthonius. And it includes developments in form and content, in terminology and function. Finally, it includes a variety of secondary materials: numerous model compositions for each exercise as well as profuse, often esoteric, comments on virtually every line of the *Progymnasmata* of Aphthonius. Accordingly, anyone who is asked, as was that schoolboy in Oxyrhynchus, "What is a chreia?" must be prepared to answer it in light of this long and rich history.

Contents and Function of the Progymnasmata. A scholiast on Aphthonius asks the question "How many *progymnasmata* are there?" and then answers it simply:

Fourteen. They are: 1) fable, 2) narrative, 3) chreia, 4) maxim, 5) refutation, 6) confirmation, 7) common place, 8) encomium, 9) censure, 10) comparison, 11) characterization, 12) description, 13) thesis, and 14) introduction of a law.[110]

This list, of course, summarizes the contents of Aphthonius' *Progymnasmata*, but it would, with only slight modifications, serve equally well for those of Hermogenes and Nicolaus,[111] and at first glance it seems to fit the textbook of Theon rather well, too. But the question of contents is not as simple as the scholiast suggests, at least early on. For a comparison of the MSS of Theon with what he actually says about the contents of his textbook shows that the fit has been forced. Indeed, scholars have long suspected that someone—an *ineptus homo*, says Oscar Hopplicher— drastically edited Theon's textbook, presumably to bring it into conformity with Aphthonius'.[112]

At any rate, Theon appears to have envisioned the contents of his textbook as follows: 1) chreia, 2) fable, 3) narrative, 4) topic, 5) description, 6) characterization, 7) encomium and censure, 8) comparison, 9) thesis, 10) law, 11) reading, 12) listening, 13) paraphrase, 14) elaboration, and 15) rebuttal.[113]

Theon's contents differ from Aphthonius' in various ways: Theon places the chreia first, not third; he has no chapter on the maxim; he incorporates refutation and confirmation in other chapters, primarily in the narrative chapter; and he has five extra exercises (nos. 11-15) which no longer appear in the Greek MSS of his textbook and which were probably excised by the *ineptus homo*.[114] Added to these substantive differences are several terminological ones: Theon uses διήγησις instead of διήγημα, τόπος instead of κοινὸς τόπος, προσωποποιία instead of ἠθοποιία, and νόμος instead of εἰσφορὰ νόμου. In other words, while the contents of the *Progymnasmata* eventually became rigidly standardized, Theon's textbook reminds us that in the earlier period variety in the number and nomenclature of exercises may have been the standard.[115]

The contents of individual chapters are formally similar. Doxapatres among others recognized this similarity, and his comment on Aphthonius' teaching methods is worth quoting in full because it applies to the others as well.

> Although there are four teaching methods, the classificatory, definitional, demonstrative, and analytical, Aphthonius uses only two in the present work; the classificatory when he classifies each of the *progymnasmata*, saying: 'One kind of fable involves human reason, another involves characterization, and one is mixed' and 'One kind of narrative is dramatic, and another historical, and another political' and similarly for the others. He uses the definitional method when he defines the exercises, saying that the fable is a fictitious story that embodies a truth and the narrative is an exposition of an incident that has happened or might happen.[116]

These twin concerns of definition and classification do in fact largely describe the content of the various chapters. In general, students first learned the definition of the form, along perhaps with an etymology of the formal term and a differentiation of the form from related ones. Then students learned to classify the form, at least into its principal types but sometimes into more subtle subtypes. At times, however, other concerns enter, especially that of manipulation of the form for compositional purposes. Other concerns include those of identifying the proper style for a form and the usefulness of the form for rhetoric.

For example, Aphthonius defines the fable, as we have seen, as a fictitious story that embodies a truth and explains why fables are sometimes called Sybaritic, Cilician, or Cyprian but usually Aesopian.[117] Then he classifies the fable according to whether it is a story about rational creatures, the characters of irrational ones, or both.[118] Since the statement of the fable's moral, its so-called "truth," can precede or follow the fable itself, Aphthonius aptly names these statements a *promythion* and *epimythion* respectively.[119] Finally, Aphthonius illustrates what he has said with the fable of the ants and cicadas, complete with *promythion* and *epimythion*.[120]

Theon's, Hermogenes', and Nicolaus' chapters on the fable are similar, although not without individual variations. Thus Theon's definition is identical,[121] but Nicolaus adds the notion of plausibility.[122] Hermogenes also speaks of Cyprian, Libyan, and Sybaritic fables,[123] but Nicolaus relates them to his classification scheme, identifying fables with rational creatures as Sybaritic, those with irrational ones as Lydian or Phrygian, and those with both as Aesopian.[124] Lastly, all go beyond Aphthonius in their attention to the manipulation, style, and rhetorical usefulness of the fable. For example, Hermogenes and Theon provide guidance on how to expand and condense, confirm and refute a fable,[125] whereas Hermogenes and Nicolaus identify the simple rather than the periodic style as proper to fable.[126] And Nicolaus notes that the fable has rhetorical usefulness in that it has the same purpose as the advisory speech and the same style as the "statement of the facts" in a speech.[127]

It would of course take us beyond the scope of this Introduction to summarize the contents of the other chapters,[128] but this one summary should suffice to indicate the general approach in all the chapters and to provide at least a basis of comparison for our discussion of the concerns of the various chapters on the chreia.

The function of the *Progymnasmata* has already been touched on above.[129] There we saw that from the time of Aphthonius and Nicolaus and especially from the time of the inclusion of Aphthonius' *Progymnasmata* in the *Corpus Hermogenianum* the various exercises in his textbook had an increasingly and explicitly rhetorical function. Indeed, we saw that the preference for προγύμνασμα over γύμνασμα apparently arose to clarify this specifically rhetorical function.

Nicolaus, we noted, pointed to the way these exercises functioned rhetorically by saying that they provided preliminary training in the various kinds of speeches and the several parts of a speech. But precisely how did these exercises function in this way, and why was such preliminary training necessary in the first place? For answers to these questions Aphthonius' commentators are particularly helpful.

One commentator answers the first question by matching the various exercises with their rhetorical counterparts:

> The *progymnasmata* provide preliminary training in the kinds of speeches and the parts of a speech insofar as some *progymnasmata* are akin to the advisory speech (for example, the fable, thesis, chreia, and maxim), others to the judicial (for example, the confirmation, refutation, and common place), and others to the panegyric (for example, the encomium, censure, and comparison).

> The *progymnasmata* also provide preliminary training in the parts of the public speech. For the fable exercises us in ideas fit for introductions, the narrative and description for statements of the facts, the confirmation and refutation for the arguments, and the common place for conclusions.[130]

In a similar passage Doxapatres adds the chreia as one of the exercises contributing to facility in the argumentative part of a speech,[131] and elsewhere he explains even more precisely how the fable supplies preliminary training in introductions:

> For just as a task of the introduction is to make the audience attentive to what will be said in the statement of the facts, so also a task of the fable is to prepare the audience for accepting the *epimythion.* Accordingly, the one who has been trained in the fable to make

someone attentive to the advice in the *epimythion* would clearly not be at a loss to compose an introduction to a speech.[132]

But why should students begin with these preliminary exercises rather than with the rhetorical speeches themselves? The answer to this second question appears as early as Theon and Quintilian but receives detailed discussion by Aphthonius' commentators. Theon answers with an apt simile: commencing rhetoric with declamations is like learning pottery on a huge storage jar.[133] In other words, it is not easy for youths, as Doxapatres says, "to grasp all at once the whole of rhetoric."[134] Hence the need for preliminary exercises, for *progymnasmata*, which take youths one step at a time through the skills required for composing the various speeches and the several parts of a speech. These exercises, therefore, function as stairsteps for carrying students to the very threshold of rhetoric.[135]

Viewed more broadly, the *Progymnasmata* thus occupied a curricular place between literary and rhetorical study.[136] Coming between the secondary and tertiary stages of education led to some overlapping in responsibility for these exercises—at least early on. Quintilian, for example, recommends that the initial exercises, including the chreia, fall to the *grammaticus*, or literary teacher, and the more advanced to the rhetor.[137] But with the increasing rhetorical perception of these exercises it is not surprising that eventually all the exercises fell to the rhetor. Thus Nicolaus speaks of them all as intended for youths who had just left the study of the poets and were now moving on to the study of rhetoric.[138]

To sum up: The contents and function of the *Progymnasmata* varied early on, as the evidence from Quintilian and especially from Theon shows. But by the time of Aphthonius and later variety gives way to standardization. Thus from Aphthonius' time on not only does the very word προγύμνασμα start to prevail but the number and sequence of these exercises become fixed — fable, narrative, chreia, maxim and so on — and their function is understood in terms of rhetoric.

In other words, students who had completed their literary study but who were not yet ready to compose the difficult rhetorical declamations began with the easier exercises of a Theon or Aphthonius and thus received preliminary training in rhetorical composition. With each exercise they learned the definition and classification of a different form of discourse, and they learned how to compose this form or otherwise manipulate it. By so doing they gained skills needed for rhetoric. And by working through all the exercises they came at last to the very threshold of rhetoric; ready to compose any of the three kinds of speeches and all the parts of a speech.

III

We have now looked where that papyrus scrap with its questions and answers about the chreia points. We have looked at the textbooks known as *Progymnasmata*, and having familiarized ourselves with them in a general way we are now ready to investigate in detail and in context their discussions of the chreia. This discussion will follow the pattern set by the textbooks themselves. That is, we will discuss the chreia in terms of definition, classification, and manipulation. Once again, we will quote numerous chreiai, not only to illustrate what, say, Theon is saying but also to demonstrate that these classroom discussions have application to the real or literary world of antiquity.

Defining the Chreia. As with the fable, the definitions of the chreia in the various *Progymnasmata* are quite similar but not identical. Perhaps the best definition for purposes of comparison is that of Aphthonius, for comparison of his with the others will allow the salient features of the chreia to become readily apparent.

Aphthonius defines the chreia as follows: "A chreia is a concise reminiscence aptly attributed to some character."[139] Four features of the chreia are discernible from this definition. The first is suggested by the word "reminiscence" (ἀπομνημόνευμα), which is itself a formal term for a saying or action.[140] Hence Hermogenes' and Nicolaus' more explicit definitions which have "a saying or an action" (λόγος ἢ πρᾶξις).[141] Hermogenes even anticipates the classification of the chreia when he adds "or a combination of both."[142] Hence an example of a chreia with a saying, with an action, and with both:

> Antisthenes, on seeing an adulterer fleeing, said: "You hapless fellow, how much danger you could have avoided for an obol."[143]

> In response to the one who said that there is no motion Diogenes got up and walked around.[144]

Jesus, on entering the Temple, began to evict the
sellers and said to them: "It is written, 'My house
shall be a house of prayer, but you have made
it a cave for brigands.'"[145]

The second feature of the definition, and one made
explicit by all, is the requirement a chreia be formulated in
a concise (σύντομος) fashion. Consequently, chreiai typically
involve only one sentence, though often a rather complex
one. A chreia in its most concise form:

Diogenes used to say that the belly is the
Charybdis of one's livelihood.[146]

A more complex example:

Anacharsis, on being asked whether there were
flutes in Scythia, said: "Why, there are not even
vineyards."[147]

At times, however, a chreia can be longer than one
sentence. Still, the chreia remains concise. For example:

Diogenes was trying to beg a mina from a prodigal.
When the latter said, "Why do you beg a triobol
from others but a mina from me?" Diogenes said:
"From the others I expect to receive something
again, but not from you."[148]

The third feature is the requirement that a chreia, to
use Aphthonius' words, must be "aptly attributed to a
character." Usually the character (πρόσωπον) is specified, such
as Diogenes in the previous example. Consequently, Theon and
Nicolaus make their definitions more precise with the phrase
"attributed to a specified character (εἴς τι ὡρισμένον
πρόσωπον)."[149] On occasion, however, the attribution can be
more general—for example, a Laconian as in Chreia 45—which
Theon seemingly accounts for in his final phrase: "or
attributed to something similar to a character."[150]

The word "aptly" (εὐστόχως) also calls for comment. Theon and Aphthonius understand the aptness to reside in the correspondence between saying (or action) and the character. Accordingly, because Diogenes was widely regarded as having begged his living, the following chreia is aptly attributed to him; it is "in character," so to speak:

Diogenes, when begging from someone, said: "If you have given to someone else, give to me, too. But if you haven't, begin with me!"[151]

Nicolaus, however, understands the aptness to reside more in the saying (or action) itself, so that the word εὐστόχως comes to mean "well-aimed," that is, appropriate to the situation.[152] Doxapatres' comment at this point is helpful. He explains:

The chreia ought to be in harmony with the occasion in question. For if, let us say, we see someone who is eager to make a profit in everything, then I could aptly say to him the line of Menander:

"Friend, look not for gain in everything."

But if we should say this to a relaxed and lazy man, the saying will not be apt.[153]

Incidentally, several authors prefer this understanding of εὐστόχος when applying it to the chreiai of various individuals: Lucian to the sayings of the Cynic Demonax,[154] Athenaeus of the harp-player Stratonicus,[155] and Diogenes Laertius of numerous philosophers.[156]

The fourth feature of the definition is only implicit in Aphthonius' word "reminiscence," which is not just any saying or action but only one that is "useful for living" (βιωφελής), as Theon's definition of this related form makes clear.[157] Hermogenes, however, underlines the chreia's usefulness when he says that generally the chreia is "useful" (χρήσιμος).[158]

Likewise, Nicolaus says that the chreia is handed on "with a view to improving some aspect of life."[159]

To be sure, the chreia's usefulness is already implied by the term itself, an implication Aphthonius draws out in the etymology of "chreia" that follows immediately upon the definition: "Since it is useful (χρειώδης), it is called 'chreia.'"[160] Theon explains:

> It has the name "chreia" because of its excellence, for more than the other (exercises) it is useful in many ways for life. Just as in the case of Homer, too, although there are many poets, we customarily call him alone "Poet" because of his excellence.[161]

The chreia, therefore, is a saying or action that is expressed concisely, attributed to a character, and regarded as useful for living. Such are the salient features of the definition of the chreia, with some clarification on the last feature provided by the etymology of the term itself.

Further clarification results with the differentiation of the chreia from two related forms: maxim and reminiscence. For example, the maxim, says Theon, is also useful for life, but it is always a saying, never an action, and it is never attributed to a character.[162] Hermogenes adds that the maxim is a mere statement, whereas the chreia is often expressed in terms of question and answer.[163]

The reminiscence, as we have seen, is a saying or action that is useful for life and so is much closer to the chreia. Indeed, it is distinguishable from the chreia primarily in being longer.[164] Consequently, while the distinction between these two forms may have worked in the classroom and the chreia further clarified by emphasis on its conciseness, still it should not be surprising if this distinction was not observed in the literary world. At any rate, Athenaeus knows of one of Machon's works as *Chreiai*[165] and refers to individual chreiai in it as reminiscences.[166] Moreover, Zeno's *Chreiai*[167] seems also to have gone under the title *Reminiscences*.[168] And what we know about the *Reminiscences* of Callisthenes[169] and Lynceus[170] suggests that they were collections of chreiai.

But even if the chreia is not as distinguishable from the reminiscence as Theon would have us believe, nevertheless the formal features of the chreia will become clearer as we move from the definition to the classification.

Classifying the Chreia. While Aphthonius' definition of the chreia allowed us to identify the main features of the textbooks' definitions, his classification does not. For Aphthonius includes only the principal classification, and Hermogenes and Nicolaus merely hint at a more complex one.[171] Consequently, when speaking of the classification of the chreia, we need to look at Theon's. His elaborate classification begins, like the others', with the principal division of chreiai into sayings, action, and mixed chreiai, but then he goes on to sub-divide them further, especially the sayings chreiai, and then to classify the sayings chreiai all over again according to the form of the saying. We will discuss and illustrate these three classifications in turn.

Theon begins his classification simply enough: "There are three main classes of chreiai. Some are sayings-chreiai, some action-chreiai, some mixed chreiai."[172] The first class, he says, includes those chreiai "which make their point by means of words without action,"[173] whereas the second includes those "which reveal some thought without speech."[174] The other textbooks agree with Theon on these two classes of chreiai,[175] but their understanding of the mixed class differs from Theon's. For Theon the mixed chreiai share features of both the sayings and action chreiai, "but make their point with the action."[176] One of his examples is Chreia 45:

A Laconian, when someone asked him where the Lacedaemonians consider the boundaries of their land to be, showed his spear.[177]

In other words, for Theon the character of a mixed chreia acts; the verbal feature it shares with the sayings chreia appears in the circumstance, i.e., the question that prompted the action.[178]

Hermogenes and the others, however, would classify this chreia as an action chreia. For them a mixed chreia requires both an action and a saying of the character.[179] Nicolaus uses this same chreia to illustrate a mixed chreia, but his recitation of it reflects this different understanding of what a mixed chreia is:

> A Laconian, on being asked where the walls of Sparta were, extended his spear (action) and said: "Here" (saying).[180]

After identifying the main classes of chreiai, Theon goes on to sub-divide the sayings and action chreiai. The sub-division of the sayings chreiai is particularly subtle and complex. He sub-divides sayings chreiai into two sub-classes and then these sub-classes even further.

The two sub-classes, or "species" (εἴδη), are termed ἀποφαντικόν and ἀποκριτικόν.[181] The εἶδος ἀποφαντικόν includes those sayings-chreiai in which the character makes a statement voluntarily (ἀποφαντικὸν κατὰ περίστασιν).[182] And yet, despite the technical language these chreiai are easy to identify. The first is simply a saying with a finite verb of saying, usually ἔφη ("he said") or ἔλεγε ("he used to say"). The second is a saying that is introduced by a participle of seeing, usually ἰδών but also θεασάμενος ("on seeing"). Here are examples of each:

> Cato *used to say* (ἔλεγε) that he liked those who turned red out of modesty more than those who turned white out of fear.[183]

> Philoxenus, *on seeing* (ἰδών) a youth turning red out of modesty, said: "Cheer up! For virtue has such a color."[184]

The εἶδος ἀποκριτικόν includes those chreiai in which the character responds to a question or to some kind of remark. Theon identifies four variations of such responsive sayings chreiai, three of them responses to questions—questions calling for a simple yes or no (ἀποκριτικὸν κατ' ἐρώτησιν), or for a longer answer (ἀποκριτικὸν κατὰ πύσμα), or for some explanation (ἀποκριτικὸν κατ' ἐρώτησιν αἰτιῶδες).[185]

Theon illustrates each of these variations with a chreia, but even so the distinctions seem too finely drawn. For one thing, chreiai in which a character answers a question with a simple yes or no are naturally rare, as in the following example:

> Diogenes, on leaving the baths said "No" (ἠρνήσατο) to the one who asked if many men were bathing, but "Yes" (ὡμολόγησε) to another who asked if a large crowd was there.[186]

For another, the characterizing participles of responsive chreiai—ἐρωτηθείς ("on being asked") and πυθομένου τινός ("when someone asked")—do not match up with the right kind of question, that is, ἐρωτηθείς with a simple question (ἐρώτησις) and πυθομένου τινός with a question calling for a longer answer (πύσμα). This distinction, then, breaks down in practice.

The third variation, a question calling for an explanation, also seems overly subtle, but at least the saying can be formally distinguished from the previous two since the explanation is expressed in a clause containing γάρ ("for") or ὅτι ("because"). Thus, if we combine the first two into one variation, that is, a question calling for an answer, and keep the third variation—a question calling for an explanation —we can illustrate them as follows:

> Socrates, *on being asked* (ἐρωτηθείς) what one should especially refrain from, said: "From shameful and illegal pleasures."[187]

> Thales, *on being asked* (ἐρωτηθείς) what the oldest of all things is, answered: "God. *For* (γάρ) he is

uncreated."[188]

Now if the three variations of questions are too finely drawn, the fourth variation, which covers all other kinds of responses, is not drawn finely enough. Theon's definition of this fourth variation amounts to little more than a miscellaneous category for non-interrogative responsive chreiai:

> Responsive chreiai are those which are based neither on a simple question nor on an inquiry; rather, they contain some remark to which the response is made.[189]

Theon's illustrative chreia (Chreia 50), which has Plato respond to Diogenes' luncheon invitation, suggests what might belong to this grab-bag category. So does the wording in Theon's definition just quoted, in particular the phrase "some remark to which (πρὸς ὅν) the response is made." At any rate, many chreiai are characterized formally by πρὸς τὸν κτλ. ("To the one who . . ."). For example:

> To those who were advising (πρὸς τοὺς συμβολεύοντας) him that he should look for his runaway slave, Diogenes said: "It is ridiculous if Manes is living without Diogenes, but Diogenes will not be able to live without Manes."[190]

Perhaps also belonging to this miscellaneous group are those chreiai in which the character responds to praise, reproach, rebuke, or simply some statement. Here are examples of such non-interrogative chreiai:

> Antisthenes, when praised (ἐπαινούμενος) once by wicked men, said: "I am afraid that I have done something wrong."[191]
>
> Anacharsis, when reproached (λοιδορούμενος) by someone because he was a Scythian, said: "I am

by birth, but not in manner of living."[192]

Diogenes, when someone rebuked (ὀνειδίζοντος) him for his poverty, said: "You poor devil, I have seen no one playing the tyrant on account of his poverty, but all do on account of their wealth."[193]

Antisthenes the Socratic, when someone stated (εἰπόντος) that war destroys the poor, said: "On the contrary, it makes many more poor."[194]

After discussing the two kinds of statement chreiai and the four kinds of responsive chreiai, Theon then introduces yet another kind of sayings chreia. He calls it a "double" chreia, although the Vatican Grammarian has a more apt term: *refutativa* ("with a rebuttal").[195] At any rate, Theon understands such a chreia to be "one with statements of two characters, either one of which creates a chreia of one character."[196] Theon illustrates with Chreia 24,[197] as does John of Sardis centuries later, but the latter in doing so adds some clarification:

> There are two classes of sayings chreiai: single and double. Single chreiai are those which have one saying made by one character — for example (cf. Chreia 24): Alexander, on seeing Diogenes sleeping, said: "To sleep all night ill suits a counsellor." Double chreiai are those which have another saying that opposes the one that had been made — for example (Chreia 24): Alexander stood over a sleeping Diogenes and said: "To sleep all night ill suits a counsellor." And Diogenes arose and said to him: "On whom the folk rely, whose cares are many."[198]

In other words, a double chreia has the sayings of two characters in which the retort of the second rebuts the first statement, as in this final example:

> There was a Roman knight drinking in the seats of the theatre, to whom Augustus sent word, saying: "If I wish to have lunch, I go home." The knight said: "Certainly, for you are not afraid that you will lose your place!"[199]

Theon proposes only a simple sub-division of action-chreiai and none at all for the mixed chreia. He distinguishes action-chreiai according to whether the character acts or is acted upon. He calls these chreiai ἐνεργητικαί and παθητικαί respectively.[200] This distinction, however, seems purely theoretical. Passive chreiai do not appear outside these textbooks, and even Theon's example, Chreia 21, appears elsewhere as a sayings chreia.[201] It looks as if Theon had to recast Chreia 21 in order for it to illustrate his passive action chreia. In any case, active action-chreiai make up a frequently encountered, if redundant, sub-division, as in this example about the madly amorous Stoic, Dionysius:

> Dionysius was once walking with some of his students, as it happened, by the brothel at which he had spent some time the day before and owed some money. Since by chance he now had the money, he stretched out his hand as all looked on and paid the money.[202]

Having discussed the principal division of the chreia as well as its sub-division, we come finally to the third division of the chreia. This division involves only the sayings-chreia, although now the classification does not depend on whether the saying is made voluntarily or is prompted by a circumstance, question, remark, or the saying of a second character. This classification depends rather on a formal consideration of the sayings themselves. More specifically,

Theon provides twelve formal categories in all. The sayings can be a maxim, a demonstration, a joke, a syllogism, an enthymeme, an example, a wish, a symbolic expression, a figure, a double entendre, a change of subject, or a combination of two or more of these.[203]

We need not illustrate all twelve, since Theon himself has done so,[204] but three examples of three categories will illustrate how formalized the sayings of chreiai are and how thoroughly reflective of literary practice the categories are. First, three chreiai whose sayings contain an ἀπόδειξις, or demonstration which is introduced by γάρ ("for"):

> Antisthenes says that it is preferable to fall among ravens than among flatterers. *For* (γάρ) the former inflict indignities on the body of a dead man, but the latter on the soul of one who is alive.[205]

> Plato, when angered by a gluttonous and disgusting slave, summoned Speusippus, his sister's son, and said as he was leaving: "Beat this slave, *for* (γάρ) I am too angry."[206]

> Diogenes said that courtesans of kings are their queens, *for* (γάρ) they do whatever the courtesans want.[207]

Next, three chreiai whose sayings contain a συλλογισμός, or syllogism with its clauses beginning with εἰ μέν . . ., εἰ δέ . . . ("If . . ., but if . . ."):

> Agesilaus was dying and ordered his friends to make nothing fabricated or copied (for so he spoke of statues). "For," he said, "*If* (εἰ) I have accomplished some noble deed, this is my memorial, *but if* (εἰ δέ) I have accomplished nothing, not all the statues in the world would be a memorial."[208]

> To the one who asked at what hour lunch should be eaten, Diogenes said: "*If* (εἰ μέν) you are rich,

whenever you want, *but if* (εἰ δέ) you are poor,
whenever you can."[209]

Jesus, on seeing someone working on the Sabbath,
said to him: "Man, *if* (εἰ μέν) you know what you
are doing, you are blessed, *but if* (εἰ δέ) you do
not, you are cursed and a transgressor of the
law."[210]

Finally, three chreiai whose sayings contain a εὐχή, or
wish, formulated with εἴθε and the optative or past tenses
of the indicative ("Would that . . ."):

Aristeides' wife, when he was busy with civic
affairs, said: "*Would* (εἴθε) that *you considered*
(ἐνόμησας) your personal affairs public and your
public affairs personal."[211]

Diogenes used to say to those who objected to
his masturbating in public: "*Would* εἴθε that *I* were
also *able* (ἠδυνάμην), by rubbing my stomach, to
bring an end to my hunger and want."[212]

Crates, the Cynic philosopher, rebuked Demetrius
of Phalerum for sending along with a bag of bread
a flask of wine, by saying: "*Would* (εἴθε) that *it*
were possible (ἦν) for springs to supply bread,
too."[213]

As a fitting way to sum up and conclude this rehearsal
of the classification of the chreia which Theon provides, we
turn to Doxapatres who demonstrates how someone might
apply this three-fold classification system to an individual
chreia. First a recitation of Chreia 51, then Doxapatres'
analysis:

Plato used to say that the off-shoots of virtue
grow by sweat and toil.

This chreia is a sayings chreia (λογική), with its
statement made voluntarily (καθ' ἐκούσιον), and it

is figurative (τροπική). It is a sayings chreia because it discloses its benefit by means of the saying. It is a voluntary statement because Plato was not prompted by some circumstance to utter this saying. And it is figurative because it has metaphorical speech."[214]

Manipulating the Chreia. Once students had learned the definition of a chreia, along with its etymology and differentiation from related forms, and had familiarized themselves with the classification of the chreia, whether in terms of Theon's elaborate system or simply in terms of the others' principal division, they turned to exercises designed to manipulate the chreia. These exercises take several forms.

One exercise eventually emerged as the standard manipulation of the chreia: the ἐργασία ("elaboration"). It first appears in Hermogenes,[215] but attains classic formulation in Aphthonius.[216] Nicolaus introduces some changes,[217] but to no avail, as is clear from the way later commentators try to fit his scheme into that of Aphthonius.[218]

At any rate, in its Aphthonian form students learn to elaborate a chreia into a short essay by discussing it according to a set list of topics: 1) praise of the character; 2) paraphrase of the saying or action; confirmation of the saying or action by stating its 3) rationale and 4) the converse; corroboration by means of 5) an analogy, 6) an historical example, and 7) an ancient testimony; and 8) a concluding epilogue.[219]

In contrast to the one exercise in Aphthonius (and in Hermogenes and Nicolaus) Theon has eight. These exercises represent a graded series[220] in which students attain an increasing level of dexterity with the chreia and thereby improve their compositional skills in general. These exercises, with brief descriptions, are as follows:

1) ἀπαγγελία, or "recitation" of an assigned
   chreia in the same words (as the teacher's)
   or also in others, as long as clarity is not
   sacrificed;[221]

2) κλίσις, or "inflection" of a chreia through the
   various cases and numbers, so that the
   character is cast in the nominative, genitive,
   dative, accusative, and vocative as well as
   in the singular, dual, and plural;[222]

3) ἐπιφώνησις, or "comment" on a chreia as to
   its being true, noble, advantageous, or
   consonant with the opinions of others;[223]

4) ἀντιλογία, or "objection" to a chreia as to
   its being the opposite of the qualities listed
   in the preceding exercise;[224]

5) ἐπεκτείνωσις, or "expansion" of a chreia by
   reciting it at greater length—for example, by
   amplifying the question and answer in the
   chreia;[225]

6) συστολή, or "condensation" of an expanded
   chreia back to its concise formulation;[226]

7) ἀνασκευή, or "refutation" of a chreia on the
   grounds that it is obscure, pleonastic,
   elliptical, impossible, implausible, false, harmful,
   useless, or shameful;[227] and

8) κατασκευή, or "confirmation" of a chreia by
   means of a short essay, complete with
   introduction, "narration" of the chreia,
   arguments, even elaboration, digressions, and
   character delineations, if need be.[228]

It is not necessary for us to discuss further each of
these exercises. They are, on the one hand, largely
straightforward and in most cases are illustrated with
examples. On the other hand, some exercises receive

extended treatment elsewhere in this volume,[229] whereas the elaboration and inflexion of a chreia, as we have said, are the subject of the second volume. Nevertheless, two exercises deserve our attention here because they have particular relevance for seeing how a familiarity with these classroom exercises can aid our analysis of chreiai as they occur in ancient literature. These exercises are recitation and expansion.

Recitation of a chreia in the classroom doubtlessly tended toward reciting with the same words as the teacher rather than with different ones. At any rate, when a Hermogenes or Nicolaus repeats a chreia or uses the same one as one of the others, the recitations show only slight variations. Thus, Nicolaus, when reciting Chreia 43, uses the plural καρποί ("fruits") on one occasion, but the singular καρπός ("fruit") on another.[230] Similarly, both Hermogenes and Nicolaus recite Chreia 26, but the latter has added the phrases "in the market-place" and "with his stick."[231] Hermogenes, however, recites this chreia once as an action chreia and once as a mixed chreia.[232]

But if students (and their teachers) recited chreiai with only slight variations at most, still they learned that recitations with different words were permissible, if clarity were not sacrificed. Accordingly, authors, with the skills and confidence of maturity, recite chreiai boldly, displaying variations that the classroom examples hardly lead us to expect. For example, Athenaeus and Diogenes Laertius both recite a chreia attributed to Aristippus but use different rather than the same words:

> Aristippus, on being soaked by the attendants of [the tyrant] Dionysius and then teased by Antiphon for putting up with it, said: "If I were just then fishing, would I have left my trade and gone away?"[233]

> Aristippus put up with Dionysius when he spat on him. When someone censured him, Aristippus

said: "Well, fishermen endure getting soaked by
the sea in order to catch goby. Shouldn't I, then,
put up with getting soaked with saliva in order
to receive a blenny?"[234]

Such great variation in recitation can occur even in the
same author, as is the case with Plutarch, who twice recites
a chreia attributed to Diogenes:

Diogenes used to say that for the one who
intends to be entirely secure it is necessary to
have good friends and ardent enemies, for the
former teach him and the latter reprimand him.[235]

Diogenes used to say that for the one in need
of security it is proper to seek out either an
excellent friend or an ardent enemy, in order
that, by being reprimanded or counseled, he might
avoid wickedness.[236]

Finally, another chreia attributed to Diogenes, this time
recited by five different authors, shows even more clearly
how literary recitations tend to be in different words rather
than the same ones. For example, Teles recites the saying
of Diogenes as a voluntary statement, what Theon terms a
καθ' ἑκούσιον.

Diogenes says that it is amazing if Manes [his
slave] is able to live without Diogenes, but
Diogenes is not able to be cheerful without
Manes.[237]

Stobaeus, however, recites this chreia, so that the saying
is now prompted by a circumstance, making it what Theon
terms a κατὰ περίστασιν.

Diogenes, when his household slave ran away, did
not fret but said: "It is terrible if Diogenes is
not able to live without him, but he can without
me."[238]

When Seneca, Diogenes Laertius, and Aelian recite this
chreia, they turn it into a responsive sayings chreia, what
Theon calls ἀποκριτικόν, since now the saying is in response
to the remarks of others.

> Diogenes' only slave ran away, but he did not
> even think it worthwhile to take him back home
> when he was pointed out to him. Rather, he said:
> "It is a disgrace if Manes can live without
> Diogenes, but Diogenes cannot without Manes."[239]

> Diogenes said to those who were advising him to
> look for his runaway slave: "It is ridiculous if
> Manes is living without Diogenes, but Diogenes will
> not be able to live without Manes."[240]

> When Diogenes left his homeland, one of his
> household slaves, Manes by name, tried to follow
> him, but could not endure his manner of life and
> so ran away. When some people advised Diogenes
> to seek after him, he said: "Is it not shameful
> that Manes has no need of Diogenes, but that
> Diogenes should have of Manes?" Now this slave
> was caught at Delphi and torn to pieces by dogs
> —a just punishment, in light of his master's name,
> for having run away.[241]

It should now be clear how differently each writer has
recited this chreia. Consequently, the wording of the saying
varies considerably. So do the circumstances (or lack of
them), which make the chreia now one sub-type of sayings
chreia, now another. Still, for all the differences the point
of the chreia is not obscured: the independence of the Cynic
from the vagaries and supposed necessities of life.

And yet, the differences in Aelian's recitation, particularly
the greater length, suggest that he is doing something more
than reciting this chreia. Aelian has in fact expanded this
chreia as well, so that it becomes a good transition to the
second of the exercises we are discussing. Manipulating a
chreia by amplifying the circumstances and saying (or action)
is another exercise that has left clear traces in ancient
literature. Two examples will suffice.

The first is a chreia attributed to Anacharsis, which
Diogenes Laertius has recited in its concise form:

> Anacharsis used to say that olive-oil is a drug
> which produces madness, since athletes, on
> anointing themselves with it, fall madly upon one
> another.[242]

Dio Chrysostom makes use of this chreia, but instead of
reciting it he expands it as follows:

> Anacharsis used to say that in each city of the
> Greeks there is a designated area (he means the
> gymnasium) where they become mad every day.
> For when they have gone there and taken off
> their clothes, they anoint themselves with a drug.
> This drug, he said, causes their madness, for
> immediately some are running, some are throwing
> one another down, while others put up their
> hands and fight an imaginary opponent, though
> others are actually beaten up. When they have
> done these things, they scrape off this drug
> and at once recover their senses, and becoming
> immediately friendly with each other, they walk
> looking down, ashamed at what they have done.[243]

Our second example of an expanded chreia comes from
the Gospel of Mark. We have already cited its concise version
from the Gospel of Luke, namely:

> Jesus, on entering the Temple, began to evict the
> sellers and said to them: "It is written, 'My house
> shall be a house of prayer, but you have made
> it a cave for brigands.'"[244]

In Mark's version of this chreia the expansions are not
as lengthy as Dio's but are apparent nonetheless.

> And so (Jesus), on entering the Temple, began
> to evict those who bought and those who sold
> in the Temple, and he overturned the tables of
> the money-changers and the seats of those who
> sold pigeons, and he kept forbidding anyone to
> carry a vessel through the Temple. And he was
> teaching and saying to them: "Is it not written,
> 'My house shall be called a house of prayer for
> all the nations'? But you have made it a cave
> for brigands."[245]

Given these literary examples of the classroom exercises
known as recitation and expansion, it should now be clear
that the manipulative exercises that students learned from
the chreia chapter of a *Progymnasmata* developed skills in
composition that served them later in literary life.
Consequently, our familiarity with the chreia chapters not
only aids us in understanding the pre-rhetorical stage of
ancient education, but also helps us in analyzing chreiai as
they occur in ancient literature. More broadly, we can now
recognize what the ancients would identify as a chreia, what
terms they would use in classifying species and subspecies
of this form, and what skills they possessed when making
use of chreiai.

IV

There remains one subject which, while not explicitly discussed
in the chreia chapters of the *Progymnasmata*, is nevertheless
implicit in various aspects of these discussions. That subject
is the historical reliability of the chreia. This subject, as

we will see, has been discussed before but not on the basis of the implications of the contents of the chreia chapters in these rhetorical handbooks.

The Chreia and the Question of Historicity. Scholars have generally been reluctant to assign much historical credibility to chreiai. Many years ago Gustav Gerhard and Kurt von Fritz, for example, argued that most chreiai attributed to Diogenes can hardly go back to the historical Diogenes. Many chreiai present the philosopher as espousing later and even contradictory views, usually those of a hedonistic or an overly rigorous Cynicism.[246] Thus a hedonistic or parasitical portrayal of Diogenes in the following chreia renders it historically dubious:

> Diogenes, while dining in a temple, was served dark bread. He picked up the loaves and threw them out, adding that nothing unclean ought to enter a temple.[247]

Conversely, an overly rigorous or misanthropic portrayal of Diogenes in the following chreia makes it equally dubious:

> Diogenes entered a theatre just as the rest were leaving. On being asked why, he said: "I make it my business to do this sort of thing in every area of life."[248]

Recently, Richard Saller has argued for a similar skepticism regarding the anecdote, although on different grounds.[249] Anthropological study of the anecdote, he says, has shown that it is among the least reliable forms of oral tradition, a conclusion he confirms for the early Roman Empire by a perusal of anecdotes in Suetonius. Saller shows that chronological and physical settings, characters, minor details, even the punchlines of anecdotes in Suetonius vary remarkably when compared with citations of the same anecdotes in other authors.[250]

The skepticism of Gerhard, von Fritz, and Saller should

not surprise us, given the discussions of the chreia in the *Progymnasmata*, especially their manipulative exercises. We have already seen that the exercises of expansion and recitation open up the chreia to considerable variation, even invention. The freedom to use "other words," as Theon puts it,[251] instead of the same ones when reciting a chreia makes it unlikely that we can recover the *ipsissima verba* or even the circumstance that prompted a saying or action.

For example, in the several extant recitations of the saying attributed to Diogenes about his runaway slave, Manes, which we quoted above. did Diogenes regard his inability to live without Manes to be something "amazing" (so Teles), "terrible" (so Stobaeus), "disgraceful" (so Seneca), "ridiculous" (so Diogenes Laertius), or "shameful" (so Aelian)? Was his remark cast in the form of a question (so Aelian) or a statement (so the others)? And was the remark in response to his learning of Manes' flight (so Stobaeus), to the advice of those who would have him seek after Manes (so Diogenes Laertius), or to the report of those who had found Manes (so Seneca)? The many variations in the recitations of this chreia make these questions unanswerable.

And yet, variations in recitation are only the beginning of problems with the historical reliability of the chreia. More problems emerge at the point of attribution. Chreiai require, say Theon and Aphthonius,[252] only aptness, not accuracy. Consequently, sayings or actions are often variously attributed, as Plutarch[253] and Diogenes Laertius[254] recognized.

For example, Plutarch attributes the following chreia to King Antigonus and the Cynic Thrasyllus:

> When Thrasyllus the Cynic asked Antigonus for a drachma, the King said: "But the gift does not befit a king." When the other responded, "Well, then, give me a talent!" the King said: "But to receive that much does not befit a Cynic."[255]

In the *Gnomologium Vaticanum*, however, this chreia is attributed to Alexander and Diogenes:

> Alexander, when Diogenes begged a drachma, said:
> "The gift does not befit a king." When Diogenes
> replied, "So give me a talent," he said: "But this
> request does not befit a Cynic."[256]

Attribution varies even more in the case of Chreia 9. At one point Diogenes Laertius attributes this chreia to Aristippus and Diogenes as follows:

> Diogenes, as he was washing off some edible
> greens, mocked Aristippus as he was passing by,
> saying: "If you had learned to eat these greens,
> you would not be a flatterer at the courts of
> tyrants." But Aristippus said: "If you knew how
> to associate with men, you would not be washing
> these greens."[257]

Elsewhere, however, Diogenes Laertius attributes this chreia to Plato and Diogenes[258] and a variant of it to the atheist Theodorus and the Cynic Metrocles.[259] Finally, the Vatican Grammarian attributes this chreia to Aristippus and Antisthenes.[260]

Just how common variation in attribution is in the literature becomes apparent from the following examples: Epictetus attributes a chreia to the Stoic Cleanthes[261] but the *Gnomologium Vaticanum* attributes it to Zeno;[262] Machon attributes a chreia to the courtesan Mania,[263] but Lynceus to the courtesan Gnathaena;[264] Diogenes Laertius attributes a chreia to Diogenes,[265] but Lynceus to the parasite Philoxenus;[266] Diogenes Laertius attributes the same chreia now to Anaxagoras,[267] now to Xenophon.[268] Lastly, Chreia 16 has multiple attributions: Theon to Damon,[269] Plutarch to Damonidas,[270] Aristodemus to Dorion,[271] and the *Gnomologium Vaticanum* to Eumonidas.[272] It is difficult, in short, not to be skeptical about the attributions of most chreiai. Mere aptness hardly assures reliable attribution.

The historical reliability of chreiai becomes even more problematic once we recognize how conventional are many circumstances that supposedly prompt a saying or action. Indeed, the very formal cues of a chreia—for example, "So and so, on *seeing* . . ." and "So and so, on *being asked* . . .—already suggest standard circumstances. What is more, even specific circumstances often appear purely conventional. For example, questions about marriage prompt many sayings, as these chreiai just from Diogenes Laertius illustrate:

> Socrates, on being asked whether one should marry, said: "You will come to regret whichever you do."[273]

> To the one who asked whether the good man should marry, Menedemus said: "Do you think I am a good man?" When he said that he was, Menedemus said: "Well, *I am married.*"[274]

> Bion, on being asked whether one should marry, said: "If you should marry an ugly woman, you will have to bear her; but if a beautiful one, you will have to share her."[275]

> Diogenes, on being asked when one should marry, said: "For young men not yet, for older ones never."[276]

In another example the question is almost surely conventional. Indeed, seldom does a prompting question seem so contrived as in these variants of a popular chreia:

> Aristippus, on being asked what he had gained from philosophy, said: "To be able to converse boldly with everybody."[277]

> Antisthenes, on being asked what he had gained from philosophy, said: "To be able to converse with myself."[278]

> Diogenes, on being asked what he had gained from philosophy, said: "If nothing else, at leasst I am prepared for every eventuality."[279]

> Xenocrates, on being asked what he had gained from philosophy, said: "Doing willingly what has been prescribed by the laws."[280]

> Ctesibus of Chalcis, on being asked by someone what he had gained from philosophy, said: "To go to dinners without paying my share."[281]

These various chreiai clearly demonstrate how elusive historicity is and why the burden of proof properly falls on those claiming historicity for any one chreia or for chreiai in general. Indeed, each part of the chreia form—the character, the prompting circumstance (if any), and the saying or action—can be manipulated in ways that do little to preserve historical reminiscence. Thus attribution to a character, needing only to be apt, can vary, so that we cannot be sure *who* said or did something. The prompting question or circumstance can also vary according to the freedoms permitted in recitation and expansion or they can simply reflect a conventional setting, so that we cannot be sure of the exact *circumstance or question* that elicited the saying or action. And, finally, the saying itself can be recited in different words, so that we cannot be sure of the exact *words* in a saying, only the general sentiment. Surely, we can use chreiai in reconstructing the life and message of, say, Diogenes or Aristippus *only if* we exercise considerable caution and sophistication.

Conclusion. It has been the purpose of this Introduction to discuss the general issues regarding the chreia and thus to provide the historical context for reading and investigating the specific rhetorical texts on the chreia that follow in this volume. Accordingly, we first surveyed the evidence for the history and popularity of the chreia outside the rhetorical tradition. We noted that the chreia as a literary form long preceded the chreia as a compositional form in the schools and that its popularity, especially among philosophers, was widespread and long-lived, as indicated by its frequent inclusion in various literary genres as well as by the collections of chreiai.

Within the rhetorical tradition we found that the chreia occupied a special place in the compositional textbooks known eventually as *Progymnasmata.* The chreia was one of several forms that prepared students for the rhetorical tasks of composing all the types of speeches and each of the parts of a speech. As with these other forms so with the chreia students learned to define, classify, and manipulate it.

We noted, furthermore, that while these discussions of the chreia served an educational purpose, they nevertheless can prove illuminating outside this context, for, as the numerous quotations of chreiai from literary sources show, students carried over the classifications and manipulations of chreiai in their use of this form in literary compositions. And we noted that the very definition of the chreia as well as the manipulations of recitation and expansion confirm scholars' suspicions, raised on other grounds, that chreiai are not likely to be historically reliable.

NOTES

1. The word χρεία is difficult to translate. Perhaps "anecdote" is the best rendering, but it is, on the one hand, too general, taking in other forms, such as the "reminiscence" (ἀπομνημόνευμα), which rhetoricians were quick to distinguish from the χρεία. On the other hand, the humorous connotation of "anecdote" fails to capture the didactic purpose of many examples of this form. Other renderings, such as "moral saying" or "moral anecdote," are too narrow or too clumsy. Consequently, we have simply transliterated the word — thus, chreia (plural: chreiai), as other scholars have done before us.

For other literature on the chreia, see, e.g., G. von Wartensleben, *Begriff der griechischen Chreia und Beiträge zur Geschichte ihrer Form* (Heidelberg: Winter, 1901) esp. 1-30 and 138-42; O. Schissel von Fleschenberg, *Novellenkränze Lukians* (Halle: Neumeyer, 1912) 3-21; M. Dibelius, *From Tradition to Gospel* (New York: Scribner's, 1935) 22-43; K. Horna, "Gnome, Gnomendichtung, Gnomologien," *RE* Suppl. 6 (1935) 74-87 (with additional comments by K. von Fritz, 87-90); H. R. Hollerbach, *Zur Bedeutung des Worts* XPEIA (Diss. Köln, 1964) esp. 74-81; A. S. F. Gow, *Machon: The Fragments* (Cambridge: Cambridge University, 1965) 12-15; H. A. Fischel, "Studies in Cynicism and the Ancient Near East: The Transformation of a Chria" in J. Neusner (ed.), *Religions in Antiquity: Essays in Memory of E. R. Goodenough* (Leiden: Brill, 1968) 372-411; Bonner, *Education in Ancient Rome*, 256-60; V. K. Robbins, "Pronouncement Stories and Jesus' Blessing of the Children: A Rhetorical Approach," *Semeia* 29 (1984) 43-74, and R. F. Hock, "Comments on the Article of Vernon K. Robbins," 97-101.

2. See, e.g., F. Susemihl, *Geschichte der griechischen Literatur in der Alexandrinerzeit* (2 vols.; Leipzig: Teubner, 1891-92) 1.31; Christ-Schmid-Stählin, *Geschichte der griechischen Literatur*, 54; and G. Rudberg, "Zur Diogenes-Tradition," *SO* 14 (1935) 22-43, esp. 23.

3. See R. Hirzel, *Der Dialog* (2 vols.; Leipzig: Hirzel, 1895) 1.145 n. 3; Wartensleben, *Begriff*, 29; G. A. Gerhard, *Phoinix von Kolophon* (Leipzig: Teubner, 1909) 248 n. 6; and Gow, *Machon*, 13 n. 1. Others, however, still maintain the other view, such as Horna-von Fritz, "Gnome," 88, and Hollerbach, *Bedeutung*, 81. Incidentally, Gow's puzzlement at von Fritz's acceptance of this view "for no visible reason" is cleared up when we realize that von Fritz also wrote the Pauly-Wissowa article on Metrocles (see *RE* 15.2 [1932] 1483-84).

4. See Plato, *Resp.* 1.329B-C, as Theon long ago pointed

out (see *Progymn.* 2 [1.158, 16–159, 4 Walz]).

5. See Diogenes Laertius, 2.85; "Chreiai, three rolls."
6. Diogenes Laertius, 6.69.
7. So Fischel, "Studies in Cynicism," 374.
8. Diogenes Laertius, 6.41. Translations of ancient texts are, unless otherwise specified, my own. Thereby I hope to allow consistency in translation to make the formal features of the chreia become all the more apparent.
9. Diogenes Laertius, 1.86.
10. Diogenes Laertius, 6.37.
11. Diogenes Laertius, 7.23.
12. Diogenes Laertius, 1.105.
13. Diogenes Laertius, 2.68.
14. Diogenes Laertius, 6.40.
15. Diogenes Laertius, 6.63.
16. See Dio, *Orat.* 72.11.
17. See Diogenes Laertius, 2.78 (Aristippus); 4.9 (Xenocrates); 63 (Carneades); 5.34 (Aristotle); 6.74 (Diogenes); and 7.177 (Sphaerus).
18. Diogenes Laertius, 6.56.
19. Diogenes Laertius, 6.6.
20. *Gnom. Vat.* 355 (p. 136 Sternbach).
21. Philostratus, *V. Soph.* 541.
22. *Gnom. Vat.* 404 (p. 152 Sternbach).
23. *Gnom. Vat.* 128 (p. 56 Sternbach).
24. *Gnom. Vat.* 82 (p. 38 Sternbach).
25. Plutarch, *Reg. et imp. apophth.* 192C.
26. Athenaeus, 13.584c.
27. Athenaeus, 6.246e.
28. See Dio, *Orat.* 72.11.
29. See Diogenes Laertius, 4.40.
30. Theodoret, *Graec. aff. cur.* 12 (PG 83.1137D).
31. See Plutarch, *Coniug. praec.* 145E.
32. See Plutarch, *De cohib. ira* 457D–E.
33. See Plutarch, *De prof. in virt.* 78F.
34. See Seneca, *ep.* 33.7–8.
35. See Menander Rhetor, 2.4 (p. 122 Russell-Wilson).
36. See, e.g., Diogenes Laertius, 1.33; 2.82; 4.4; and Athenaeus, 4.162e; 6.250f; 8.345d; 10.437e; and 12.548d.
37. See, e.g., Diogenes Laertius, 2.75; 9.27; and Athenaeus, 10.422c–d and 437e–f.
38. See, e.g., Diogenes Laertius, 1.63; 5.21; 6.89; and Athenaeus, 8.350e–352c.
39. See Diogenes Laertius, 6.4 (Antisthenes), 32 (Diogenes), 95 (Metrocles); 7.26 (Zeno) and 172 (Cleanthes). Susemihl (*Geschichte*, 2.242 n. 25) suspects that material about Chrysippus in 7.181 and Zeno in 7.2 also came from Hecato's

Chreiai. Only the latter, however, seems correct.

40. See Diogenes Laertius, 6.33 (Metrocles), 91 (Zeno); and 9.11, which names Ariston as the source of a chreia attributed to Socrates which Diogenes Laertius cited in 2.22. The source is presumably Ariston's *Chreiai* (cf. 7.163).

41. See Diogenes Laertius, 2.84-85 (Aristippus); 5.81 (Demetrius); 6.80 (Diogenes); 7.36 (Persaeus) and 175 (Cleanthes).

42. These chreiai are conveniently collected in Gow, *Machon*, 35-54.

43. See Stobaeus, 2.31.89 (p. 216 Wachsmuth); 3.7.28 (p. 316 Hense); and 3.13.42 (p. 462).

44. These chreiai are collected in V. Rose, *Aristoteles Pseudepigraphus* (Leipzig: Teubner, 1865) 613-15. Rose not only denies their Aristotelian origin, but also proposes Ariston (cf. Diogenes Laertius, 7.163) as their actual collector (so pp. 611-13). Susemihl (*Geschichte*, 1.66 n. 248) accepts Rose's first thesis but is properly cautious about the second.

45. See PSI 1.85 (=Pack² 2287). TEXT AND TRANSLATION OF THIS PAPYRUS WILL APPEAR IN THE SECOND VOLUME OF *The Chreia in Ancient Rhetoric.*.

46. So A. Körte, "Literarische Texte mit Ausschluss der christlichen," *Archiv* 7 (1924) 225-58, esp. 228-29.

47. For fuller discussion of the *Progymnasmata* than is possible here, see especially Bonner, *Education in Ancient Rome*, 250-76, which focuses on the early imperial period; and G. L. Kustas, "The Function and Evolution of Byzantine Rhetoric," *Viator* 1 (1970) 55-73, esp. 57-64, and Hunger, *Die hochsprachliche profane Literatur*, 1.92-120, both of which treat the late imperial and Byzantine periods. Cf. also Kennedy, *Greek Rhetoric*, 54-72. Among older works see especially E. Jullien, *Les Professeurs de Littéärature dans l'ancienne Rome* (Paris: Leroux, 1895) 282-331, which remains the fullest discussion of the Latin evidence, and Reichel, *Quaestiones progymnasmaticae*, which emphasizes introductory questions of dating, sources, etc. Finally, in many ways the best discussions of the *Progymnasmata* are the *Pauly-Wissowa* articles by W. Stegemann on Theon (*RE* 5A [1934] 2037-54) and on Nicolaus (*RE* 17 [1936] 424-57).

48. On the dating of Theon, see Stegemann, "Theon," 2037-39, and the "Introduction" to Theon, below pp. 63-64.

49. See Theon, *Progymn.* 1 (1.146.9-10 Walz), and the discussion in Stegemann, "Theon," 2048-49.

50. See esp. Quintilian 6-19 but also *Inst.* 2.4.1-42. The former passage refers to fable, maxim, and chreia, the latter to narrative, encomium and censure, common place, and thesis. Cf. further Jullien, *Les Professeurs*, 293-95.

51. See Quintilian, *Inst.* 2.1.1-12.

52. See Suetonius, *De Rhet.* 1, which refers to condensation and expansion of narratives as well as to confirmation and refutation of fables.
53. See Cicero, *De orat.* 1.6.23; cf. Quintilian, *Inst.* 3.1.20. Cf. further Jullien, *Les Professeurs*, 282–83.
54. See *Rhet. ad Heren.* 4.44.56–57. Cf. further Reichel, *Quaestiones progymnasmaticae*, 12–19.
55. See *Rhet. ad Alex.* 1436a 25 and Bonner, *Education in Ancient Rome*, 250.
56. So Bonner, *Education in Ancient Rome*, 250. More precise, however, is K. Barwick ("Die Gliederung der Narratio in der rhetorischen Theorie und ihre Bedeutung für die Geschichte des antiken Romans," *Hermes* 63 [1928] 261–87, esp. 282–83), who posits the second century B.C.
57. Statements in Theon not only suggest he added exercises, such as the encomium (see *Progymn.* 1 [1.151, 4–6 Walz]), but may even have begun the practice of defining each exercise and differentiating them from similar forms (see *Progymn.* 1 [1.147, 3–10]).
58. On this plausible origin of these textbooks, see Stegemann, "Nikolaos," 447.
59. See John Argyropulus, *Prol. Syll.* 10 (p. 157, 6–11 Rabe).
60. The evidence for Paul of Tyre and the following rhetors, which is largely from the *Suda*, is conveniently collected by H. Rabe (ed.), *Aphthonii Progymnasmata* (Rhetores Graeci 10; Leipzig: Teubner, 1926) 52–70, esp. 55 (for Paul).
61. See Rabe, *Aphthonii Progymnasmata*, 54. It should be pointed out here that the *Suda* articles on Minucianus the elder and younger are confused. The writer of the *Progymnasmata* is Minucianus the elder. For clarification, see O. Schissel, "Die Familie des Minukianos," *Klio* 21 (1926) 361–73, and W. Stegemann, "Minukianos (1)," *RE* 15 (1932) 1975–86, esp. 1975–76 and 1984–86.
62. It is possible that Harpocration also wrote a *Progymnasmata.* At any rate, Rabe (*Aphthonii Progymnasmata*, 54) cites a marginal comment in a Vatican MS of Doxapatres that names Harpocration along with Theon as people who put the chreia before the narrative in the sequence of *progymnasmata.* And yet the *Suda* article on Harpocration does not say that he wrote a *Progymnasmata*.
63. Text in H. Rabe (ed.), *Hermogenis Opera* (Rhetores Graeci 6; Leipzig: Teubner, 1913) 1–27. An English translation is available in C. S. Baldwin, *Medieval Rhetoric and Poetic* (New York: Macmillan, 1928) 23–38.
64. See Rabe, *Aphthonii Progymnasmata*, 54. Cf. further J. Brzoska, "Epiphanius (8)," *RE* 11 (1907) 195–96.
65. See Rabe, *Aphthonii Progymnasmata*, 54–55. Cf. also W.

Stegemann, "Onasimos," *RE* 35 (1939) 406-08, esp. his comment (col. 407) that the reference to *Progymnasmata* in the *Suda* article on Onasimus may equally refer a collection of model exercises as to a theoretical textbook on these exercises as we are talking about here.

66. See Rabe, *Aphthonii Progymnasmata*, 55.

67. See Rabe, *Aphthonii Progymnasmata*, 55-56. The fragment, which comes from the chapter on the maxim, is preserved by Nicolaus (see *Progymn.* 5 [pp. 27, 14-28,8 Felten]).

68. The fragments in Rabe, *Aphthonii Progymnasmata*, 57-70. Cf. further S. Glöckner, "Sopatros (10)," *RE* 2nd reihe 5 (1927) 1002-06.

69. Text in Rabe, *Aphthonii Progymnasmata*, 1-51. An English translatioin is available in R. Nadeau, "The *Progymnasmata* of Aphthonius in translation," *SM* 19 (1952) 264-85.

70. See Rabe, *Aphthonii Progymnasmata*, 56-57.

71. Text in J. Felten (ed.), *Nicolai Progymnasmata* (Rhetores Graeci 11; Leipzig: Teubner, 1913). There is no translation of this textbook.

72. It is possible, e.g., that P. Mich. inv. 6 (=Pack^2 2294) is a fragment of a chapter on the fable from some *Progymnasmata*. For text, translation, and discussion, see J. G. Winter, "Some Literary Papyri in the University of Michigan Collection," *TAPA* 53 (1922) 128-41, esp. 136-41.

73. See the "Introduction" to Aphthonius, below pp. 212-16.

74. See also the brief comment on terminology by Kennedy, *Greek Rhetoric*, 55.

75. See Theon, *Progymn.* 1 (1.151, 1-6 Walz).

76. See Theon, *Progymn.* 1 (1.148, 12 Walz).

77. See Theon, *Progymn.* 1 (1.157, 3 Walz).

78. See Theon, *Progymn.* 1 (1.149, 4 Walz).

79. See Hermogenes, *Progymn.* 8 (p. 19, 1 Rabe); 10 (p. 23, 16 and 21), and 12 (p. 26, 11).

80. See Sopater, *frag.* 8 (p. 65, 19 Rabe).

81. See Aphthonius, *Progymn.* 5 (p. 10, 18-19 Rabe).

82. See esp. Aphthonius, *Progymn.* 13 (p. 42, 6-7 Rabe). Cf. also Aphthonius, *Progymn.* 7 (p. 17, 13) and 10 (p. 32, 2).

83. See, e.g., Nicolaus' usage in his introductory chapter (*Progymn.* 1 [p. 1, 15-16 and 5, 11-18 Felten]).

84. See Priscian, *Praeexer.* 8 (3.437, 14 Keil), 10 (439, 6 and 9), and 12 (440, 2). For the passages in Hermogenes, see above n. 79.

85. For Theon, see the *Suda* s.v. Θέων (2.702, 18 Adler). For MS EVIDENCE ON HERMOGENES, SEE RABE'S NOTE ON THE TITLE OF THE TEXTBOOK.

86. So, e.g., John of Sardis, *Comm. in Aphthon.* (p. 194, 5-9 Rabe).

87. See Rabe's note on the title of the textbook.
88. See *Prol. Syll.* 8 (p. 76, 1-6 Rabe), 9 (p. 137, 5-21), and 11 (p. 168, 13-20).
89. "The rationale for the title" (ἡ αἰτία τῆς ἐπιγραφῆς) is one of eight standard topics for discussing a book. See the list in *Prol. Syll.* 8 (p. 73, 11-17 Rabe).
90. Doxapatres, *Hom.* (2.275, 17 Walz).
91. Cf. Aphthonius, *Progymn.* 5 (p. 10, 18-19 Rabe).
92. For example, Theon (*Progymn.* 1 [p. 148, 18-20 Walz]) says that the exercise of προσωποποιία ("characterization") is of benefit not only for writers of speeches but also for writers of history, dialogue, and poetry.
93. Nicolaus, *Progymn.* 1 (p. 5, 12-18 Felten).
94. See the Suda s.v. Ἀφθόνιος (1.432, 10-11 Adler); ἔγραψεν εἰς τὴν Ἑρμογένους τέχνην Προγυμνάσματα..
95. Doxapatres, *Hom.* (2.128, 21-129, 1 Walz). On the *gymnasmata* or declamations, see now D. A. Russell, *Greek Declamation* (New York; Cambridge, 1983).
96. See, e.g., the numerous such compositions, edited by Walz under the name of Nicolaus, in *Rhetores Graeci*, 1.266-420.
97. For the latter term, see Nicolaus 10 and 14. Cf. also Doxapatres, *Hom.* (2.192, 14-19 Walz).
98. See Aphthonius 23-79.
99. See Libanius, *Progymn.* (8.63-102 Foerster).
100. See Nicolaus, *Progymn.* (1.272, 20-278, 3 Walz).
101. See Doxapatres, *Hom.* (2.282, 12-286, 6 Walz).
102. See, e.g., the elaborations of chreiai attributed to Nicepherus (1.442, 11-449, 24 Walz), Georgius (1.553, 20-555, 8), and to an unknown writer (1.602, 1-605, 18).
103. See British Museum Add MS 37516 (=Pack² 2711), edited by F. G. Kenyon (*JHS* 29 [1909] 29-40, esp. 29-31). Cf. also Diomedes (1.310 Keil) and Doxapatres, *Hom.* (2.192, 21-193, 4 Walz).
104. The various *prolegomena* to Aphthonius' textbook collected by H. Rabe (ed.), *Prolegomenon Sylloge* (Rhetores Graeci 14; Leipzig: Teubner, 1931), esp. nos. 8, 9, 10, and 11.
105. Text in H. Rabe (ed.), *Ioannis Sardiani Commentarium in Aphthonii Progymnasmata* (Rhetores Graeci 15; Leipzig: Teubner, 1928) esp. 34-55 (on the chreia).
106. Text in Walz, *Rhetores Graeci*, 2.81-564, esp. 247-86 (on the chreia).
107. See, e.g., Doxapatres, *Hom.* (2.104, 16-18 Walz), and Kustas, *Studies in Byzantine Rhetoric*, 24-25.
108. Seven of the eight fragments of Sopater come from John of Sardis; for references, see Rabe's index s.v.
109. For details, see the "Introduction" to Nicolaus, below pp. 238-39.
110. Anon. Schol. (2.567, 7-10 Walz): μῦθος, διήγημα, χρεία, γνώμη,

ἀνασκευή, κατασκευή, κοινὸς τόπος, ἐγκώμιον, ψόγος, σύγκρισις, ἠθοποιία, ἔκφρασις, θέσις, εἰσφορὰ τοῦ νόμου.

111. Hermogenes and Nicolaus share Aphthonius' number and order of *progymnasmata*, once we realaize they put refutation and confirmation together and likewise encomium and censure. Nicolaus also has an introductory chapter.

112. For details, see Stegemann, "Theon," 2040-42. For the reference to the *ineptus homo*, see O. Hopplicher, *De Theone, Hermogene, Aphthonioque Progymnasmatum scriptoribus* (diss. Virceburg, 1884) 47. Rabe *(PhW* 51 [1931] 1240-41) places the date of this revision in the sixth century or slightly later.

113. This list is reconstructed from Theon's more rambling discussion of his sequence of exercises (cf. *Progymn.* 1 [1.157, 3-158, 12 Walz]). Cf. further Stegemann, "Theon," 2042.

114. On these other exercises, see Stegemann, "Theon," 2040-42.

115. This variety is also clear from the brief comments of Quintilian and the Vatican Grammarian, on whom see the "Introductions" below, pp. 117-38 and 275-78. More variety would also be likely if we still had such second century textbooks as those of Paulus of Tyre and Minucianus of Athens.

116. Doxapatres, *Hom.* (2.130, 20-131, 6 Walz). Much the same thing appears in *Prol. Syll.* 8 (p. 78, 12-27 Rabe) and 11 (p. 169, 20-30).

117. See Aphthonius, *Progymn.* 1 (p. 1, 6-10 Rabe).

118. See Aphthonius, *Progymn.* 1 (p. 1, 11-14 Rabe).

119. See Aphthonius, *Progym.* 1 (pp. 1, 15-2, 2 Rabe).

120. See Aphthonius, *Progymn.* 1 (p. 2, 3-12 Rabe).

121. See Theon, *Progymn.* 3 (1.173, 5 Walz).

122. See Nicolaus, *Progymn.* 2 (p. 6, 9-10 Felten). Cf. also Sopater, *frag.* 1 (p. 59, 2-5 Rabe).

123. See Hermogenes, *Progymn.* 1 (p. 1, 9-10 Rabe).

124. See Nicolaus, *Progymn.* 2 (pp. 6, 20-7, 4 Felten).

125. On expanding and condensing the fable, see Hermogenes, *Progymn.* 1 (pp. 2, 11-3, 14 Rabe), and Theon, *Progymn.* 3 (1.177, 17-19 Walz). On confirming and refuting the fable, see Theon, *Progymn.* 3 (1.178, 15-181, 23).

126. See Hermogenes, *Progymn.* 1 (p. 3, 15-16 Rabe).

127. See Nicolaus, *Progymn.* 2 (pp. 8, 12-9, 15 Felten).

128. For brief discussions of the contents of all the chapters, see Bonner, *Education in Ancient Rome*, 254-73, and Kennedy, *Greek Rhetoric*, 60-66. For more detailed discussion, see Reichel, *Quaestiones Progymnasmaticae*, 46-114.

129. See above, pp. 13-14.

130. Anonymous, *Prol. Syll.* 8 (p. 75, 7-17 Rabe).

131. See Doxapatres, *Prol. Syll.* 27 (p. 363, 2-3 Rabe).

132. Doxapatres, *Hom.* (2.125, 15-22 Walz).
133. See Theon, *Progymn.* 1 (1.146, 3-6 Walz). Cf. Quintilian, *Inst.* 1.9.1.
134. Doxapatres, *Hom.* (2.136, 18-19 Walz).
135. The imagery of stairsteps comes from Doxapatres (cf. *Hom.* [2.138, 16-17 Walz]). For the considerable skills needed for rhetoric, see Russell, *Greek Declamation*, 40-73.
136. For the stages of ancient education, see now Bonner, *Education in Ancient Rome*, 165-327.
137. See Quintilian, *Inst.* 1.9 and 2.1.78.
138. See Nicolaus 13-19.
139. Aphthonius 2-3.
140. So Theon 7-8.
141. See Hermogenes 2-3 and Nicolaus 45.
142. See Hermogenes 3.
143. Diogenes Laertius, 6.4.
144. Diogenes Laertius, 6.39.
145. Luke 19.45-46.
146. Diogenes Laertius, 6.51.
147. Diogenes Laertius, 1.104.
148. Stobaeus, 3.15.9 (p. 478 Hense).
149. See Theon 3 and Nicolaus 46-47.
150. See Theon 4. On the distinction between specified and general characters, see also Hermogenes, *Progymn.* 9 (p. 20, 19-23 Rabe): "There is characterization (ἠθοποιία) of both specified and unspecified characters (καὶ ὡρισμένων καὶ ἀορίστων προσώπων). Of unspecified; for example, what words someone might say to members of his household when he is about to go on a journey; and of specified; for example, what words Achilles might say to Deidameia when he was about to go off to the war."
151. Diogenes Laertius, 6.49. On Diogenes begging his living, see Diogenes Laertius, 6.6, 38, 46, 56, 59, 60, 62, 67, and G. A. Gerhard, "Zur Legende vom Kyniker Diogenes," *ARW* 15 (1912) 388-408, esp. 397-99.
152 See Nicolaus 45. Note that Nicolaus connects εὔστοχος adjectivally to λόγος ἢ πρᾶξις, not adverbially to ἀναφέρουσα, as Aphthonius does.
153. Doxapatres, *Hom.* (2.251, 12-18 Walz).
154. See Lucian, *Demonax* 12 and 39.
155. See Athenaeus, 8.348d.
156. See Diogenes Laertius, 2.78 (Aristippus); 4.9 (Xenocrates), 63 (Carneades); 5.34 (Aristotle); 6.74 (Diogenes); and 7.177 (Sphaerus).
157. See Theon 7-8.
158. See Hermogenes 4.
159. See Nicolaus 47-48.

160. Aphthonius 4.
161. Theon 25-28.
162. See Theon 9-18.
163. See Hermogenes 19-22.
164. See Theon 20-21.
165. See Athenaeus, 13.577d.
166. See, e.g., Athenaeus, 8.348e and 13.579d.
167. See Diogenes Laeretius, 6.91.
168. See Diogenes Laertius, 7.4. On the identity of these two writings, see Susemihl, *Geschichte*, 1.56 n. 190.
169. For the fragments, see Athenaeus, 8.350e-352c.
170. The fragments are scattered throughout Athenaeus, sometimes identified as coming from his *Reminiscences* (so 6.241d, 248d-e; 10.434d; 13.583f, 584b-f, and presumably 8.344c) and sometimes from his *Sayings* ('Αποφθέγματα) (so 6.245a, 245d-246a, and 8.337d-e). On the identity of these two works, see Susemihl, *Geschichte*, 1.488 n. 9, and A. Körte, "Lynkeus (6)," *RE* 13 (1927) 2472-73, esp. 2472.
171. See Aphthonius 5-17. For hints of a more complex classification of the chreia, see Hermogenes 27-29 and Nicolaus 131-37.
172. Theon 29-31.
173. Theon 31-32.
174. Theon 96-97.
175. See Hermogenes 5-11, Aphthonius 5-12, and Nicolaus 70-76.
176. See Theon 105-07.
177. Theon 111-13.
178. Theon's other example of a mixed chreia (Chreia 54) is formulated similarly.
179. See Hermogenes 11-12, Aphthonius 13, and Nicolaus 76-77.
180. Nicolaus 77-79.
181. For what follows see Theon 36-83.
182. See Theon 37-45.
183. Plutarch, *De poet. aud.* 29E.
184. *Gnom. Vat.* 548 (p. 197 Sternbach).
185. See Theon 46-73.
186. Diogenes Laertius, 6.40.
187. Stobaeus, 3.5.32 (p. 265 Hense).
188. Stobaeus, 1.1.29a (p. 34 Wachsmuth).
189. Theon 74-76.
190. Diogenes Laertius, 6.55.
191. Diogenes, 6.5.
192. *Gnom. Vat.* 15 (p. 10 Sternbach).
193. Stobaeus, 4.33.26 (pp. 806-07 Hense).
194. Stobaeus, 4.9.10 (p. 323 Hense).

195. See Vatican Grammarian 15-22.
196. Theon 86-88.
197. See Theon 88-93.
198. John of Sardis, *Comm. in Aphthon.* (p. 41, 2-11 Rabe).
199. Quintilian, *Inst.* 6.3.63.
200. See Theon 96-104.
201. See Diogenes Laertius, 6.51.
202. Athenaeus, 10.437f.
203. See Theon 115-23.
204. See Theon 124-89.
205. Stobaeus, 3.14.17 (p. 474 Hense).
206. Ps.-Plutarch, *De lib. educ.* 10D.
207. Diogenes Laertius, 6.63.
208. Plutarch, *Reg. et imp. apophth.* 191D.
209. Diogenes Laertius, 6.40.
210. Luke 6.5D. Cf. Chreia 27.
211. Stobaeus, 3.39.30 (p. 728 Hense).
212. Athenaeus, 4.158f.
213. Athenaeus, 10.422c-d.
214. Doxapatres, *Hom.* (2.260, 10-17 Walz).
215. See Hermogenes 31-62.
216. See Aphthonius 18-78.
217. See Nicolaus 162-80.
218. See Anon. Schol. (2.588, 20-31 Walz).
219. Aphthonius 18-22.
220. So correctly Schissel, *Novellenkränze*, 5.
221. See Theon 195-98.
222. See Theon 199-275.
223. See Theon 276-97.
224. See Theon 298-308.
225. See Theon 309-12 and 317-33.
226. See Theon 313-17.
227. See Theon 334-83.
228. See Theon 384-405.
229. See esp. the "Introduction" to Theon, below, pp. 68-74.
230. See Nicolaus 73 and 84.
231. See Nicolaus 75-76.
232. See Hermogenes 10-15.
233. Athenaeus, 12.544d.
234. Diogenes Laertius, 2.67.
235. Plutarch, *Quom. adul. ab amico internosc.* 74C.
236. Plutarch, *De prof. in virt.* 82A.
237. Teles, *frag.* IV[A] (p. 42 O'Neil).
238. Stobaeus, 4.19.47 (p. 430 Hense).
239. Seneca, *De tranqu. an.* 8.7.
240. Diogenes Laertius, 6.55.
241. Aelian, *V. H.* 13.28 (p. 164 Dilts).

242. Diogenes Laertius, 1.104.
243. Dio, *Orat.* 32.44.
244. Luke 19.45-46.
245. Mark 11.15-17.
246. See Gerhard, "Legende," 390-95, and K. von Fritz, *Quellenuntersuchungen zu Leben und Philosophie des Diogenes von Sinope* (*Philologus* Suppl. 18, 2; Leipzig: Dieterich'sche, 1926) 41-47.
247. Diogenes Laertius, 6.64. Cf. Gerhard, "Legende," 401.
248. Diogenes Laertius, 6.64. Cf. Gerhard, "Legende," 395, and G. A. Gerhard, *Phoinix von Kolophon* 67-68.
249. See R. Saller, "Anecdotes as Historical Evidence for the Principate," *G & R* 27 (1980) 69-83.
250. See Saller, "Anecdotes," 74-79.
251. See Theon 195-98.
252. See Theon 2-3 and Aphthonius 2-3.
253. See esp. Plutarch, *Apophth. Lacon.* 218A.
254. See Diogenes Laertius, 1.33; 2.13, 35, 82, 102; 4.48; 6.26, 36, and 42.
255. Plutarch, *Reg. et imp. apophth.* 182E. Plutarch recites this chreia again (cf. *De vitios. pudor.* 531E), though without naming the Cynic, as does Seneca (cf. *De ben.* 2.17.1).
256. *Gnom. Vat.* 104 (p. 49 Sternbach).
257. Diogenes Laertius, 2.68.
258. See Diogenes Laertius, 6.58.
259. See Diogenes Laertius, 2.102.
260. See Vatican Grammarian 15-22.
261. See Epictetus, 4.1.173.
262. See *Gnom. Vat.* 295 (p. 113 Sternbach).
263. See Athenaeus, 13.578e.
264. See Athenaeus, 13.584c.
265. See Diogenes Laertius, 6.55.
266. See Athenaeus, 6.246a.
267. See Diogenes Laertius, 2.13.
268. See Diogenes Laertius, 2.55.
269. See Theon 154-57.
270. See Plutarch, *De aud. poet.* 18D.
271. See Athenaeus, 8.338a.
272. See *Gnom. Vat.* 284 (p. 110 Sternbach).
273. Diogenes Laertius, 2.33.
274. Diogenes Laertius, 2.128.
275. Diogenes Laertius, 4.48.
276. Diogenes Laertius, 6.54.
277. Diogenes Laertius, 2.68. Cf. *Gnom. Vat.* 36 (p. 17 Sternbach).
278. Diogenes Laertius, 6.6.
279. Diogenes Laertius, 6.63. Cf. *Gnom. Vat.* 182 (p. 74

Sternbach).
    280. *Gnom. Vat.* 417 (p. 146 Sternbach). Cf. Plutarch, *De virt. mor.* 446E, and *Adv. Colot.* 1124E.
    281. Athenaeus, 4.162e-f.

THE CHREIA DISCUSSION OF
AELIUS THEON OF ALEXANDRIA

Introduction, Translation and Comments

by

RONALD F. HOCK
EDWARD N. O'NEIL

INTRODUCTION

I

Life and Writings. Little is known about Theon. In the MS tradition of the *Progymnasmata* he is simply identified as "Theon the sophist."[1] The *Suda* provides a few more details: that our sophist was an Alexandrian and called Aelius — hence his usual designation as Aelius Theon of Alexandria. The *Suda* also provides a partial list of Theon's other writings, all of them, so far as we can tell, of a strictly rhetorical nature, but none of them extant: a handbook on rhetoric; commentaries on Xenophon, Isocrates, and Demosthenes; rhetorical speeches; inquiries on the composition of a speech; and much else.[2]

Still, the information provided by the *Suda* is not without its own problems of interpretation, such as whether the handbook on rhetoric should be distinguished, as assumed above, from the *Progymnasmata.* The problem arises in the punctuation of the list of Theon's writings: whether the words τέχνη περὶ προγυμνασμάτων should be left unpunctuated and so understood as referring to a "rhetorical handbook concerning the *progymnasmata*," or whether a comma should be placed after τέχνη, thus distinguishing a rhetorical handbook from the *Progymnasmata*, as the editor of the *Suda* assumes.[3]

In either case it is more important to note that the *Suda* is too sketchy to help us decide the more significant issues of dating Theon or of his relationship to other men of the same name, especially the Stoic rhetorician referred to by Quintilian.[4] On the one hand, Ulrich von Wilamowitz-Moellendorf is hesitant to identify Theon with Quintilian's Stoic, citing the popularity of the name Theon. Nevertheless, he admits that the characterization of Theon as a Stoic is not incompatible with what can be known about him from the *Progymnasmata.*[5] On the other hand, Georg Reichel argues vigorously for identifying these Theons, amassing many parallels to Theon's language and ideas from Stoic sources, such as the strikingly similar distinction between ἐρώτημα and πύσμα in Diogenes Laertius' account of Stoic dialectic and in Theon's sub-division of responsive chreiai[6] — to cite just one example from Theon's chreia chapter.[7]

As a result, we find frequent references to the Stoicism of our author[8] and a general consensus that he was a near contemporary of Quintilian.[9] By these estimates Theon was therefore a rhetorician of the mid or late first century A.D. rather than of the fourth or fifth century, as previous scholars thought.[10]

It should be noted, however, that this earlier dating, which is based less on hard evidence than on soft arguments,[11] is not as secure as the current unanimity might lead us to assume. In fact, confirmation of this dating has not been forthcoming. For example, the discovery of the first papyrus fragments of the *Progymnasmata*, dated to the fourth or fifth century,[12] has not necessitated an early dating, as has happened in the case of, say, Chariton's romance *Callirhoe*.[13] Likewise, the presumed contact between Theon and Quintilian is not borne out by a comparison of their classifications of the chreia, Otto Schissel von Fleschenberg's claims notwithstanding.[14] Nor does Quintilian betray knowledge of Theon's rather distinctive notion of placing the chreia exercise first among the *progymnasmata*, preferring instead the usual sequence: fable, narrative, chreia.[15] In other words, even if Quintilian in fact refers to our Theon (a conclusion that would require a fuller investigation than is possible here), still it must be said that this thesis is not confirmed when tested on the data regarding the chreia. In short, although most scholars accept a first century dating for Theon, we cannot assume that it is thereby assured.

Such, then, is the prevailing opinion about the few biographical details regarding our author: known as Aelius Theon and as a Stoic, he lived in Alexandria during the mid or late first century A.D. and wrote a considerable, though now largely lost, body of rhetorical writings. The one extant volume, his *Progymnasmata*, is the earliest surviving example of this type of rhetorical handbook.

The Progymnasmata of Theon. Theon's *Progymnasmata* has reached us in a truncated and confused condition. A considerable portion has disappeared completely—at least in the Greek MSS. What is more, the chapters which remain have been rearranged in an order never intended by the author. We need not describe this editorial activity fully[16] but merely sketch its main features and provide details only where the discussion of the chreia is concerned.

The Greek MSS of Theon's *Progymnasmata* end with his chapter "On Law" and, on closer inspection, they end abruptly, after discussing in detail only one of the eight ways for refuting a law that Theon had listed at the start of this chapter.[17] Since it is not Theon's practice, as is clear from the other chapters including the chreia chapter, to leave any item of such a list undiscussed, it is virtually certain that the law chapter is incomplete. Furthermore, from statements Theon makes in his introductory chapter[18] it is also likely that five other *progymnasmata*, all of them following the *progymnasma* "On Law," were dropped (though preserved in the Armenian version). And finally, the remaining *progymnasmata* were rearranged and, at least in the chapter "On Narrative," divided up. All this editorial activity, it has been argued, took place in the sixth century, presumably in order to make Theon's number and sequence of *progymnasmata* conform to those of Hermogenes, Aphthonius, and Nicolaus.[19]

It is here that this editorial activity bears on the chreia chapter. For its present position as the third *progymnasma* (behind the fable and narrative) is not Theon's intended order. Originally, he placed the chreia chapter first. This fact is clear from Theon's own statement that the *progymnasmata* are to begin "with the chreia, for it is short and easy to remember; then with the fable and the narrative."[20] This sequence is also assumed in his advice to the teacher to have examples of each *progymnasma* for his students, since Theon suggests sources for these examples in the sequence chreia, fable, narrative, etc.[21]

In putting the chreia exercise first Theon is apparently being innovative. In any case, Theon is occasionally remembered for placing the chreia exercise first[22] and is probably responsible for the later debate over the proper placement of the chreia in the *progymnasmata* series—a debate found, for example, in Nicolaus.[23]

II

Theon's Discussion of the Chreia. Theon's discussion[24] is clearly the longest of the chreia chapters in the extant *Progymnasmata.* And yet, his discussion lacks several subjects that were taken up by Hermogenes, Aphthonius, and Nicolaus. Especially noteworthy is the lack of the chreia manipulation called ἐργασία, or "elaboration" of the chreia, which occupies so prominent a place in Hermogenes and Aphthonius.[25] And Theon, unlike Nicolaus, is not concerned with emphasizing how facility with the chreia develops rhetorical skills needed to compose speeches.[26]

Still, despite these omissions, the discussion of the chreia in Theon conforms in the main to those of the other *Progymnasmata.* That is, Theon discusses the chreia in terms of (1) definition (lines 2-35), (2) classification (lines 36-189), and (3) manipulation (lines 190-404).

(1) Theon's discussion of matters which pertain to definition is very similar to what we find in the corresponding sections of the other *Progymnasmata.* First comes the definition itself: "A chreia is a concise statement or action which is attributed with aptness to some specified character or to something analogous to a character."[27] Then follows the related but separate comparison and contrast of the chreia with the maxim and reminiscence.[28] And following that is the suggested etymology of the word "chreia."[29]

Theon's definition is similar to those found in the other *Progymnasmata.* Nevertheless, it is not without its own distinctive features. Thus, while he shares with others most of his terms (conciseness, aptness, and attribution to a specified character), Theon is alone in using ἀπόφασις ("statement") rather than the more usual λόγος ("saying") of Hermogenes and Nicolaus.[30]

The difference in meaning between ἀπόφασις and λόγος is slight, to be sure, but two reasons can be given for Theon's choice. First, ἀπόφασις, which is regularly used in definitions of the maxim,[31] allows him to indicate the close relationship between chreiai and maxims. This comparison is necessary in the chreia chapter because Theon does not include a separate chapter on the maxim, as do Hermogenes and the rest. The second reason for using ἀπόφασις is that Theon prefers technical terms based on this root — for example, ἀποφαντικόν (a species of chreia containing a "statement").[32]

In short, however much Theon and the others are dependent on traditional formulations, we should not regard them as repetitive and unimaginative bearers of that tradition, as, say, Henri I. Marrou does,[33] but rather as careful and self-conscious writers whose individuality is to be recognized and appreciated.

(2) Theon's individuality is especially clear in the classification section of his discussion of the chreia. For while he gives the usual division (διαίρεσις) of the chreia into sayings, action, and mixed chreiai,[34] Theon also provides an elaborate subdivision (ὑποδιαίρεσις) of both the sayings and action chreiai,[35] a subdivision only hinted at in Hermogenes and Nicolaus[36] and missing altogether in Aphthonius.

This subdivision, it will be recalled from the General Introduction,[37] distinguishes chreiai in which the character a) makes a statement, either with or without a prompting circumstance;[38] b) responds to questions of various kinds or to some word or remark;[39] and c) makes a statement only to be rebutted by a second character.[40] Theon's subdivision of the action chreia is simpler. He merely distinguishes between action chreiai in which the character is credited with some action and those in which he is said to be acted upon.[41]

As if these distinctions were not enough, Theon, it will

be recalled, goes on to provide still another classification of the chreia, or ἐπιδιαίρεσις.[42] Now chreiai are classified according to the ways an ἀπόφασις can be expressed, such as maxim, logical demonstration, syllogism, wish—twelve forms in all.[43]

Theon's elaborate classification has much to commend it. This classification alerts us (as presumably it did his students) to the many formal variations that could be used in composing chreiai. What is more, this classification system is remarkably close to chreiai as they are encountered in ancient literature, as has been amply demonstrated in the General Introduction.[44] In short, Theon provides us with a subtle and accurate analysis of the chreia that is contemporary with the phenomenon it attempts to describe.[45]

(3) The manipulation of the chreia is Theon's third section and so makes his discussion formally similar to the structure of the chreia chapters in the other *Progymnasmata*. But here the similarity ends, for instead of manipulating the chreia by means of "elaboration"[46] Theon provides his students with a series of eight graded exercises, or better, with four pairs of exercises: recitation and inflexion, positive and negative comment, expansion and condensation, refutation and confirmation.[47]

Recitation (ἀπαγγελία), as Theon puts it, is reporting an assigned chreia as clearly as possible (σαφέστατα) by using the same words or by using others.[48] Of interest here is Theon's point that clarity rather than mere repetition is the aim of recitation. For thus is explained the many variations that are found when a chreia is recited by several authors or even several times by the same author. For example, in Chreia 45 Theon has the Laconian being asked where Sparta's boundaries are,[49] whereas in Nicolaus the question concerns Sparta's walls(!).[50] Similarly, in Chreia 57 Theon himself varies his wording, preferring now "Socrates," now "Socrates the philosopher."[51] Incidentally, greater variation is encountered in other occurrences of this chreia. Thus one recitatiton has "King Archelaus" instead of Theon's "the Great King," whereas another recitation lengthens Theon's report of Socrates' ἀπόφασις.[52]

The second manipulative exercise is inflexion.[53] It is obviously related to recitation, for here, too, the chreia is simply reported. But now the concern is not so much clarity as correctness in the case endings of the name of the πρόσωπον and related words when they are recited in the various numbers and cases. With the latter several phrases are suggested, so that the cases are all possible. Thus, the phrase "the saying of Diogenes is remembered" puts "Diogenes" in the genitive, whereas the phrases "it occurred to Diogenes to say" and "they say that Diogenes said" put "Diogenes" in the dative and accusative cases.[54]

Inflexion of chreiai has been much maligned as excessively pedantic and, especially in the dual and plural, clearly absurd, as even Nicolaus perceived.[55] Still, such rote exercise was necessary, to judge from a student's declension of a chreia that has been preserved, complete with errors (not unexpectedly) in the dative plural participle.[56] And in defense of Theon it should be added that even he was aware that only the accusative would be used outside the classroom. For in his treatment of the fable he says: "One should inflect fables and the chreia into the numbers and oblique cases, but one should especially practice with the accusative because the classical authors have recited the majority of fables in this way."[57] So also with the chreia; when a chreia is not recited in the nominative, it is cast in the accusative, that is, dependent on "they say."[58] Accordingly, in his actual classroom practice Theon probably stressed the accusative when his students were doing this exercise.

Having learned to recite a chreia clearly and inflect it correctly, students then learned how to comment on a chreia. The third and fourth exercises involve instructions on adding a positive comment (ἐπιφωνεῖν) or a negative one (ἀντιλέγειν). The comments are derived from standard rhetorical *topoi* or lists in which arguments are conveniently identified and arranged. Thus, to comment positively on a chreia students are instructed to argue that it is true, noble, advantageous, or consonant with the sentiments of distinguished people.[59] To comment negatively required only that the opposite judgments be made.[60]

Theon's examples using Chreia 38 suggest that the comments be a sentence in length, but in actual practice only one word might be sufficient. At any rate, Plutarch comments on a saying of Dionysius as being "true,"[61] and Athenaeus adds that a saying of Bion is "noble."[62] Conversely, Plutarch judges a saying of Bias to be "not noble."[63]

The fifth and sixth exercises further develop the students' facility with the chreia itself. Now, however, clarity and correctness are assumed as students learn, in the fifth exercise, to expand (ἐπεκτείνειν) a chreia from its usual sentence length into a paragraph by expanding the chreia's question and answer and by saying more about its character and circumstances.[64] In the sixth exercise, where students condense (συστέλλειν) a chreia, they learn to work in reverse.

Theon's example shows clearly what is intended by these exercises. He offers Chreia 37 in the following expanded form:

> Epameinondas, the Theban general, was, of course, a good man in time of peace, but when war against the Lacedaemonians came to his country, he displayed many outstanding deeds of great courage. As a Boeotarch at Leuctra, he triumphed over the enemy, and while campaigning and fighting for his country, he died at Mantineia. While he was dying of his wounds and his friends were lamenting among many things that he was dying childless, he smiled and said: "Stop weeping, friends, for I have left you two immortal daughters: two victories of our country over the Lacedaemonians, the one at Leuctra, who is the older, and the younger, who is just now being born at Mantineia."[65]

This expanded chreia can also be condensed back to its normal concise form as follows:

Epameinondas, as he was dying childless, said to his friends: "I have left two daughters—the victory at Leuctra and the one at Mantineia."[66]

Theon's seventh manipulative exercise is called "refutation" (ἀνασκευή). It takes up the analytical aims of ἐπιφώνησις and ἀντιλογία. Now, however, the analysis is more advanced, since it is done in terms of nine categories instead of only four as before. The nine categories seem divisible into three groups—those pertaining to matters of style (obscurity, pleonasm, ellipsis), of logic (impossibility, implausibility, untruth), and of morality (inappropriateness, uselessness, shamefulness).[67]

To judge from Theon's examples of this exercise,[68] students were presumably given several chreiai to refute. The students then read them in light of these categories, selecting whatever category that seemed a suitable basis for criticizing a specific chreia. Theon himself, for example, recites Chreia 62 as follows:

A Sybarite, on seeing the Lacedaemonians living a life of toil, said he did not wonder that in their wars they do not hesitate to die, for death is better than such a life.[69]

Theon then refutes this chreia on moral grounds, pronouncing it "shameful." For, he explains, the Sybarite made his "statement in an effeminate manner and one that is not in keeping with a manly character."[70]

At first, one is inclined to criticize this exercise and especially Theon's treatment of it. The exercise seems mechanical, and Theon is hardly correct in his estimation of the chreia quoted immediately above. Indeed, far from espousing a shameful way of life, Chreia 62 promotes just the opposite, as Stobaeus recognized when he included this chreia in his *Anthology* under the topic "On the love of toil."[71]

And yet, on second thought these criticisms may be too harsh. After all, the exercise is part of a *progymnasma*, and the first one at that, so that it is designed for students who are taking their first steps in composing and thinking for themselves. Seen thus, the nine categories at least have a formal utility, providing students with various analytical perspectives from which to judge a chreia. Presumably, with experience students could recognize, say, pleonasm (the second of the categories) in a chreia attributed to Aristippus that Athenaeus recites rather loquaciously.[72] Students could then recite this chreia as concisely as Diogenes Laertius has done.[73]

The eighth exercise should be "confirmation" (κατασκευή), which is not only the analytical partner of refutation or ἀνασκευή, but is also the exercise Theon himself had announced in the list of exercises which introduced the section devoted to manipulative exercises.[74]

Indeed, not only does Theon not explicitly identify this exercise as "confirmation," he also speaks enigmatically of "each part of the chreia" (ἕκαστον μέρος τῆς χρείας) or of its "main parts" (τὰ ἀνωτάτω μέρη),[75] and he refers elliptically to some *topoi* or standard arguments that are to be used in this exercise.[76] And, to make matters still more confusing, Theon seems to envision, as we shall see, both a beginners' and an advanced form of this exercise. Consequently, any discussion of this exercise must remain somewhat tentative.

Fortunately, though, a comparison of this section with the corresponding (and larger) section of Theon's fable chapter allows us to clarify what he says here about this last exercise with the chreia. Thus the fable chapter also contains the twin manipulations of refutation and confirmation of fables,[77] but with respect to the latter Theon explicitly calls it "confirmation."[78] Therefore, in the chreia chapter we must assume that Theon also understood this eighth exercise to be "confirmation," even if he did not say so.

Similarly, Theon refers to "each part of the fable"

(ἕκαστον μέρος τοῦ μύθου)[79] and to specific *topoi*, at least for refutation of fables (as he does for chreiai). Indeed, these *topoi* are quite similar to those for refutation of chreiai: obscurity, implausibility, impropriety, ellipsis, pleonasm — eleven in all.[80] But Theon explicitly says of confirmation of fables that it involves arguing "from the opposite *topoi*" (ἐκ τῶν ἐναντίων τόπων).[81] Furthermore, on the basis of the examples of these *topoi* in refutation of fables and chreiai,[82] it becomes clear that the μέρη of a fable or chreia are the "details" that are arguably obscure, implausible, etc. Accordingly, confirmation of fables and chreiai — for neither of which does Theon provide any examples — would presumably involve identifying details that are arguably clear, plausible, etc.

    In one respect, however, the confirmation of chreiai differs from that of fables in that besides the *topoi* already identified Theon adds that advanced students[83] can take their starting points for argument from the more plentiful and subtle *topoi* that are normally used in the later *progymnasma* known as "thesis."[84] Thus these students can argue that the parts or details of a chreia are feasible, according to nature and the customs of all peoples, easy, praiseworthy, pious, necessary, advantageous, to name a few of these thesis *topoi.*

    With these clarifications we can now summarize the main features of Theon's last exercise with the chreia, what we are probably justified to call "confirmation." Students begin with an introduction (προοίμιον) that is designed for each specific chreia.[85] Then the chreia itself is set forth or recited.[86] Then follow the arguments, with beginning students making use of arguments which are opposite of those they used to refute chreiai, whereas the more advanced students appeal to the *topoi* associated with theses. In any case, the students may use as many arguments as possible.[87] Finally, they can also make use of amplifications, digressions, and character delineations where feasible.[88] All in all, confirmation turns out to be a rather sophisticated exercise.

    With "confirmation" Theon's series of eight manipulative

exercises comes to an end—and thereby his discussion of
the chreia. That discussion—involving matters of definition,
classification, and manipulation—surely provided his students
with a thorough introduction to this literary form and just
as surely served his overall goal of producing in his students
a "facility with language and a good moral character."[89]

The Text of Theon's Progymnasmata. The two critical
editions of Theon that scholars usually cite are those of
Christian Walz and Leonard Spengel.[90] These editions, however,
are not only old (1832 and 1854 respectively). They are also
inadequate, as Italo Lana's monograph on the MS tradition
of Theon amply attests.[91] Spengel, for example, merely took
over Christoph Finckh's 1834 edition, which was not based
on a personal inspection of the MSS, and Walz did little better,
consulting only one MS. Consequently, the need for an
adequate critical edition has long been felt.

Hans Herter's announced edition for the Teubner *Rhetores
Graeci* series was never published, since the materials for
the edition, including Hugo Rabe's notes, were destroyed
during the bombing of the Second World War.[92] In 1959 Lana
also announced a critical edition of Theon, but that edition
has not yet appeared.

Chreia Project member James Butts is also preparing a
critical edition of Theon based on his own collation of the
four Greek MSS as well as on the recently published papyrus
fragment and the Armenian version. His edition is far enough
along so that we can use his text for the chreia chapter
in this volume, although the *apparatus criticus* has been
considerably reduced in light of the different purposes of
this study.

Finally, an English translation of the whole of Theon, the
first in any modern language, will accompany Butts's text.

NOTES

1. See, e.g., Codex Pariesiensis 2918: Θέωνος σοφιστοῦ Προγυμνάσματα as discussed in Walz, *Rhetores Graeci*, 1.140.

2. See the *Suda* (2.702, 17-29 Adler): Ἀλεξανδρεύς, σοφιστής, ὃς ἐχρημάτισεν Αἴλιος. ἔγραψε Τέχνην, Περὶ Προγυμνασμάτων, ὑπόμνημα εἰς Ξενοφῶντα, εἰς τὸν Ἰσοκράτην, εἰς Δημοσθένην, Ῥητορικὰς ὑποθέσεις. καὶ Ζητήματα περὶ συντάξεως λόγου, καὶ ἄλλα πλείονα.

3. For fuller discussion, deciding in favor of the latter alternative, see W. Stegemann, "Theon (5)," *RE* 5A (1934) 2037-54, esp. 2039-40. Stegemann's article remains the fundamental study of Theon.

4. Quintilian, *Inst.* 3.6.48 and 9.3.76.

5. See U. von Wilamowitz-Moellendorf, "Asianismus und Attizismus," *Hermes* 35 (1900) 1-52, esp. 6-7.

6. Compare Diogenes Laertius, 7.66 with Theon 50-54.

7. See Reichel, *Quaestiones Progymnasmaticae*, 23-30.

8. See, e.g., Christ-Schmid-Stählin, *Geschichte der griechischen Literatur*, 461.

9. See, e.g., R. W. Smith, *The Art of Rhetoric in Alexandria* (The Hague: Nijhoff, 1974) 133.

10. For a mid-first century A.D. dating, see Wilamowitz, "Asianismus," 6-7, and Reichel, *Quaestiones Progymnasmaticae*, 30. For a late first or early second century dating, see L. Radermacher, "Hermogenes (22)," *RE* (1912) 865-77, esp. 877, and Christ-Schmid-Stählin, *Geschichte der griechischen Literatur*, 461. Stegemann ("Theon," 2037-38) considers all views and decides on A.D. 50-100. This dating is accepted, without discussion, by more recent studies: A. Lesky, *A History of Greek Literature* (New York: Crowell, 1966) 843; R. W. Smith, "Theon, Aelius of Alexandria," in D. C. Bryant (ed.), *Ancient Greek and Roman Rhetoricians: A Biographical Dictionary* (Columbia, MO: Artcraft, 1968) 97-98; and Kennedy, *Art of Rhetoric*, 616.

11. Apart from Quintilian's presumed reference to Theon, scholars have argued for their dating by placing Theon in the context of developments in early imperial literary history. On the one hand, scholars look to Theon's place in the trends toward Atticism (so, e.g., E. Norden, *Die antike Kunstprosa* [3rd ed.; Leipzig: Teubner, 1915] 273 n. 2). Or, on the other hand, they note rhetoric's appropriation of the chreia from the grammarian and so see Theon as an early representative of it, given his "grammatical" concern with the declension of the chreia (see Theon 199-275), a concern that drops out by the time of Hermogenes (so Radermacher, "Hermogenes," 877, and O. Schissel von Fleschenberg, *Novellenkränze Lukians*

[Halle: Neumeyer, 1912] 3-4. Such arguments are seldom compelling, as Stegemann ("Theon," 2038) recognizes.

12. See M. Gronewald, "Ein Fragment aus Theon, *Progymnasmata*, *ZPE* 24 (1977) 23-24.

13. See, e.g., Lesky, *History of Greek Literature*, 857.

14. See O. Schissel von Fleschenberg, "Die Einteilung der Chrie bei Quintilian," *Hermes* 68 (1933) 245-48. For further discussion and critique of Schissel's theses, see E. O'Neil's "Introduction to Quintilian" (below, p. 133).

15. See Quintilian, *Inst.* I.9.2-3.

16. See further Stegemann, "Theon," 2040-42, and I. Lana, *I Progimnasmi di Elio Teone* (Turin: Universita di Torino, 1959) 156-71.

17. See Theon, *Progymn.* 13 (1.254, 16-20 Walz).

18. See Theon, *Progymn.* 1 (1.158, 9-12 Walz).

19. Cf. Stegemann, "Theon," 2041-42.

20. Theon, *Progymn.* 1 (1.157, 3-6 Walz).

21. See Theon, *Progymn.* 2 (1.158, 16-159, 4 Walz).

22. See H. Rabe (ed.), *Aphthonii Progymnasmata* (Rhetores Graeci 10; Leipzig: Teubner, 1926) 54.

23. See Nicolaus 2-44. Cf. Hermogenes, *Progymn.* 2 (p. 4.7-8 Rabe).

24. Previous treatments of Theon's chapter on the chreia include: Reichel, *Quaestiones Progymnasmaticae*, 46-49; Schissel, *Novelenkränze*, 3-12; Stegemann, "Theon," 2046; and Bonner, *Education in Ancient Rome*, 256-60.

25. See Hermogenes 331-63 and Aphthonius 24-79.

26. See Nicolaus 138-62.

27. Theon 2-4.

28. Theon 5-24.

29. Theon 25-28.

30. Theon 2. Cf. Hermogenes 2 and Nicolaus 45.

31. See, e.g., Aristotle, *Rhet.* 2.21 (1394 a). Cf. Aphthonius, *Progymn.* 4 (p. 7, 2-3 Rabe).

32. See Theon 36-45.

33. See H. I. Marrou, *History of Education in Antiquity* (New York: Sheed and Ward, 1956) 172-75.

34. Theon 29-31.

35. Theon 36-104.

36. See Hermogenes 27-30 and Nicolaus 131-37.

37. See pp. 28-33.

38. Theon 36-45.

39. Theon 46-83.

40. Theon 84-95.

41. Theon 96-104.

42. See pp. 33-35.

43. Theon 115-89.

44. See pp. 29-35.
45. For some critical remarks on Theon's classification, however, see pp. 29-30, 33.
46. See Hermogenes 31-63, Aphthonius 24-79, and Nicolaus 163-81.
47. For the list, see Theon 190-94.
48. Theon 196-98.
49. Theon 111-13.
50. Nicolaus 77-79.
51. See Theon 70 and 347-48.
52. See *Gnom. Vat.* 496 (p. 183 Sternbach) and Plutarch, *De lib. educ.* 6A.
53. Theon 199-275.
54. Theon 227-28, 255-57, and 265-66.
55. See Nicolaus 35-38. For modern disparagement, see, e.g., Marrou, *History of Education*, 175.
56. See Brit. Mus. Add. mss 37516 and Bonner, *Education in Ancient Rome*, 258.
57. Theon, *Progymn.* 3 (1.176, 6-10 Walz).
58. Examples are legion. A sampling of chreiai cast in the accusative: Musonius, *Frag.* 17 (p. 110, 5-7 Lutz); Plutarch, *De tuenda san.* 136D; and Athenaeus, 4.138d. Examples from literature of chreiai cast in the other cases are very rare. For chreiai in the dative case, see Plutarch, *Conviv.* 615A, and Dio, *Orat.* 66.26.
59. Theon 276-97, esp. 278-80.
60. Theon 298-99.
61. See Plutarch, *Ad princ. inerud.* 782C.
62. See Athenaeus, 10.421e.
63. See Plutarch, *Quom. adul. ab amico internosc.* 61C.
64. Theon 309-12.
65. Theon 318-33.
66. Theon 314-17.
67. Theon 334-38.
68. Theon 339-83.
69. Theon 377-81.
70. Theon 381-82.
71. See Stobaeus, 3.29.96 (p. 658 Hense).
72. Athenaeus, 12.544c.
73. See Diogenes Laertius, 2.73.
74. For the list of exercises, see Theon 190-194, esp. 194: ἀνασκευάζομεν καὶ κατασκευάζομεν..
75. See Theon 384 and 399.
76. See Theon 386.
77. See Theon, *Progymn.* 3 (1.178, 15-181, 23 Walz).
78. See Theon, *Progymn.* 3 (1.181, 13-14 Walz).
79. Theon, *Progymn.* 3 (1.179, 11 Walz).

80. See Theon, *Progymn.* 3 (1.179, 12-16 Walz).

81. Theon, *Progymn.* 3 (1.181, 13-14 Walz); "Now we shall confirm from the opposite *topoi.*"

82. For the refutation of fables, see Theon, *Progymn.* 3 (1.179, 16-181, 13 Walz). For refutation of chreiai, see Theon 339-83.

83. See Theon 392-93: τοῖς δὲ ἤδη τελειοτέροις.

84. See Theon, *Progymn.* 12 (1.244, 19-245, 15 Walz).

85. See Theon 395-97.

86. See Theon 400-01.

87. See Theon 402. Cf. 384-94.

88. See Theon 402-04.

89. Theon, *Progymn.* 1 (1.148, 12-14 Walz).

90. C. Walz, *Rhetores Graeci* (9 vols.; Stuttgart: Cottae, 1832-36, repr. Osnabrück: Zeller, 1968) 1.137-262; and L. Spengel, *Rhetores Graeci* (3 vols.; Leipzig: Teubner, 1853-56, repr. Frankfurt: Minerva, 1966) 2.57-130.

91. See Lana, *Progimnasmi*, 84-89.

92. For the announcement of Herter's edition, see Stegemann, "Theon," 2053. For its destruction during World War II, see the review of Lana's book by A. E. Douglas in *CR* 11 (1961) 164-65, esp. 164.

SIGLA

A = consensus codicum LPMMa

L = Mediceus Laurenzianus plut. LV.10, Biblioteca Medicea Laurenziana, Florence. saec. XIII.

L^1 = qui codicem L transcripsit.

L^2 = qui codicem L correxit (= R^3).

P = Parisinus 2918, Bibliotheque Nationale, Paris. saec. XIV.

P^1 = qui codicem P transcripsit.

P^2 = qui codicem P correxit.

M = Estensis 116 (= α. P. 5.14), Biblioteca Estensis, Modena. saec. XV.

M^1 = qui codicem M transcripsit.

M^2 = qui codicem M correxit.

Ma = Marcianus, gr. cl. X.1 (= 1374), Biblioteca Nazionale Marciana, Venice. saec. XVI.

R = Theonis edition princeps: *Theonis Rhetoris De Modo Dec lamandi Libellus*, ed. Angelo Barbato (Rome, 1520).

R^1 = qui primus edit. prin. correxit.

R^2 = qui secundus edit. prin. correxit.

R^3 = qui tertius edit. prin. correxit (=L^2).

Arm^a = Theonis liber in Armeniacum convertus, MS 8371 of the Matenadaran. State Museum of Erevan). saec. XVII. *Theonis Progymnasmata Armeniace et Graece* , ed. Agap Manandrian (Erevan, 1938).

Note

The *sigla* for the remaining authors in this volume, viz. Quintilian, Hermogenes, Priscian, Aphthonius, Nicolaus and the Vatican Grammarian, are the same as those in the standard texts which we have used.

TEXT
AND
TRANSLATION

Περὶ Χρείας

Χρεία ἐστι σύντομος ἀπόφασις ἢ πρᾶξις μετ᾽
εὐστοχίας ἀναφερομένη εἴς τι ὡρισμένον πρόσωπον
(201,20)   ἢ ἀναλογοῦν προσώπῳ.
Παράκειται δὲ αὐτῇ γνώμη καὶ ἀπομνημό-   5
νευμα, πᾶσα γὰρ γνώμη σύντομος εἰς πρόσωπον
ἀναφερομένη χρείαν ποιεῖ. καὶ τὸ ἀπομνημόνευμα δὲ πρᾶξίς ἐστιν ἢ λόγος βιωφελής.
Διαφέρει δὲ ἡ μὲν γνώμη τῆς χρείας τέτρασι
τοῖσδε· (1) τῷ τὴν χρείαν πάντως ἀναφέρεσθαι   10
(202,5)   εἰς πρόσωπον, τὴν δὲ γνώμην οὐ πάντως· (2) καὶ
τῷ ποτὲ μὲν τὸ καθόλου, ποτὲ δὲ τὸ ἐπὶ μέρους
ἀποφαίνεσθαι τὴν χρείαν, τὴν δὲ γνώμην τὸ
καθόλου μόνον· (3) ἔτι δὲ τῷ χαριεντίζεσθαι τὴν
χρείαν ἐνίοτε μηδὲν ἔχουσαν βιωφελές, τὴν   15
δὲ γνώμην ἀεὶ περὶ τῶν ἐν τῷ βίῳ χρησίμων
(202,10)   εἶναι· (4) τέταρτον ὅτι ἡ μὲν χρεία πρᾶξις
ἢ λόγος ὑπάρχει, ἡ δὲ γνώμη λόγος ἐστὶ μόνον.
Τὸ δὲ ἀπομνημόνευμα δυσὶ τοῖσδε κεχώρισ-
ται τῆς χρείας· (1) ἡ μὲν γὰρ σύντομος, τὸ   20
δὲ γὰρ ἀπομνημόνευμα ἔσθ᾽ ὅτε ἐπεκτείνεται
καὶ (2) ἡ μὲν ἀναφέρεται εἴς τινα πρόσωπα,
τὸ δὲ ἀπομνημόνευμα καὶ καθ᾽ ἑαυτὸ μνημον-
(202,15)   εύεται.
Εἴρηται δὲ χρεία κατ᾽ ἐξοχὴν ὅτι μᾶλλον   25
τῶν ἄλλων πρὸς πολλὰ χρειώδης ἐστὶ τῷ βίῳ,
καθάπερ καὶ Ὅμηρον πολλῶν ὄντων ποιητῶν κατ᾽
ἐξοχὴν τοῦτον μόνον καλεῖν εἰώθαμεν Ποιητήν.

In multis per sectionem locis aliter atque Walz et Spengel tacite
interpunximus. 5 γνώμη om. haud recte Hein. ἀπομνημόνευμα Walz]
-ματα mss et edd. om.   10 et   12 τῷ] τὸ PMa   13 ἀποφαίνεσθαι
AR] ὑπο- Dox unde Camer.   13-15 τὴν δὲ ... χρείαν AR' (in mg.)
et Dox] om. R unde Camer.   19-21 δυσὶ ... ἀπομνημόνευμα AR'
(in mg.)] om. R unde Camer.

On the Chreia

A chreia is a concise statement or action which is attributed with aptness to some specified character[1] or to something analogous to a character.[2]

Closely related to the chreia are maxim and reminiscence.[3] For every concise maxim, if it is attributed to a character, produces a chreia. And the reminiscence is an action or saying that is useful for living.[4]

The maxim, however, differs from the chreia in these four ways: 1) The chreia is always attributed to a character, while the maxim never is. 2) The chreia sometimes makes a general statement, sometimes a specific one, while the maxim makes only a general one. 3) Furthermore, the chreia is witty, sometimes containing nothing useful for living, while the maxim is always concerned with matters useful in life. And 4) the chreia is an action or saying, while the maxim is only a saying.

The reminiscence is distinguished from the chreia in these two ways: 1) The chreia is concise, while the reminiscence is sometimes expanded. And 2) the former is attributed to various characters, while the reminiscence is also told by itself.[5]

It has the name "chreia" because of its excellence, for more than the other excercises it is useful in many ways for life. Just as in the case of Homer, too, although there are many poets, we customarily call him alone "Poet" because of his excellence.

(202,20)

Τῆς δὲ χρείας τὰ ἀνωτάτω γένη τρία· αἱ
μὲν γάρ εἰσι λογικαί, αἱ δὲ πρακτικαί, αἱ δέ   30
μικταί. λογικαὶ μέν εἰσιν αἱ χωρὶς πράξεως
διὰ λόγων ἔχουσαι τὸ κῦρος· οἷον (Chreia 22)
" Διογένης ὁ φιλόσοφος ἐρωτηθεὶς ὑπό τινος πῶς
ἂν ἔνδοξος γένοιτο ἀπεκρίνατο, ' ῞Οτι ἥκιστα
δόξης φροντίζων '."   35
Τῶν δὲ λογικῶν εἴδη δύο· ἀποφαντικὸν
καὶ ἀποκριτικόν. τοῦ δὲ ἀποφαντικοῦ αἱ μέν
εἰσι καθ' ἑκούσιον ἀπόφασιν· οἷον (Chreia 40)

(203,5)

" Ἰσοκράτης ὁ σοφιστὴς τοὺς εὐφυεῖς τῶν μαθητῶν θεῶν παῖδας ἔλεγεν εἶναι. " αἱ δὲ κατὰ   40
περίστασιν· οἷον (Chreia 23) " Διογένης ὁ
Κυνικὸς φιλόσοφος ἰδὼν μειράκιον πλούσιον
ἀπαίδευτον εἶπεν, ' Οὗτός ἐστι ῥύπος περιηργυρωμένος '." οὐ γὰρ ὁ Διογένης ἁπλῶς ἀπεφήνατο,
ἀλλ' ἐξ ὧν εἶδεν.   45

(203,10)

῎Ετι καὶ τοῦ ἀποκριτικοῦ εἰσιν εἴδη τεσ-
σαρα. (1) τό τε κατ' ἐρώτησιν καὶ (2) τὸ κατὰ
πύσμα καὶ (3) τὸ κατ' ἐρώτησιν αἰτιῶδες καὶ
(4) τὸ ὁμωνύμως τῷ γένει λεγόμενον ἀποκριτικόν.
διαφέρει δὲ τοῦ πύσματος ἡ ἐρώτησις ὅτι πρὸς   50
μὲν τὴν ἐρώτησιν συγκαταθέσθαι δεῖ μόνον ἢ

(203,15)

ἀρνήσασθαι οἷον ἀνανεῦσαι ἢ κατανεῦσαι ἢ διά
γε τοῦ "ναὶ" ἢ τοῦ "οὗ" ἀποκρίνασθαι. τὸ δὲ
πύσμα μακροτέραν ἀπαιτεῖ τὴν ἀπόκρισιν.
(1) Κατ' ἐρώτησιν μὲν οὖν ἐστιν, οἷον   55
(Chreia 49) " Πιττακὸς ὁ Μιτυληναῖος ἐρωτηθεὶς
εἰ λανθάνει τις τοὺς θεοὺς φαῦλόν τι ποιῶν
εἶπεν, ' Οὔ, οὐδὲ διανοούμενος '." μετὰ γὰρ τὴν
ἀπόφασιν τὸ προστιθέμενον περισσόν ἐστιν, ἐπεὶ
καὶ ἀφαιρεθέντος αὐτοῦ ἐπήρκει ἡ ἀπόφασις.   60

---

34 ὅτι om. PMa et ex corr. P² 43 ῥύπος LPM¹ et edd.] ἵππος M²R
Darm, Dox, Plan   53 ἢ τοῦ οὗ MR] ἢ οὗ LPMa. 58 οὔ, οὐδὲ L²P(in
eras.)MMaR, unde Camer.] οὐδὲ L Darm, Dox, Plan 60 ἀπήρκει Finckh

There are three main classes of chreiai.[6] Some
are sayings-chreiai, some action-chreiai, some mixed
chreiai. Sayings-chreiai are those which make their
point in words without action. For example (Chreia
22),[7] *"Diogenes the philosopher, on being asked by
someone how he could become famous, responded:
By worrying as little as possible about fame."*

Of sayings-chreiai there are two species:
statement and response. Of the statement species
some are in the form of an unprompted statement.
For example (Chreia 40), *Isocrates the sophist used
to say that gifted students are children of gods.*
Others arise out of a specific circumstance. For
example (Chreia 23), *Diogenes the Cynic philosopher,
on seeing a rich young man who was uneducated,
said: "This fellow is silver-plated filth."* For
Diogenes did not simply make a statement, but did
so in reaction to what he saw.

In addition, there are four species of responses:
1) to a simple question, 2) to an inquiry, 3) to a
question calling for an explanation, and 4) the
"responsive" species which is ambiguously
designated by the name of the class.[8] A simple
question differs from an inquiry in that with a simple
question one need only agree or disagree: for
example, shake the head "no" or nod "yes," or
answer with a "yes" or "no." An inquiry, however,
requires that the answer be longer.

So, then, 1) a response to a simple question.
For example (Chreia 49), *Pittacus of Mitylene, on
being asked if anyone escapes the notice of the
gods in committing some sinful act, said: "No, not
even in contemplating it."* For after the negative
particle the additional phrase is superfluous, since
even with it removed the negative would be
sufficient.

(204,5)

(2) Ἡ δὲ πρυσματικὴ τοιαύτη ἐστίν· οἷον
(Chreia 64) " Θεανὼ ἡ Πυθαγορικὴ φιλόσοφος
ἐρωτηθεῖσα ὑπό τινος ποσταία γυνὴ ἀπ'ἀνδρὸς
καθαρὰ εἰς τὸ Θεσμοφορεῖον κάτεισιν εἶπεν,
'Ἀπὸ μὲν τοῦ ἰδίου παραχρῆμα, ἀπὸ δὲ τοῦ   65
ἀλλοτρίου οὐδέποτε'."

(204,10)

(3) Αἱ δὲ κατ' ἐρώτησιν αἰτιώδεις εἰσιν
ὅσαι χωρὶς τῆς πρὸς τὴν ἐρώτησιν ἀποκρίσεως
καὶ αἰτίαν τινὰ ἔχουσιν ἢ συμβουλὴν ἢ τι τοιοῦτον, οἷον (Chreia 57) " Σωκράτης ἐρωτηθεὶς   70
εἰ εὐδαίμων αὐτῷ δοκεῖ ὁ Περσῶν βασιλεύς,
' Οὐκ ἔχω λέγειν, ' εἶπε, ' μηδὲ γὰρ εἰδέναι πῶς
ἔχει παιδείας '."

(205,5)

(4) Ἀποκριτικαὶ δέ εἰσιν αἱ μήτε κατ'
ἐρώτησιν μήτε κατὰ πύσμα, λόγον δέ τινα   75
ἔχουσαι πρὸς ὅν ἐστιν ἡ ἀπόκρισις· οἷον (Chreia
50) "Πλάτων ποτὲ Διογένους ἀριστῶντος ἐν ἀγορᾷ
καὶ καλοῦντος αὐτὸν ἐπὶ τὸ ἄριστον, ' Ὦ Διόγενες,' εἶπεν, 'ὡς χαρίεν ἄν ἦν σου τὸ ἄπλαστον
εἰ μὴ πλαστὸν ἦν '." οὔτε γὰρ Διογένης περί   80
τινος ἠρώτα τὸν Πλάτωνα, οὔτε ὁ Πλάτων πυν-
θάνεται αὐτοῦ, ἀλλ'ἁπλῶς πρὸς τὸ ἄριστον καλεῖ
αὐτόν, ὅπερ ἐστὶ τῶν οὐδετέρων.

(205,10)

Ἔστι δὲ παρὰ ταῦτα καὶ ἄλλο εἶδος, ἐμ-
πῖπτον εἰς τὰς λογικάς, καλούμενον διπλοῦν.   85
διπλῆ δέ ἐστι χρεία ἡ δύο προσώπων ἀποφάσεις
ἔχουσα, ὧν καὶ ἡ ἑτέρα μεθ'ἑνὸς προσώπου
χρείαν ποιεῖ· οἷον (Chreia 24) " Ἀλέξανδρος
ὁ τῶν Μακεδόνων βασιλεὺς ἐπιστὰς Διογένει
κοιμωμένῳ εἶπεν (Il. 2.24)·   90

(205,15)

οὐ χρὴ παννύχιον εὕδειν βουληφόρον ἄνδρα.

καὶ ὁ Διογένης ἀπεκρίνατο (Il. 2.25)·

ὦ λαοί τ'ἐπιτετράφαται καὶ τόσσα μέμηλεν. "

---

63 ποσταία Arm³ Darm, Dox, Plan] ποία AR 84 ἐμπῖπτον Finckh]
ἐμπῖπτον AR et edd. plures, cf. autem Hdn. *Tech. rel.* II.10. 93
τόσσα Hom. mss unde R³ (in mg.)] τόσα AR

2) The chreia with an inquiry is like this, for example (Chreia 64), *Theano the Pythagorean philosopher, on being asked by someone how long after intercourse with a man does a woman go in purity to the Thesmorphorion, said: "With your own, immediately; with another's, never."*

3) Chreiai containing an explanatory response to a question are those which, apart from the answer to the question, also have some explanation or advice or some such thing. For example (Chreia 57), *Socrates, on being asked whether the Persian king seemed happy to him, said: "I can't say, for I can't know where he stands on education."*

4) "Responsive" chreiai are those which are based neither on a simple question nor on an inquiry; rather, they contain some remark to which the response is made. For example (Chreia 50), *Once when Diogenes was having lunch in the market-place and invited him to lunch, Plato said: "Diogenes, how charming your unpretentiousness would be, if it were not so pretentious."* For neither has Dioigenes questioned Plato about anything, nor does Plato inquire of him. Rather, one simply invites the other to lunch. And this belongs to neither of the species.

In addition to these, there is another species falling within the sayings-chreiai which is called "double." A double chreia is one with statements of two characters, either one of which creates a chreia of one character. For example (Chreia 24), *Alexander the Macedonian king stood over Diogenes as he slept and said (Il. 2.24):*

"To sleep all night ill suits a counsellor."
and *Diogenes responded (Il. 2.25):*
"On whom the folk rely, whose cares are many."

ἦν γὰρ καὶ οὕτω χρεία μὴ προστιθεμένης τῆς
ἀποκρίσεως.   95
        Πρακτικαὶ δέ εἰσιν αἱ χωρὶς λόγου ἐμ-
(205,20) φαίνουσαί τινα νοῦν. τῶν δὲ πρακτικῶν αἱ μέν
          εἰσιν ἐνεργητικαί, αἱ δὲ παθητικαί. ἐνεργή-
          τικαὶ μὲν ὅσαι δηλοῦσί τινα ἐνέργειαν· οἷον
          (Chreia 25) " Διογένης ὁ Κυνικὸς φιλόσοφος   100
          ἰδὼν ὀψοφάγον παῖδα τὸν παιδαγωγὸν τῇ βακ-
          τηρίᾳ ἔπαισε. " παθητικαὶ δὲ αἱ πάθος τι ση-
(205,25) μαίνουσαι· οἷον (Chreia 21) " Διδύμων ὁ αὐλητὴς
          ἁλοὺς ἐπὶ μοιχείᾳ ἐκ τοῦ ὀνόματος ἐκρεμάσθη. "
          Μικταὶ δέ εἰσιν ὅσαι τοῦ μὲν λογικοῦ   105
          καὶ τοῦ πρακτικοῦ κοινωνοῦσιν, ἐν δὲ τῷ πρακ-
          τικῷ τὸ κῦρος ἔχουσιν· οἷον (Chreia 54) " Πυ-
          θαγόρας ὁ φιλόσοφος ἐρωτηθεὶς πόσος ἐστὶν ὁ
(206,5)   τῶν ἀνθρώπων βίος, ἀναβὰς ἐπὶ τὸ δωμάτιον παρ-
          έκυψεν ὀλίγον, δηλῶν διὰ τούτου τὴν βραχύ-   110
          τητα. " καὶ ἔτι (Chreia 45) " Λάκων ἐρομένου
          τινὸς αὐτὸν ποῦ τοὺς ὅρους τῆς γῆς ἔχουσι
          Λακεδαιμόνιοι ἔδειξε τὸ δόρυ. " τὰ μὲν οὖν
          εἴδη τῶν χρειῶν ταῦτά ἐστι.
          Προφέρονται δὲ (1) αἱ μὲν γνωμολογικῶς,   115
(206,10) (2) αἱ δὲ ἀποδεικτικῶς, (3) αἱ δὲ κατὰ χαρι-
          εντισμόν, (4) αἱ δὲ κατὰ συλλογισμόν, (5) αἱ
          δὲ κατὰ ἐνθύμημα, (6) αἱ δὲ κατὰ παράδειγμα,
          (7) αἱ δὲ κατ᾽εὐχήν, (8) αἱ δὲ συμβολικῶς,
          (9) αἱ δὲ τροπικῶς, (10) αἱ δὲ κατὰ ἀμφι-   120
          βολίαν, (11) αἱ δὲ κατὰ μετάληψιν, (12) αἱ
          δὲ συνεζευγμένως, ἐξ οἵων δήποτε τῶν προ-
(206,15) ειρημένων τρόπων συγκείμεναι.
          (1) Γνομολογικῶς μὲν οἷον (Chreia 10)
          "Βίων ὁ σοφιστὴς τὴν φιλαργυρίαν μητρόπολιν   125
          ἔλεγε πάσης κακίας εἶναι. "

---

101 ὀψοφάγον] ἀδδηφάγον Darm, Dox, Plan 103 Διδύμων L Sard, Darm,
Dox, Plan] Δίδυμος L²(corr.)PMMaR et edd. 110 τούτου AR unde
Finckh] τοῦτο Camer., Hein., unde Walz. 121 μετάληψιν Armᵃ Dox]
ἀντίληψιν AR et edd. pr. 125 Βίων] ὁ Βίας Darm, Dox, Plan

For even as it was, this was a chreia without the addition of the response by Diogenes.

Action-chreiai are those which reveal some thought without speech. Of action-chreiai some are active, some are passive. The active are those which show some aggressive act. For example (Chreia 25), *Diogenes the Cynic philosopher, on seeing a boy who was a gourmand, struck the paidagogus with his staff.* The passive are those pointing out something experienced.[9] For example (Chreia 21), *Didymon the flute-player, on being convicted of adultery, was hanged by his namesake.*[10]

Mixed chreiai are those which share characteristics of both the sayaings-species and the action-species but make their point with the action. For example (Chreia 54), *Pythagoras the philosopher, on being asked how long human life is, went up to his bedroom and peeked in for a short time, showing thereby its brevity.* And also (Chreia 45), *A Laconian, when someone asked him where the Lacedaemonians consider the boundaries of their land to be, showed his spear.* These, then, are the species of chreiai.

Chreiai are expressed; 1) in the manner of a maxim, 2) in the manner of an explanation,[11] 3) with wit, 4) with a syllogism, 5) with an enthymeme, 6) with an example, 7) with a wish, 8) in a symbolic manner, 9) in a figurative manner, 10) with double entendre, 11) with a change of subject, 12) in a combination of the forms mentioned above.

1) "In the manner of a maxim." For example (Chreia 10), *Bion the sophist used to say that love of money is the mother-city of every evil.*

(2) Ἀποδεικτικῶς δὲ οἷον (Chreia 41)
" Ἰσοκράτης ὁ ῥήτωρ παρῄνει τοῖς γνωρίμοις
προτιμᾶν τῶν γονέων τοὺς διδασκάλους ὅτι οἱ
μὲν τοῦ ζῆν μόνον, οἱ δὲ διδάσκαλοι καὶ τοῦ 130
(207,5) καλῶς ζῆν αἴτιοι γεγόνασιν. " τὴν γὰρ ἀπόφασιν αὐτοῦ Ἰσοκράτης μετὰ ἀποδείξεως ἐξ-
ενήνοχε.

(3) Κατὰ χαριεντισμὸν δὲ οἷον (Chreia 48)
" Ὀλυμπιὰς πυθομένη τὸν υἱὸν Ἀλέξανδρον 135
Διὸς αὐτὸν ἀποφαίνειν, ‘ Οὐ παύσεται οὗτος, ’
ἔφη, ‘ διαβάλλων με πρὸς τὴν Ἥραν ’;"

(4) Συλλογιστικῶς δὲ οἷον (Chreia 27)
"Διογένης ὁ φιλόσοφος ἰδὼν μειράκιον περισσῶς
καλλωπιζόμενον, εἶπεν, ‘ Εἰ μὲν πρὸς ἄνδρας 140
ἀτυχεῖς, εἰ δὲ πρὸς γυναῖκας ἀδικεῖς ’."

(5) Ἐνθυμηματικῶς δὲ οἷον (Chreia 58)
(208,5) "Σωκράτης ὁ φιλόσοφος Ἀπολλοδώρου τινὸς γνωρίμου λέγοντος αὐτῷ, ‘ Ἀδικῶς σου θάνατον
κατέγνωσαν Ἀθηναῖοι ’, γελάσας ἔφη, ‘ Σὺ δὲ 145
ἐβούλου δικαίως ’;" προσενθυμεῖσθαι γὰρ ἡμᾶς
δεῖ ὅτι ἄρα βέλτιον ἀδικῶς ἢ δικαίως κατ-
(208,10) εγνῶσθαι, ὅπερ ἐν τῇ χρείᾳ δοκεῖ παραλελεῖφθαι
δυνάμει δηλούμενον.

(6) Κατὰ παράδειγμα δὲ οἷον (Chreia 3) 150
"Ἀλέξανδρος ὁ Μακεδόνων βασιλεὺς παρακαλού-
μενος ὑπὸ τῶν φίλων συναγαγεῖν χρήματα εἶπεν,
‘ Ἀλλὰ ταῦτα οὐκ ὤνησεν οὐδὲ Κροῖσον ’."

(7) Εὐκτικῶς δὲ οἷον (Chreia 16) " Δάμων
ὁ παιδοτρίβης χωλοὺς ἔχων τοὺς πόδας κλαπ- 155
(208,15) έντων αὐτοῦ τῶν ὑποδημάτων ἔφη ‘ Εἴθε ἐναρμόσειε τῷ κλέπτῃ ’."

(8) Συμβολικῶς δὲ οἷον (Chreia 4) " Ἀλὲξ-

---

132 αὐτοῦ Finckh] αὐτοῦ AR et edd. plures 135 υἱὸν AR] om. (fort.
recte) edd. pr. 136 αὐτὸν Hein.] αὐτὸν AR unde Camer. 146 προενθυ-
L 146-7 γὰρ ἡμᾶς δεῖ om. R (in mg.R¹) ἡμᾶς] ὑμᾶς Walz 149 δυνάμει
om. (fort. recte) R add. in mg. R¹ 152 εἶπεν om. M 153 ἀλλὰ ταῦτα
M² (in mg.) unde R et edd.; om. A

2) "In the manner of an explanation." For example (Chreia 41), *Isocrates the rhetor used to advise his students to honor their teachers before their parents, because the latter are the cause only of living, while teachers are the cause of living nobly.* For Isocrates made his statement with an explanation.

3) "With wit." For example (Chreia 48), *Olympias, on hearing that her son Alexander was proclaiming himself the offspring of Zeus, said: "Won't this fellow stop slandering me to Hera?"*

4) "In the manner of a syllogism."[12] For example (Chreia 27), *Diogenes the philosopher, on seeing a youth dressed foppishly, said: "If you are doing this for husbands, you are accursed; if for wives, you are unjust."*

5) "In the manner of an enthymeme."[13] For example (Chreia 58) *Socrates the philosopher, when a certain student named Apollodorus said to him, "The Athenians have unjustly condemned you to death," said with a laugh: "But did you want them to do it justly?"* For we must further deduce that it is surely better to be condemned unjustly than justly, and it is this very point which appears to have been omitted in the chreia, though the implication is clear.

6) "With an example." For example (Chreia 3), *Alexander the Macedonian king, on being urged by his friends to amass money, said: "But it didn't help even Croesus."*

7) "In the manner of a wish."[14] For example (Chreia 16), *Damon the gymnastic teacher whose feet were deformed, when his shoes had been stolen, said: "May they fit the thief."*

8) "In a symbolic manner." For example (Chreia 4), *Alex-*

ανδρος ὁ τῶν Μακεδόνων βασιλεὺς ἐρωτηθεὶς ὑπό
τινος ποῦ ἔχει τοὺς θησαυρούς, ' Ἐν τούτοις, ' 160
ἔφη δείξας τοὺς φίλους. "
 (9) Τροπικῶς δὲ οἷον (Chreia 51) " Πλάτων
(208,20) ὁ φιλόσοφος τοὺς τῆς ἀρετῆς κλῶνας ἔφη ἱδρῶτι
καὶ πόνοις φύεσθαι. "
 (10) Κατὰ ἀμφιβολίαν δὲ οἷον (Chreia 165
42) " Ἰσοκράτης ὁ ῥήτωρ συνισταμένου αὐτῷ παιδίου καὶ ἐρωτῶντος τοῦ συνιστάντος τίνος αὐτῷ
δεῖ, εἶπε, ' Πινακιδίου ΚΑΙΝΟΥ καὶ γραφειδίου
ΚΑΙΝΟΥ '." ἀμφιβαλλόμενον γὰρ πότερον " νοῦ καὶ
(209,5) πινακιδίου " λέγει ἢ " πινακίδος καινῆς καὶ 170
καινοῦ γραφειδίου. "
 (11) Κατὰ μετάληψιν δέ ἐστιν ὅταν τὸ
λεγόμενον καὶ τὸ ἐρωτώμενον ἐπ᾽ἄλλο τις ἀπο-
κρινόμενος μεταλαμβάνῃ. οἷον (Chreia 53) " Πύρρος ὁ τῶν Ἠπειρωτῶν βασιλεὺς ζητούντων τινῶν 175
παρὰ πότον πότερος κρείττων αὐλητὴς Ἀντι-
(209,10) γεννίδας ἢ Σάτυρος, ' Ἐμοὶ μέν, ' εἶπε, ' στρα-
τηγὸς Πολυσπέρχων '."
 (12) Ὁ δὲ συνεζευγμένος τρόπος οὐκ ἄδηλός
ἐστιν, ὅτι πολλαχῶς γίνεται· ἢ γὰρ γνωμικῷ 180
χαριεντισμῷ συμπλακήσεται ἢ παραδείγματι συμ-
βολικῷ ἢ ἀμφιβολίᾳ καὶ μεταλήψει ἢ ἁπλῶς καθ᾽
(209,15) ὅσους καὶ ἄλλους τρόπους δύναται συγγενέσθαι
συζυγία, ἤτοι δυοῖν ἢ καὶ πλειόνων τρόπων εἰς
μίαν χρείαν παραλαμβανομένων. οἷον (Chreia 185
28) " Διογένης ὁ Κυνικὸς φιλόσοφος ἰδὼν μειράκιον ἐκ μοιχοῦ λίθους βάλλον, ' Παῦσαι, ' ἔφη,
' παιδίον, μὴ ἀγνοοῦν παίσῃς τὸν πατέρα '." ἔχει
γὰρ ἅμα καὶ συμβολικῶς καὶ χαριέντως ἡ ἀπόφασις.

168-9 ΚΑΙΝΟΥ LPMaArmᵃ] καὶ νοῦ MR 169 ἀμφιβαλλόμενον Camer.
unde edd.] -μένου AR; ἄδηλον Darm, Dox, Plan. 174 Πύρρος]
Ἐπαμινώνδας Darm, Dox, Plan. 176 Ἀντιγεννίδας AR] -γενίδας
Camer., Hein., Schef.; -γενίδης Suda, Darm, Dox, Plan 187 μοιχοῦ
LPR¹ (in mg.) Darm, Dox, Plan] τοίχου M (ex corr.) unde R et edd.
pr.; βάλλον· παῦσαι L(βάλλων)PM Armᵃ] β. εἰς ἀγοράν· π. M²(in mg.)
unde R et edd. plur. β. εἰς πλῆθος· π. Darm, Dox, Plan β. εἰς ὄχλον·
π. D.L. 6.62.

ander the Macedonian king, on being asked by
someone where he had his treasures, pointed to his
friends and said: "In these."

9) "In a figurative manner." For example (Chreia
51), *Plato the philosopher used to say that the off-*
shoots of virtue grow by sweat and toil.

10) "With double entendre." For example (Chreia
42), *Isocrates the rhetor, when a boy was being*
enrolled with him and when the one who was enrolling
him asked what the boy needed, said: "A new tablet
and a new stylus." For it is ambiguous whether he
means "a mind and a tablet," or "a new tablet and
a new stylus."[15]

11) "With a change of subject" occurs whenever
someone in replying changes the subject and the
question to something else. For example (Chreia 53),
Pyrrhus the king of Epirus, when some people were
debating over wine whether Antigennidas or Satyrus
was the better flute-player, said: "In my opinion,
Polysperchon is the better general."

12) The combined form is obvious because it
occurs in many combinations. For it will be a
combination of sententious wit or symbolic example
or double entendre and change of subject, or it
can, in short, be a combination of as many different
forms as possible, with two or even more forms
being combined in one chreia. For example (Chreia
28), *Diogenes the Cynic philosopher, on seeing a*
youth who was the son of an adulterer throwing
stones, said: "Stop, boy! You may unwittingly hit your
father!" For his statement is at once both symbolic
and witty.

Γυμνάζονται δὲ κατὰ τὰς χρείας (1) τῇ   190
ἀπαγγελίᾳ, (2) τῇ κλίσει, (3) ἐπιφωνήσει, (4)
(210,5)   τῇ ἀντιλογίᾳ, (5) ἐπεκτείνομέν τε καὶ (6) συστέλλομεν τὴν χρείαν. πρὸς δὲ τούτοις (7) ἀνασκευάζομεν καὶ (8) κατασκευάζομεν.
            (1) Καὶ ἡ μὲν ἀπαγγελία φανερά ἐστι.   195
ῥηθεῖσαν γὰρ χρείαν πειρώμεθα κατὰ τὸ δυνατὸν
αὐτοῖς ὀνόμασιν ἢ καὶ ἑτέροις σαφέστατα
ἑρμηνεῦσαι.
(210,10)   (2) Ἡ δὲ κλίσις ἐστι ποικίλη. τὰ γὰρ ἐν
τῇ χρείᾳ πρόσωπα εἰς τοὺς τρεῖς ἀριθμοὺς ἐν-   200
αλλάττομεν· καὶ τοῦτο οὐχ ἁπλῶς, ἀλλ᾽ οἷον ἑνὸς
πρὸς ἕνα [δύο] πρὸς δύο καὶ [πλείους] πρὸς
πλείους. καὶ πάλιν δυοῖν πρὸς ἕνα καὶ πρὸς δύο
καὶ πρὸς πλείους. ἔτι δὲ πλειόνων πρὸς ἕνα
(210,15)   καὶ πρὸς δύο καὶ πρὸς πλείους. προκειμένης   205
γὰρ χρείας, ὅτι (Chreia 40) " Ἰσοκράτης ὁ
ῥήτωρ τοὺς εὐφυεῖς τῶν μαθητῶν θεῶν παῖδας
ἔλεγεν εἶναι, " οὕτω κλίνομεν· ἑνὸς μὲν πρὸς
ἕνα, οἷον " Ἰσοκράτης ὁ ῥήτωρ τὸν εὐφυέα τῶν
μαθητῶν θεῶν παῖδα ἔλεγεν εἶναι. " δυοῖν δὲ   210
(210,20)   πρὸς δύο· " Ἰσοκράτεε τὼ ῥήτορε τὼ εὐφυέε
τῶν μαθητῶν θεῶν παῖδε ἐλεγέτην εἶναι. " πλειόνων δὲ πρὸς πλείους· " Ἰσοκράτεις οἱ ῥήτορες
τοὺς εὐφυεῖς τῶν μαθητῶν θεῶν παῖδας ἔλεγον
εἶναι. "   215
            Φανερὸν δὲ ἐκ τούτων πῶς καὶ τοὺς ἄλλους
τρόπους κλινοῦμεν. μεταλαμβάνονται γὰρ καὶ
(210,25)   εἰς τὰς πέντε πτώσεις, ἀλλ᾽ἐπεὶ τῶν χρειῶν αἱ
μέν εἰσιν λογικαί, αἱ δὲ πρακτικαί, αἱ δὲ ἐκ
ἀμφοῖν τούτοιν μικταί, καὶ τούτων αὖ ἕτερά   220
ἐστιν εἴδη, καθ᾽ἕκαστον αὐτῶν πειρασόμεθα
διδάσκειν τὴν κλίσιν ἐπὶ παραδείγματος.

---

202 δύο et πλείους del. Finckh 204-5 ἔτι δὲ ... πρὸς πλείους om.
R (add. in mg. R¹, qui pro πλειόνων exhibit πλεῖον unde Walz) et
edd. pr. 207 εὐφυεῖς AR¹ (in mg.)] τὸν εὐφυέα R εὐφυέας Camer.,
Hein. unde Walz; μαθητῶν om. Hein. unde Walz 212 θεῶν] θεοῦ Camer.,
Hein. unde Walz 216 τούτων] τούτου PMa

There are also exercises with chreiai in 1)
recitation, 2) inflexion, 3) comment, and 4) objection.
We also 5) expand and 6) condense the chreia. In
addition, we 7) refute and 8) confirm it.

And so 1) "Recitation" is obvious. For we try
to the best of our ability to report the assigned
chreia very clearly in the same words or in others
as well.

2) "Inflexion" is complex. For we change the
characters in the chreia into the three numbers.
And we do not do this unilaterally, but, for example,
from singular to singular, and to dual, and to plural.
And again, from dual to singular, and to dual, and
to plural. Further, from plural to singular, and to
dual, and to plural.[16] For in the case of a previous
chreia—namely (Chreia 40), *Isocrates the rhetor
used to say that gifted students are children of
gods*—we inflect in this way: singular to singular,
for example, *Isocrates the rhetor used to say that
the gifted student is a child of gods.* Dual to dual:
*The two rhetors named Isocrates used to say that
the two gifted students are two children of gods.*
Plural to plural: *The rhetors named Isocrates used
to say that gifted students are children of gods.*[17]

It is obvious from these examples how we will
inflect in the other ways, too. For chreiai are also
changed into the five cases. But since some chreiai
are sayings-chreiai, some action-chreiai, and some
a mixture of both of these, and since each of these
classes is further divided into several species, we
will try to demonstrate for each of these its
inflection with an example.

'Η μὲν οὖν ὀρθὴ οὐδεμίαν ἔχει δυσκολίαν,
κατὰ γὰρ αὐτὴν ἑκάστη τῶν χρειῶν εἴωθε προ-
φέρεσθαι.   225
(211,5)   Τὴν δὲ γενικὴν πτῶσιν οὕτω κλινοῦμεν·
ἐὰν μὲν λογικὴ ᾖ χρεία, προσθήσομεν αὐτῇ " τὸ
ῥηθὲν μνήμης ἔτυχε " ἢ " λόγος ἀπομνημονεύεται
εἰπόντος. " τὸ μὲν οὖν πρότερον μετὰ τὴν ἀπ-
αγγελίαν ὅλης τῆς χρείας εὐπρεπές ἐστιν ἐπ-   230
ενεκεῖν οἷον (Chreia 40) " Ἰσοκράτους τοῦ
(211,10)   ῥήτορος τοὺς εὐφυεῖς τῶν μαθητῶν θεῶν παῖδας
λέγοντος εἶναι τὸ ῥηθὲν μνήμης ἔτυχε. " τὸ δὲ
δεύτερον μεσούσης αὐτῆς καὶ τῆς ἀποφάσεως
ἀρχομένης, οἷον (Chreia 49) " Πιττακοῦ τοῦ   235
Μιτυληναίου ἐρωτηθέντος εἰ λανθάνει τις τοὺς
θεοὺς φαῦλόν τι ποιῶν λόγος ἀπομνημονεύεται
(211,15)   εἰπόντος, ' Οὐδὲ διανοούμενος '."
'Αρμόττει δὲ μᾶλλον τὸ μὲν " λόγος ἀπομνημονεύεται " πάσαις ταῖς λογικαῖς χρείαις   240
πλὴν τῆς καθ'ἑκούσιον ἀπόφασιν, ταύτῃ γὰρ
" τὸ ῥηθὲν μνήμης ἔτυχεν. "
'Εὰν δὲ πρακτικὴ ᾖ χρεία, εἰ μὲν παθητικὴ
εἴη, προσθετέον " τὸ συμβὰν μνήμης ἔτυχεν. " εἰ
(211,20)   δὲ ἐνεργητική, " τὸ πραχθὲν μνήμης ἔτυχεν. "   245
ὁμοίως δὲ καὶ ἐπὶ τοῦ μικτοῦ. ἐπὶ τέλει μέν-
τοι τῶν χρειῶν καὶ τούτων ἕκαστον προσθετέον,
οἷον (Chreia 21) " Διδύμωνος τοῦ αὐλητοῦ ἀλόντος
ἐπὶ μοιχείᾳ καὶ ἐκ τοῦ ὀνόματος κρεμασθέντος
τὸ συμβὰν μνήμης ἔτυχε. " καὶ (Chreia 25)   250
" Διογένους τοῦ Κυνικοῦ φιλοσόφου ἰδόντος
(211,25)   ὀψοφάγον παῖδα καὶ τὸν παιδαγωγὸν τῇ βακτηρίᾳ παίσαντος τὸ πραχθὲν μνήμης ἔτυχε. "

224 τὴν αὐτὴν MR; ἑκάστην PMMaR 227 χρεία LPMa] ἢ χρεία MR. 243
ἢ χρεία M 245 ἐνεργετική Walz, sed unde nescimus. 248 Διδύμωνος
L (in ras.) Darm, Dox, Plan] Διδύμου L² (ex corr.) PMMaR et edd.
plur.

So then, the nominative holds no difficulty, for
each of the chreiai is customarily cited in this case.

In the genitive case we will inflect in this way.
If it is a sayings-chreia, we will add to it "the
statement is remembered" or "the saying is recalled
of the one speaking." It is good style to add the
former after the recitation of the whole chreia.
For example (Chreia 40),[18] *Isocrates the rhetor's*
statement, when he said gifted students are children
of gods, is remembered. It is good style, however,
to add the second phrase in the middle of the
chreia and at the beginning of the statement. For
example (Chreia 49), *Pittacus of Mitylene's saying,*
on being asked if anyone escapes the notice of the
gods in committing some sinful act, is recalled, when
he said: "Not even in contemplating it."

The phrase "the saying is recalled" suits all the
sayings-chreiai better except the one in the form
of an unprompted statement. For to this one the
phrase "the statement is remembered" is better
suited.

Should it be an action-chreia, and if it is passive,
the expression "the experience is remembered"
should be added. If, however, it is active, "the act
is remembered" should be added, and the same holds
true for the mixed class[19] of chreia. One ought,
however, to add each of these expressions at the
end of the chreiai. For example (Chreia 21), *Of*
Didymon the flute-player, who was convicted of
adultery and hanged by his namesake, the
experience is remembered. Also (Chreia 25), *Of*
Diogenes the Cynic philosopher, who saw a boy who
was a gourmand and struck the paedagogus, the act
is remembered.

Τῇ δὲ δοτικῇ ἐπὶ πάσης χρείας πλὴν τῆς
παθητικῆς προσθήσομεν τὸ " ἔδοξεν " ἢ τὸ   255
"ἐφάνη" ἢ τὸ "ἐπῆλθεν" ἢ καὶ τὸ "παρέστη" ἤ
τι τῶν τοιούτων. οἶον (Chreia 23) " Διογένει
(211,30)   τῷ Κυνικῷ φιλοσόφῳ ἰδόντι μειράκιον πλούσιον
ἀπαίδευτον ἔδοξεν εἰπεῖν, ' Οὗτός ἐστι ῥύπος
περιηργυρωμένος '." ἐπὶ μὲν τῆς παθητικῆς   260
προσθήσομεν τὸ " συνέβη. " οἶον (Chreia 20)
" Διδύμωνι τῷ αὐλητῇ ἁλόντι ἐπὶ μοιχείᾳ συνέβη ἐκ τοῦ ὀνόματος κρεμασθῆναι. "
              Ἐπὶ δὲ τῆς αἰτιατικῆς προσθήσομεν καθ-
(212,5)   όλου ἐπὶ πάσης χρείας τὸ " φασὶ, " τὸ " λέγ-   265
εται. " οἶον (Chreia 23) " Διογένην τὸν
Κυνικὸν φιλόσοφον ἰδόντα μειράκιον πλούσιον
ἀπαίδευτον φασὶν εἰπεῖν (ἢ λέγεται), ' Οὗτός
ἐστι ῥύπος περιηργυρωμένος '."
              Ἡ δὲ κλητικὴ σαφής ἐστι, ποιησόμεθα   270
γὰρ τὸν λόγον πρὸς παρὸν ἡμῖν πρόσωπον, ἐφ'
(212,10)   ὃ ἡ χρεία ἀναφέρεται. οἶον (Chreia 23) " Διόγενες Κυνικὲ φιλόσοφε, ἰδὼν μειράκιον πλούσιον
ἀπαίδευτον εἶπας, ' Οὗτός ἐστι ῥύπος περιηργυρωμένος '."   275
              (3) Ἐπιφωνεῖν δέ ἐστιν ἀποδεχομένους
οἰκείως καὶ συντόμως τὸ λεγόμενον διὰ τῆς
χρείας ἢ ὡς ἀληθές ἐστιν ἢ ὡς καλὸν ἢ ὡς σύμ-
(212,15)   φερον ἢ ὡς καὶ ἄλλοις τὸ αὐτὸ τοῦτο ἔδοξεν
ἀνδράσι δεδοκιμασμένοις. οἶον (Chreia 38)   280
" Εὐριπίδης ὁ ποιητὴς τὸν νοῦν ἡμῶν ἑκάστου
ἔφησεν εἶναι θεόν. " ἐπιφωνήσομεν δὲ ἐκ μὲν
τοῦ ἀληθοῦς οὕτως· θεὸς γὰρ ὄντως ἑκάστῳ ὁ
νοῦς ἐφ'ἃ μὲν συμφέρει προτρέπων ἡμᾶς, ἀπ-
(212,20)   είργων δὲ τῶν ζημιούντων. ἐκ δὲ τοῦ καλοῦ   285
οὕτω· καλὸν γὰρ ἕκαστον μὴ ἐν χρύσῳ καὶ
ἀργύρῳ νομίζειν εἶναι τὸν θεόν, ἀλλ'ἐν ἑαυτῷ.

---

259 ῥύπος LMR] ῥῦπος P² (ex corr.) Ma ἵππος P¹ (in ras.) Darm,
Dox, Plan 262 Διδύμωνι L² (ex corr.) PMMaR et edd. plur. 268 ῥῦπος
PMa. 272 ὅ] ᾧ (sic) PMa 274 ῥύπος PMa 285 ἐκ δὲ] δὲ om. Walz

In the dative case, in every chreia except the
passive we will add the expression "it seemed best"
or "it appeared best" or "it occurred" or even
"it came to mind" or some such phrase. For example
(Chreia 23), *To Diogenes the Cynic philosopher, on
seeing a rich young man who was uneducated, it
seemed best to say: "This fellow is silver-plated
filth."* In the passive chreia we will add the
expression "it was the experience." For example
(Chreia 21), *To Didymon the fluteplayer who was
convicted of adultery it was the experience to be
hanged by his namesake.*

In the accusative case we will generally add to
any chreia the words "they say," "it is said." For
example (Chreia 23), *They say (or it is said) that
Diogenes the Cynic philosopher, on seeing a rich
young man who was uneducated, said: "This fellow
is silver-plated filth."*

The vocative case is straight-forward. For we
will directly address the character before us, to
whom the chreia is attributed. For example (Chreia
23), *You, Diogenes, Cynic philosopher, on seeing a
rich young man who was uneducated, said: "This
fellow is silver-plated filth."*

3) It is also possible for those who approve
of what has been fittingly and concisely said in
a chreia to comment that it is true or noble or
advantageous or that the saying has also appealed
to other men of distinction. For example (Chreia 38),
*The poet Euripides has said that the mind of each
of us is a god.* We will add comments on its being
true like this: "the mind in each of us really is a
god, directing us toward what is advantageous and
keeping us from injurious things." On its being noble,
like this: "it is indeed noble for each of us to believe
that god exists not in gold and silver but in
himself."

100 THE CHREIA IN ANCIENT RHETORIC

(212,25)

ἐκ δὲ τοῦ συμφέροντος οὕτως·...ἵνα μὴ διὰ
μακροῦ κεῖσθαι τὸ τιμωροῦν οἰόμενοι πολλὴν
τοῦ ἀδικεῖν ἔχοιμεν εὐχέρειαν. ἐκ δὲ τῆς   290
τῶν εὐδοκίμων μαρτυρίας, ὅταν ᾖ σοφὸν ἢ
νομοθέτην ἢ ποιητὴν ἢ ἄλλον τινὰ τῶν διωνο-
μασμένων λέγωμεν ὁμογνωμονεῖν τῷ ῥηθέντι.
οἷον ἐπὶ τῆς προκειμένης χρείας φήσομεν (Od.
18. 136-37)·   295

    τοῖος γὰρ νόος ἐστὶν ἐπιχθονίων ἀνθώπων,
    οἷον ἐπ' ἦμαρ ἄγῃσι πατὴρ ἀνδρῶν τε θεῶν τε.

(213,5)

(4) Ἀντιλέγομεν δὲ ταῖς χρείαις ἐκ τῶν
ἐναντίων, ὡς (Chreia 41) πρὸς τὸν Ἰσοκράτην
εἰπόντα ὅτι τοὺς διδασκάλους προτιμητέον   300
τῶν πατέρων, οἱ μὲν γὰρ τὸ ζῆν ἡμῖν, οἱ δὲ
διδάσκαλοι τὸ καλῶς ζῆν παρέσχοντο. φαμὲν
γὰρ ἀντιλέγοντες ὅτι οὐκ ἐνῆν καλῶς ζῆν, εἰ
μὴ τὸ ζῆν οἱ πατέρες παρέσχοντο. εἰδέναι δὲ
δεῖ ὅτι οὐ δυνατὸν ἀντιλέγειν πάσῃ χρείᾳ   305

(213,10)

πολλῶν καλῶς καὶ ἀμέμπτως εἰρημένων ὥσπερ
οὐδὲ πάσας ἐστιν ἐπαινεῖν διὰ τὸ τινων εὐθὺς
προσπίπτειν τὴν ἀτοπίαν.

(5) Ἐπεκτείνομεν δὲ τὴν χρείαν ἐπειδὰν
τὰς ἐν αὐτῇ ἐρωτήσεις τε καὶ ἀποκρίσεις,   310
καὶ εἰ πρᾶξις τις ἢ πάθος ἐνυπάρχῃ, μηκύν-
ομεν.

(213,15)

(6) Συστέλλομεν δὲ τὸ ἐναντίον ποιοῦντες,
οἷον σύντομος μὲν χρεία (Chreia 37) " Ἐπαμεινώνδας ἄτεκνος ἀποθνήσκων ἔλεγε τοῖς φίλοις,   315
' Δύο θυγατέρας ἀπέλιπον, τήν τε περὶ Λεῦκτρα
νίκην καὶ τὴν περὶ Μαντίνειαν '." ἐκτείνωμεν
δὲ οὕτως· Ἐπαμεινώνδας ὁ τῶν Θηβαίων στρατη-
γὸς ἦν μὲν ἄρα καὶ παρὰ τὴν εἰρήνην ἀνὴρ
ἀγαθός, συστάντος δὲ τῇ πατρίδι πολέμου   320

---

288 lacunam recte suspexit Scheff. 314 Ἐπαμεινώνδας MR] -ινώνδας
LPMa 316 Λεῦκτρα MR] Λεύκτραν LPMa unde Walz 317 ἐκτείνωμεν
PMa Armᵃ] -ομεν LM et edd. -τένομεν R 318 Θηβαίων MaR² (in mg.)]
Ἀθηναίων LPMR

On its being advantageous, like this:[20] ". . . so that
by supposing that punishment is not long delayed
we will not have a great deal of tolerance for wrong
doing." On the basis of testimony of renowned
persons: whenever we say that a wise man or
legislator or poet or some other well-known person
agrees with the saying. For example, in the case
of the preceding chreia we will say (*Od.* 18.136-37):

> The mind of earthly men is like the day
> Which the father of men and gods brings on.

4) We also object to chreiai from the opposite
points of view, as, for example (Chreia 41), against
Isocrates' saying that one should honor teachers
before parents, since the latter have offered us
the chance to live but teachers the chance to live
nobly. We say in objecting to this idea that it is
impossible to live nobly, unless our parents have
given us the chance to live. One must realize,
however, that it is impossible to object to every
chreia, since many have been expressed properly
and faultlessly. In the same way it is not possible
to praise all of them because some fall into outright
absurdity.

5) We expand the chreia whenever we enlarge
upon the questions and responses in it, and upon
whatever act or experience is in it.

6) We condense by doing the opposite. For
example, a concise chreia (Chreia 37): *Epameinondas,*
as he was dying childless, said to his friends: "I
have left two daughters — the victory at Leuctra
and the one at Mantineia." Let us expand like this:
Epameinondas the Theban general was, of course,
a good man in time of peace, and when war against

(213,20)   πρὸς Λακεδαιμονίους πολλὰ καὶ λάμπρα ἔργα
            τῆς μεγαλοψυχίας ἐπεδείξατο. βοιωταρχῶν μὲν
            περὶ Λεῦκτρα ἐνίκα τοὺς πολεμίους, στρατευ-
            όμενος δὲ ὑπὲρ τῆς πατρίδος καὶ ἀγωνιζόμενος
            ἀπέθανεν ἐν Μαντινείᾳ. ἐπεὶ δὲ τρωθεὶς   325
            ἐτελεύτα τὸν βίον, ὀλοφυρομένων τῶν φίλων
(213,25)   τά τε ἄλλα καὶ διότι ἄτεκνος ἀποθνήσκοι,
            μειδιάσας, " παύσασθε, " ἔφη, " ὦ φίλοι, κλαί-
            οντες, ἐγὼ γὰρ ὑμῖν ἀθανάτους δύο καταλέλοιπα
            θυγατέρας, δύο νίκας τῆς πατρίδος κατὰ   330
            Λακεδαιμονίων, τὴν μὲν ἐν Λεύκτροις τὴν
            πρεσβυτέραν, νεωτέραν δὲ τὴν ἄρτι μοι γενο-
            μένην ἐν Μαντινείᾳ.
                (7) Ἀνασκευαστέον δὲ ἔτι τὰς χρείας·
(214,5)   ἐκ τοῦ ἀσαφοῦς, ἐκ τοῦ πλεονάζοντος, ἐκ τοῦ   335
            ἐλλείποντος, ἐκ τοῦ ἀδυνάτου, ἐκ τοῦ ἀπιθά-
            νου, ἐκ τοῦ ψευδοῦς, ἐκ τοῦ ἀσυμφόρου, ἐκ τοῦ
            ἀχρήστου, ἐκ τοῦ αἰσχροῦ.
                Ἐκ μὲν τοῦ ἀσαφοῦς· ὡς εἰ λέγομεν τὸν
            Ἰσοκράτην (cf. Chreia 42) μὴ σαφῶς διωρικέ-   340
            ναι ὧν δεῖται πρὸς ῥητορείαν τὸ συνιστάμενον
(214,10)   αὐτῷ παιδίον. ὁμοίως δὲ ἔχει καὶ (cf. Chreia
            21) ἡ Διδύμωνος τοῦ αὐλητοῦ, οὐ γὰρ ἅπασι
            σαφές ἐστι τὸ " ἐκ τοῦ ὀνόματος ἐκρεμάσθη. "
                Ἐκ δὲ τοῦ πλεονάζοντος· ἐπειδὰν λέγ-   345
            ηταί τι οὗ ἀφαιρεθέντος οὐδὲν ἧττον διαμένει
            ἡ χρεία. οἷον (Chreia 57) " Σωκράτης ὁ φιλό-
            σοφος ἐρωτηθεὶς εἰ εὐδαίμων αὐτῷ δοκεῖ ὁ
(214,15)   Περσῶν βασιλεύς, ‘ Οὐκ ἔχω λέγειν, ’ ἔφη, ‘ μὴ
            γὰρ εἰδέναι πῶς ἔχει παιδείας ’." ἐπλεόνασε   350
            γὰρ οὐ μόνον πρὸς τὴν ἐρώτησιν ἀποκρινόμενος,

---

323 Λεῦκτρα MR] Λεύκτρα Ma Λεύκτραν P unde Walz Λύκτραν L 328
ἔφη om. MR (in mg. R¹) 329 καταλέλοιπα] κατέλιπα PMa. 339 ὡς εἰ
λέγομεν PMa Armᵃ] ὡς ἐλέγομεν LMR ὡς εἰ λέγοιμεν Camer., Hein.
unde Walz 340 διωρικέναι] διακρῖναι PMa 343 Διδύμωνος L (in ras.)
Darm, Dox, Plan] Διδύμου L² (ex corr.) PMMaR et edd.

the Lacedaemonians came to his country, he displayed many outstanding deeds of great courage. As a Boeotarch at Leuctra, he triumphed over the enemy, and while campaigning and fighting for his country, he died at Mantineia. While he was dying of his wounds and his friends were lamenting, among other things, that he was dying childless, he smiled and said: "Stop weeping, friends, for I have left you two immortal daughters: two victories of our country over the Lacedaemonians, the one at Leuctra, who is the older, and the younger, who is just now being born at Mantineia."

7) Furthermore, one must refute chreiai: for obscurity, for pleonasm, for ellipsis, for impossibility, for implausibility, for falsity, for unsuitability, for uselessness, for shamefulness.

"For obscurity:" as if we say that Isocrates (cf. Chreia 42) did not identify clearly what the boy being enrolled with him needed for a course in rhetoric.[21] The chreia (cf. 21) about Didymon the flute-player is similar. For the expression "being hanged by his namesake" is not clear to everyone.[22]

"For pleonasm:" whenever something is said which, if it is taken away, the chreia nonetheless remains. For example (Chreia 57), *Socrates the philosopher, on being asked whether the Persian king seemed happy to him, said: "I can't say, for I can't even know where he stands on education."* For he has been pleonastic not only in responding to the question,

ἀλλὰ καὶ τῆς ἀποκρίσεως αἰτίαν εἰπών, οὐκ
ἀναμείνας εἴπερ ἄρα ἐπανερωτήσει, ὅπερ οὐκ
ἦν κατὰ Σωκράτην ἄνδρα διαλεκτικὸν ὄντα.

(214,20)   Ἐκ δὲ τοῦ ἐλλείποντος· ὅταν δείκνυμεν   355
μὴ καλῶς (cf. Chreia 17) φάμενον τὸν Δημοσ-
θένην ὑπόκρισιν εἶναι τὴν ῥητορικήν· πολλῶν
γὰρ καὶ ἄλλων εἰς αὐτὴν δεόμεθα.

Ἐκ δὲ τοῦ ἀδυνάτου· ὡς ἃν φῶμεν πρὸς
τὸν Ἰσοκράτην (cf. Chreia 40) μὴ δυνατὸν ἐκ   360
θεῶν ἀνθρώπους γενέσθαι, μηδ'ἃ ν εὐφυεῖς ὦσιν.

Ἐκ δὲ τοῦ ἀπιθάνου· ὅτι μὴ εἰκός ἐστιν
(215,5)   (Chreia 6) Ἀντισθένην Ἀττικόν γε ὄντα, παραγενόμενον Ἀθήνηθεν εἰς Λακεδαίμονα, ἐκ τῆς
γυναικωνίτιδος λέγειν εἰς τὴν ἀνδρωνῖτιν   365
ἐπιέναι.

Ἐκ δὲ τοῦ ψευδοῦς· ὅτι μὴ ἀληθῶς (Chreia
10) " ὁ Βίων ἔλεγε τὴν φιλαργυρίαν μητρόπολιν
εἶναι τῆς κακίας, " μᾶλλον γὰρ ἀφροσύνη ἐστίν.

Ἐκ δὲ τοῦ ἀσυμφόρου· ὅτι βλαβερῶς   370
(215,10)   παραινεῖ (Chreia 56) Σιμωνίδης παίζειν ἐν
τῷ βίῳ καὶ περὶ μηδὲν ἁπλῶς σπουδάζειν.

Ἐκ δὲ τοῦ ἀχρήστου· ὅσον εἰ φαίνοιτο
πρὸς οὐδὲν ὠφέλιμον τὸ ῥηθὲν τῷ βίῳ.

Ἐκ δὲ τοῦ αἰσχροῦ· ὁπόταν αἰσχρὰν   375
καὶ ἐπονείδιστον ἀποφαίνωμεν τὴν χρείαν.
οἷον (Chreia 62) " ἀνὴρ Συβαρίτης ἰδὼν Λακε-
(215,15)   δαιμονίους ἐπιπόνως ζῶντας οὐ θαυμάζειν ἔφησεν
ὅτι ἐν τοῖς πολέμοις οὐκ ὀκνοῦσιν ἀποθνήσκειν,
ἄμεινον γὰρ εἶναι τὸν θάνατον τοῦ τοιούτου   380
βίου. " πάνυ γὰρ μαλακῶς καὶ οὐκ ἀνδρείου
τρόπου τὴν ἀπόφασιν ἐποιήσατο. ἐκ μὲν οὖν
τούτων ἀνασκευαστέον.

357 καὶ τὴν PMMaR.   373 ὅσον] οἷον Hein. et edd. rec.

but also in providing the explanation for his
response without waiting to see whether the person
was even going to ask a further question. This was
not at all like Socrates, who was one to use dialectic.

"For ellipsis:" whenever we show that
Demosthenes did not speak properly in saying that
(Chreia 17) *rhetoric is simply delivery.* For we need
many other things for rhetoric.[23]

"For impossibility:" as though we say to
Isocrates (cf. Chreia 40) that it is impossible for
people to be born from gods, even if they are
gifted.

"For implausibility:" because it is unlikely that
(Chreia 6) *Antisthenes,* who was of course an
Athenian, *said on coming from Athens to Lacedaemon
that he was coming from the women's quarters to
the men's.*[24]

"For falsity:" because (Chreia 10) *Bion said*
untruthfully *that love of money is the mother-city
of evil.* Rather, the evil is ignorance.[25]

"For unsuitability:" namely (Chreia 56) Simonides'
*advice to play in life and to be entirely serious
about nothing* is harmful.

"For uselessness:" to the extent that the
saying should appear useful for nothing in life.

"For shamefulness:" whenever we pronounce the
chreia shameful and disgraceful. For example (Chreia
62), *A Sybarite, on seeing the Lacedaemonians living
a life of toil, said he did not wonder that in their
wars they do not hesitate to die, for death is better
than such a life.* For he made a statement in a
very effeminate manner and one that is not in
keeping with a manly character. So then, one should
refute on the basis of these reasons.

(216,5)

(8) Πρὸς ἕκαστον δὲ μέρος τῆς χρείας
ἀρξάμενον ἀπὸ τῶν πρώτων ἐπιχειρεῖν δεῖ,　　385
ἐξ ὅσων τόπων ἐὰν δυνατὸν ᾖ. μὴ λανθανέτω
γὰρ ἡμᾶς ὅτι οὐχ οἷόν τέ ἐστιν ἐν πάσαις ἐκ
πάντων ἐπιχειρεῖν.

Τὴν μέντοι τάξιν τῶν ἐπιχειρημάτων ποι-
ησόμεθα, καθὰ καὶ τῶν τόπων ἐκτιθέμεθα. οἱ　　390
αὐτοὶ δ'ἂν εἶεν καὶ πρὸς τὴν τῶν γνωμῶν
ἀνασκευήν τε καὶ κατασκευήν. τοῖς δὲ ἤδη
τελειοτέροις προσήκει τὰς ἀφορμὰς λαμβάνειν

(216,10)
καὶ ἐκ τῶν πρὸς τὰς θέσεις ἡμῖν παραθησομένων.

Χρὴ δὲ τὸ προοίμιον μὴ τοιοῦτον εἶναι,　　395
ὥστε ἐφαρμόττειν ἑτέραις χρείαις, ἀλλ'ἴδιον
τῆς ὑποκειμένης. τοῦτο δ'ἂν καλῶς γένοιτο
ἐπί τε χρείας καὶ μύθου καὶ τῶν ἄλλων ἀπάντων,

(216,15)
ὅταν ἐξ ἑνὸς ἢ δύο τῶν ἀνωτάτω μερῶν τὰς ἀφορμὰς τῶν προοιμίων λαμβάνωμεν. μετὰ δὲ τὸ　　400
προοίμιον αὐτήν τε τὴν χρείαν ἐκθετέον, εἶτα
ἐξῆς τὰς ἐπιχειρήσεις. χρηστέον δὲ ἐνταῦθα
καὶ αὐξήσεσι καὶ παρεκβάσεσι καὶ ἤθεσιν, οἷς
δυνατόν ἐστιν.

386 τόπων] τρόπων R (in mg., corr. R¹)　391 εἶεν] εἶναι PMa.　402
δὲ om. R (add. in mg. R¹).

8) It is necessary, however, to provide
arguments for each part of the chreia,[26] beginning
with the first ones, using as many topics as
possible. For let us not ignore the fact that it
is impossible in the case of every chreia to argue
from every topic.

We will arrange the arguments just as we also
set forth the order of topics. The same topics,
moreover, could be used for refuting and confiming
maxims. It is appropriate, however, for more
advanced students to start from those topics
which we have postponed to the chapter on theses.

Now the introduction must not be such that it
fits other chreiai. Rather, it should be special to
the chreia which follows. This would be correct for
a chreia, a fable, and all other exercises, whenever
we take the starting points for the introduction
from one or two of the main parts. After the
introduction one should set forth the chreia itself;
then, in order, the arguments. Here one must use
elaborations, digressioins, and character
delineations, where there is an opportunity for
them.

1. Although at times πρόσωπον seems to have the general meaning of "person," the contrived nature of the chreia and its frequent use of dialogue and dramatic situations make the basic and limited meaning of the noun more appropriate. Consequently, here and throughout the translations we render πρόσωπον with "character," i.e., one who plays a role.

2. The phrase ἢ ἀναλογοῦν προσώπῳ is strange and obscure. Furthermore, it does not appear in the other definitions of the chreia. Nevertheless, in a later chapter Theon distinguishes between general characters—a husband or a general—and such specified characters (ὡρισμένα πρόσωπα) as Cyrus and Datis (cf. *Progymn.* 10 [1.235, 11-18 Walz]). In his definition of the chreia, however, Theon places the specified character first and identifies it with the words εἴς τι ὡρισμένον πρόσωπον. Included here would be all chreiai attributed to such specified characters as Alexander, Diogenes, and Isocrates. But nowhere does Theon's definition cover a chreia without a specified character, such as the Laconian of Chreia 45 or the Sybarite of Chreia 62—nowhere, that is, unless the phrase ἀναλογοῦν πρόσωπον covers it.

Since Theon has just used the phrase ὡρισμένον πρόσωπον, he may have retained the adjective in his mind and thus understood, or intended us to understand, ὡρισμένῳ with προσώπῳ. The phrase, however, remains obscure.

3. No really good English equivalent of ἀπομνημόνευμα is available. A literal translation is perhaps "memoir," but this word has a restricted meaning and usually implies an autobiographical account. The Greek term has no such restricted connotation. Consequently, we have chosen the word "reminiscence" which retains some of the etymological sense of the Greek without the restriction of "memoir." The chief drawback of "reminiscence" is the difficulty in retaining Theon's play on the noun and its related verb in lines 23-24.

4. Plutarch has an interesting play on these words in the introduction to his *Regum et Imperatorum Apophthegmata* (172C). In fact, the introduction as a whole is valuable evidence of the role of the chreia and reminiscence in ancient literature.

5. The phrase καθ' ἑαυτὸ μνημονεύεται is troublesome, and Theon could surely have found a better way to make his point. Yet the general context seems to indicate the meaning: The preceding words (ἀναφέρεται εἴς τινα πρόσωπα) repeat the idea of 2-4 and again stress the fictional nature of the chreia. Since Theon's contrast here between chreia and reminiscence

hinges on this very point, he seems to be saying that the reminiscence is not arbitrarily attributed to a character. Since it recounts a real event, either an action or saying, which is complete with the identity of the actual person, there can be no manipulating of history. The reminiscence must be reported as it happened, in and of itself. Xenophon's *Memorabilia* is an example of this distinction.

 6. Theon uses γένος for the three main divisions of the chreiai and εἶδος for the following sub-divisions. But see Comment 8 below.

 7. Here and throughout the translations chreiai are numbered for easy reference to the "Catalogue of Chreiai," where all the chreiai from these rhetorical discussions are collected and discussed.

 8. Notice that Theon writes γένει ("class") here, although he obviously means εἶδος ("species"), for the ambiguity lies in calling this fourth sub-division the same name as the ἀποκριτικὸν εἶδος itself.

 Apparently, one of Theon's sources had arranged the γένη —or the εἴδη—in a different way, and he is attempting to make some corrections. His use of ὁμωνύμως seems to imply disagreement with his source, but his own discussion of the subject is far from clear.

 9. Or perhaps "suffered," for πάθος admits both meanings.

 10. For clarification of the phrase ἐκ τοῦ ὀνόματος, see Comment 22 below.

 11. Cf. Aristotle, *Post. Anal.* 1.6 (75a 12): ἐπίσταται ἀποδεικτικῶς. Much of Theon's technical vocabulary seems to have been derived, directly or indirectly, from Aristotle. See also Comments 12 and 13 below.

 12. For the term see, e.g., Aristotle, *Post. Anal.* 1.6 (74b 11), and *Prior Anal.* 1.1 (24b 11).

 13. For the term see, e.g., Aristotle, *Prior Anal.* 2.27 (70a 11), and *Rhet.* 1.1.11 (1355a 6).

 14. Or "prayer."

 15. The double entendre arises from the fact that in Greek the letters ΚΑΙΝΟΥ can be read as either καινοῦ ("new") or as καὶ νοῦ ("and a mind"). There is, of course, no way to retain the pun in English.

 16. This passage has caused considerable trouble for scribes and editors alike (see the apparatus). The best way to demonstrate Theon's arrangement here is with a chart:

```
        A           B           C
```

1 ἑνὸς πρὸς ἕνα καὶ [δύο] πρὸς δύο καὶ [πλείους] πρὸς πλείους
2 δυοῖν πρὸς ἕνα καὶ πρὸς δύο καὶ πρὸς πλείους
3 πλείον⟨ων⟩ πρὸς ἕνα καὶ πρός δύο καὶ πρὸς πλείους

The first word in each line refers to the πρόσωπον, and it is genitive because it depends on some such word as λόγος, πρᾶξις, or ἀπόφασις. Troubles arose when scribes failed to realize that Theon cut across his three categories when he selected his examples (see lines 205-15) and chose (using the designations of the chart) 1A, 2B, and 3C.

17. The expressions "the two rhetors named Isocrates" and "the rhetors named Isocrates" are attempts to render the dual and plural numbers of the singular Ἰσοκράτης.

18. Here and in all the versions of the chreiai which follow it is impossible to reflect exactly the Greek word order in English.

19. The neuter τοῦ μικτοῦ requires a neuter noun, no doubt γένος —hence our rendering: "for the mixed class of chreia." Note, however, that just above in lines 240 and 243 Theon uses the feminine forms of the adjectives for the classes: sayings-chreiai and action chreiai.

20. As Scheffer saw, something has obviously fallen from the text here. He suggested that the missing Greek was something like this: "for it is of advantage to believe that there is a god in our mind" so that etc. Walz and Finckh quote Scheffer's suggestion in a note, but, like Spengel, they fail to indicate a lacuna in the text.

21. Theon is referring, of course, to the ambiguity of the letters ΚΑΙΝΟΥ. Cf. above Comment 15.

22. The obscurity here arises from the fact that we must supply Didymon's name, so that ἐκ τοῦ ὀνόματος becomes ἐκ τῶν Διδύμων and hence also ἐκ τῶν διδύμων, that is, "by his testicles," as explained in an anonymous scholion on Aphthonius (2.17, 21-23 Walz).

23. Rhetoricians usually regarded invention, arrangement, expression, and memory as equally necessary for rhetoric as delivery (see, e.g., Quintilian, *Inst.* 3.1.1).

24. The implausibility presumably stems from an Athenian like Antisthenes comparing Athens and Sparta, to the detriment of the former. Hence perhaps the attribution elsewhere to Diogenes of Sinope (so Diogenes Laertius, 6.59).

25. Theon can hardly refute Bion's statement as untrue. He is merely rejecting a popular notion (cf. 1 Tim. 6.10 and the "Catalogue of Chreiai") in favor of a more philosophical one, ignorance (ἀφροσύνη) being the opposite of the principal

virtue of self-control (σωφροσύνη) (cf., e.g., Plato's *Protag.* 332E, and Diogenes Laertius, 7.93).

26. On the meaning of "each part of the chreia" and indeed on the whole of this last section, see the discussion of this troublesome passage in the "Introduction" to Theon, above p. 72.

DISCUSSION OF PRELIMINARY EXERCISES OF
MARCUS FABIUS QUINTILIANUS

Introduction, Translation and Comments

by

EDWARD N. O'NEIL

INTRODUCTION

I

Life and Writings. Marcus Fabius Quintilianus (c. A.D. 30-100) remains for us one of the famous and influential men of letters in the Silver Age of Latin literature. His *Institutiones Oratoriae* achieved a great reputation in antiquity and retained it throughout the Middle Ages. Even today, in an age which cares little for the subject, his name remains synonymous with ancient rhetorical education.

Yet, despite his fame as a rhetorician and teacher, only scanty information about his personal life has survived. Moreover, the little that we know or can estimate has already been said many times. There is no need to serve up the *crambe repetita*[1] again.

Who has not heard that Quintilian was born in Spain around A.D. 30, that he came to Rome as a young man, mingled in high society, became a famous *rhetor* and under Vespasian was probably the first teacher to receive a salary from the state? Tradition also reports that he became a wealthy man and that after twenty years of teaching he retired to write his famous work on rhetoric. Domitian appointed him tutor of his two great-nephews, the sons of Flavius Clemens,[2] and this association brought Quintilian the *ornamenta consularia*.[3]

Sometime before his retirement, he married a young girl who bore him two sons and died before she was nineteen. Neither son survived boyhood, and grief at their deaths overwhelmed the father. He attempted to console himself with his writing, but rhetoric can offer little real consolation to the soul.[4] The date of Quintilian's death in unknown, but scholars generally agree in placing it no later than A.D. 100.

This much, and not a great deal more, appears in many editions of the *Institutiones Oratoriae* as well as in numeerous handbooks and encycolpaedias.[5] It must suffice here. We can add nothing new, and so we turn our attention to Quintilian's writings.

For all practical purposes, Quintilian is the author of a single work, the *Institutiones Oratoriae* in twelve books. He himself refers to certain speeches and essays of his, some of which were published without his authorization,[6] but none of these compositions has survived. In addition, there is the so-called *Declamationes Quintilianeae*, a two-part collection of some 388 rhetorical pieces, but these brief compositions cannot be the work of the great teacher, though they may be in part derived form his teachings.[7]

The *Institutiones Oratoriae* deals with the training of an orator from early childhood to the grown man who has become a polished orator. In broad outline, this *magnum opus* is arranged as follows, book by book:

1: Elementary education.
2: Education under a rhetor; nature and use of rhetoric.
3: Origin, parts and function of rhetoric; *status*.
4-6: Detailed structure of a speech.
7: Arrangement (*dispositio*).
8: Style.
9: Figures of thought and speech.
10: Critique of Greek and Latin authors; *imitatio*; practical details of composition.
11: Physical aspects of oratory: memory, delivery, gesture, dress.
12: The complete orator in action: his character, learning, skill; styles of oratory; age for retirement and activities in retirement.

II

Institutiones Oratoriae 1.9.1-1.10.1. The general subject of Book I is elementary education, and part of the discussion concerns the *grammaticus*, i.e., teacher of literature, and his role in the system. In chapter 9 Quintilian examines the elementary exercises for which the *grammaticus* is primarily responsible, and this section is the focus of our attention. In order, however, to give the discussion its proper setting, the first part of chapter 10 is included in the following summary.

The arrangement is fairly simple—up to a point.[8] Lines 1-4 serve as a transition from the previous section: *ratio loquendi* (2) refers back to 1.4-7, *enarratio auctorum* (2-3) refers to 1.8. Then Quintilian turns (4-5) to *quaedam dicendi primordia*. Among these "preliminary exercises" the first (6-9) is the *fabella* (fable), then (9-14) *recitatio* of poetic passages and in sequence (14-19) *sententia* (maxim), *chria* and an item which seems to bear the designation *aetiologia*. From this confusing and problematic passage (see below) Quintilian turns to the *chria* (19-32) and finally (32-33) to the *narratiuncula* (simple narrative).

At this point he turns abruptly from his condensed treatment of the preliminary exercises to a discussion of the respective roles and responsibilities of the *grammaticus* and *rhetor* in the education system (33-36). Then, finally, after an apology for the brevity of his treatment (37-39), he glances ahead (39-42) to the topics he will next discuss, i.e., the remaining sections of the ἐγκύκλος παιδεία: music (1.10.9-33), mathematics (1.10.34-39), vocal training (1.11.1-4) and physical training (1.11.15-19).

Such a summary, or course, does little more than identify the various items which Quintilian touches on in this section and consequently makes several unsupported assumptions. Several problematic words and phrases, however, require closer study. Quintilian's *"quaedam dicendi primordia"* present at least four problems: 1) the phrase itself, 2) the exercise with poetic passages (9-14), 3) the problem of *aetiologia* (15, 18), and 4) the meaning of *narratiuncula* (32). The analysis of each problem must often touch upon that of the others, yet it is better to keep the discussions separated as far as that is possible.

1) Meaning of *quaedam dicendi primordia*. This phrase has attracted little attentioin because critics have assumed that Quintilian means by it nothing more or less than *progymnasmata*. This assumption, however, is incorrect but contains just enough of the truth to conceal the author's real reasons for employing the unusual expression.

There are three reasons. First, as earlier discussions have shown,[9] the term *progymnasmata* was not used to designate these classroom exercises until sometime after Quintilian and Theon. If a regular term existed at all among the Greeks, it was *gymnasmata*. And yet, even this designation was apparently unsatisfactory to Quintilian, and this point leads to his other reasons for employing the term *quaedam dicendi primordia*.

First, although he is concerned with elementary exercises which were—or at least became—a part of the standard *progymnasmata*, Quintilian at most includes only the first four, viz. fable, maxim, chreia, and narrative. As his discussion clearly shows, these four are the only exercises which a *grammaticus* should handle. Consequently, here in 1.9 he turns aside after *narratiunculae* to a discussion of the respective roles of a *grammaticus* and *rhetor*. When he later returns to his treatment of the exercises (2.4), he has in mind the *rhetor* and those students who have now advanced beyond the *grammaticus*. Thus the second reason for Quintilian's avoidance of the term *progymnasmata* is that he discusses only a few of those exercises.

The last reason is that he apparently adds two exercises which do not appear in the standard *progymnasmata*. After *fabella* he inserts (9-14) an exercise based on the paraphrase and recitation of poetic passages. Then, after *sententia* and *chria* he refers (15 and 18) to an exercise which seems to involve a rhetorical figure. Each of these exercises will be examined in detail below.

In summary, then, Quintilian neither uses nor has in mind the designation *progymnasmata* because 1) this term did not yet exist, 2) he is not considering all the classroom exercises here and 3) he adds two exercises which seem never to have achieved the status of a regular exercise. His choice of terms is deliberate and expressive, expecially the indefinite adjective *quaedam* which at once renders the whole phrase more general and less technical. This one word alone is a clear signal that Quintilian is deviating from the usual treatment of the subject.

2) Nature of the exercise with poetic passages (9-14). The problem here concerns the discussion in lines 6-14. Do these lines deal only with the fable or does Quintilian add a similar but different exercise which involves the paraphrase and recitation of poetic passages?

For several reasons the answer must be, as F. H. Colson long ago demonstrated,[10] that the discussion involves two separate exercises. The break comes with the words *versus primo solvere* (9). In the first place, the term "Aesop's Fables" refers to a species of fable,[11] and these compositions were usually written in prose. The noun *versus* can, of course, refer to a line of prose, but Quintilian's phrase *versus . . . solvere*, contrary to H. E. Butler's interpretation,[12] means "to express in prose," thus demonstrating that he has poetic models in mind, not "Aesop's Fables."

J. P. Postgate, who recognized only one exercise here, attempted to get around the reference to Aesop's Fables by suggesting that Quintilian actually refers to the fables of Phaedrus.[13] Yet, if this were his intention, Quintilian would surely have named his author. As a matter of fact, it is apparent in several places that he has Greek, not Latin, models in mind; cf. *putant* (25) and *dicunt* χρειῶδες (28-29).

The chief argument against two separate exercises is the syntax of the Latin and in particular the construction of *condiscant* (9). This verb clearly governs the two preceding infinitives *narrare* (7) and *exigere* (9) as well as the three which follow: *solvere* (9), *interpretari* and *vertere* (10). If we are to punctuate the text in such a way that the two exercises are distinct, we must do something about *condiscant*.

Colson, despite his belief that Quintilian discusses two exercises, printed a colon after *condiscant* in his edition.[14] Later both Helmut Rahn[15] and Michael Winterbottom[16] used the same mark. Butler, who apparently recognized only one exercise, printed a semi-colon.[17] Neither mark is satisfactory. The colon implies that the second statement follows logically on the first; the semi-colon begs the question. Yet the fact remains that, whatever punctuation we use, we must understand *condiscant* with the words that follow the mark.

The only alternative is to emend the text and insert a second *condiscant*. Yet emendation is an unlikely solution because of Quintilian's avowed brevity in this chapter (cf. 37), so we are left with the need to supply the verb. An editor, however, must also give a clear indication of exactly where the discussion of one exercise ends and that of the second begins. Whether the solution in this text is an improvement or not, we have elected to place a period after *condiscant* and in the translation repeat the verb with the words that follow.

However the passage is punctuated, two points are clear: Quintilian discusses two separate exercises, and he intends for the reader to understand *condiscant* as the main verb with both. The Latin is awkward, but the author's attempt at brevity is the cause.

There is another problem in this passage. Quintilian's statement (12-14) that the task of paraphrasing and reciting is *consummatis professoribus difficile* has prompted several critical comments and interpretations. Uncertainty about the meaning of these words is reasonable, for the exercise under discussion, whether it involves fables or poetic passages, is expressly designed for young students who are still under the tutelage of the *grammaticus*. How then can such a teacher expect his charges to cope with an exercise that is a challenge even for him?

Yet apparently Quintilian expects it, for later in 10.5.8, where he has in mind those students who are working under a *rhetor*, he points out that paraphrase itself *utilisima est exercitationi difficultas*. Apparently, then, his philosophy advocates throwing the young student into deep water and forcing him to swim. In fact, he voices this same philosophy earlier in 1.1.30 where he discusses the learning of syllables and says

> Syllabis nullum compendium est; perdiscendae omnis
> nec, ut fit plerumque, difficillima quaeque earum
> differenda, ut in nominibus scribendis depre-
> hendantur.

> For syllables there is no short cut. All must be
> learned thoroughly, nor, as frequently happens,
> should the most difficult ones be postponed with
> the result that they (sc. students) are caught
> making errors in the writing of words.

Despite Quintilian's later evaluation of paraphrase and his
earlier comment on learning syllables, some editors have been
troubled by his statement here in 1.9 and have attempted
to alter the obvious sense of the words either by emending
the text or by interpreting the phrase in a way that differs
from a normal understanding. For example, Colson rejects the
suggestion of Spalding that *consummatis professoribus* is
ablative and means "with accomplished teachers."[18] Colson is
right, for the ablative is impossible. No Roman could have
understood   anything   but   the   dative   with   *difficile*.
Furthermore, had Quintilian intended the idea which Spalding
suggested, he would probably have written *apud consummatos
professores* (cf. 15).

Colson   himself   is   more   attracted   to   the   emendation
suggested by Sarpe, who wanted to read *profectibus*, but
this word seems equally impossible. The sense of Quintilian's
phrase surely points to people, but *profectus* in Quintilian —
and seemingly everywhere else — refers to "progress," not
to those making progress. For the latter sense we need
profectis or even *illis profectis*, and in combination with
consummatis either expression is extremely awkward, if not
impossible.

In summary, then, the words *consummatis professoribus
difficile* refer   to   an   exercise   involving   paraphrase   and
recitation of poetic passages. Moreover, despite what at first
glance appears to be a curious statement, the text is sound.
We must accept the fact that Quintilian advocated a "sink

or swim" philosophy in the early training of boys.

3) The problem of *"aetiologia"* (15 and 18). Actually the problem is a three-fold one: a) the manuscript evidence for *aetiologia* and for *ethologia*, the reading which most editors have adopted; b) the meaning of the two words; c) Quintilian's apparent confusion of the term with *chria*.

a) The evidence for *aetiologia* and *ethologia* has been discussed by Colson[19] and more especially by R. P. Robinson,[20] both of whom have shown that no manuscript authority whatsoever exists for *ethologia* in Quintilian 1.9 and very little for it in Suetonius' *De Gram.* 4.7, the passage which editors have invariably cited as a parallel.

It was Raphaël Regius who first (1493) printed *ethologia* in Quintilian and Beroaldus (Filippo Beroaldo) who emended (1504) the text of Suetonius and printed *ethologia* on the basis of Regius' emendation. This reading remained standard in both texts, with editors of one author citing the emended text of the other to justify the term, until Colson and Robinson examined the problem more than four hundred years later.

The matter should have been settled then, with *aetiologia* restored to the text. Indeed, in 1970 Winterbottom wrote, "It is, I hope, unnecessary to argue about *aetiologia* since Colson's note,"[21] and this is the reading which he printed in his critical text. Two years later, however, Helmut Rahn printed *ethologia*, apparently unaware of the work of Colson, Robinson and Winterbottom.[22] At any rate, the revised Teubner edition (1959) of Radermacher-Buchheit[23] prints *ethologia* and fails to list *aetiologia* even in the apparatus. And to crown the list of futility, the new *Oxford Latin Dictionary*[24] cites both Quintilian and Suetonius for *ethologia* but for *aetiologia* lists only Seneca's *Epist. Mor.* 95.65, without a reference to the other two authors.

Here the matter stands today, and unfortunately here it will probably remain for a long time. The Teubner text will ensure the continuing legitimacy of *ethologia* in most of Europe; the *OLD* will take care of England, the United States and most of the English speaking world, and any defense of *aetiologia* will likely prove futile.[25] Yet, to repeat an undeniable fact: the manuscript evidence indicates that both Quintilian and Suetonius wrote *aetiologia*, not *ethologia*. Such evidence, however, is not enough. The reading must also make sense in the context, and to this matter we can now turn.

   b) The meaning of *aetiologia* and *ethologia*. In this analysis of the problem Colson and Robinson cite Seneca's *Epist. Mor.* 95.65, the only passage in which both words appear, where they are defined, and where Seneca even says that the *grammatici* use the word *aetiologia*. The passage runs as follows:

> Posidonius believes that not only the preceptual (*praeceptio*)—for nothing prevents our using this word—but also persuasion, consolation and exhortation are necessary. To these he adds "the investigation of causes," *aetiologia*—for I see no reson why we should not venture to use this term since the *grammatici*, guardians of the Latin language, use it in their own right. He says that description of individual virtues will also be useful. This description Posidonius calls *ethologia;* some people call it *characterismos*, which describes the signs and distinguishing marks of individual virtues and vices by which similar things are distinguished from one another.

At first glance, this passage seems to provide us with the necessary information to distinguish *aetiologia* and *ethologia*. The former, says Seneca, means investigation of causes and is a word used by the *grammatici;* the latter is the same as *characterismos*, which means a description of signs and distinguishing marks of individual virtues and vices. Yet Seneca makes it clear throughout his discussion that he is concerned with Posidonius' moral system of philosophy, not with rhetorical or grammatical terminology as such.[26] His reference to the *grammatici* merely justifies his use of a loan word and in no way implies the existence of a regular exercise called *aetiologia*. He has made a similar apology in the opening remark after using *praeceptio* to translate Posidonius' παραινετική.[27] In this instance he gives the Latin word a sense that is outside its normal range of meaning, and for that reason he calls attention to the fact by saying "for nothing prevents our using this word."

Thus in his effort to express some of Posidonius' terms, Seneca felt it necessary to give a new meaning to one standard Latin word[28] and to use two Greek words which were apparently not in regular use in Latin. But to repeat, philosophy is the subject here, not rhetorical principles, exercises or terminology. This passage offers just one example of the fact that some words were technical terms in both philosophy and rhetoric.

The evidence for *ethologia*, however, either as a philosophical or rhetorical term, is sparse. Except for the passage of Seneca, it seems to appear only in Charisius.[29] In his section entitled *De schemate dianoeas* (*On Figures of Thought*) he lists fifteen *species*, and the fourth in the list is *ethologia*. Unfortunately, Charisius provides no definition (although he does so for the other items in the list) and merely cites an example.[30] Yet the appearance of *ethologia* here is proof that some authorities at least considered it a rhetorical figure.

For *characterismos*, which Seneca equates with *ethologia*, there is better evidence. Several Latin grammarians list it as a standard *schema dianoeas*: Rutilius Lupus,[31] the anonymous *Carmen de Figuris*[32] and *Schemata Dianoeas*,[33] and Isidore.[34] Although the definitions in these authors differ slightly, the basic meaning of *characterismos* is clear; it is a verbal picture of a person designed to describe both his outer appearance and his inner attitude. Such a definition, while close to that of Seneca (or Posidonius), is not really in total agreement. The grammarians stress a description of a person; Seneca emphasizes description of the outward signs of a virtue or vice. Furtherlmore, even the *grammatici* do not consider *characterismos* to be an exercise. To them it

is a rhetorical figure, a status which Quintilian himself
explicitly denies the term (9.3.99).

What about *aetiologia?* Here the evidence is more plentiful,
and only a summary is possible. It appears to be a fairly
regular term in philosophy and rhetoric, but its meaning in
the two areas differs, at least in part.

Among philosophers *aetiologia* may mean either
"investigation of causes" or "statement of causes," i.e.,
"explanation." The first meaning, as we have seen, is the
one which Posidonius, as interpreted by Seneca, uses.[35] It
also appears in Epicurus[36] and perhaps Democritus.[37] In the
terminology of the Sceptics, however, *aetiologia* means
"statement of causes." For example, Sextus Empiricus[38]
discusses eight "modes" (τρόποι) which Aenesidemus proposed
for refuting every δογματικὴ αἰτιολογία.[39]

In rhetorical and grammatical texts, *aetiologia* always
means "statement of causes." This is its meaning in such Latin
writers as Rutilius Rufus,[40] Julius Rufinanus,[41] the *Carmen de
Figuris*,[42] *Schemata Dianoeas*,[43] Isidore[44] and St. Augustine.[45]
Among Greek writers the same definition appears in three
works bearing the title Περὶ σχημάτων.[46] In addition,
ps.-Aristeides, who offers no precise definition of αἰτιολογία,
analyzes six different passages from literature[47] in such a
way that he clearly understands the term in exactly the
same way as the other writers.

Any one of the definitions may suffice, but that of Isidore
is as clear as most: *aetiologia est cum proponimus aliquid
eiusque causam et rationem reddimus* ("Aetiology is when we
make some statement and add its reason and rationale"). Such
a definition, even though of a figure rather than an exercise,
clarifies Quintilian's phrase in line 15: *subiectis dictorum
rationibus*. As Robinson has observed, these words refer only
to the term which immediately precedes them.[48] Since they
make no sense with *ethologia* while defining *aetiologia*
accurately, the latter word must be what Quintilian wrote.

In fact, he may elsewhere describe just such an exercise.
As part of his discussion of *theses*, he says (2.4.26):

My teachers used to prepare us for conjectual
cases by a type of exercise that was both useful
and enjoyable. They would instruct us to ask and
to explore such questions as "Why among the
Lacedaemonians is Venus armed?" and "Why is
Cupid considered a boy as well as winged and
armed with arrows and a torch?" and similar
topics where we investigated intent, and the
question of intent is frequent in debates. This
exercise can appear to be a type of chreia.

Such an exercise as this is obviously concerned with
assigned questions for which the student was expected to
provide an answer and rationale. Thus it at least resembles
an *aetiologia* and may in fact be one; certainly it cannot
be an *ethologia*. Yet, despite his own fond memories of the
activity, Quintilian assigns no name to it. He merely says that
it can resemble a type of chreia, and that remark is strange.
Without a complete recasting of the material, such examples
as Quintilian cites cannot resemble any form of a chreia that
is known to us. Be that as it may, in his mind this exercise
which to us seems to resemble an *aetiologia* could appear
to be a type of chreia. And in chapter 9, line 15 it is the
aetiologia that he sets side by side with the chreia.

Consequently, despite some ambiguity and uncertainty —
much of which results from Quintilian's brevity — *aetiologia*
must be the correct reading in line 15. By its nature it is
a rhetorical figure which is used as an exercise by the
grammatici. That they did indeed employ it, or that at least
Quintilian considered it appropriate for them to do so, is clear
from his remark that such exercises *apud grammaticos
scribantur* (16).

c) Quintilian's apparent confusion of *aetiologia* and *chria*.
No explanation of *aetiologia* in line 15 can solve the problem
of its appearance in line 18. Consider what the text says:

Of all these exercises the principle is the same,
the form different in that the maxim is a general
statement; the aetiology is associated with
characters. Of the chreiai there are several
traditional types.

Quintilian seems to say that the three exercises are alike
in principle, purpose, rationale. This is a correct observation.
He continues by pointing out that the form of each is
different and apparently explains how this evaluation is true.
Like every other ancient authority, he first identifies the
maxim as a general statement (his *brevitas* leaves unsaid the
fact that a maxim is not associated with a character), but
then he inexplicably says that the *aetiologia* is associated
with characters, the very distinction which we are
accustomed to read about the chreia. About the nature of
the chreia he says absolutely nothing before beginning his
classification of the form, and even in the light of his brevity
the omission is strange.

Colson[49] long ago suggested that after *continetur* (19) the
text should read *ut chria. Harum plura*, etc. This is an
ingenious emendation paleographically, but it confuses the
matter by failing to make the real and necessary distinction
between *aetiologia* and *chria*.

More recently, Winterbottom[50] has suggested an
emendation designed to make the distinction. He proposed
adding *rebus, chria* after *aetiologia* (18), with the sense then
being "the aetiology is associated with subjects, the chreia
with characters." As evidence for this addition of *rebus*
Winterbottom cited the definition in the anonymous *Schemata
dianoeas:*[51] αἰτιολογία *est cum causam alicuius rei et rationem
subicimus.*

This reading is very close to what is needed, but *rebus*
still misses the mark, nor is it easy to explain how it could
have fallen from the text. Each of the three exercises —
maxim, chreia and aetiology — must be concerned with a *res*,
i.e., a subject. The very use of *alicuius* to modify *rei* in
the definition of the *Schemata dianoeas* shows that *rei* is

not the key word. What distinguishes *aetiologia* from both the maxim and the chreia is its connection with "statement of cause."

A better reading, therefore, is *aetiologia causis, chria personis continetur:* "aetiology is associated with causes, chreia with characters." Were it not clumsy, *rationibus* instead of *causis* would be possible. It is the term which Quintilian uses in line 15 to identify the *aetiologia*, and it also occurs in the definition of Isidore and the anonymous *Schemata dianoeas.* On the other hand, *causa* also appears in the two definitions. It too gives the proper sense here and is palaeographically more feasible.

In summary, then, the text of lines 17-19 makes an erroneous and incomplete statement as it stands in all editions, and only an emendation can bring any sense to the passage. It is long past time to restore to Quintilian's text, if not his *ipsissima verba*, at least the sense which he surely intended. That sense is expressed by *aetiologia causis, chria personis continetur*, and that is what the text of this volume offers.

4) The meaning of *"narratiunculae"* (32). The last exercise which Quintilian mentions in his treatment of quaedam dicendi primordia is *narratiunculae*, but he fails to define the term. He merely says that *narratiunculae* are used in profusion by poets and should be handled, not for the purpose of eloquence, but to impart information.[52]

What, then, are *narratiunculae* and what part did they play in the educational process? Quintilian himself clarifies these points later (2.4.1-2) when he returns to the subject of exercises which are suitable for advanced students. He says that with the *rhetor* boys should begin on subjects which resemble those they have learned *apud grammaticos*. He then identifies three species of narrative: fictional (*fabula*) which has its place in tragedies and poems and which is far removed not only from truth, but even from the semblance of truth; and third, historical narrative (*historia*) in which an historical event (*res gesta*) is set forth.

At this point Quintilian makes it clear when the student should study each narrative form: "We have assigned the poetic species to the *grammatici;* with the *rhetor* the historical should be the beginning since it is at once more forceful and truthful." Clearly by "poetic species" he means the first two: *fabula* and *argumentum.* And, although he does not expressly say so, these two are what he refers to here in chapter 9 as *narratiunculae.* They are the passages, "used in profusion by the poets," which the young student takes from his reading (16) of tragedies, comedies and other poetic works, and which he studies with the *grammaticus* (15).

These are the simpler forms of *narratio* and thus more appropriate for the young student. For this reason, Quintilian —or his source—has employed a diminutive form of *narratio*, for that is what *narratiuncula* is.[53] In the progression of exercises, narrative is the last form which the student handles with the *grammaticus* and the first he turns to after he has advanced to the *rhetor.*

Thus, it is no coincidence that in chapter 9 Quintilian turns from his brief reference to *narratiunculae* to a discussion, also brief, of the mutual roles of the *grammaticus* and *rhetor.*

Classification of the Chreia. Some critics have been troubled by Quintilian's treatment of the chreia because it is neither as complete nor as lucid as other classifications of the form. The tendency has been to try and force his concise remarks into a conformity with the rhetorical works which we possess, but the efforts have met with failure. Quintilian is simply not adhering to the methods of any author or tradition known to us.

The fact is that in the first century A.D. rhetorical theory was still in a fluid state. These preliminary exercises, which only later acquired the name *Progymnasmata*, had not yet achieved the full status of a unified *gradus*, nor had the treatment of individual exercises yet been given a set form. Even the definitions apparently varied from writer to writer or, as Theon seems to suggest,[54] did not yet exist for every form. Whatever the exact situation — and lack

of solid evidence renders it uncertain — it is best to take
Quintilian at his word and not attempt to fit him into a mold
which may not have existed until a much later date.

That Quintilian does indeed differ from the Greek
rhetoricians in his classification of the chreia is readily
apparent from the brief and general nature of the following
outline:

  A. Definition of chreia (19)
  B. Classification of chreia (19-30)
    1. Sayings-chreia (20-25)
    2. Action-chreia (25-30)
  C. Declension of chreia (30-32).

A glance at the corresponding sections in Theon,
Hermogenes, Nicolaus or even the very concise Aphthonius
shows just how curtailed Quintilian's analysis is. Consider first
his definition. If we follow the reading of the manuscripts,
he gives no definition, and even if we emend the text as
we must for other reasons[55] and print (19) *chria personis
continetur*, the definition is still far less precise than any
of the others. It does little more, in fact, than distinguish
the chreia from the *sententia* and *aetiologia*. Yet for Quintilian
this general identification was apparently sufficient.

Then when we move on to his opening statement in the
classification proper (19-20), there is confusion unless we
assume that, unlike the Greek rhetoricians, Quintilian does not
use *genera* (γένη) in the technical sense of "classes." Yet
this assumption becomes fact not only when we consider the
discussion which follows, but also when we recall his comment
in 2.4.26 that a certain exercise which he has just described
can appear to be a *genus chriae*. By this phrase, as the
context shows, he does not mean a "class" but rather, in
a more general and non-technical sense, a "type" of chreia.

The same meaning of *genera* must be his intention here
in line 19, for otherwise his statement that *chriarum plura
genera traduntur* is nonsense in the light of the discussion
that follows. Elsewhere we regularly find three "classes" of

chreiai: sayings (λογικαί: *dicti*), action (πρακτικαί: *facti*) and mixed (μικταί: *mixti*). Quintilian, however, uses no such technical terms or distinctions and has been content merely with the description of some "types" of chreiai: *unum simile sententiae, quod est positum in voce simplici* ("one resembling a maxim in that it is cast in the form of a simple statement"); *positum in respondendo* ("cast in the form of a response"); and *huic non dissimile* ("one not unlike this one").

The point is that in later classifications these three *genera* are not separate "classes." Rather they are three *species* (εἴδη) of the same *genus:* i.e., of the sayings-chreia. The species are, to use Theon's arrangement and terminology,[56] 1) ἀποφαντικὸν καθ' ἐκούσιον ἀπόφασιν (an unprompted statement which Quintilian expresses with *in voce simplici*); 2) ἀποκριτικόν (in response to a question); and 3) another ἀποφαντικόν but in particular an ἀποφαντικὸν κατὰ περίστασιν ("a statement in response to a circumstance").

By separating his first and third examples Quintilian demonstrates two points: first that he is not using a technical distinction between *genus* and *species* and secondly that Theon is not his source, at least at this point. Yet the use of *traduntur* (20) shows clearly that Quintilian is following some source, some tradition. Therefore, we are led to the conclusion that in the first century A.D. no such precise form had yet been developed for classifying these preliminary exercises as appears later in the standard *Progymnasmata*.

The same lack of precision is apparent in the next part of Quintilian's classification. From the three examples of sayings-chreiai he turns abruptly, with only *etiam* (25) to mark the turn, to what is actually the second *genus* of chreia in other classifications: *in ipsorum factis esse chriam putant*. Yet these few words raise a number of questions. First, although anyone who is familiar with the Greek *Progymnasmata* quickly realizes that by the use of *factis* Quintilian is referring to the action-chreia, he must still be troubled by the vagueness of the expression. In particular, *ipsorum* lacks the precision we find elsewhere. Quintilian surely means *personarum,* but why his aversion to that noun? He has, after all, used it just above in line 19. And why *ipsorum* rather than *ipsarum?*

Then, who is the subject of *putant?* It is surely not that notorius and indefinite third person. Can it be *Graeci?* Quintilian uses the name in lines 35 and 42, so why not here? Or is he making a general reference to his source or sources as he does with *traduntur* (20)? We can only guess at an answer.

Finally, we must consider the chreiai which Quintilian cites as examples. The first (Chreia 14) resembles several others (i.e., 23, 25, 26) which appear frequently in the Greek rhetoricians and elsewhere, but in each of the others the πρόσωπον is Diogenes. Indeed, the type of action depicted here is quite appropriate to the traditional character of Diogenes but very uncharacteristic of Crates, who seems to have possessed a reputation for being calmer and more gentle in his relationships with people.[57] Yet Quintilian uses Crates as the πρόσωπον who saw an uneducated boy and beat his paedagogus. Has he found this chreia in his source or has he altered another chreia for some reason? No reason for the change is apparent, but if it was Quintilian's source that used the chreia with Crates, then once again we are left with the thought that neither Theon nor any tradition known to us was his source.

Quintilian's second example of an action-chreia also raises some questions. First, he says (27) that it is *paene par ei* ("almost like it," i.e., the first example). But then he adds (28-29) *quod tamen eodem nomine appellare non audent sed dicunt* χρειῶδες ("which they nevertheless do not venture to call by the same name but instead call it 'chreia-like'"), and these words themselves raise question. That is, is the example really a chreia? What is Quintilian's source? What does he mean by χρειῶδες?

The anecdote about Milo, who used to carry the bull which he had grown accustomed to carry as a calf, does not conform to any definition of chreia which we possess, not in verbal structure, not in content or in tone — or does it? Theon would not have considered it a chreia, nor would Hermogenes, Aphthonius, or Nicolaus, but Quintilian is not following their rules. His own definition is at most *chria personis continetur*, and, because the action of the anecdote is connected with Milo as the *persona*, it conforms to his definition. Those who are accustomed to catalogue rhetorical forms in accordance with the definitions and classifications of later *Progymnasmata* may feel some dissatisfaction with Quintilian's appraisal, but it is readily apparaent that in his choice of examples he is consistent with his own definition.

Where did he find this definition? What is his source for the anecdote/chreia about Milo of Crotona? Many stories about this man's extraordinary strength and enormous appetite appear in such writers as Herodotus (3.137), Diodorus (12.9), Pausanias (6.14.5-8) and Athenaeus (10.412f). In fact, his strength became proverbial as a passage in Petronius (sec. 25) shows, and some form of the proverb is probably the ultimate source of Quintilian's version. Yet nowhere else does Milo appear as the πρόσωπον of a chreia. Thus the source of his example, like that of his definition of the chreia, must remain hidden to us.

The final question here concerns the meaning of χρειῶδες. By the definitions of a chreia in other authors, every chreia is χρειώδης, i.e., "useful." Yet apparently Quintilian means something different. He seems to understand the word to mean "chreia-like," but no lexicon recognizes this meaning of χρειώδης, nor does such a word as χρειοίδης seem to exist. Yet Quintilian attributes his use of the term to others (*dicunt*), so it apparently had some authority. But once again that authority cannot be Theon or any tradition known to us.

These matters have troubled more than one critic.[58] In their unwillingness to see in Quintilian's discussion either an error or, despite other obvious discrepancies, a departure from the standard classification of the chreia, they have attempted to explain away the differences by suggesting that his two action-chreiai reflect the two species of that class: ἐνεργητικαί and παθητικαί (cf. Theon 91-99).

Their suggestions are wrong. It is true that Quintilian's example about Crates is an action-chreia whose action is active (ἐνεργητική). Theon himself uses a similar chreia (Chreia 26) as his own example of this species. But the anecdote about Milo cannot, by any stretching of the imagination, qualify as an action-chreia in which the action is passive (παθητική), i.e., where the πρόσωπον suffers an adverse experience because of something he has done. For a typical chreia of this species see Chreia 21 (Didymon).

So once again Quintilian's classification differs from those of Theon and the later writers of *Progymnasmata*. He is apparently unaware of the elaborate system of διαίρεσις such as we find in Theon, and, no matter how unsatisfactory his arrangement may seem to us, it is unfair to attempt to force upon his brief discussion of the chreia all the details which later developed.

Another case in point here is Quintilian's silence about the third class of chreia, the mixed-chreia. By its very nature, this class could not have developed until the first two were well established and easily identified. Since in Quintilian's system this preliminary stage seems not to have been fully developed, it is unlikely that he even thought about a class which possessed characteristics of the first two. For that reason, he has nothing to say about a mixed chreia.

On the other hand, he is well aware of one primary function of the chreia *apud grammaticos* and includes (30-32) a brief reference to the exercise called *declinatio* (κλίσις): *In his omnibus et declinatio per eosdem ducitur casus et tam factorum quam dictorum ratio est* ("In all these, too, declension is done in the same cases, and the method is the same for both action-chreiai and sayings-chreiai").

The first part of this sentence confused H. E. Butler,[59] who apparently never took the trouble to consult either the Greek rhetoricians or Latin grammarians. Yet, to anyone who has looked at such passages Quintilian's remarks here seem

straightforward, even if compressed. By *in his omnibus* he
refers to the examples which he has just used or to all
chreiai. The sense is the same in either case. The words *per
eosdem ducitur casus* mean simply that any chreia can be
declined in the six cases of Latin, that some cases are not
more appropriate to sayings-chreiai, some to action-chreiai.
The point is that declension was designed primarily to teach
the young students form and syntax, and consequently the
actual sense of the Latin in the various cases was
unimportant. One need only glance at, for example, Theon's
treatment of this exercise (199-275) to see how contrived
and artificial some of the maneuvers become.[60] Quintilian, with
his usual brevity, is saying simply that the sense of the
chreia in these manipulations makes no difference; form is
the primary concern.

The same simplified approach is reflected by his final
observation here: *tam factorum quam dictorum ration est.* The
key word is, of course, *ratio* which refers to the method
by which someone can introduce a chreia so that each oblique
case follows logically and syntactically. For example, Theon
(226-75) lists several phrases which are appropriate for
introducing a chreia in the various cases, some for sayings-
chreiai, some for action-chreiai. He even subdivides and
provides phrases for action-chreiai which are active, and
those which are passive. Quintilian, whether or not he was
familiar with such complicated exercises, here advoctes a
simple approach: treat every chreia alike and merely decline
it without introducing complication. This attitude is quite in
keeping with his view that the chreia, as one of the *quaedam
dicendi primordia*, is a simple exerecise and one designed
expressly for the young student who is still under the
tutelage of a *grammaticus*.

With this observation on *declinatio* Quintilian concludes his
discussion of the chreia. He has used less than a hundred
words, but even so he has devoted much more space to the
chreia than to any other of the *quaedam dicandi primordia*.
To *fabula* he allows three lines (6-9); to *recitatio* he gives

three more (9-12); the *sententia* receives hardly a sentence of its own (18); and the *aetiologia* really has only two brief remarks (15 and 18); and finally, *narratiunculae* are dismissed in one brief sentence (32-33).

Obviously, then, the chreia stood in a position of special importance in Quintilian's limited set of elementary exercises. It has a similar position of prominence in Theon's fuller sequence of exercises and retained it in the works of the later *rhetores*.

Quintilian's Contribution to the Development of the Chreia. Rather than contribution, however, we should perhaps say role in the history of the development, for it seems likely that he was content merely to report the *status quo*. His very brevity in discussing matters which he is at pains to insist properly belong to the *grammaticus* rather than to the *rhetor* points to his relative lack of professional interest in all these early exercises.

Lack of interest probably caused him to expend little time and effort on developing the material which he found ready at hand. Instead, he has handled the subject, as he must, but he has only touched upon it, sketched an outline as it were, and hastened on to the subjects in which he as a *rhetor* has an interest and feels qualified to make evaluations and contributions. This interest has undoubtedly caused his abrupt change of subject from the last preliminary exercise to the duties of *grammatici* and *rhetores* (33ff.).

One remark which Quintilian makes on this subject deserves comment. He says (35-36) *Graeci magis operum suorum et onera et modum norunt* ("The Greeks have a better understanding of the importance and scope of their tasks"). He means, of course, that the Greek *rhetores* and *grammatici* share the teaching responsibility as he himself thinks is proper. This observation may have been true in Quintilian's day, but from the vantage point of almost twenty centuries later it appears incorrect.

The tug-of-war to which he refers here and elsewhere seems to have become two separate contests, one Greek and one Roman. Among the Greeks the *rhetores* eventually pulled the preliminary exercises into their curriculum and assumed responsibility for teaching them as the first steps in a young man's training to become an orator. Then, and only then, these exercises acquired the designation of *Progymnasmata* as opposed to the simple *Gymnasmata* which Theon uses.

Among the Romans, the *grammatici* eventually pulled all the elementary exercises into their sphere of influence. The very trend which Quintilian attacks here continued, and the Roman *rhetores* soon limited themselves to such exercises as *controversiae* and *suasoriae*. These developments show themselves today in a very concrete and practical way: when we consult Greek writers on the subject of these elementary exercises, we turn to editions of *Rhetores Graeci*, but when we need Roman writers, we turn to *Grammatici Latini*.

This brief and general evaluation of the history of the elementary exercises naturally includes the chreia. This exercise regularly stood first or third in the sequence, and Quintilian insists that it, along with fable, maxim, simple narrative, etc., is a proper vehicle for instruction by the *grammaticus*. For this reason he gives only a summary of how students should use it. He is not interested, as later *rhetores* were, in its application to the training of students for writing speeches.

Consequently, he treats the chreia as an exercise that is effective for its purpose but one that is still very elementary. He offers nothing new and perhaps simplifies what he knows. Therefore, to criticize his treatment of the chreia and fault him for lack of consistency with the standard *Progymnasmata* is unfair and unscholarly. To do so is much the same as comparing, for example, the verses of Gnaeus Naevius with Vergil's *Aeneid* and expecting the early poet to conform to the rules of the great Roman epic.

Like the early verses of Naevius, Quintilian's discussion of the *quaedam dicendi primordia* in general and of the chreia in particular has an historical significance. It is interesting and even important for providing insight into conditions of first-century education, but as an analysis of the material which can stand beside such works as those of Theon, Hermogenes and Ajphthonius it falls short. We should consider Quintilian's discussion little more than an historical curiosity.

NOTES

1. Juvenal, *Sat.* 7.154.

2. This man was Domitian's cousin and his colleague (for four months in A.D. 95) in the consulship. The Emperor had designated Clemens' two sons to succeed him and had changed their names to Vespasian and Domitian (Suetonius, *Dom.* 15). Then shortly after the conclusion of Clemens' consulship, Domitian suddenly ordered him to be executed and his wife Domitilla, herself a relative of the Emperor, to be banished on the charge of ἀθεότης. This charge, as Cassius Dio says (67.14.2), was at this same time leveled against many who ἐς τὰ τῶν Ἰουδαίων ἤθη ἐξοκέλλοντες ("drifted into the ways of the Jews").

The clear implication in these events is that Clemens and his wife, as well as many others, had become Christians. If this premise is correct, we have evidence for at least a minor persecution of Christians toward the end of Domitian's reign (cf. *CAH* 11.31-32, 42, and 255). Whatever the situation, we hear no more of Clemens' two sons after A.D. 96, but the trouble that beset their family never touched Quintilian.

3. One of the honors conferred by emperors upon men who had distinguished themselves in some way. It gave the recipient the rights of an ex-consul in matters of dress, attendence and precedence at public festivities, and in burial ceremonies.

4. This comment is true despite Quintilian's impressive and moving description of his grief in the Preface to Bk. 6. Such rhetoric can be helpful only when, as Wordsworth says of poetry (*Lyrical Ballads*, 2nd ed., preface), it "takes its origin from emotion recollected in tranquility."

5. See, e.g., J. Duff, *A Literary History of Rome in the Silver Age* (London: Benn, 1960) 311-14.

6. See Quintilian, *Inst.* 1, pref. 7.

7. Cf. S. F. Bonner, "Roman Oratory" in M. Platnauer (ed.), *Fifty Years (and Twelve) of Classical Scholarship* (Oxford: Blackwell, 1968) 416-64, esp. 453-54. The best edition is still that of C. Ritter, *M. Fabii Quintiliani Declamationes quae supersunt CXIV* (Leipzig: Teubner, 1884).

8. For convenience and consistency the lines of this passage are numbered consecutively as we have done for each of the authors studied in this volume. The standard chapter and section numbers also appear.

9. See "General Introduction," above, pp. 12-15.

10. See F. H. Colson, "Phaedrus and Quintilian, 1.9.2," *CR* 33 (1919) 59-61, esp. 60.

11. Cf., e.g., the discussion of Theon in his chapter on μῦθος (*Progymn.* 3 [1.172, 9-174, 5 Walz]).

12. See Butler's translation in *Quintilian* (4 vols; Loeb Classical Library; London: Heinemann, 1921-22) 1.157.

13. See J. P. Postgate, "Phaedrus and Seneca," *CR* 33 (1919) 19-24, esp. 23. Later Postgate ("Quintilian, 1.9.2," *CR* [1919] 108) accepted Colson's view.

14. *M. Fabii Quintiliani Institutionis Oratoriae Liber I* (Cambridge, 1924).

15. *M. Fabii Quintiliani Institutionis Oratoriae Libri XII* (2 vols.; Darmstadt: Wissenschaftliche Buchgesellschaft, 1972).

16. *M. Fabii Quintiliani Institutionis Oratoriae Libri Duodecim* (2 vols.; Oxford: Clarendon, 1970).

17. See Butler's text in *Quintilian*, 1.156.

18. Cf. Colson, *Liber I*, 117.

19. See F. H. Colson, "Quintilian 1.9 and the 'Chria' in Ancient Education," *CR* 35 (1921) 150-54.

20. See R. P. Robinson, "*Ethologia* or *Aetiologia* in Suetonius' *De Grammataicis* 4 and Quintilian, 1.9," *CPh* 15 (1920) 370-79.

21. See M. Winterbottom, *Problems in Quintilian* (*BICS* Suppl. 25; London: Institute of Classical Studies, 1970) 67.

22. Rahn says (p. xv) that he is merely using Radermacher's Teubner text (see below n. 23), not establishing his own text.

23. *M. Fabii Quintiliani Institutionis Oratoriae Libri XII* (2 vols.; Leipzig: Teubner, 1959).

24. See *Oxford Latin Dictionary* s.v. *ethologia*.

25. See, e.g., G. Kennedy (*Quintilian* [New York: Twayne, 1969] 45), who fails, however, to make it clear whether he reads *ethologia* or *aetiologia* when he says ". . . short written exercises describing a saying or action with some kind of moral value." Yet his concluding remark in the same paragraph is certainly incorrect:

> Quintilian does not explain the technique very fully, but we know these and other exercises from Greek handbooks of composition called *progymnasmata* such as that published soon after Quintilian's time by Aelius Theon.

Whether Theon was later or earlier than Quintilian, his *Progymnasmata* does not include an exercise called *aetiologia* or *ethologia*, nor does any other standard *Progymnasmata*. Quintilian has clearly used a tradition quite different from any with which we are acquainted.

26. For a good discussion of this point, see A. Dihle, "Posidonius' System of Moral Philosophy," *JHS* 93 (1973) 50-57,

esp. 53. Dihle correctly assumes that Seneca is concerned here only with philosophy and consequently omits any reference to rhetoric.
27. On the sense of *praeceptio* here, see Dihle, "Posidonius' System," 56 n. 34. His suggestion that παραινετική (which he spells incorrectly) is the term of Posidonius may not be as certain as he implies. The word appears nowhere in the fragments of Posidonius collected by L. Edelstein and I. F. Kidd (*Posidonius: The Fragments* [Cambridge, 1972]).
28. The *Oxford Latin Dictionary s.v. praeceptio* fails to include this meaning and lists Seneca's passage under the meaning "the inculcation of rules, instructions."
29. See Charisius, *Art. Gram.* 4.5 (pp. 371–72 Barwick).
30. *Trag. Incert.* 149 Ribbeck.
31. Rutilius, 2.7 (1.16, 1 Halm).
32. *Carmen de Figuris* 148 (1.69,148 Halm).
33. *Schemata Dianoeas* 9 (1.72,31 Halm).
34. Isidore, *Etym.* (2.21,40 Lindsay).
35. In the fragments of Posidonius αἰτιολογία appears twice with the meaning "statement of cause," but in each case the word seems to be that of the author who refers to Posidonius and not that of the philosopher. Cf. *Frag.* 18.38 (Edelstein-Kidd)=Simplicius, *In Arist. Physica* 2.2 (193b23) and *Frag.* 223.21=Strabo, 17.3.10.
36. See Epicurus, *ep.* 2 (p. 42, 14 Usener): ἅπασα ἡ τῶν μετεώρων αἰτιολογία ματαία ἔσται ("Every investigation of the causes of astronomical phenomena will be in vain").
37. See Democritus, *Frag.* 118 (Diels). The statement is just a bit peculiar. It appears in Eusebius (*EP* 14.27.4) in a quotation from Dionysius, the bishop of Alexandria, and it is expressed in the form of a chreia: Δημόκριτος . . . ἔλεγε βούλεσθαι μᾶλλον μίαν εὑρεῖν αἰτιολογίαν ἢ τὴν Περσῶν οἱ βασιλείαν γενέσθαι ("Democritus . . . used to say that he would rather discover one αἰτιολογία than for the Persian Empire to come into his possession").
The phrase εὑρεῖν αἰτιολογίαν is strange. Certainly one cannot discover an "investigation of a cause," so that meaning is ruled out. To discover a "statement of cause" or explanation makes some sense perhaps, but the idea seems awkward. The usual expression is αἰτίαν εὑρεῖν as we see, e.g., in the humorous incident which Plutarch (*Quaes. Conv.* 1.10.2 [628C-D]) describes where Democritus wants αἰτίαν τῆς γλυκύτητος εὑρεῖν of a cucumber which, as it turns out, his serving-woman has stored in a honey jar.
The use of αἰτιολογία in *Frag.* 118 seems tautological. Perhaps by the third (or fourth) century the compound word had lost its original force and had come to mean little more

than the simple αἰτία. For this reason, either Dionysius or Eusebious, in reporting the chreia about Democritus, used αἰτιολογία for αἰτία.

38. See Sextus, *Pyrrh. Hyp.* 1.17.180–86. The technique of Aenesidemus reminds one of an ἐργασία or at least of an elaborate ἀνασκευή.

39. An attested use of αἰτιολογία appears also in Philodemus' *De deis* 1.10 (p. 17 Diels), but the context has been lost completely. Still, one expects this Epicurean to use the word in the same way as his master.

40. Rutilius Rufus, 11.19 (1.21, 8 Halm).

41. Julius Rufianus, 8 (1.40, 19 Halm). Rufianus has an interesting, and apparently unique, association of αἰτιολογία with ἀπόφασις ("statement").

42. *Carmen de Figuris* 25–27 (1.64, 25–27 Halm).

43. *Schemata Dianoeas* 17 (1.73, 17 Halm).

44. Isidore, *Etym.* (2.31, 39 Lindsay).

45. See Augustine, *De Gen. ad Lit. Imperf.* 2, and *De Utilitate Credendi* 5.

46. Alexander Numenius 8 (8.438, 9ff. Walz); Zonaeus 6 (8.675, 5ff.); and an anonymous work (8.699, 25ff.).

47. See ps.-Aristeides, *Rhet.* (pp. 7, 17; 30, 14 and 19; 73, 23; 82, 9; 92, 3; and 114, 2 Schmid). Each section in which the word appears is fairly long and must be read to see how the author understands the word.

48. See Robinson, "*Ethologia* or *Aetiologia*," 378.

49. See Colson, "Quintilian 1.9," 151 n. 5. Cf. Colson, *Liber I*, 119.

50. See Winterbottom, *Problems in Quintilian*, 68, but in his edition he has left the emendation in his apparatus.

51. Cf. also the definition of Isidore quoted above.

52. It is of some interest to note that in the only other occurrence of the word the younger Pliny boasts (*ep.* 6.33.8) of using *narratiunculae* for the sake of eloquence. There is some evidence that Pliny was a student of Quintilian; in *ep.* 2.14.9 he calls him *praeceptor meus* and in *ep.* 6.6.3 he says that he attended Quintilian's lectures. Apparently, therefore, we have another example here of a student failing to follow his mentor's teaching.

53. Since the word seems to occur only in Quintilian and Pliny, who was probably his student, we may have an indication that *narratiunculae* is an invention of Quintilian himself.

54. See Theon, *Progymn.* 1 (1.147, 2–10 Walz).

55. See discussion, pp. 127–28, above.

56. Cf. lines 35–79. Quintilian's first type is the same as that of Theon in 36–39; the second equals Theon 53–58; the third Theon 39–43. Like every Latin writer, Quintilian omits

a distinction between κατ'ἐρώτησιν and κατὰ πύσμα. Even the Greeks themselves were not always careful to separate the two.

57. Cf., however, Diogenes Laertius, 6.88, but the people whom Crates here drives away with his βακτηρία are kinsmen.

58. See, e.g., O. Schissel, "Die Einteilung der Chrie bei Quintilian," *Hermes* 68 (1933) 245-48, esp. 248. He provides a *stemma* in an effort to compare the διαίρεσις of Theon and Quintilian. But Schissel's confusion about Quintilian's purpose nullifies the usefulness of the study.

59. See Butler's comment in *Quintilian*, 158 n. 1.

60. For a complete declension of a chreia in Latin, see Diomedes (1.310 Keil). This passage will appear in vol. 2 of *The Chreia in Ancient Rhetoric*.

TEXT
AND
TRANSLATION

9. Et finitae sunt partes duae quas haec
professio pollicetur, id est ratio loquendi et enarratio
auctorum, quarum illam *methodicen*, hanc *historicen* vocant.
adiciamus tamen eorum curae quaedam dicendi primordia
quibus aetatis nondum rhetorem capientis instituant.   5
(2) Igitur Aesopi fabellas, quae fabulis nutricularum
proxime succedunt, narrare sermone puro et nihil se
supra modum extollente, deinde eandem gracilitatem stilo
exigere condiscant. versus primo solvere, mox mutatis
verbis interpretari, tum paraphrasi audacius vertere,   10
qua et breviare quaedam et exornare salvo modo poetae
sensu permittitur. (3) Quod opus, etiam consummatis
professoribus difficile, qui commode tractaverit cuicum-
que discendo sufficiet. sententiae quoque et chriae et
aetiologiae subiectis dictorum rationibus apud gram-   15
maticos scribantur, quia initium ex lectione ducunt;
quorum omnium similis est ratio, forma diversa, quia
sententia universalis est vox, aetiologia <causis,
chria> personis continetur. (4) Chriarum plura genera
traduntur; unum simile sententiae, quod est positum   20
in voce simplici: "dixit ille" aut "dicere solebat";
alterum quod est in respondendo: "interrogatus ille,"
vel "cum hoc ei dictum esset, respondit"; tertium huic
non dissimile: "cum quis dixisset aliquid" vel "fecis-
set." (5) Etiam in ipsorum factis esse chriam putant,   25
ut (Chreia 14) "Crates, cum indoctum puerum vidisset,
paedagogum eius percussit." et aliud paene par ei,

---

14 chriae vel *Jullien* 15 aetiologiae B] aethio- A aethimo- *aut*
ethimo- *aut* ethymo- *alii* ethologiae *Regius et edd. multi.* 17
Num quarum? *cf. supra v.3.* 18 aetiologia B] aetimo- A
ethymo- *alii* ethologia *Regius et edd. multi.* aetologia causis,
chria *temptavi* aetiologia rebus, chria *Winterbottom.*
continetur ut et chria. Harum *Colson.*

9. And now two sections which this profession offers have been completed; that is, the art of speaking and the interpretation of authors.[1] They call the former *methodice*, the latter *historice*.[2] But let us add to their study certain elementary rules of speaking for the benefit of those whose age has not yet prepared them to enroll with a rhetor. (2) These young boys, then,[3] should learn how to recite Aesop's fables, which are the immediate successor of nursery tales, in language that is natural[4] and not unduly embellished and then to execute the same simplicity of style in writing. They should also learn first to render verses in prose, then to recite[5] them in different words, then to turn with more confidence to paraphrase in which it is permissible to abridge[6] or embellish certain elements, provided the poet's meaning remains intact. (3) The one who can successfully handle this task, difficult even for accomplished instructors, will be capable of learning anything. Maxims, too, and chriae, as well as aetiologies, with the reason for the saying added, should be written under the guidance of teachers of literature because these forms have their origin in reading. Of all these exercises, the principle is the same, the form different, in that the maxim is a general statement, the aetiology is connected <with reasons, the chria> with characters. (4) In the case of chriae, there are several traditional types: one resembles the maxim in that it is cast in the form of a simple statement: "He said" or "He used to say." A second is cast in the form of a reply: "On being asked" or "When this had been said to him, he replied." A third type is not unlike this: "When someone had said" or "done something." (5) They also believe that a chria occurs in the actions of characters, as (Chreia 14) *Crates, when he saw an uneducated boy, struck his paedagogus.* And there is another type almost its equivalent,

quod tamen eodem nomine appellare non audent, sed dicunt
χρειῶδες, ut (Chreia 47) "Milo, quem vitulum adsueverat
ferre, taurum ferebat." in his omnibus et declinatio   30
per eosdem ducitur casus et tam factorum quam dictorum
ratio est. (6) Narratiunculas a poetis celebratas
notitiae causa, non eloquentiae, tractandas puto. ce-
tera maioris operis ac spiritus Latini rhetores re-
linquendo necessaria grammaticis fecerunt. Graeci   40
magis operum suorum et onera et modum norunt.

10. Haec de grammatice, quam brevissime potui,
non ut omnia dicerem sectatus, quod infinitum erat, sed
ut maxime necessaria. nunc de ceteris artibus quibus
instituendos priusquam rhetori tradantur pueros ex-   40
istimo strictim subiungam, ut efficiatur orbis ille
doctrinae, quem Graeci ἐγκύκλιον παιδείαν vocant.

which they nevertheless do not venture to call by the same name but instead call "chreia-like," as (Chreia 47) *Milo used to carry the bull which he had grown accustomed to carry as a calf.* In all these types, too, declension in done for both action-chriae and sayings-chriae. (6) Simple narratives, used in profusion[7] by poets, should, in my opinion, be handled for the sake of imparting knowledge,[8] not for style. By neglecting the rest of the more serious and ambitious subjects, Latin rhetors have made them necessary subjects for the teachers of literature. The Greeks have a better understanding of the importance and scope of their tasks.

10. These matters which are concerned with the teaching of literature I have treated as briefly as I could, not attempting to say everything, which would be an endless task, but only what is most essential. Now I will add some brief remarks on the other skills in which I think boys should be trained before they are turned over to the rhetor, so that the well-known "Cycle of Learning" which the Greeks call *encyclios paideia* can be rounded off.[9]

COMMENTS

1. Since most of the problems concerning the preliminary exercises and the chreia in particular are discussed in the introduction, the comments here concentrate on philological matters.

2. Neither μεθοδική nor ἱστορική seems to occur as a technical term in Greek, and only Diomedes (Keil 1.482,31-483,1) uses *historice*. But even in Diomedes the word refers to a species of narrative poetry (i.e. historical) and has nothing to do with the meaning which Quintilian gives it.

3. This use of *igitur* is Ciceronian. The word serves, not as an inferential conjunction, but as a particle to introduce a new subject. Cf. the use of δ'οὖν (Denniston, *Greek Particles*, 463-64).

4. The word *purus* means more than "natural." It also refers to purity and correctness of style.

5. *Interpretari* refers to the Greek (and Roman) practice of recitation, i.e. ἀπαγγελία.

6. *Breviare* is a rare word. Quintilian uses it four times and Manilius once. The more common verb is *contrahere*.

7. Most translators render *celebratas* with "made famous." This is a regular meaning of the word, but just as common (and perhaps more so than translators have allowed) is the original sense of "crowded," i.e. "frequent, given currency," hence "used in profusion." As often in such matters, English rather than Latin is the cause of the uncertainty. For a possible parallel to *celebratas* here see Quint. 2.10,2.

8. *Notitiae causa:* "for the sake of imparting knowledge." Although the standard dictionaries do not make the fact plain, *notitia* (like most verbal nouns) can be active or passive. Quintilian uses the word four times; in 1.10,33 and 6.4,8 it has a passive meaning, i.e. knowledge acquired; in 12.11,8 and here in line 32 it means the imparting of knowledge.

9. For a brief but adequate treatment of the ἐγκύκλιος παιδεία see P. J. Enk's article "Encyclopaedic Learning" in the *Oxford Classical Dictionary*, 2nd ed., p. 383, together with his short bibliography. See also Stanley F. Bonner, *Education in Ancient Rome*, 77-8, 102-3 and his extensive bibliography, 380ff. This excellent book is probably the best treatment of Roman education.

THE CHREIA DISCUSSION OF

HERMOGENES OF TARSUS

Introduction, Translation and Comments

by

BURTON L. MACK
EDWARD N. O'NEIL

INTRODUCTION

I

Life and Writings. The information which has reached us about the life of Hermogenes in meager, confused and, in part at least, fanciful and seemingly malicious. Our earliest notice is a brief statement in the Epitome of Cassius Dio (71.1.2) that the Emperor Marcus Aurelius was not reluctant to attend Hermogenes' lectures on rhetoric. The chief ancient source, however, is Philostratus' *Vitae Sophistarum* (577-78).[1] The only other certain references to Hermogenes in antiquity are those of two fifth century Neoplatonists, Syrianus[2] and the younger Sopater.[3] The former says, moreover, that he has found no life of Hermogenes other than the one of Philostratus. The remaining sources are Byzantine writers, scholiasts and commentators.[4]

Scholars have attempted to establish some order in the chaos which the various sources have caused, but they have been unable to reach a consensus of opinion either about the genuineness of the material or its reliability. For example, Hugo Rabe has examined all the references and postulated a double tradition about the life of Hermogenes.[5] Ludwig Radermacher, using the same data, insisted that Rabe's analysis was incorrect and saw everything either derived from Philostratus or the result of invention and confusion on the part of later writers.[6]

This is not the place to discuss the intricacies of the tradition, interesting as such problems may be, or to attempt a solution of an apparently insoluable problem. Instead it must be enough to list the pieces of information, or rather allegations, which have reached us and to limit comments to points of clarification.

From various statements which have come down to us we can summarize the life of Hermogenes as follows: He was born in A.D. 161[7] at Tarsus,[8] the son of a wealthy man[9] named Callippus.[10] His teacher was the sophist Scopelian[11] of Clazomenae, who taught at Smyrna and numbered among his

pupils the famous Herodes Atticus.[12] By the time Hermogenes
was fifteen,[13] he had acquired such a reputation as a skilled
orator and extemporaneous speaker (the usual repertoire of
a sophist) that in A.D. 176[14] the Emperor Marcus Aurelius
attended one of his sessions at Tarsus and heard him speak.
He was so impressed with the youth's ability that he
presented him with lavish gifts.

At age 17 (or 18, 19, 20, etc.)[15] Hermogenes began to write,
and presumably it was during the next few years that he
wrote his Περὶ τῶν στάσεων, Περὶ εὑρέσεως, Περὶ ἰδέων, Περὶ μεθόδου
δεινότητος, Προγυμνάσματα and whatever else he may have
composed. During this period of writing activity, or as a result
of it, he acquired the nickname Θυστήρ, i.e., Scratcher or
Polisher, with a sarcastic reference either to his irascible
temper or to the emphasis which he placed on the need to
polish compositions.[16]

When Hermogenes was 24 or 25,[17] he supposedly became
deranged and lost all his artistic powers, a misfortune which
elicited cruel jokes from his contemporaries and a
contemptuous attitude on the part of Philostratus.[18] He lived
to advanced old age[19] and died in relative obscurity.[20] After
his death, his body was examined, and it was discovered that
his heart was covered with hair and enlarged beyond that
of a human being.[21]

From such a list of obscure, unsubstantiated and even
fanciful statements only the most general outline of the life
and career of Hermogenes in discernible to us. Yet it is all
that we have or are ever likely to have. From these remarks
we can at least know the approximate time when Hermogenes
lived and wrote, but most important of all, of course, is our
possession of his writings. And we know from other sources
that among rhetoricians these works enjoyed a vogue which
endured for several centuries.[22]

Not until the fifth century, however, do we find anyone
attributing specific works to Hermogenes. The first person
we know about is Syrianus, who names him as the author
of the Περὶ στάσεων,[23] Περὶ ἰδέων[24] and Περὶ μεθόδου δεινότητος.[25]

Later tradition has generally confirmed Hermogenes as the author of these three works.[26]

The case for the Περὶ εὑρέσεως is not so clear. Hermogenes himself[27] refers to a work with this title as one of his own compositions, and both Syrianus[28] and Lachares[29] cite passages from the document we possess. Yet these two commentators attribute it to Apsines,[30] and Syrianus at least intimates[31] that he has not seen the Περὶ εὑρέσεως to which Hermogenes refers.

Thus the implication appears rather strong that the Περὶ εὑρέσεως which is extant is not the composition of Hermogenes. With this conclusion both Rabe[32] and Radermacher[33] agree, and each supports his position with arguments based on the differences in style and content between the Περὶ εὑρέσεωας and the works which are generally acknowledged as genuine.

Whatever the truth may be about the Περὶ εὑρέσεως, the fact remains that Hermogenes' τέχνη ῥητορική[34] as a whole became standard in the Byzantine world. The sheer number of manuscripts, epitomes and commentaries in ample evidence of his continuing popularity and importance, at least in the rhetorical tradition. Despite the subsequent fame of Aphthonius, Hermogenes' works continued to exert an influence, and we must not forget that it was at Byzantium that Priscian translated the *Progymnasmata* into Latin.

In the West, however, Hermogenes remained virtually unknown for centuries. Only through Priscian's translation of the *Progymnasmata*, which was generally considered to be Priscian's own composition, did he exert any influence. Then early in the fifteenth century a Greek emigrant by the name of Georgius Trapezuntius[35] came to Italy and introduced the Greek rhetorical tradition, including the writings of Hermogenes.[36] And the Latin West was awakened to one more new reality from the East.

The Greek texts, however, did not become widely available until the appearance of the *editio princeps* of the *Rhetores Graeci* by Aldus Manutius in 1508-1509. Soon afterwards the writings of Hermogenes acquired a place in rhetorical training similar to what they had long held in the East.[37]

In modern scholarship the assessment of Hermogenes is mixed. In an age when good speaking—not to mention good writing—is all but a lost art, many scholars dismiss Hermogenes along with most ancient rhetoricians and pronounce their complicated rules and analyses as "barren, scholastic complexities."[38] Rhetoric has become a topic to which many must of necessity refer but about which very few have any first hand knowledge.[39]

For those who are acquainted with the history of rhetoric and appreciate its development and its influence on almost every form of writing Hermogenes stands as a great systematizer of the Greek rhetorical tradition.[40] Of particular importance are his sequential theory of the στάσεις and the development of a theory of style. Both theories were studied and put into practice by leading figures of the Renaissance,[41] and they in turn exerted a strong influence on modern rhetorical theory.

The Progymnasmata. The authenticty of this work which is traditionally attributed to Hermogenes has long been a subject of debate. Rabe[42] summarized the arguments for and against Hermogenean authorship, as follows: For: 1) All MSS attribute the work to Hermogenes, and 2) The commentaries of John of Sardis, John Doxapatres (on the *Progymnasmata* of Aphthonius) and the three scholia on the Περὶ στάσεων all name Hermogenes as the author of the *Progymnasmata*.

The arguments against are: 1) One scholion on the Περὶ στάσεων says that some attribute the *Progymnasmata* to Libanius (Codd. Paris 1983 and 2977 [=7.511, 3-4 Walz]); 2) Two MSS of Priscian's translation have a *subscriptio* designating the author as Hermogenes or Libanius; 3) Syrianus fails to include the *Progymnasmata* in his list of Hermogenes' works; and 4) No scholia on the *Progymnasmata* exist.

Rabe chose to ignore the first set of evidence as well as the negative nature of much of the data in his second set and concluded that the author was no longer known in the fifth and sixth centuries and that the attributions to

Libanius and Hermogenes were merely conjectures.

Radermacher agrees with Rabe's evaluation and goes so far as to say that the *Progymnasmata* "ist dürftig und schwerlich von der Hand des H(ermogenes)."[43] Since Rabe and Radermacher, other critics have held the same position, most notably George L Kustas,[44] who of course cites Rabe.

On the other hand, Stanley F. Bonner refers to Rabe's rejection of Hermogenes as the author but otherwise seems to follow the traditional assumption that Hermogenes wrote the work.[45] George Kennedy, however, gives no hint at any uncertainty of authorship and names Hermogenes as the author.[46]

As for Rabe's arguments, they are far from persuasive. Rather, they seem to be in keeping with the fad of nineteenth century, especially in Germany, whereby ancient texts were frequently re-written to suit modern notions,[47] and where works were declared anonymous rather than the product of the author to whom they had been traditionally assigned. That occasionally such claims were correct — or at least could not be proved incorrect — only encouraged more such attempts.

In the case of Hermogenes and this *Progymnasmata*, Rabe and those who accept his thesis may be correct. But they may also be wrong. In either case, we have the document, and, whether Hermogenes or "anonymous" is the author, at least some of the evidence points to a strong possibility that it was composed in the period between Theon and Aphthonius. Even Rabe[48] and Radermacher[49] agree with this supposition.

The evidence which points to a time between Theon and Aphthonius may be summarized as follows: 1) The emphasis on a rhetorical use of the exercises rather than, as in Theon, on a less restricted use; 2) Changes in the order of the exercises — for example, the chreia chapter being moved from first to third position,[50] and the chapter on description being put after characterization; 3) New exercises, such as the chapter on the maxim and an independent chapter on refutation and confirmation; and finally 4) The attempt in the treatment of each subject to simplify and clarify the discussion.

When we examine Aphthonius' *Progymnasmata*, we see that it retains the basic order, not of Theon, but of this set of exercises. Further, Aphthonius adds two chapters of his own by separating confirmation and refutation and by balancing the chapter on encomium with one on censure. He even continues the trend toward simplification and adds completely worked out models as examples of each exercise.

None of this evidence proves that Hermogenes wrote the *Progymnasmata* which passes under his name. Indeed, we know of at least two other men living in roughly the same period who dealt with the same subject: Paulus of Tyre and Minucianus (the elder) of Athens.[51] On balance, however, the evidence favors Hermogenes. The positive attributions of the manuscripts, commentaries and scholia point directly to him, and the negative arguments hardly point in any other direction. Were it not for the nineteenth century penchant for questioning traditional attributions, Hermogenes would be the acknowledged author of the *Progymnasmata* which we possess. This volume assumes Hermogenean authorship.

II

Hermogenes' Discussion of the Chreia. In Hermogenes' *Progymnasmata* this chapter, as we have seen, stands third after μῦθος and διήγημα. It has three main sections: 1) Definition (lines 2-4); 2) Classification, including differentiation from other forms (5-30); and 3) Outline of a prescribed elaboration, i.e., ἐργασία (31-61).

Compared with the treatment of the chreia in the *Progymnasmata* of Theon and Nicolaus, the discussion of Hermogenes is very brief. The definition itself lacks several elements found in the other two, yet clearly it agrees with them in principle. Likewise, the classification omits all but a general reference (cf. 27-30) to the sub-types of the chreia which are so prominent in Theon's analysis. Nor does he list the modes in which the ἀπόφασις of the chreia occurs.

In fact, the reader gets the impression that for Hermogenes the definition and classification are minor but necessary preliminaries to the main point of the chapter. This center piece, as it were, is the ἐργασία, and Hermogenes' emphasis on this exercise or manipulation provides the most striking difference between his chapter and that of Theon. It may also be the most important feature of Hermogenes' treatment of the chreia.

To such an extent does he concentrate on the ἐργασία that, once he has completed his discussion of it, he abruptly ends the chapter, thus emphasizing the importance of the manipulation in his own mind. Nowhere does he even hint at the declension (κλίσις) or, say, refutation (ἀνασκευνη) of a chreia. For him the ἐργασία alone is worthy of discussion.[52]

The pattern of the ἐργασία which he provides contains eight steps or sections:

1) ἐγκώμιον (Encomium; praise)

2) παράφρασις (Paraphrase)

3) αἰτία (Rationale)

4) κατὰ τὸ ἐναντίον (Statement from the opposite)

5) ἐκ παραβολῆς (Statement from analogy)

6) ἐκ παραδείγματος (Statement from example)

7) ἐκ κρίσεως (Statement from authority)

8) παράκλησις (Exhortation)

This pattern of eight points closely resembles a set of seven which the author of the *Rhetorica ad Herennium* (4.43.56-58) calls *tractatio* and which he uses to elaborate a maxim.[53] There is another similarity between Hermogenes' ἐργασία and the *tractatio:* both are designed to train the student to use the rhetorical form as the starting point for a single, elaborate speech rather than, as in Theon, for a series of short, relatively simple essays, each based on some aspect of the same fable, chreia, etc.[54]

This difference between Theon's treatment and that of the other two is significant for more than one reason. First, the very fact that a Roman rhetorician of the first century B.C. utilized a standard rhetorical form in this way indicates that Greek theorists had already worked out the details of such exercises.[55] Thus, when Hermogenes applies the same type of elaboration to a chreia, he seems to be following a tradition that is older than Theon.

Secondly, Theon could not have been unaware of the tradition. Therefore he must have made changes deliberately and in keeping with his own view that the early exercises should be kept simple. That he indeed considered the elaboration an exercise which should be reserved for advanced students is clear from his statement at the end of his introductory chapter: "We will make use of reading, recitation, and paraphrase from the beginning, but we will use the elaboration (ἐξεργασία) and, to an even greater extent, the rebuttal only when we have acquired some skill."[56] Yet, whether Theon ever included elaboration in any later chapter is debatable, for no such exercise appears in our text of his *Progymnasmata*.

In any case, Theon broke with tradition; Hermogenes followed it, and subsequent writers followed him, not Theon. Aphthonius, in his usual succinct fashion, devotes most of his chapter to an ἐργασία, and his popularity insured the continued use of the elaboration with the chreia throughout the rest of antiquity.

Even earlier than Aphthonius, however, Libanius composed four such ἐργασίαι which in length and wealth of detail far exceed anything we might expect from Hermogenes' or Aphthonius' brief treatments. As Bonner, with slight hyperbole, says about one of Libanius' ἐργασίαι, it is "so lucid and natural that, if one did not already know the pegs on which it was hung, one would not suspect it to be an artificial composition at all."[57]

This application of the ἐργασία, then, which reached such a high point of development, may have begun in a much earlier period. For us, however, it begins with Hermogenes, who saw it as the basis for writing one specific rhetorical composition rather than a mere elementary exercise designed to help the young student analyze a piece of literature.

The Text of Hermogenes. The text used in this volume is that of Rabe, who has edited the standard text of all of Hermogenes' writings, published as volume 6 of the Teubner *Rhetores Graeci* series.[58] A translation of the whole of the *Progymnasmata* is available.[59]

NOTES

1. The dating of Dio and Philostratus cannot be precise. Evidence points to Dio's publishing his work sometime after A.D. 222 and no later than 229. Philostratus' *Vitae Sophistarum* appeared no earlier than 230 and perhaps as late as 238. In any case, the two appear to be independent witnesses for the meeting between Hermogenes and the Emperor.
2. See Syrianus, *In Hermogenem Comm.* (2.1, 8ff. Rabe).
3. See Sopater, Σχόλια εἰς τὰς στάσεις (5.8, 1ff. Walz).
4. A full list appears in H. Rabe's "Aus Rhetoren-Handschriften. 1. Nachrichten über das Leben des Hermogenes," *RhM* 62 (1907) 247-62, esp. 247-55.
5. See Rabe, "Nachrichten," 247-51.
6. See L. Radermacher, "Hermognes (22)," *RE* 8 (1912) 865-877, esp. 867.
7. This date depends solely on two points: a) that Hermogenes met Marcus Aurelius in 176 and b) that he was 15 years old at the time. On the first point, see n. 14; on the second, see n. 13.
8. Philostratus, *V. Soph.* 577.
9. Cf. Codd. Paris 1983 (11th c.) f. 7v., and 2977 (11th c.). Rabe ("Nachrichten," 247) doubts this piece of information.
10. Sopater, Σχόλια εἰς τὰς στάσεις (5.8, 25 Walz). Cf. Rabe, "Nachrichten," 247: "Die überlieferung ist verdächtig."
11. Cod. Paris. 1987 f.7v, but this bit of information cannot be any more correct than the statement of the *Suda* that Musonius heard Hermogenes. Scopelian flourished in the reign of Domitian and was too old in the reign of Hadrian to go on an embassy to the Emperor on behalf of Smyrna (cf. Philostratus, *V. Soph.* 521). Certainly, as Christ-Schmid-Stählin (*Geschichte der griechischen Literatur*, 771 n. 5) pointed out long ago, "dieser (sc. Scopelian) kann in den siebzieger Jahren des 2. Jhs. nicht mehr doziert haben."

As Radermacher ("Hermogenes," 868) observes, the ancients liked to set up teacher-student successions, but the choice of Scopelian is strange. A more logical candidate could easily have been found, even though Scopelian is reputed to have had students from all over the East (cf. Philostratus, *V. Soph.* 518).
12. Philostratus, *V. Soph.* 521.
13. Philostratus, *V. Soph.* 577, at least implies that the meeting between Hermogenes and Marcus occurred when the youth was fifteen. The source of this age, however, may be nothing more than an interpretation of a sentence from the speech which Hermogenes supposedly delivered before

the Emperor (Philostratus, *V. Soph.* 578): "Behold! I come
before you, Emperor, as a rhetor needing a paedagogus, a
rhetor awaiting manhood."

14. As Rabe ("Nachrichten," 259) says: "176 (nicht 175)."
Yet numerous histories, encyclopedias, etc. cannot decide
between 175 and 176. It is true that beyond the bare notice
that Marcus visited Hermogenes and heard him declaim we
have no evidence for a contact between the two, but on
the assumption that the meeting was historical and that it
occurred during the period in which tradition places it, some
reasonable interpretation is possible.

First, a brief summary of Marcus' activities in the latter
part of A.D. 175 and most of 176:

After the assassination of Avidius Cassius (August 175)
which abruptly ended the Eastern uprising against the
Emperor, Marcus felt that it was imperative for him to make
an appearance in these regions in order to win back the
goodwill of the people. Accordingly, in August 175 or very
shortly thereafter, he set out on a journey across Asia
Minor, through Syria and southward to Alexandria. After a
brief stay here, he retraced his steps northward to Syria,
then by the main roads to Tarsus, through the Cilician Gates
to Halala, where his wife Faustina suddenly died. From Halala
he journied eastward to Smyrna, where he met Aelius
Aristeides, and from there he sailed to Athens. In Athens
he was initiated into the Eleusinian Mysteries (Aug/Sept 176)
and also established four chairs of philosophy as well as
two chairs of rhetoric. In the latter part of November 176,
after fifteen months of travel, Marcus returned to Rome.

Now, any meeting between Marcus and Hermogenes during
this period undoubtedly took place on the return portion of
the journey summarized above. Several factors point to the
probability of this statement. First, on the outward journey
in the months immediately following the uprising, Marcus was
surely too occupied with affairs of state to think very much
about rhetoric and youthful rhetoricians.

Secondly, Faustina died on the return journey (cf. Julius
Capitolinus' *Life* of Marcus Aurelius 26.3-4 and Cassius Dio,
72.28,3-29,1, both of whom place her death after Marcus' visit
to Alexandria). She died at Halala, afterwards renamed
Faustinopolis, which was situated just north of the Cilician
Gates. Furthermore, her death must have occurred sometime
in the late spring or summer of 176 since by August 176 Marcus
had already visited Smyrna and was in Athens.

Third, Tarsus, where we must assume Hermogenes was at
this time, was an important highway junction. Several

important roads met there, including the east-west road between Syria and the regions west of Cilicia and the north-south road which led through the Cilician Gates into central Asia Minor. Marcus' entourage probably approached Tarsus from the east and departed by the road leading northward. While in Tarsus, Marcus heard Hermogenes declaim, and, since the distance from Tarsus to Halala is less than a hundred miles, that event occurred only a very short time before Faustina's death. In any case, both the meeting with Hermogenes and the death of the Empress took place in 176 (not 175).

15. At age 17, according to Syrianus, Proleg. ad Περὶ ἰδέων (7.40, 6 Walz); at age 18, according to Sopater, Σχόλια εἰς τὰς στάσεις (5.8, 26 Walz). At age 19 or 20, according to the *Suda* (s.v. Ἑρμογένης [2.415, 9-12 Adler]). See also the passage quoted below in n. 22 which may point to a tradition (possibly Neoplatonic) that Hermogenes had written at least some of his works before age 17.

16. More likely the appellation referred to his insistence on polished writing, and this notion finds some support from Plutarch's remarks about Isocrates in *De glor. Athen.* 350D-E where he says that Isocrates had grown old, not in polishing and sharpening weapons of war but rather in welding and joining together antitheses, clauses, etc., all but polishing and proportioning them with chisels and files (κολαπτῆρσι καὶ ξυστῆρσι).

17. At age 24, according to the *Suda* (2.415, 5 Adler). At age 25, according to Sopater, Σχόλια εἰς τὰς στάσεις (5.8, 28 Walz); *Proleg. ad* Περὶ στάσεων (7.40, 9 Walz), and others.

18. Philostratus, *V. Soph.* 577-78.

19. Philostratus (*V. Soph.* 578) says ἐν βαθεῖ γήρᾳ, a phrase which he uses nowhere else even though he discusses sophists who lived into their 70s, 80s and even later. The closest verbal parallel is ἐς γῆρας βαθύ which he uses of Scopelian (*V. Soph.* 515), who also died ἀκέραιός τε καὶ ἄρτιος. On Scopelian, see n. 11 above.

Philostratus' statement about Hermogenes raises some serious questions (cf. Rabe, "Nachrichten," 268). When he wrote in 230 or at least no later than 238, Hermogenes would have been 69 or at most 77, but the rhetorician was already dead. Can we assume that for Philostratus this was "advanced old age" in the case of Hermogenes when it was not for the other sophists? Apparently, for otherwise all our dating is faulty.

20. Philostratus' phrase is εἷς τῶν πολλῶν νομιζόμενος (*V. Soph.* 578), which may suggest nothing more than the fact that Hermogenes was no longer prominent among sophists.

And yet the remark of Antiochus which Philostratus quotes in this same passage ("This Hermogenes, who in childhood was an old man, in old age a child") suggests that he was still prominent enough to rate a barb. Nobodies seldom arouse hostility. Then there is Philostratus' *Life*. Admittedly it is brief and very hostile, but why did he write it about "one of the many"?

21. Although at first glance this description may seem silly, it probably contains symbolism that is indicative of one traditional view of Hermogenes. There are two separate elements here, the hairiness and the size of the heart, but both are associated with the ancient belief that the heart was the seat of intelligence. There are many references to this belief, but one needs only to read only such passages as Plato, *Theaet.* 194C-195A, and Pliny, *H.N.* 11.70.183-85, to see that the enlarged heart symbolized intelligence and the hairy heart not only bravery and resoluteness, but cleverness as well.

In addition, there was, e.g., the tradition that the heart of the Spartan general Lysander was found after death to be hairy (cf. Eustathius on *Iliad* 1.189), and Plutarch (*Lys.* 28) says of him that he was χαλεπὸς ὀργὴν διὰ τὴν μελαγχολίαν ἐπιτείνουσαν εἰς γῆρας. This observation may bring us close to the picture of Hermogenes which Philostratus, whom the *Suda* follows, presents.

In summary, then, the remark of the *Suda* is not unique. There are numerous references to such conditions of the heart after death, and in almost every case the reputation of the man involved was less than perfect. Certainly that is the case with Hermogenes.

For much of the information here, as well as many other pertinent references, we are indebted to Prof. John Scarborough of the University of Kentucky who, in his work on the Committee for the History of Medicine and Science, is recognized as an expert on the subject of ancient medicine.

22. Among these sources is one which neither Rabe nor Radermacher mentions and which Schmid-Stählin fail to associate with the discussion of Hermogenes, although they cite it elsewhere. In the section on Claudius Ptolemaeus, the author of the so-called *Tetrabiblos* (cf. Christ-Schmid-Stählin, *Geschichte der griechischen Literatur*, 896-904, esp. 897 n. 1) they cite a *Life* of Ptolemy which appears before the *Tetrabiblos*:

> This Ptolemy flourished in the period of Hadrian and survived even to the reign of Marcus Antoninus (i.e., Marcus Aurelius). In this period,

too, Galen won distinction for his medical art as did the grammarian Herodian and Hermogenes, the writer on rhetorical art (περὶ τέχνης ῥητορικῆς).

According to most modern estimates, Ptolemy's dates were c. 100-178 A.D. If this dating is accurate, we may have evidence here that Hermogenes had written his compositions — or at least some of them — by 178 when he was 17 years old. Even if we consider this evidence negligible, there remains the obvious point that a later scribe — though one tradition claims that the Neoplatonist Porphyry was the original author — thought that it was sufficient to identify Ptolemy's period by naming Hermogenes as one of three contemporary writers.

23. See Syrianus, *In Hermogenem Comm.* (1.1, 7-12 Rabe).

24. See Syrianus, *In Hermogenem Comm.* (1.96, 6-11 Rabe).

25. See Syrianus, *In Hermogenem Comm.* (2.1,9-3, 2 Rabe).

26. But tradition is not unanimous about the third work, and both Rabe (*Hermogenis Opera*, ix-xii) and Radermacher ("Hermogenes," 872-73) do their best to disprove Hermogenean authorship.

27. See Hermogenes, Περὶ ἰδέων (p. 378, 19 Rabe).

28. See Hermogenes, Περὶ ἰδέων (p. 36, 22 Rabe).

29. A fifth century rhetorician whom Studemund identified as the author of the scholia to the Περὶ ἰδέων which appears in Codex Parisinus 1983 as well as in 2977. See Rabe's comment on Περὶ εὑρέσεως (p. 183, 19 Rabe) and in the preface to his *Hermogenis Opera*, vi-ix.

30. A third century sophist and rhetorician, and a friend of Philostratus, who on that account refrains from including him in his *Vitae Sophistarum* (cf. 628). Cf. Christ-Schmid-Stählin, *Geschichte der griechischen Literatur*, 937-38.

31. See Syrianus, *In Hermogenem Comm.* (2.3, 4 Rabe): "He (sc. Hermogenes) has left another treatise on the parts of the public speech, as he himself intimates in his τέχνη τῶν στάσεων . . ."

32. See Rabe, *Hermogenis Opera*, vi-ix.

33. See Radermacher, "Hermogenes," 873-77.

34. See n. 22 above and the passage in which the author of Ptolemy's *Life* uses the singular form of the term in an apparent reference to more than one rhetorical work of Hermogenes. For a recent discussion of Hermogenes' place in the rhetorical tradition of these centuries, see Kustas, *Studies in Byzantine Rhetoric*, 5-26.

35. Or George Trebizond of Crete, as J. Montfasani suggests in his *George of Trebizond: A Biography and a Study of his Rhetoric and Logic* (Columbia Studies in the Classical Tradition 1; Leiden: Brill, 1976) 4-5. This volume is the product

of hard work, careful research and close reasoning and is
a mine of information not only for George Trebizond himself
but for the whole period of the Italian Renaissance. See also
Kennedy, *Rhetoric . . . from Ancient to Modern Times*, 199-205.
For some unaccountable reason A. Patterson (*Hermogenes and
the Renaissance: Seven Ideas of Style* [Princeton: Princeton
Univ., 1970]) omits any reference to this very important
Renaissance figure. In a discussion of Hermogenes and the
role of his rhetorical works in the Renaissance such an
omission is inexcusable.

36. He reached Italy, according to Montfasani (*George of
Trebizond*, 8-9) in 1416. On his introduction of Hermogenes'
works to the Latin West, see Montfasani, *George of Trebizond*,
17-18, 26, 248-57, 325 *et passim*.

37. For Hermogenes' role in the Renaissance, see, in
addition to the works cited in n. 35, J. E. Sandys, *A History
of Classical Scholarship* (3 vols.; Cambridge: Cambridge Univ.,
1903-1908) 2.1-163.

38. D. A. Russell, "Greek Rhetoric," *OCD*² (1970) 921.

39. One result — and cause — of this situation is the fact
that many of the Greek rhetorical works have not even been
edited, much less translated into a modern language, in the
past seventy years. For many of these texts we must still
depend on the old edition of Walz.

40. See, e.g., the analysis of Kennedy, *Rhetoric . . . from
Ancient to Modern Times*, 165.

41. See Montfasani, *George of Trebizond*, 248-55.

42. See Rabe, *Hermogenis Opera*, iv-vi.

43. See Radermacher, "Hermogenes," 877.

44. See Kustas, *Studies in Byzantine Rhetoric*, 19-20.

45. See Bonner, *Education in Ancient Rome*, 368 n. 7.

46. See Kennedy, *Rhetoric . . . from Ancient to Modern Times*,
165 *et passim*. See also Montfasani, *George of Trebizond*, 249.
He dismisses the *Art* of Hermogenes, including the
Progymnasmata, with a single sentence, yet he seems to
assume the work is genuine.

47. As just one example, one need only look at the Teubner
text, and expecially the apparatus, of R. Foerster's edition
of Libanius. Change after useless change has been made in
the text, and the most frequent word in the apparatus is
scripsi.

48. See Rabe, *Hermogenis Opera*, vi.

49. See Radermacher, "Hermogenes," 877.

50. Hermogenes says in his chapter on διήγημα (*Progymn.*
2 [p. 4,7-8 Rabe]) that some people place the chreia before
the διήγημα. We also read in a scholion to Doxapatres (as
cited in H. Rabe [ed.], *Aphthonii Progymnasmata* [Rhetores

Graeci 10; Leipzig: Teubner, 1926] 54) that Theon and the second century rhetorician Harpocration also placed the chreia in this position.

51. See Rabe, *Aphthonii Progymnasmata*, 54-55.

52. In fact he makes his attitude clear in lines 30-31 when he says, "But now let us move on to the chief matter (ἐπὶ τὸ συνέχον), and this is the elaboration."

53. Cf. Bonner, *Education in Ancient Rome*, 259. As he correctly observes (cf. 369 n. 66), H. Caplan, the editor of the Loeb edition of the *Rhetorica ad Herennium*, follows an erroneous tradition in calling the exercise a chreia (p. 370 n. d).

54. Yet Theon, too, seems to have in mind an essay-length composition when he discusses the various arguments that should be used in the κατασκευή of a chreia (cf. Theon 384-405). This exercise, however, is quite different from the ἐργασία.

55. So Bonner, *Education in Ancient Rome*, 259.

56. Theon, *Progymn.* 1 (1.158, 10-12 Walz).

57. Bonner, *Education in Ancient Rome*, 259.

58. H. Rabe (ed.), *Hermogenis Opera* (Rhetores Graeci 6; Leipzig: Teubner, 1913) 1-27.

59. See C. Baldwin, *Medieval Rhetoric and Poetic* (New York: Macmillan, 1928) 23-38.

TEXT
AND
TRANSLATION

(6,5)

Χρεία ἐστὶν ἀπομνημόνευμα λόγου τινὸς ἢ
πράξεως ἢ συναμφοτέρου σύντομον ἔχον δήλωσιν
ὡς ἐπὶ τὸ πλεῖστον χρησίμου τινὸς ἔνεκα.
Τῶν δὲ χρειῶν αἱ μέν εἰσι λογικαί, αἱ δὲ   5
πρακτικαί, αἱ δὲ μικταί· λογικαὶ μέν, αἷς

(6,10)
λόγος ἔνεστι μόνον, οἷον (Chreia 52) " Πλάτων
ἔφησε τὰς Μούσας ἐν ταῖς ψυχαῖς τῶν εὐφυῶν
οἰκεῖν. " πρακτικαὶ δέ, ἐν αἷς πρᾶξις μόνον,
οἷον (Chreia 26) " Διογένης ἰδὼν μειράκιον   10
ἀτακτοῦν τὸν παιδαγωγὸν ἐτύπησε. " μικταὶ δὲ
αἱ μῖξιν ἔχουσαι λόγου καὶ πράξεως, οἷον (cf.
Chreia 26) " Διογένης ἰδὼν μειράκιον ἀτακτοῦν
τὸν παιδαγωγὸν ἐτύπτησε λέγων· ' τί γὰρ τοιαῦτα
ἐπαίδευες; '"   15

(6,15)
Διαφέρει δὲ χρεία ἀπομνημονεύματος
μάλιστα τῷ μέτρῳ· τὰ μὲν γὰρ ἀπομνημονεύματα
καὶ διὰ μακροτέρων ἂν γένοιτο, τὴν δὲ χρείαν
σύντομον εἶναι δεῖ. γνώμης δὲ διαφέρει τῷ

(7,1)
τὴν μὲν ἐν ἀποφάνσει ψιλῇ λέγεσθαι, τὴν δὲ   20
χρείαν πολλάκις <καὶ> κατὰ ἐρώτησιν καὶ κατὰ
ἀπόκρισιν· καὶ πάλιν τῷ τὴν μὲν χρείαν καὶ ἐν
πράξεσιν εἶναι, τὴν δὲ γνώμην ἐν λόγοις μόνον·
καὶ πάλιν τῷ τὴν μὲν χρείαν τὸ πεποιηκὸς

(7,5)
πρόσωπον ἔχειν ἢ εἰρηκός, τὴν δὲ γνώμην ἄνευ   25
προσώπου λέγεσθαι.
Λέγεται δὲ περὶ διαφορᾶς χρειῶν πλεῖστα
παρὰ τοῖς παλαιοῖς, ὅτι αἱ μὲν αὐτῶν εἰσιν ἀποφαντικαί, αἱ δὲ ἐρωτηματικαί, αἱ δὲ πυσματικαί.

19: Post δεῖ add. PΖ (fort. ex Theone 22–24), om. LbPhg et Prisc.
ἔτι δὲ ὅτι ἡ μὲν ἀναφέρεται εἴς τινα πρόσωπα, τὸ δὲ ἀπομνημόνευμα
καὶ καθ'αὑτὸ μνημονεύεται. Quae verba accipiunt Walz et Spengel,
omisit Rabe propter Prisciani silentium.
21: καί ex Dox (2.305,9 W) addit Rabe et laudat Prisc. qui "etiam"
in hoc loco ostendit.

On the Chreia[1]

A chreia is a reminiscence of some saying or
action or a combination of both which has a concise
resolution,[2] generally[3] for the purpose of something
useful.

Some are sayings-chreiai, some action-chreiai,
some mixed chreiai. Sayings-chreiai are those in
which there is only speech; for example (Chreia 52)
*Plato said that the Muses dwell in the souls of the
gifted*. Action-chreiai are those in which there is
only action; for example (Chreia 26) *Diogenes, on
seeing a youth misbehaving, beat the paedagogus*.
Mixed chreiai are those with a mixture of speech
and action; for example (cf. Chreia 26) *Diogenes, on
seeing a youth misbehaving, beat the paedagogus
and said "Why were you teaching such things?"*
A chreia differs from a reminiscence mainly
in its length, for reminiscences may occur also
in greater lengths, but the chreia must be
concise.[4] A chreia differs from a maxim in that
the maxim is expressed in a simple statement,
but the chreia is frequently expressed also with
a question and an answer. And further, they
differ in that the chreia has to do with actions,
but the maxim has to do only with words. And
further, they differ in that the chreia has a
character who has acted or spoken,[5] but the
maxim is expressed without a character.

On the different species[6] of chreiai, it is said,
mainly in the older writers,[7] that some of them are
statements, some responses to simple questions,
and some responses to enquiries requiring an
explanation.

(7,10)   Ἀλλὰ νῦν ἐπὶ τὸ συνέχον χωρῶμεν, τοῦτο   30
          δέ ἐστιν ἡ ἐργασία. ἐργασία τοίνυν οὕτως ἔστω·
          (1) πρῶτον ἐγκώμιον διὰ βραχέων τοῦ εἰπόντος ἢ
          πράξαντος, εἶτα (2) αὐτῆς τῆς χρείας παράφρασις,
          εἶτα (3) ἡ αἰτία.
          Οἷον (Chreia 43) " Ἰσοκράτης ἔφησε τῆς   35
          παιδείας τὴν μὲν ῥίζαν εἶναι πικρὰν, τὸν δὲ
(7,15)   καρπὸν γλυκύν. "
          (1) Ἔπαινος· " Ἰσοκράτης σοφὸς ἦν, " καὶ
          πλατυνεῖς ἠρέμα τὸ χωρίον.
          (2) Εἶθ' ἡ χρεία· " εἶπε τόδε, " καὶ οὐ   40
          θήσεις αὐτὴν ψιλὴν ἀλλὰ πλατύνων τὴν ἑρμηνείαν.
          (3) Εἶτα ἡ αἰτία· " τὰ γὰρ μέγιστα τῶν
          πραγμάτων ἐκ πόνων φιλεῖ κατορθοῦσθαι, κατορ-
(7,20)   θωθέντα δὲ τὴν ἡδονὴν φέρει. "
          (4) Εἶτα κατὰ τὸ ἐναντίον· " τὰ μὲν γὰρ   45
          τυχόντα τῶν πραγμάτων οὐ δεῖται πόνων καὶ τὸ τέ-
          λος ἀηδέστατον ἔχει, τὰ σπουδαῖα δὲ τοὐναντίον. "
          (5) Εἶτα ἐκ παραβολῆς· " ὥσπερ γὰρ τοὺς
          γεωργοὺς δεῖ πονήσαντος περὶ τὴν γῆν κομίζεσθαι
          τοὺς καρπούς, οὕτω καὶ τοὺς λόγους. "   50
          (6) Εἶτα ἐκ παραδείγματος· " Δημοσθένης
(8,5)   καθείρξας ἑαυτὸν ἐν οἰκήματι καὶ πολλὰ μοχθήσας
          ὕστερον ἐκομίζετο τοὺς καρπούς, στεφάνους καὶ
          ἀναρρήσεις. "
          (7) Ἔστι δὲ καὶ ἐκ κρίσεως ἐπιχειρῆσαι,   55
          οἷον " Ἡσίοδος μὲν γὰρ ἔφη (Op. 289)
          τῆς δ' ἀρετῆς ἱδρῶτα θεοὶ προπάροιθεν ἔθηκαν,
(8,10)   ἄλλος δὲ ποιητής φησι (Epicharmus, Fr. 287 Kaibel)
          τῶν πόνων πωλοῦσιν ἡμῖν πάντα τἀγαθ' οἱ θεοί."
          (8) Ἐν δὲ τῷ τέλει παράκλησιν προσ-   60
          θήσεις, ὅτι χρὴ πείθεσθαι τῷ εἰρηκότι ἢ πε-
          ποιηκότι.
          Τοσαῦτα πρὸς τὸ παρόν· τὴν δὲ τελεωτέραν
          διδασκαλίαν ὕστερον εἴσῃ.

But now let us move on to the chief matter,[8] and
this is the elaboration.[9] Accordingly, let the elaboration
be as follows: (1) First, an encomium, in a few words,
for the one who spoke or acted. Then (2) a paraphrase
of the chreia itself; then (3) the rationale.

For example[10] (Chreia 43) *Isocrates said that
education's root is bitter, its fruit is sweet.*

(1) Praise:[11] "Isocrates was wise," and you amplify
the subject moderately.

(2) Then the chreia: "He said thus and so," and you
are not to express it simply[12] but rather by amplifying
the presentation.

(3) Then the rationale: "For the most important
affairs generally succeed because of toil, and once they
have succeeded, they bring pleasure."

(4) Then the statement from the opposite: "For
ordinary affairs do not need toil, and they have an
outcome that is entirely without pleasure; but serious
affairs have the opposite outcome."

(5) Then the statement from analogy: "For just as
it is the lot of farmers to reap their fruits after
working with the land, so also is it for those working
with words."

(6) Then the statement from example: "Demosthenes,[13]
after locking himself in a room and toiling long, later
reaped his fruits: wreaths and public acclamations."

(7) It is also possible[14] to argue from the statement
by an authority. For example, Hesiod said (*Op.* 289):

In front of virtue gods have ordained sweat.

And another poet says (Epicharmus, *Fr.* 287 Kaibel):

At the price of toil do the gods sell every good to us."

(8) At the end you are to add an exhortation to
the effect that it is necessary to heed the one who
has spoken or acted.

So much for the present; you will learn the more
advanced instruction later.[15]

COMMENTS

1. The introduction to Hermogenes discusses both the structure of this chapter and the author's general treatment of the subject. These comments concentrate on the clarification of specific words and phrases.

2. "Concise resolution": Hermogenes alone associates σύντομος with a part of the chreia rather than with the chreia as a whole. Theon says (line 2) σύντομος ἀπόφασις ἢ πρᾶξις where, in effect, each noun represents the whole chreia. Aphthonius (line 2) uses the adjective to modify ἀπομνημόνευμα which, again, is synonymous with the whole chreia. In Hermogenes, however, as the word order itself indicates and as Priscian's translation (line 4) proves, the adjective modifies δήλωσιν.

This use of δήλωσις, too, seems unique in the definitions of the chreia (but cf. Aphthonius' use of τὸ δηλοῦν in line 7 and Nicolaus, line 110), and a precise English equivalent is impossible. The word means "disclosure, revelation, demonstration" by either verbal or physical means. If a chreia were a more complicated form, "dénouement" would be appropriate, for δήλωσις indicates the outcome, the "point" of the anecdote. Priscian uses *demonstratio* which is an accurate translation, but even the Latin noun, as a rhetorical term, lacks a close English correspondence.

3. "Generally": with the phrase ἐπὶ τὸ πλεῖστον Hermogenes implies that a chreia need not always be useful (for living) despite the etymology of χρεία. Theon also attempts a similar disclaimer (lines 14-17) and later includes ἀχρηστία as one reason for refuting a chreia. Yet in his subsequent reference (lines 373-74) to the χρεία ἄχρηστος he fails to provide an example. The only reason Theon gives for the uselessness of a chreia is wit, and Nicolaus (lines 78-109) responds to this notion and, in effect, refutes the statement of Theon: a chreia can be both witty and useful for living as Chreia 16 or 48 proves.

4. After this sentence some MSS add two sentences (see apparatus) which Walz, followed as usual by Spengel, emends and prints in his edition. Rabe omits them because they are identical to a passage in Theon (lines 22-24) and because Priscian fails to translate them. See Priscian, comment 14, esp. 14h.

5. Notice that here in lines 24-25 and again in 61 Hermogenes uses the perfect tense of the two participles, but in lines 33-34 he uses the aorist. This variation is deliberate, for with the aorist he refers to the actual, i.e. the historical, person who is to be praised. With the perfect

tense, however, he refers to the πρόσωπον of the chreia who "has spoken or acted" and thus, in effect, continues to do so. Thus, as usual, the perfect tense is the equivalent of the present, while the aorist is the preterit.

6. "Different species" translates διαφορά which seems to be an Aristotelian term. See, for example, *Metaph.* 10.1057b7; cf. Plutarch, *Ad Stoic.* 1075C. Priscian's *differentia* (line 27) has the same technical sense.

7. "Older writers" may include Theon. Yet Hermogenes ignores, or at least departs from, the tradition to which he here refers. He is clearly not interested in such sub-classifications as Theon includes (lines 36–95). For Priscian's strange translation of Hermogenes' sentence see Priscian, comment 19.

8. On the implication of τὸ συνέχον see the introduction for a discussion of Hermogenes' emphasis on the ἐργασία.

9. Although the ἐργασία is the most important feature of Hermogenes' chapter on the chreia (and consequently of Priscian's as well), as it is also of Aphthonius' chapter, this study is postponing a full analysis of the exercise to Volume II which will present texts of those authors who deal with both κλίσις and ἐργασία; e.g. Libanius, Nicolaus and Diomedes.

10. The paragraphing here differs from that of other editions for two reasons. First, Hermogenes apparently uses οἶον to introduce the example, not just of Chreia 43, but of the whole ἐργασία which follows. Unless we understand οἶον in this way, the remaining treatment of the ἐργασία has no introduction. Secondly, the new paragraph here serves to point up an oddity in Hermogenes' arrangement of material. He begins (lines 32–34) with a list of the steps in an ἐργασία, but after only the third step he stops and introduces a sample chreia. Then after the chreia, and without a word of direction, he reverts to step one (but changing ἐγκώμιον to ἔπαινος and continues without interruption through the eight steps.

Such an arrangement is illogical and unlike any other method of listing which we find in the rhetoricians (cf., for example, the very clear presentation in Aphthonius, lines 19–22, 26–79). The first thought is that the Greek which gave the other five steps in the first list has fallen from the text. On the other hand, Priscian's version (lines 32–35) presents the material in exactly the same way, and this agreement points unmistakably to the reliabiltiy of the Greek — unless we can assume that the missing portion fell out in antiquity sometime after A.D. 225 and before about 525. Such an assumption may be unpalatable to textual critics, but the fact remains that, as Hermogenes' and Priscian's texts stand, the arrangement of material is curious and unsatisfactory.

11. Notice that Hermogenes writes ἔπαινος here after using ἐγκώμιον in line 32. The change seems to be deliberate, for ἔπαινος is the more general term. Aphthonius probably employs the same technique by using (line 19) ἐγκωμιαστικός.

12. "Simply" translates ψιλήν which means "unadorned, unelaborated, unslanted (in the speaker's view)." Despite his failure to repeat παράφρασις from line 33, Hermogenes is discussing paraphrase, and he seems to have in mind the use of the διήγησις of a speech. See Nicolaus, lines 153-62; cf. Quint. 4.2,2-4 et passim.

13. See Plutarch, Demosth. 849B-C; cf. ps. Plutarch, Vit. dec. orat. 844D.

14. "It is also possible": this phrase suggests that "Statement by authority" was not yet a regular part of the ἐργασία (can Hermogenes be the innovator?). As with other aspects of the ancient rhetorical tradition, the ἐργασία may not yet have received its final form before Hermogenes' day. That this fluid state of the art existed may be indicated by Rhet. ad Her. 4.44,57 where, contrary to what the Loeb editor, Harry Caplan, says (p. 373, note e), the section on "Testimony of the ancients" is not a part of the elaboration of the maxim. The section is, however, a regular part of the ἐργασία of the chreia in Aphthonius, Libanius, Nicolaus. Priscian, of course, reflects the optional nature of Hermogenes' statement by using the subjunctive form of the verb: argumenteris (line 58).

15. The combination of διδασκαλίαν and εἴση suggests that the person to whom Hermogenes addresses this remark (and whom he may have in mind throughout the Progymnasmata) is the teacher. The noun means "instruction by a teacher," and to say to a student "you will learn the instruction" is illogical. What he says is "you will learn the instruction (which you are to impart to your students)." In short, Hermogenes is obviously writing for teachers.

Priscian omits this last sentence (see Priscian, comment 31). Could his copy have been lacking these words? See, however, the conclusion of Ch. 6 on κοινὸς τόπος (14.14-15 Rabe) where a similar statement appears but which Priscian fails to translate.

THE CHREIA DISCUSSION OF
PRISCIAN

Introduction, Translation and Comments

by

EDWARD N. O'NEIL

INTRODUCTION

Life and Writings. Priscian stands on the threshold of the Middle Ages. He represents, so to speak, the end of the ancient grammatical and rhetorical tradition among the Romans. He collected and systematized the rules of Latin grammar, syntax and rhetoric, and he filled his works with quotations from numerous Greek and Latin works, fragments which in many cases would otherwise have perished.

His grammar in eighteen books, the famous *Institutiones Grammaticae*, became one of the great textbooks of Medieval Europe. Its popularity is attested by the more than a thousand manuscripts which survive and by the numerous references to Priscian as a master teacher as well as by the countless allusions to and adaptations of his *magnum opus*.[1]

Despite this widespread fame, we know very little about Priscian himself, but the following bits of information are generally held to be true. From his surname Caesariensis scholars have deduced that he was born at Caesarea in Mauritania[2] or at least received his education there. The dates of his birth and death are still debated, but he was probably born around the middle of the fifth century A.D. and died in the first part of the sixth century.[3]

Priscian himself tells us that his teacher was a man named Theoctistus:[4]

> . . . noster praeceptor Theoctistus, omnis eloquentiae decus, cui quicquid in me sit doctrinae post deum imputo.

This statement, especially the words *post deum*, also indicates that Priscian was a Christian, but there is even better evidence. In his translation of the *Periegesis* of Dionysius, Priscian has removed allusions to pagan subjects and substituted Christian ones.

Another proof that he was a Christian is the fact that

he became a teacher of grammar at Constantinople and received a salary from the state, for non-Christians could not at this time be on the official payroll.

That he was actually in Constantinople (which Priscian calls Byzantium) is attested by his statement in *Inst. Gram.* I.22 (II.17, 13-14 Keil):

> et epigrammata, quae egomet legi in tripode vetustissimo Apollinis, qui stat in Xerolopho Byzanti, sic scripta:

and he then quotes the inscription.

We should get some idea of Priscian's approximate dates by looking at the men to whom he dedicated his various works. Yet even here we encounter problems because the identities, and hence the dates, of these men are often far from certain. For example, Priscian dedicates his *Institutiones Grammaticae* to a man named Julian, whom he addressed as *consul ac patricius*.

Unfortunately, even with this reference to Julian's official position, no one has yet been able to make a convincing identification of this man with any other Julian. As early as 1565 Huber Goltz[5] sought to identify him with the reputed jurist and author of a Latin epitome of the *Novellae* of Justinian.[6] But since this work was completed no earlier than 555, the author seems too young to have been *consul ac patricius* at the time Priscian made his dedication — unless, of course, our other dates are incorrect.

Recently, M. Salaman[7] has suggested that Julian is the same man who was an Egyptian official and a poet who contributed some seventy-one epigrams to the so-called Cycle of Agathias. The few details we know about this poet who also involved himself in political matters are suggestive. Since at least two epigrams refer to events of 532, his dates are reasonably close to those of Priscian and those of Priscian's friend. Furthermore, he is referred to as ἀπὸ ὑπάρχων (ex-prefect), but ex-prefect is not ex-consul or *patricius*. In short, Salaman's suggestion is tempting but not persuasive, and it is certainly not conclusive.[8]

We are on firmer ground when we turn to the panegyric in verse which Priscian wrote on Anastasius, the controversial emperor who ascended the Eastern throne in 491 at the age of 60 and died in 518. The date of the panegyric is unknown, and critics have varied in placing it somewhere between 512 and 518. Still, this six-year span is as definite a date as we have about Priscian's life.[9]

Three of his smaller works, *De Figura Numerorum, De Metris Terentii,* and the one in which we are especially interested, *De Praeexercitamentis,*[10] Priscian dedicated to a man named Symmachus. Most critics identify him as Quintus Aurelius Memmius Symmachus, who wrote numerous works, including a *Roman History* in seven books.[11] He was also consul in 485, and in 525 he was executed by Theodoric in the same affair that brought about the death of Boethius, the pupil and son-in-law of Symmachus.[12]

None of these dates is conclusive or even very limiting, but taken together they give us at least an approximate time for Priscian's life.[13] Yet, some contradictory evidence exists,[14] and scholars are still far from being unanimous in their dating of Priscian and his writings.

De Praeexercitamentis. Unfortunately, nothing helps us date Priscian's translation of Hermogenes' *Progymnasmata;* nor, for that matter, is the point important here. What is important is the nature and value of the translation itself.

Its value lies in the fact that this version of Hermogenes' work was the only one available for almost a thousand years. The *Progymnasmata,* written toward the end of the second century A.D.,[15] became a standard work on the subject and rmained one until Aphthonius published his own *Progymnasmata* late in the fourth or early in the fifth century.

Even then Aphthonius' work did not immediately gain its eventual widespread popularity. For awhile there may have been a period of uncertainty and dispute among rhetoricians over the relative merits of those two, as well as other similar, works. It was apparently during this time that Priscian, for reasons now unknown to us, selected Hermogenes' *Progymnasmata* as his model rather than that of Aphthonius or some other rhetorician.

As a result, even after Hermogenes' own work lost its position of influence and fell into virtual oblivion, the Latin version, aided by the popularity of the translator,[16] gained new importance and acquired a great reputation in late antiquity down into the Middle Ages. In this way, Priscian preserved, however imperfectly and unintentionally, Hermogenes' *Progymnasmata* until a copy of the Greek text was found and the work regained its proper place in the rhetorical literature.

Priscian's translation is, on the whole, an accurate one.[17] In fact, in one place in the chreia chapter he follows the Greek so closely that his Latin is incorrect.[18] Yet he frequently adds words or omits some, and on occasion he expands and seems to offer a brief explanation of Hermogenes' discussion.

Despite these differences, Priscian's translation serves as a good check on Hermogenes' treatment of the *progymnasmata* as a whole and, in particular, of the section on the chreia. For this reason, his section on *usus* is placed immediately after its Greek original in this volume.[19]

NOTES

1. For a short account of the ebb and flow of Priscian's popularity in the Middle Ages, see D. L. Clark, "The Rise and Fall of *Progymnasmata* in Sixteenth and Seventeenth Century Grammar Schools," *SM* 19 (1952) 259–63, esp. 260–61.

Clark, however, does not inspire us with much confidence in his accuracy. In at least one place he has made a serious error of fact. He says (p. 260) that the edition of Priscian's *Praeexcercitamenta* is Hertz (he means Martin Hertz). In fact, the editor is Keil himself as anyone can see by glancing at the title page which faces p. 384 and more especially by reading the "*Praefatio Henrici Keilii*" on pp. 387–402.

In these pages, Keil gives full credit to Hertz for all his work on the threee smaller pieces which appear on pages 404–56, but for some reason Hertz declined to edit them. Keil undertook the task. Clark apparently looked only at the first title page of the volume, the one for Priscian's *Institutiones Grammaticae*, vol. 2. Hertz did indeed edit this larger work.

2. Cf. Schanz-Hosius-Krüger, *Geschichte der römischen Literatur*, 222, which quotes a *Life* of Priscian which says *sed quidam adfirmant, Caesaream istam, de qua Priscianus oriundus fuit, coloniam Africae esse*. On the other hand, Hertz (2.xiv) quotes a 13th c. MS which says that Priscian came from Caesarea in Cappadocia.

For some strange reason, F. A. Wright and T. A. Sinclair (*A History of Later Latin Literature* [London: Routledge, 1931; repr. London: Dawsons, 1969] 93) say "Priscianus of Caesarea (in Spain)." Although there were several cities of this name, none seems to have been located in Spain. Cf. W. Smith, *A Dictionary of Greek and Roman Geography* (3 volumes; London: Murray, 1873; repr. New York: AMS, 1966) 1.469–70.

3. M. Salaman, "Priscianus und seine Sch'lerkreis in Konstantinopel," *Philologus* 123 (1979) 91–96, esp. 92, is a bit more specific, at least about his death. He says 1 October 527 A.D.

4. *Inst. Gramm.* 2.51 (2.238, 7 Keil). The same man is referred to in *Cassiodorii Excerpta* (8.213, 1 Keil). Cf. Schanz-Hosius-Krüger, *Geschichte der römischen Literature*, 221. The name appears in various forms in the MSS, but most editors have accepted "Theoctistus."

5. Cf. W. Smith, *Dictionary of Greek and Latin Biography and Mythology* (3 vols.; London: Murray, 1844; repr. New York: AMS, 1967) 2.650, cites Goltz and the preface of his edition of the Epitome of the *Novellae*.

6. Although A(veril) and A(lan) Cameron ("The Cycle of

Agathias," *JHS* 86 [1966] 6-25, esp. 13) discuss this "Julianus Antecessor," they make no reference to Goltz's identifying him with Priscian's friend.

7. See Salaman, "Priscianus," 94-95.

8. For a detailed study of this Julian, see Cameron and Cameron, "Cycle," 12-14, and R. C. McCail, "The Cycle of Agathias: New Identifications Scrutinised," *JHS* 89 (1969) 87-88.

9. Cf. A(lan) Cameron, "The Date of Priscian's *De laude Anastasii*, *GRBS* 15 (1974) 313-16.

10. These titles vary slightly. The forms here are those adopted by Keil.

11. Schanz-Hosius-Krüger, *Geschichte der römischen Literatur*, 83-84.

12. For a detailed discussion of Boethius and Symmachus, their lives, relationship and deaths, see T. Hodgkin, *Italy and Her Invaders* (8 vols.; 2nd ed.; Oxford: Clarendon, 1896) 3.466-518, esp. 472ff. This old work has yet to be superceded.

13. One other datable piece of evidence is available. Theodorus, pupil of Priscian, completed a transcription of the *Institutiones* in 526-527 at Constantinople. Cf. Schanz-Hosius-Krüger, *Geschichte der römischen Literatur*, 230. At the very least, we have here a *terminus ad quem* for the compostion of this work.

14. Aldhelm, *De metris* 142 (ed. R. Ehwald, *Monumenta Germ. Hist.* 15 [1913] p. 203, 15), says that the Emperor Theodosius II, who lived 401-450, copied out Priscian's entire grammatical work in his own hand (*propriis palmarum digitulis*).

From what we know of this emperor and the way in which his sister Pulcheria controlled his life, such a project seems quite in keeping. But if Theodosius made such a copy even at the end of his life, it is impossible for Priscian to have written his work by that time and still be alive to compose the panegyric on Anastasius in 518, or even in 512. Therefore, either this piece of information is incorrect or almost every other source is wrong.

Schanz-Hosius-Krüger (*Geschichte der römischen Literatur*, 230) suggest that Aldhelm, knowing about Theodosius as a *"Bücherschreiber,"* confused the emperor with Priscian's pupil Theodorus. This explanation is as good as any, for Aldhelm seems to have been a bit of a *poseur* and not always careful about his facts. Cf. J. Sandys, *A History of Classical Scholarship* (3 vols.; Cambridge, 1920; repr. New York: Hafner, 1958) 1.465-67 and the bibliography on 467 n. 1.

15. This date is probably accurate only if Hermogenes is the author of this *Progymnasmata*. The question of authorship is discussed above in the "Introduction" to Hermogenes (see pp. 158-60). On the whole, the evidence points to Hermogenes

of Tarsus as the author.

16. Clark ("Rise and Fall," 260) points out that as late as the sixteenth century the general belief was that Priscian's work was his own composition rather than a translation from Greek.

17. Cf. A. Luscher, *De Prisciani studiis Graecis* (Diss. Breslau, 1912) for a detailed, but not entirely satisfactory analysis. Luscher was inclined to be much too mechanical in his comparisons.

18. Cf. Comment 14, section 9, to the translation.

19. Since the "Introduction" to Hermogenes deals with the subject, scope and structure of the chapter on the chreia, most of the discussion in this section, including the notes to the translation, assume a familiarity with Hermogenes' treatment in an attempt to avoid as much repetition as possible.

TEXT
AND
TRANSLATION

Usus est, quem Graeci χρείαν vocant commemoratio orationis alicuius vel facti vel
utriusque simul, celerem habens demonstrati-
onem, quae utilitatis alicuius plerumque   5
causa profertur.

Usuum autem alii sunt orationales, alii
activi. orationales sunt quibus oratio inest
sola, ut (Chreia 52) "Plato dicebat Musas in
animis esse ingeniosorum." activi vero in   10

(431,35) quibus actus inest solus, ut (Chreia 26)
"Diogenes, cum vidisset puerum indecenter agen-
tem, pedisecum virga percussit." vel mixti,
si addas "... percussit dicens 'quare sic
erudiisti?'"   15

Interest autem inter usum et commem-
orationem hoc, quod usus breviter profertur,
commemorationes vero, quas ἀπομνημονεύματα
Graeci vocant, longiores sunt. sententiae
vero differt, quod sententia indicative pro-   20

(432,5) fertur, usus vero saepe etiam per interroga-
tionem et per responsionem. praeterea, quod
usus etiam in actu solet inveniri, sententia
vero in verbis tantum. et quoniam usus habet
omnimodo personam quae fecit vel dixit, sen-   25
tentia vero sine persona dicitur.

Traduntur tamen differentiae usuum plures
a veteribus. alii enim sunt indicativi, alii
interrogativi.

(432,10) Sed nunc ad instans veniamus, hoc est ad   30
operationem et ordinationem ad usus pertinen-
tium capitulorum. disponendum igitur sic: (1)
primum laus breviter dicatur eius qui dixit
vel fecit, deinde (2) expositio ipsius usus,
hinc (3) causa.   35

2: quem P] quam (*ob genus vocis* chria) RVS, 8: *post* activi *add.* alii mixti
ς. 13: mixti ς] mixtae PRVS. 17: commemorationes RVS. 19: longiora PVS.

On Usus[1]

Usus, which the Greeks call chreia, is a reminiscence[2] of some saying[3] or action, or of both together, with a quick[4] resolution.[5] It generally serves some useful purpose.[6]

Some are sayings-chreiai, some action-chreiai.[7] Sayings-chreiai are those in which there is only speech. For example (Chreia 52) *Plato used to say*[8] *that the Muses exist in the minds of the gifted.* Action-chreiai, however, are those in which there is only action. For example (Chreia 26) *Diogenes, when he saw a boy misbehaving, struck the paedagogus*[9] *with his rod.*[10] Or they are mixed chreiai if you add[11] "*... he struck, saying 'Why have you been teaching*[12] *like this?'"*

There is, moreover, this difference between a chreia and a reminiscence: a chreia is set forth briefly,[13] but reminiscences, which the Greek call ἀπομνημονεύματα, are longer.[14] It differs, however, from the maxim in that the maxim is set forth in declarative form,[15] whereas the chreia is often set forth with a question and answer as well. Furthermore, the chreia is customarily found[16] in an action also, but the maxim only in words. And they differ since in every case[17] the chreia has a character who has acted or spoken, whereas the maxim is expressed without a character.

Several different species of chreiai,[18] however, are handed down by older writers:[19] some are declarative, some interrogative.

But now let us come to the important matter, that is the elaboration and arrangement of the sections which pertain to chreiai.[20] So, then, the order should be this:[21] (1) First, praise[22] of the one who has spoken or acted should be briefly expressed, then (2) a paraphrase of the chreia itself, then (3) the rationale.

Ut (Chreia 43) "Isocrates dicebat stirpem quidem doctrinae esse amaram, fructum vero dulcem."

(1) Laus: "Isocrates sapiens fuit," et producis pedetemptim locum.   40

(432,15)   (2) Postea sequatur elocutio ipsius usus, non oportet tamen ipsum per se ponere, sed latius eum interpretari.

(3) Deinde a causa: "maxima enim factorum per laborem perfici solent, perfecta vero afferunt iucunditatem."   45

(4) Deinde utendum a contrario: "nam vilissimae rerum non egent labore et finem taeterrimum habent, studiossimae vero res ex contrario."   50

(432,20)   (5) Posthac a comparatione: "quomodo enim agricolas oportet laborantes in terra accipere fructus, sic etiam eloquentes."

(6) Deinde ab exemplo: "Demosthenes inclusit sese in aediculis ad legendum et multo labore post accepit fructur: coronas et praedicationes."   55

(7) Praeterea ab iudicio argumenteris, ut "Hesiodus quidem dixit (*Op.* 289):

(432,25)   Virtutis sudorem di longe posuere.   60
alius poeta dixit (Epicharmus, *Fr.* 287 Kaibel):
     Laboribus vendunt dei nobis omnia bona.
(8) Post omnia inferes exhortationem, quod oportet parere illi qui dixit aut fecit.

60: virtuti *Ascens.* virtutis viam asperam dii fecere *Ald.* sudore ç; dei PRVS.
In subscriptione operis (v. paginam 440 Keilii) hoc legitur quod "Prisciani sophistae ars praeexercitaminum secundum Hermogenen vel Libanium explicit feliciter." RV.

For example[23] (Chreia 43) *Isocrates used to say*[24] *that education's root is bitter but its fruit is sweet.*

(1) Praise: "Isocrates was wise," and you amplify the topic point by point.[25]

(2) Then should follow the recitation of the chreia itself, but you should not set it forth just as it is, but rather express it more fully.[26]

(3) Then a statement of the rationale:[27] "For the most important deeds are usually accomplished by toil, but once accomplished they bring pleasure."

(4) Then a statement of the opposite should be used:[28] "For the most disreputable matters require no toil, and they have a very disgraceful end; but those requiring the most careful attention are just the opposite."

(5) After this the statement from analogy:[29] "For just as it is the lot of farmers to reap fruit by working on the land, so too is it for those expressing their thoughts well."

(6) Then the statement from example: "Demosthenes shut himself up in his house in order to read and, after much toil, later received its fruits: crowns and public proclamations."

(7) In addition, you may support the argument by a statement of authority. For example, "Hesiod, of course, said (*Op.* 289)[30]

Ere virtue, sweat the gods by far ordained.

Another poet said (Epicharmus, *Fr.* 287 Kaibel)

At the price of toil do the gods sell every good to us."

(8) At the end you are to add an exhortation to the effect that it is necessary to heed the one who has spoken or acted.[31]

COMMENTS

1. Priscian seems to be the only Latin writer to translate χρεία. Others, e.g., Quintilian, Diomedes, Isidore, the Vatican Grammarian, simply transliterate and write either *chreia* or *chria*. The closest anyone else comes to a translation is Julius Rufianus (*De figuris sententiarum et elocutionis* 18 [= 1.43, 24,25 Halm]), who says: *applicatur huic figurae* (i.e. διάνοια) *etiam* χρεία, *sententia necessaria.*

Despite Priscian's unusual practice, it seems best to use "chreia" in the translation rather than the awkward and at times ambiguous fourth declension term "*usus.*" The only exceptions are in the title and the first sentence.

2. As Priscian eventually explains below (line 18), his *commemoratio* translates ἀπομνημόνευμα. For the simple *memoratio*, see Vatican Grammarian (line 1).

3. Priscian uses *oratio* instead of the usual *dictum*, but he apparently understands λόγος in the usual sense which it has in these definitions. At least as early as Cicero (*ND* 1.44.123; *Tusc. Disp.* 5.16.46) *oratio* can have the meaning of "speech" in the sense of human utterance.

4. Hermogenes uses σύντομος in the sense of "concise." Priscian, however, understands the word in its temporal sense which is also common. But see line 17 where he renders the same word with *breviter*. Cf. Comments 13 and 14.

5. On δήλωσις which Priscian translates with *demonstratio* see Comment 2 to the translation of Hermogenes.

6. Priscian reverses Hermogenes' χρησίμου τινός by making the Greek adjective into a Latin noun and the pronoun into a pronominal adjective. To reflect the change, the English here differs from that in the translation of Hermogenes.

7. Notice that Priscian omits mixed chreiai here, although he includes them in his opening sentence and again in lines 13-15. Some MSS fill the omission by adding *alii mixti* to reflect Hermogenes' αἱ δὲ μικταί. They may be correct.

8. Priscian changes Hermogenes' aorist ἔφησεν to the imperfect *dicebat*, perhaps because he considers the Greek tense as a gnomic aorist. He makes the same change in Chreia 43 (line 36 below). In Nicolaus (cf. 136-37) and in the anonymous scholia (2.588, 5-6 Walz) this statement appears in a responsive chreia, and consequently the same grammatical situation does not arise.

9. Latin writers regularly transliterate παιδαγωγός, but Priscian, as he does in the case of χρεία-*usus*, translates with the relatively rare *pedisecus*. This noun normally refers to a slave who is assigned menial tasks and who has nothing

to do with education or the guarding of boys. Instead, a
pedisecus usually serves as a "page, footman," etc. (see,
e.g., Plautus, *Aul.* 501, *Mil. Glor.* 1009; Nepos, *Cim.* 4.2) or
represents an even more menial servant, e.g., a "lackey" (cf.
Cicero, *De Domo* 42.110; *Ad Att.* 2.16.1).

The only other passage where *pedisecus* may be a
translation of παιδαγωγός is, curiously enough, *Rhet. ad Her.*
4.52.65. The text, however, is very uncertain, and the reading
is an emendation: *"Heus," inquit, "Gorgia," pedisequo puerorum,
"absconde pueros, defende, fac ut incolumis ad adulescentiam
perducas"* ("Listen, Gorgias," he says to the boys' attendant,
"hide them, defend them, be sure that you bring them safely
to young manhood.")

10. Priscian adds *virga* to his translation of Hermogenes'
version of the chreia. Perhaps his familiarity with similar
passages (e.g., Chreia 25) caused an automatic addition. Or,
of course, the practice of ἀπαγγελία, which permitted such
alterations, may have led the change which is, after all, slight
and logical.

11. Here Priscian makes some small changes in Hermogenes'
wording, but the general sense remains unchanged. In
particular, where Hermogenes repeats the whole chreia in
order to add the remark of Diogenes, Priscian repeats only
the verb before making the addition.

12. For Hermogenes' imperfect ἐπαίδευες Priscian writes the
perfect *erudiisti.* Others (e.g., Nicolaus, *Progymn.* (1.272, 23
Walz) and Libanius, *Progymn.* (8.74, 3 Foerster) have the
present tense.

13. Here Priscian interprets σύντομος in a non-temporal
sense, i.e., *breviter*="concisely" or "with brevity." Cf.
Comments 4 and 14.

14. This passage, when compared with Hermogenes' words,
presents a number of problems, though even the Greek is
not free of difficulties. There are, in fact, eight separate
elements to the overall problem.

    a) Where Hermogenes says διαφέρει δὲ χρεία
       ἀπομνημονεύματος, Priscian correctly
       translates with *interest autem inter usum et
       commemorationem.*

    b) Hermogenes' μάλιστα τῷ μέτρῳ (a phrase which
       some editors have suspected) becomes simply
       hoc quod in Priscian. This is an economical and
       idiomatic way of expressing the Greek
       thought, but even so the Latin is not very
       close to the Greek.

    c) Where Hermogenes begins his comparison with

the reminiscence, Priscian strangely reverses the order and begins with the chreia. And where Hermogenes ends the comparison with the chreia, Priscian concludes with the reminiscence.

d) Furthermore, in neither phrase is Priscian's translation entirely accurate. For Hermogenes' καὶ διὰ μακροτέρων ἂν γένοιτο. Priscian says simply *longiores sunt*, thus missing the effect of καί ("also" or perhaps "even") and of the potential optative. Thus Hermogenes says that the reminiscences can be longer; Priscian says that they are.

e) The same situation exists in the two phrases on the chreia. Hermogenes says τὴν δὲ χρείαν σύντομον εἶναι δεῖ ("the chreia must be concise"). Yet Priscian says simply *usus breviter profertur* ("The chreia is set forth briefly"), and in the process (cf. Comment 13) he gives a meaning to σύντομος that differs from the one he used earlier (cf. Comment 4). Hermogenes says that the chreia must be concise; Priscian says simply that it is.

f) Another rather peculiar situation is the fact that Priscian has waited until now to explain that *commemoratio* is his translation of ἀπομνημόνευμα. Why has he postponed the definition? The term occurs first in line 1 where it would have been logical to insert the words *quem* ἀπομνημόνευμα *Graeci vocant*. Of course, one can argue that in the same sentence he has already defined *usus* and that two such definitions in the same sentence would be awkward. Yet he has already defined *usus* once (cf. 3.431, 5–6 Keil), and so a repetition is redundant. Yet an early definition of *commemoratio* seems quite in order. Even so, it is not even with the second occurrence of the noun that Priscian identifies his translation; it is the third.

g) Next, just as he began this passage with a close translation of Hermogenes' words, so he begins the next sentence with an even closer one. Where the Greek says γνώμης δὲ διαφέρει, Priscian writes *sententiae vero differt*, retaining the genitive case with a verb expressing difference. This construction is, of course, regular in Greek, but surely no such usage exists in Latin. *Differt* may take the ablative (with or without a preposition) or *inter* and the accusative, but the genitive or even the dative (which *sententiae* may be in form) seems impossible. And yet Priscian may use a genitive of separation in an even stranger way below in his translation of Hesiod's line. See comment 30.

h) The final difference in the two passages may indicate a deeper problem. In Hermogenes' text some codices add two sentences just before the words γνώμης δὲ διαφέρει (line 19): ἔστι δὲ ὅτι ἡ μὲν ἀναφέρεται εἴς τινα πρόσωπα. τὸ δὲ ἀπομνημόνευμα καὶ καθ'αὐτὸ μνημονεύεται. Walz (and Spengel of course) changed ἔστι to ἔτι and printed the two sentences. Rabe, following the other codices, omitted the words. His reasons for the omission are: 1) The words are identical with a passage in Theon (cf. 22-24) and were probably borrowed to make Hermogenes' discussion conform at this point with that of Theon; and 2) Priscian has not translated the sentences.

Rabe may be correct in omitting the words, for they do not sound like Hermogenes. Yet in view of all the points made above, Rabe's reliance on Priscian at this point may not be well placed. Whatever the reasons for Priscian's changes in this section, the fact remains that while he begins and ends with a very close translation of Hermogenes' words, between these two points he reverses the order of the Greek discussion, makes an awkward identification and fails to retain some of the important nuance of the original. Can we then be so sure that Priscian is a reliable witness of Hermogenes' text here? There is room for doubt.

15. Priscian's *quod sententia indicative profertur* translates τῷ τὴν μὲν ἐν ἀποφάνσει ψιλῇ λέγεσθαι, and for once the translation is more lucid and succinct than the original.

16. In place of τῷ . . . εἶναι Priscian writes *solet inveniri*. The use of *solet* is perhaps a legitimate translation of the Greek articular infinitive which can express an habitual

situation, but *inveniri* may have a significance that is not present in Hermogenes' version. The use of *inveniri* resembles the language of Nicolaus (cf. 48-49), who uses εὑρίσκεται. In Nicolaus the implication is that a chreia is an invention, a contrived vignette, which of course it is. Consequently, it is tempting to read in Priscian's choice of term a suggestion that such inventions can be made with an action-chreia as well as a sayings-chreia.

Some legitimate objections against this interpretation are possible. As Priscian's sentence stands, *inveniri* must, like Hermogenes' εἶναι, be understood with the following clause as well: *sententia vero in verbis tantum*. It is true that the idea of invention applies equally well to the maxim, but this seems a strange place and method of making such an observation. Furthermore, like several other Latin verbs, *inveniri* can be a vivid substitution for *esse*.

Nevertheless, Priscian's choice of substitution, if that is all *inveniri* is, remains interesting and perhaps even provocative.

17. The use of *omnimodo* here is interesting because nothing in the Greek of Hermogenes accounts for it. In fact, the Latin here is not unlike the language of Theon's discussion of the same subject (cf. Theon 10-11) where the adverb πάντως appears twice. The Latin translation of πάντως is *omnimodo*. Can Priscian have momentarily remembered Theon's definition?

18. Like Hermogenes' διαφοραί, *differentiae* indicates "different types" or "different species." The Greeks differ in their classification of sayings-chreiai: Theon gives four types, Nicolaus gives two; Aphthonius says nothing on the subject. Hermogenes himself identifies three types (cf. 29-30): ἀποφαντικαί, ἐρωτηματικαί and πυσματικαί. Priscian, however, even though he is translating Hermogenes, follows the practice of all Latin writers on the subject (see, e.g., Quintilian 22-25; Vat. Gram. 10-15) and omits the distinction between ἐρωτηματικαί and πυσματικαί.

19. For some reason Priscian has changed the sense of Hermogenes' Greek and in doing so has introduced an incongruity. The Greek says λέγεται δὲ περὶ διαφορᾶς χρειῶν πλεῖστα παρὰ παλαιοῖς ὅτι . . .: "But it is said about the different species of chreiai, mostly in older writers, that. . . ." Priscian has made "species" the subject of his verb and converted the adverb πλεῖστα into an adjective with "species." As a result, he says that "several species" are handed down, but then he identifies only two. Logically he should have written *duae* or *duplices*, for surely *plures* implies more than two.

20. Here Priscian expands the Greek. For τοῦτο δέ ἐστιν ἡ ἐργασία he offers *hoc est ad operationem et ordinationem*

ad usus pertinentium capitulorum. With the expansion he adds a new thought, for by itself *operatio* translates ἐργασία.

21. Again Priscian expands, and for the simple οὕτως ἔστω he writes *disponendum igitur sic.* He makes the same use of a gerundive in line 47: *utendum.*

22. Hermogenes uses ἐγκώμιον here (line 32) but ἔπαινος in the subsequent example (line 38). Priscian retains *laus* in both places.

23. On the significance of the new paragraph here see comment 10 to Hermogenes. Priscian may not, in fact, have understood the Greek as we suggest, for even though *ut* is a close verbal translation of οἷον, it seems too weak to introduce an entire section. On the whole, however, it seems better to be consistent in the arrangement of the two passages. Besides, the reasons for re-arranging the Greek text also apply to the Latin version.

24. On the change from aorist to imperfect, see comment 8 above.

25. Priscian's *pedetemptim* translates ἠρέμα, but the two words can give an almost opposite sense. The Greek suggests "quietly, unobrusively," or as we have rendered it, "moderately." The Latin implies "carefully, step-by-step." This sense is obvious in rhetorical passages where *pedetemptim* is joined with *caute.* Whether or not the change of Priscian is deliberate, his advice seems to point to a more detailed expansion of the *laus* than Hermogenes had in mind. It is, in effect, a reversal of Nicolaus' warning (cf. lines 163-67) that the ἔπαινος should not be extended διὰ πάντων τῶν ἐγκωμιαστικῶν κεφαλαίων and thus become longer than the ὑπόθεσις itself.

26. Priscian's translation of this section raises questions and may indicate that his text of Hermogenes differed from ours or, more likely, that he had the same text but found it expedient to make changes. At this point Hermogenes says εἶθ'ἡ χρεία· "εἶπε τόδε·" καὶ οὐ θήσεις οὐτὴν ψιλήν, ἀλλὰ πλατύνων τὴν ἑρμηνείαν. Priscian translates with *postea sequatur elocutio ipsius usus; non oportet tamen ipsum per se ponere, sed latius interpretari.*

There are four points of difference here:

1) For εἶθ'ἡ χρεία Priscian writes *postea . . . elocutio ipsius usus.*

2) Priscian adds *sequatur.*

3) The phrase εἶπε τόδε is not represented in the Latin.

4) The awkward construction of the Greek καὶ

οὐ θήσεις . . . ἑρμηνείαν, where the reader must understand θήσεις after ἀλλά in order to have a construction for πλατύνων, has been smoothed out by Priscian, whose two infinitives *ponere* and *interpretari* are parallel and depend on *oportet*.

Now, of these four points, the first can be explained. Priscian simply expands the Greek to include what it must mean (cf. comment 12 to Hermogenes). The fourth point, too, probably represents no problem. Priscian has merely interpreted the Greek and expressed it clearly and reasonably smoothly.

But the second and third points are more troublesome. There is nothing in the Greek to explain *sequatur*, nor anything in the Latin to suggest εἶπε τόδε. Walz, *ad loc.*, cites Ward's suggestion of ἑσπέτω for εἶπε τόδε, thus attempting to solve both problems at once. Rabe, however, ignores the suggestion, and he is probably correct.

Nonetheless, *sequatur* is unnecessary and obtrusive. Priscian regularly indicates sequence with such words as *deinde, hinc, posthac, posterea* and, as here, *postea*. But nowhere else in the *Praeexercitamina* does he use any form of *sequor* for this or any other purpose. Yet several passages elsewhere present lists similar to the one here where he could have used some form of this verb. His failure to do so suggests that *sequor* was not part of his technical vocabulary any more than ἕπομαι was a part of Hermogenes'.

Arguments *ex silentio* are dangerous and vain. Still, the fact remains that either *sequatur* reflects something lost from the Greek or Priscian has elected in just this one place to use that verb when he expanded. As for εἶπε τόδε, these words are unnecessary and just a bit obscure. Priscian again may have elected to omit them because he considered them unimportant to the sense.

So one can explain away the individual differences in this passage, but in a final analysis the fact remains that Priscian has altered the Greek in a way that is uncharacteristic of him.

27. The Greek has εἶτα ἡ αἰτία and does not begin to use the phrase with ἐκ until the fourth item (line 48). Priscian begins with the preposition here: *deinde a causa*.

28. On the surface, the Latin is fairly close to the Greek, but on closer inspection the translation gains—of loses— ideas. In both versions there is discussion of the theme πόνος (*labor*) vs. ἡδονή (*iucunditas*, a regular but weak translation), but Priscian's choice of vocabulary, deliberate or not, is

stronger than that which Hermogenes has used. For example, both *vilissimae rerum* and *finem taeterrimum* are more pejorative than their counterparts, τὰ τυχόντα τῶν πραγμάτων and τὸ τέλος ἀηδέστατον (although his adjective gains strength from the play on ἡδονή), and *studiossimae res* is much stronger and more vivid than τὰ σπουδαῖα. Apparently a bit of Roman Stoicism (or at least anti-Epicureanism) has crept into Priscian's version.

29. Priscian makes some changes in the section on analogy and in doing so alters the sense. Where the Greek has the aorist participle active πονήσαντες to express time prior to δεῖ, the Latin has *laborantes* expressing time contemporary with *oportet*. The reason for the change is, of course, obvious: Latin has no past active participle except with deponent verbs. To retain the original sequence Priscian would have needed to use a verbose construction and destroy the succint expression of the chreia.

There is a second point of difference: for the elliptical οὕτω καὶ περὶ λόγους Priscian writes *sic etiam eloquentes*. He may have intended nothing more with the participle than Hermogenes did with his prepositional phrase, but the Latin seems to imply more than the Greek. F. H. Colson (*M. Fabii Quintiliani Institutionis Oratoriae Liber I* [Cambridge: Cambridge University, 1924] xxii) points out that "the idea of *'eloquentia'* always carried with it wealth of thought as well as wealth of words." In addition, *eloquor* here seems to express the idea of action. That is, just as *laborantes* refers to physical laboring, so *eloquentes* indicates the mental activity in *loquentia*, i.e. of a *rhetor*. In an effort to express these ideas in English, the translation appears to expand the Latin. It also differs from the translation of Hermogenes.

30. Priscian's line is technically a dactylic hexameter, but it is an extremely clumsy one. Every foot, except the fifth, is a spondee, and the third has dieresis but no caesura. As a result, the conflict of ictus and accent everywhere except the sixth foot renders the line intolerable. In addition, Priscian has done some violence to Latin grammar. In his attempt to translate Hesiod's line in the same order, word for word (except δέ), he uses *virtutis* as a genitive of separation (cf. above, line 19 and comment 14g) with *longe*. Neither such a genitive nor such a use of *longe* seems to occur elsewhere. In short, his attempt at a literal translation has resulted in bad verse and worse Latin.

31. Priscian omits the final sentence of Hermogenes' section (lines 63-64), and any speculation on his reason for doing so is probably futile. Nonetheless, it is interesting and

perhaps suggestive that Priscian has omitted the only remarks of Hermogenes which are clearly directed to teachers. Cf. comment 15 to Hermogenes.

THE CHREIA DISCUSSION OF

APHTHONIUS OF ANTIOCH

Introduction, Translation and Comments

by

JAMES R. BUTTS
RONALD F. HOCK

INTRODUCTION

I

Life and Writings. Evidence about the life of Aphthonius is scarce. The *Suda* says only that Aphthonius was a σοφιστής and that he composed a *Progymnasmata* for the τέχνη of Hermogenes.[1] The title σοφιστής appears in references to Aphthonius in the writings of such Byzantine scholars as John Doxapatres and John Argyropulus,[2] and it has the nearly unanimous support of the MS tradition of the *Progymnasmata*.[3] Moreover, no one ever questions the claim that Aphthonius composed (or "fathered," as Argyropulus puts it[4]) the *Progymnasmata*.[5]

Still, these two facts, even if uncontested, do not allow us to place Aphthonius in a specific historical context. For that we must turn to Argyropulus, who adds the information that Aphthonius came from Syrian Antioch and that he was a pupil of Libanius and, less clearly, of Phasganius.[6] Argyropulus' testimony is, of course, late, but confirmation of some of it comes from a letter of Libanius to Aphthonius. This letter, written in A.D. 392, expresses Libanius' delight in Aphthonius' "toils" and specifically in his having written "many things," all of which "nobly manifest the seed."[7] The language clearly suggests a teacher-pupil relationship and thus places Aphthonius' student years in Antioch sometime between that time and 354 when Libanius opened his school in Antioch.[8] Unfortunately, Libanius does not say where Aphthonius was living and presumably teaching at the time of the letter.

Attempts to locate Aphthonius more precisely have not been successful. For example, in the nineteenth century several scholars tried to argue that Aphthonius' model ἔκφρασις, which is a vivid description of the Serapeum and Acropolis at Alexandria, shows that he must have lived in this city and indeed that he composed the *Progymnasmata* before 391, the date of the temple's destruction.[9] This argument, however, fails to convince because the features

of the Serapeum were familiar outside of Alexandria and
because the memory of it lived long after its destruction.[10]
Moreover, the vividness of Aphthonius' description is
precisely what this exercise is intended to accomplish. Thus
the vividness says more about Aphthonius' rhetorical skill
than about his place and time. Consequently, we must be
content to place Aphthonius in the late fourth-early fifth
century and locate him in Antioch for at least part of his
life.

Of the "many things" that Aphthonius wrote very little
has survived. Besides the *Progymnasmata*, only a collection
of forty fables is extant,[11] but Photius refers, in passing,
to some μελέται, or practice exercises, of Aphthonius.[12]
Nothing more about them is known, but some scholars plausibly
suggest that they were a collection of model exercises for
the various *progymnasmata*, of which the fable collection is
only a part.[13]

The "Nachleben" of Aphthonius' Progymnasmata. The influence of Aphthonius' little book on European culture — at
first in the Greek East and then in the Latin West — is
all out of proportion to its size. Indeed, it is hard to
overestimate the impact of Aphthonius on European rhetoric
and education, an impact that lasted well into the seventeenth
century.

When Aphthonius wrote his little book, no one could have
predicted its later importance and influence. His book was
just one of many. Aphthonius' predecessors in teaching
youths the essentials of composition still had readers, as
recently published papyrus fragments of Theon's
Progymnasmata attest.[14] In addition, a younger contemporary
of Aphthonius, Sopater, was to write another such
textbook,[15] as would Nicolaus still later. Moreover, Priscian
was to select Hermogenes' *Progymnasmata*, not Aphthonius',
for translation into Latin. Thus, even after a century or so
Aphthonius' textbook had not yet assumed its dominance.

It was not long, however, before Aphthonius' textbook
did become dominant, largely as the consequence of its

inclusion in the *Corpus Hermogenianum* sometime in the first half of the sixth century.[16] Moreover, since the *Corpus Hermogenianum* soon proved victorious over the *Progymnasmata* and advanced rhetorical treatises of Minucianus, the *Progymnasmata* of Aphthonius was assured of preservation.[17] In fact, the *Progymnasmata* appear in the two main classes of Hermogenes mss, introducing Hermogenes' *De statibus, De inventione, De formis orationis*, and *De methodo gravitatis*.[18] Accordingly, the *Suda* is, strictly speaking, wrong in saying that Aphthonius composed his textbook *for* the technical treatises of Hermogenes,[19] although by that time the ms tradition made it appear so.

Later tradition may well be right, however, on another point: the reason for selecting Aphthonius' textbook over the others. Thus Argyropulus says: "Since Hermogenes' *Progymnasmata* seemed unclear and hard to understand (insofar as it contained no model exercises), many other rhetors offered their *Progymnasmata* to replace his, and among that group was the sophist Aphthonius, whose *Progymnasmata* was the preferred one for reading since it was clearer."[20] The greater clarity of Aphthonius derived, as Doxapatres explains, from his use of model exercises for each *progymnasma*.[21] In other words, whatever the actual circumstances of selection, Aphthonius' model exercises probably made his textbook stand out.

At any rate, in its lead-off position in the *Corpus Hermogenianum* the textbook of Aphthonius served as introductory exercises, as *progymnasmata*, for the actual rhetorical instruction in Hermogenes' several treatises. The *Progymnasmata* functioned, as Doxapatres puts it, "to anoint and quicken youths to the study of Hermogenes' writings."[22]

The importance of Aphthonius' *Progymnasmata*, therefore, derives from its (originally unforseen) association with the τέχνη of Hermogenes. Accordingly, as the *Corpus Hermogenianum* emerged as the standard rhetorical curriculum, Aphthonius' *Progymnasmata* achieved virtual canonical status in Byzantine education. This status is apparent in several ways. It is obvious, for example, from the casual way in which, say, Nicephorus Blemmydes' autobiography refers to Aphthonius (and Hermogenes) when speaking of his early education.[23]

More important, George Kustas has demonstated the extent to which the *progymnasmata* predisposed Byzantine writers to make use of literary forms they had learned from Aphthonius. Kustas thus explains their predilection for the description (ἔκφρασις) and the letter, which they had learned in the context of characterization (ἠθοποιία).[24]

Nothing so attests to Aphthonius' status, however, as the emergence of scholarly reflection on the *Progymnasmata* in the form of commentaries, prolegomena, scholia, and epitomes. As early as the sixth century commentaries begin to appear, although the earliest commentary to survive comes only from the middle of the ninth century, namely that of John of Sardis.[25] During the latter part of the tenth century John Geometres wrote a commentary on Aphthonius,[26] but it survives only in the numerous quotations of the most extensive commentary of all, that of Doxapatres.[27]

In addition to these line by line, even phrase by phrase, commentaries, the prolegomena tried to provide more general discussion of Aphthonius' *Progymnasmata*. The prolegomena, which Hugo Rabe has conveniently collected in his *Proglegomenon Sylloge*,[28] typically discuss eight topics: 1) the purpose of Aphthonius' *Progymnasmata*, 2) its usefulness, 3) its authenticity, 4) its place in the sequence of rhetorical textbooks, 5) the reason for its title, 6) the division of *progymnasmata* according to their similarity to one of the types or parts of a speech, 7) its didactic methods, and 8) the reason for preferring the *Progymnasmata* of Aphthonius to all others.[29]

We hardly need to add the numerous scholia on and an epitome of the *Progymnasmata*[30] to appreciate the status of Aphthonius in Byzantine education and literature. Indeed, it is not surprising that one writer even composed an epigram for Aphthonius' little book:

If your heart's set on rhetoric, my friend,
Aphthonius' practices I recommend.[31]

Aphthonius' influence, however, was not restricted to the
Greek East. His *Progymnasmata* reached the Latin West
sometime during the fourteenth or fifteenth century.
Rhetoric was now emerging from the long shadows which the
disciplines of grammar and dialectic had cast over it. For
example, humanist scholars, in their zeal to recover classical
culture, discovered the complete text of Quintilian and even
long forgotten rhetorical texts, such as Cicero's *De oratore*,
Orator, and *Brutus*. They also welcomed the arrival of
traveling Greek scholars like George Trebizond, who
introduced the rhetorical works of Hermogenes into Italy. And
finally they translated Greek rhetorical works into Latin,
including Aphthonius' *Progymnasmata*.[32]

The first Latin translation of Aphthonius was that of
Joannes Maria Catanaeus in 1507.[33] Rudolphus Agricola followed
with another in 1532.[34] These translations were destined to
go through numerous printings—the former eleven, the latter
seven. Other translations continued to appear,[35] but the most
popular by far was Reinhold Lorich's, which between 1542 and
1689 went through seventy-three printings from presses
throughout Europe.[36]

The importance of the Latin Aphthonius in European
education is therfore obvious, as Julius Brzoska long ago
pointed out.[37] No one, however, has yet to study adequately
the importance of Aphthonius in the American colonies. For
example, copies of Lorich's Aphthonius crossed the Atlantic
where Harvard students used them,[38] presumably each Friday
when Henry Dunster, the College's first president, lectured
on rhetoric.[39] In the eighteenth century the classicist James
Logan of Philadelphia had copies of the *Progymnasmata* of
Aphthonius (and Theon) in his library,[40] but by this time the
actual use of Aphthonius in the classroom was in irreversible
decline in America—and in Europe.[41]

And so the eighteenth century marks the end of the
Nachleben of Aphthonius' *Progymnasmata*. By any standard

its influence is remarkable. Within a century or so Aphthonius'
little book had risen above all its competitors, and for a
millenium or so it first dominated Byzantine education and
literature, then spread its influence to Western Europe, and
even found a place, however short-lived, in America.

II

Aphthonius' Discussion of the Chreia. After chapters on the
fable and narrative, Aphthonius turns his attention to the
chreia. This discussion is far shorter than Theon's 404 lines,
and at 79 lines is only slightly longer than Hermogenes' 63
lines. Indeed, Aphthonius' discussion is closer to that of
Hermogenes in more than length. As we shall see, it is also
sometimes similar in content. Nevertheless, it is not necessary
to claim, as Brzoska does, that Aphthonius "doubtlessly had
the *Progymnasmata* of Hermogenes in front of him."[42]

In any case, Aphthonius organizes his discussion, as had
Theon and Hermogenes, around the three general topics of
definition (lines 2-4), classification (5-17), and manipulation
(18-79). He restricts himself, however, only to the essentials,
especially in regard to definition and classification.

For example, Aphthonius' definition of the chreia is the
briefest we have, a mere nine words in Greek: "A chreia is
a concise reminiscence aptly attributed to some character"
(2-3). There follows an etymology of the word "chreia" (not
in Hermogenes), but instead of using an elaborate analogy
to explain the etymology, as Theon (cf. 25-28) had, Aphthonius
says simply: "Since it is useful (χρειώδης), it is called 'chreia'"
(4). And unlike both Theon (cf. 9-24) and Hermogenes (cf. 16-26),
Aphthonius leaves out any discussion of what distinguishes
a chreia from a reminiscence or maxim, at least in this
chapter.[43]

Aphthonius' economy of thought and expression is even
more apparent in his classification of the chreia. Gone are
Theon's complex subdivisions of sayings chreiai (36-95; cf.
Hermogenes 27-29) as well as Theon's alternate formal
classification of ἀποφάσεις (115-89).[44] All that remains is the

simple διαίρεσις (cf. 16) of the chreia into sayings, action, and mixed chreiai (5-6). Aphthonius defines each and provides an example (6-16), but of special interest is his definition of the mixed chreia, since it agrees with Hermogenes' (cf. 11-12) in assigning both the saying and action to the principal character in the chreia (13). In contrast, Theon placed the emphasis on the action and let the verbal part be merely a question put to the principal character.[45]

Aphthonius also follows Hermogenes in the manipulation section of his discussion, in that he includes only the elaboration exercise, or ἐργασία (18-79; cf. Hermogenes 30-63) rather than Theon's series of eight manipulative exercises (190-404). Aphthonius also agrees with Hermogenes in having eight parts to the elaboration, although he differs, at least terminologically, on the last two parts. He prefers calling the seventh part μαρτυρία παλαιῶν to Hermogenes' ἐκ κρίσεως (21; cf. Hermogenes 55) and the eighth ἐπίλογος βραχύς to Hermogenes' παράκλησις (21-22; cf. Hermogenes 60).

In one respect, however, Aphthonius' discussion is an improvement over Hermogenes. Thus, whereas both illustrate the elaboration exercise by means of Chreia 43, only Aphthonius does so completely and independently of his enumeration of the eight parts. Aphthonius' elaboration is fifty three lines long, a detailed and coherent short essay. In contrast, if one were to extract the elaboration from Hermogenes' discussion of the eight parts, it would be only twenty lines long. He only hints at what the encomium might contain (cf. Hermogenes 38-39) and provides no illustration whatever of the paraphrase (cf. 40-41) and exhortation (cf. 60-62); elsewhere his illustration is always briefer than that of Aphthonius. As a result, Aphthonius' complete and independent elaboration of Chreia 43 (cf. Aphthonius 23-79) more clearly demonstrates to teacher and student alike what the elaboration of a chreia ought to look like.

The Text of Aphthonius. We are fortunate that Aphthonius has had Hugo Rabe as his most recent editor, whom Wilhelm Schmid has called *codicorum Graecorum indagator oculatissimus.*[46] Not surprisingly, then, Rabe's edition, published as volume 10 of the Teubner *Rhetores Graeci* series,[47] has been judged by one reviewer as a model of editing.[48] Accordingly, the text used in this volume is Rabe's, although with a few changes, all clearly identified.

A translation of Aphthonius' entire *Progymnasmata* has long been available.[49]

NOTES

1. The *Suda* (1.432 Adler) says: Ἀφθόνιος, σοφιστής, ἔγραψεν εἰς τὴν Ἑρμογένους τέχνην Προγυμνάσματα.
2. For Aphthonius as a σοφιστής, see Doxapatres, *Hom.* (2.128, 17-18; 134, 23; and 137, 31 Walz), and Argyropulus, *Prol. Syll.* 10 (p. 157, 9 Rabe; cf. also *Prol. Syll.* 11 [p. 167, 29]). Note, however, that John of Sardis prefers τεχνικός (see, e.g., *Comm.* [pp. 98, 10 and 255, 24 Rabe]).
3. On the MSS see H. Rabe (ed.), *Aphthonii Progymnasmata* (Rhetores Graeci 10; Leipzig: Teubner, 1926) iii-ix and esp. xxii.
4. On Aphthonius as πατήρ of this *Progymnasmata*, see Argyropulus, *Prol. Syll.* 10 (p. 156, 9 Rabe).
5. Note the unequivocal confidence of an anonymous scholion on Aphthonius: "That the book of *Progymnasmata* is genuinely that of Aphthonius is obvious from the unanimity of those who comment on it. For all accept the *Progymnasmata* as belonging to Aphthonius" (*Prol. Syll.* 11 [p. 167, 16-19 Rabe]). Cf. also Doxapatres, *Hom.* (2.127, 4-7 Walz).
6. See Argyropulus, *Prol. Syll.* 10 (p. 156, 10-11 Rabe): Ἀφθόνιος Ἀντιοχεὺς ὁ Σύρος, ὁ Λιβανίου τοῦ Fasganίου μαθητής. Rabe in his apparatus notes that one MS has καί instead of τοῦ and hence understands Phasganius as a second teacher of Aphthonius.
7. See Libanius, *ep.* 985 (11.189 Foerster). The letter also refers to a close friendship between Aphthonius and Eutropius, an orator and friend of Libanius (cf. J. Brozoska, "Aphthonius (1)," *RE* 1 [1884] 2797-2800, esp. 2797).
8. So Rabe, *Aphthonii Progymnasmata*, xxii-xxiii.
9. For a convenient summary of this discussion, see Rabe, *Aphthonii Progymnasmata*, xxiii. For the description itself, see Aphthonius, *Progymn.* 12 (pp. 38, 3-41, 11 Rabe).
10. On the destruction of the Serapeum and its legacy, see J. Schwartz, "La Fin du Serapeum d' Alexandrie," in *Essays in Honor of C. Bradford Welles* (ed. A. Samuel; American Studies in Papyrology, 1966) 97-111, and A. Rowe and B. Rees, "The Great Serapeum of Alexandria," *BJRL* 39 (1957) 485-520.
11. For the fables of Aphthonius, see A. Hausrath and H. Hunger (eds.), *Corpus fabularum Aesopicarum* (2nd ed.; Leipzig: Teubner, 1959) I.2.133-51.
12. See Photius, *Bibl.* 133 (2.105 Henry).
13. See further Brzoska, "Aphthonios," 2797.
14. See M. Gronewald, "Ein Fragment aus Theon, *Progymnasmata*," *ZPE* 24 (1977) 23-24.
15. See S. Glöckner, "Sopatros (10)," *RE* 3A (1927) 1002-1006. The considerable fragments of this *Progymnasmata* are

collected in Rabe, *Aphthonii Progymnasmata*, 57-69.

16. On the dating of the emergence of the *Corpus Hermogenianum*, see Kustas, *Studies in Byzantine Rhetoric*, 19-20. Cf. also H. Rabe (ed.), *Prolegomenon Sylloge* (Rhetores Graeci 14; Leipzig: Teubner, 1936) xix-xxiii, and Hunger, *Die hochsprachliche profane Literatur*, 1.77.

17. On the victory, see Kustas, *Studies in Byzantine Rhetoric*, 5-26. In contrast, only the title of the *Progymnasmata* of Minucianus has survived; see the *Suda* s.v. Μινουκιανός (3.398 Adler). On the *Suda's* conflation of biographical information about Minucianus the younger with bibliographical information of Minucianus the elder, the writer of the *Progymnasmata*, see W. Stegemann, "Minoukianos (1)," *RE* 15 (1932) 1975-86, esp. 1975.

18. See Kustas, *Studies in Byzantine Rhetoric*, 23.

19. See the *Suda* s.v. Ἀφθόνιος (1.432 Adler): εἰς τὴν Ἑρμογένους τέχνην.

20. Argyropulus, *Prol. Syll.* 10 (p. 157, 6-11 Rabe).

21. See Doxapatres, *Hom.* (2.131, 15-18 Walz).

22. Doxapatres, *Hom.* (2.129, 9-10 Walz).

23. Text available in A. Heisenberg (ed.), *Nicephori Blemmydae curriculum vitae et carmina* (Leipzig: Teubner, 1896) 2.

24. See Kustas, *Studies in Byzantine Rhetoric*, 44-61. For the influence of other *progymnasmata* on literary forms, see G. Kustas, "The Function and Evolution of Byzantine Rhetoric," *Viator* 1 (1970) 55-73, esp. 57-64.

25. On John of Sardis, see Kustas, *Studies in Byzantine Rhetoric*, 23-24. Text available in H. Rabe (ed.), *Ioannis Sardiani Commentarium in Aphthonii Progymnasmata* (Rhetores Graeci 15; Leipzig: Teubner, 1928).

26. Geometres' commentary is referred to by Doxapatres (see *Hom.* [2.104, 16-18 Walz]). Cf. also Kustas, *Studies in Byzantine Rhetoric*, 24-25.

27. On Doxapatres, see Kustas, *Studies in Byzantine Rhetoric*, 25-26. Text in Walz, *Rhetores Graeci*, 2.81-564.

28. See *Prol. Syll.* 8-11 (pp. 73-170 Rabe).

29. See esp. *Prol. Syll.* 8 (pp. 74-79 Rabe), 9 (pp. 127-140), and 11 (pp. 167-170).

30. See, e.g., the scholia on Aphthonius included by Walz, *Rhetores Graeci*, 1.257-62; 2.1-68, 565-684. The epitome, made by Matthew Camariotes in the 15th c., is likewise included by Walz (*Rhetores Graeci*, 1.121-126).

31. Anon., *Prol. Syll.* 11 (p. 167, 21-22 Rabe). The translation is by Edward O'Neil.

32. On the emergence of rhetoric during these centuries, see further Kennedy, *Rhetoric . . . from Ancient to Modern*

Times, 195-219. On the Latin translations of Aphthonius, see D. L. Clark, "The Rise and Fall of *Progymnasmata* in Sixteenth and Seventeenth Century Grammar Schools," *SM* 19 (1952) 259-63, esp. 261-62.

33. Clark, "Rise and Fall," 261. Clark corrects both Brzoska ("Aphthonios," 2800) and Rabe (*Aphthonii Progymnasmata*, ix) who know only the 1513 (or second printing) of Catanaeus' Aphthonius. A copy of the 1507 edition, Clark says, is in the Bodleian Library.

34. See Kennedy, *Rhetoric . . . from Ancient to Modern Times*, 208.

35. See the chart showing the editions and translations in Clark, "Rise and Fall," 262.

36. Clark, "Rise and Fall," 261-62.

37. See Brzoska, "Aphthonios," 2798.

38. See S. E. Morison, *Harvard College in the Seventeenth Century* (Cambridge: Harvard, 1936) 172-85, esp. 177. Cf. also A. O. Norton, "Harvard Textbooks and Reference Books of the Seventeenth Century," *CSM* 28 (1933), 361-438, esp. 385-86.

39. President Dunster refers to the lectures on rhetoric in his "New Englands First Fruits." Text in S. E. Morison, *The Founding of Harvard College* (Cambridge: Harvard, 1935) 432-46, esp. 435-36.

40. See E. Wolf 2nd, *The Library of James Logan of Philadelphia* (Philadelphia: The Library Company of Philadelphia, 1974) 15-16 (Aphthonius) and 484 (Theon).

41. By the early 18th c. at Harvard Aphthonius was yielding to the rhetorical manuals of William Dugard and Thomas Farnaby (so Morison, *Harvard College*, 146 and 177-78). More onimously, Clark ("Rise and Fall," 262-63) emphasiszes that the last printing of Lorich's Aphthonius in 1689 coincides with the emergence of a demand for a more scientific and less rhetorical curriculum.

42. Brzoska, "Aphthonios," 2798. That there are many similarities between Aphthonius and Hermogenes (and even Theon) is clear. See the collection of parallel passages in O. Hopplicher, *De Theone, Hermogene, Aphthonique Progymnasmaticum scriptoribus* (Virceburg: Becker, 1884) 5-14. But that these similarities require the literary dependence of Aphthonius on Hermogenes (or even on Theon) is not so clear. For the similarities, on the one hand, seem more impressive in the isolation of Hopplicher's lists but appear more scattered and haphazard when read in context. Aphthonius hardly seems to have followed Hermogenes. On the other hand, if Aphthonius did use sources (which seems likely), he may just as easily have used sources which are no longer extant.

43. Aphthonius does distinguish the chreia from the maxim, but not until the chapter on the maxim. He says there (cf. *Progymn.* 4 [p. 8, 7-10 Rabe]) that the chreia differs from the maxim in that 1) the chreia occasionally contains an action, whereas the maxim always is a saying, and 2) the chreia requires a character, whereas the maxim is expressed without a character. Note that Aphthonius thus anticipates Nicolaus who also reserves this discussion until the chapter on the maxim. Nicolaus' discussion, however, is long enough that we have appended that discussion to the text of the chreia chapter (cf. Nicolaus 185-214).

44. On Theon's elaborate classification, see pp. 27-34.

45. On Theon's peculiar understanding of the mixed chreia, see pp. 26-27.

46. Cited by G. Ammon in his review of Rabe (*PhW* 49 [1929] 929-36, esp. 929).

47. For bibliographical information, see above n. 3.

48. See Ammon's review (*PhW* 49 [1929] 929).

49. R. Nadeau, "The *Progymnasmata* of Aphthonius in Translation," *SM* 19 (1952) 264-85.

TEXT
AND
TRANSLATION

Χρεία ἐστὶν ἀπομνημόνευμα σύντομον εὐστόχως ἐπί τι πρόσωπον ἀναφέρουσα.

(4,1)　　Χρειώδης δὲ οὖσα προσαγορεύεται χρεία.
Τῆς δὲ χρείας τὸ μέν ἐστι λογικόν, τὸ δὲ　　　　　5
πρακτικόν, τὸ δὲ μικτόν. καὶ λογικὸν μὲν τὸ
τῷ λόγῳ δηλοῦν τὴν ὠφέλειαν· οἷον (Chreia 51)

(4,5)　　"ὁ Πλάτων τοὺς τῆς ἀρετῆς κλῶνας ἱδρῶτι καὶ
πόνοις ἔλεγε φύεσθαι." πρακτικὸν δὲ τὸ πρᾶξιν
σημαῖνον· οἷον (Chreia 54) "Πυθαγόρας ἐρωτηθείς,　　10
ὅσος ἂν εἴη τῶν ἀνθρώπων ὁ βίος, βραχύ τι φανεὶς
ἀπεκρύψατο· μέτρον τοῦ βίου τὴν θέαν ποιούμενος."
μικτὸν δὲ τὸ ἐξ ἀμφοτέρων, λόγου καὶ πράξεως·

(4,10)　　οἷον (cf. Chreia 26) " Διογένης μειράκιον ἑωρακὼς
ἀτακτοῦν τὸν παιδαγωγὸν ἔπαισεν ἐπειπὼν ‘Τί γὰρ　　15
τοιαῦτα παιδεύεις;’" ἡ μὲν οὖν διαίρεσις αὕτη
τῆς χρείας.

’Εργάσαιο δὲ αὐτὴν τοῖσδε τοῖς κεφαλαίοις·
(1) ἐγκωμιαστικῷ, (2) παραφραστικῷ, (3) τῷ τῆς
αἰτίας, (4) ἐκ τοῦ ἐναντίου, (5) παραβολῇ, (6)　　　　20

(4,15)　　παραδείγματι, (7) μαρτυρίᾳ παλαιῶν, (8) ἐπιλόγῳ
βραχεῖ.

Χρεία λογική
(Chreia 43)

’Ισοκράτης τῆς παιδείας τὴν μὲν ῥίζαν ἔφη
πικράν, γλυκεῖς δὲ τοὺς καρπούς.　　　　　　　　25

(1) Θαυμάσαι δίκαιον ’Ισοκράτην τῆς τέχνης,
ὃς ὄνομα αὐτῇ κατεφάνη λαμπρότατον, καὶ ὅση τις

(4,20)　　ἦν ἀσκῶν ἐπεδείξατο. καὶ κηρύττει τὴν τέχνην·
οὐκ αὐτὸς ἐκ ταύτης κεκήρυκται. ὅσα μὲν τοίνυν
ἢ βασιλεῦσι νομοθετῶν ἢ παραινῶν τοῖς καθ’　　　　30
ἕκαστον τὸν τῶν ἀνθρώπων εὖ πεποίηκε βίον,
μακρὸν ἂν εἴη διεξελθεῖν, ἀλλ’ οἷα περὶ τῆς
παιδείας ἐφιλοσόφησεν.

On the Chreia

A chreia is a concise reminiscence aptly attributed to some character.[1]

Since it is useful, it is called "chreia."

Of the chreia there is the sayings-class,[2] the action-class and the mixed class. The sayings-class is the one which demonstrates its utility[3] by a saying. For example (Chreia 51) *Plato used to say that the off-shoots of virtue grow by sweat and toil.* The action-class is the one which depicts an action. For example (Chreia 54) *Pythagoras, on being asked how long human life can be, was visible for a short time and disappeared, making his visibility the measure of life.* The mixed class is the one which is composed of both, a saying and an action. For example (cf. Chreia 26) *Diogenes, having seen a youth misbehaving, struck the paedagogus, adding, "Why are you teaching such things?"* This, then, is the classification of the chreia.

You can elaborate the chreia under the following headings: (1) Encomiastic, (2) Paraphrastic, (3) Of the Rationale, (4) From the opposite, (5) Analogy, (6) Example, (7) Testimony of the Ancients, (8) Short Epilogue.

A Sayings-Chreia
(Chreia 43)

Isocrates said that education's root
is bitter, its fruits sweet.

(1) It is right to admire Isocrates for his art, for he gave it distinction by his illustrious name and by his practice showed how important it was.[4] And so he is a herald for this art; he himself has not been heralded by it. How often, moreover, either as lawgiver to kings or adviser to individuals he has benefitted the life of mankind would be a long story to set forth in detail.[5] But what a philosophy of education he had!

(5,5)   (2) Ὁ παιδείας, φησίν, ἐρῶν πόνων μὲν
ἄρχεται, πόνων δὲ ὅμως τελευτώντων εἰς ὄνησιν.   35
καὶ ἃ μὲν ἐφιλοσόφησε ταῦτα τοῖς δὲ ἐφεξῆς
θαυμασόμεθα.
            (3) Οἱ γὰρ παιδείας ἐρῶντες τοῖς τῆς
παιδείας ἡγεμόσι συνεξετάζονται, παρ'οἷς καὶ
(5,10)   τὸ προσελθεῖν φοβερὸν καὶ τὸ διαλιπεῖν ἀμαθ-   40
έστατον. φόβος ἀεὶ τοῖς παισὶ περιγίνεται
καὶ παροῦσι καὶ μέλλοσσι. διδασκάλους παιδα-
γωγοὶ διαδέχονται φοβεροὶ μὲν ἰδεῖν, αἰκιζόμενοι
δὲ φοβερώτεροι. φθάνει τὴν πεῖραν τὸ δέος καὶ
διαδέχεται τὸ δέος ἡ κόλασις· καὶ τὰ μὲν   45
(5,15)   ἁμαρτήματα τῶν παίδων μετέρχονται, οἰκεῖα δὲ
τὰ κατορθώματα κρίνουσι. τῶν παιδαγωγῶν οἱ
πατέρες εἰσι χαλεπώτεροι, τὰς ὁδοὺς ἀνακρίνοντες,
προελθεῖν ἐπιτάττοντες, καὶ τὴν ἀγορὰν ὑπο-
πτεύοντες. κἂν δέῃ κολάζειν, ἀγνοοῦσι τὴν   50
φύσιν. ἀλλ'ἐν τούτοις ὢν ὁ παῖς εἰς ἄνδρας
(5,20)   ἐλθὼν ἀρετῇ περιστέφεται.
            (4) Εἰ δέ τις ταῦτα φοβούμενος φύγῃ μὲν
τοὺς διδασκάλους, ἀποδράσει δὲ τοὺς πατέρας,
τοὺς δὲ παιδαγωγοὺς ἀποστροφῇ, παντελῶς τῶν   55
λόγων ἐστέρηται καὶ μετὰ τοῦ δέος τοὺς λόγους
(6,1)   ἀφῄρηται. ταῦτα δὴ πάντα τὴν Ἰσοκράτους ἔπεισε
γνώμην πικρὰν ὀνομάσαι τῆς παιδείας τὴν ῥίζαν.
            (5) Ὥσπερ γὰρ οἱ γῆν ἐργαζόμενοι πόνῳ μὲν
τῇ γῇ τὰ σπέρματα καταβάλλουσι, τοὺς δὲ καρ-   60
(6,5)   ποὺς ἡδονῇ μείζονι συγκομίζονται, τὸν αὐτὸν
τρόπον οἱ παιδείας ἀντιποιούμενοι πόνῳ τὴν εἰς
ἔπειτα δόξαν εἰλήφασι.

---

53 φύγῃ (φύγηι) PAc et m.2 supr. Vc; φύγοι (m. post.) Vc, unde
Walz et Spengel; φεύγει Vind., unde Rabe. 54 ἀποδράσει PV, unde
Rabe] ἀποδράσειε (ε add. m. post.) PcBa, unde Walz et Spengel. 55.
ἀποστροφῇ temptavimus] ἀποστραφείη codd. om. (η add. m. post. Ba),
unde edd. om.

(2) The lover of education,[6] he says, begins with toil
but toil which nevertheless ends in profit. And so this
was his philosophy; and in the words that follow we will
express our admiration of it.

(3) For lovers of education are reckoned among the
leaders of education, at whose school it is both fearsome
to appear, and from which it is very foolish to stay
away. Fear is always beneficial to boys, both present
and future.[7] Teachers are succeeded by paedagogi who
are fearful to behold and more fearful when they are
inflicting punishment.[8] Apprehension precedes the
endeavour[9] and chastisement succeeds the apprehension.
And so they assail the mistakes of the boys but
consider their work done correctly as only proper.
Harsher than the paedagogi are the fathers as they
closely examine the paths they are following, insist that
they make progress and regard the market-place with
suspicion.[10] And if there is need to chastise, they are
ignorant of human nature.[11] Still, by being in such
circumstances, the boy, on reaching manhood, is still
crowned with virtue.

(4) If, however, anyone in fear of all this avoids his
teachers, avoids his parents by running away, avoids
his paedagogi because of his aversion to them, he comes
to be completely without their guidance and in ridding
himself of his apprehension also rids himself of their
guidance.[12] All these things, then, influenced Isocrates'
decision to call education's root bitter.

(5) For just as those who till the land sow the seeds
in the land with toil and then gather the fruits with
greater pleasure, in the same way those who pursue
education with toil attain the subsequent reputation.

(6,10)

(6) Τὸν Δημοσθένους ὅρα μοι βίον, παντὸς
μὲν ὄντα φιλοπονώτερον ῥήτορος, γεγονότα δὲ   65
παντὸς εὐκλεέστερον. καὶ γὰρ τοσοῦτον αὐτῷ
σπουδῆς περιῆν, ὡς καὶ τὸν κόσμον παραιρεῖσθαι
τῆς κεφαλῆς, κόσμον ἄριστον τὸν ἐξ ἀρετῆς
ἡγησάμενον· καὶ πόνοις ἀνάλωσεν, ἃ πρὸς ἡδονὰς
ἀναλίσκουσιν ἕτεροι.   70

(6,15)

(7) Διὸ θαυμάσαι τὸν Ἡσίοδον δεῖ τραχεῖαν
εἰπόντα τῆς ἀρετῆς τὴν ὁδόν, τὴν δὲ ἄκραν ῥᾳδίαν,
τὴν αὐτὴν Ἰσοκράτει γνώμην φιλοσοφήσαντα. ὃ
γὰρ Ἡσίοδος ὁδὸν ἀπεφήνατο, Ἰσοκράτης ῥίζαν
ἐκάλεσαν· ἐν διαφόροις ὀνόμασι μίαν ἀμφότεροι   75
δηλοῦντες διάνοιαν.

(8) Πρὸς ἃ δεῖ βλέποντας Ἰσοκράτην θαυμάζειν κάλλιστα περὶ τῆς παιδείας φιλοσοφήσαντα.

(6) Consider, if you will, the life of Demosthenes which was more industrious than any orator's and has become more acclaimed than any. Indeed, his life so excelled in zeal that he even removed the adornment from his head,[13] regarding the best adornment to be what comes from virtue. And so he spent on toil what others spend on pleasures.

(7) Therefore, one must admire Hesiod for saying that virtue's road is rough but its summit smooth,[14] since he taught the same sentiment as Isocrates. For what Hesiod termed a "road," Isocrates called a "root," both pointing to a single thought with different words.

(8) When these points are considered, we must admire[15] Isocrates, whose philosophy of education is best.

COMMENTS

1. Aphthonius' definition of the chreia is so brief that a principal feature of the chreia, i.e., the saying or action (λόγος ἢ πρᾶξις) feature that is elsewhere so central, seems to have been left out. But not really, for Aphthonius' choice of "reminiscence" (ἀπομνημόνευμα) makes up for the seeming deficiency. Theon, we recall, defined this related form as an action or saying (πρᾶξις ἢ λόγος) that is useful for living (cf. Theon 7-8).

2. Aphthonius is again brief, though not to the point of obscurity, for the neuter article (τό) clearly presupposes the noun γένος ("class"). Hence our translation.

3. Perhaps ὠφέλεια might even be translated by "point." Note also the use of δηλοῦν here, on which see the full discussion in Comment 2 on the translation of Hermogenes.

4. For similar assessments of Isocrates' talent and importance, see, e.g., Cicero, *De Orat.* 2.22.94, and esp. Hermogenes, Περὶ ἰδεῶν (pp. 397, 14-398, 14 Rabe). For modern discussion, see H. I. Marrou, *A History of Education in Antiquity* (New York: Sheed & Ward, 1956) 79-91.

5. This statement, as John of Sardis (*Comm. in Aphthon.* [p. 52, 2-3 Rabe]) recognized, is an example of the rhetorical figure known as *paraleipsis*, or pretending to "pass over" something and still call attention to it (cf. *Rhet. ad Alex.* 1438b 6-7). Its use is especially appropriate here since it allows Aphthonius in effect to say more than he actually does and thus to fulfill the requirement that an introduction be brief.

6. The use of erotic language, i.e., οἱ παιδείας ἐρῶντες, in an educational context should not go unnoticed, as it is especially characteristic of education in antiquity. Cf. Marrou, *History of Education*, 26-35, esp. 31-32: "Throughout Greek history the relationship between master and pupil was to remain that between a lover and his beloved: education remained in principle not so much a form of teaching, an instruction in techniques, as an expenditure of loving effort by an elder concerned to promote the growth of a younger man who was burning with desire to respond to this love and show himself worthy of it."

7. In what follows we have a vivid, if somewhat onesided, picture of a boy's school day. This picture focuses on the fear—the fear of failure, the fear of punishment—that was an ever present reality as the boy went first to the teacher, then home for study with the paidagogus, and then was examined by his father. This frightening picture can be easily confirmed. Thus for the sequence teachers, paedagogi, and

parents, see, e.g., Quintilian, *Inst.* 1.1.25; for the fear that attended learning, see, e.g., Plutarch, *De recta rat. aud.* 47B; Dio, *Orat.* 72.10; and esp. the school day of Kottalos as seen in Herodas' third mime. See also Comments 8, 9, and 11 below.

Still, given the function of this picture in Aphthonius' ἐργασία, namely, to provide the rationale (αἰτία) of the saying of Isocrates about education being a largely toilsome and painful experience, we must recognize that this picture is also one-sided. Thus for balance, see, e.g., Diogenes Laertius, 6.30–31, and Bonner, *Education in Ancient Rome*, 38–46. For another picture of a school day, which stresses different details, see ps.-Lucian, *Am.* 44–45.

8. For examples of punishing paedagogi (and teachers), see Herodas, 3.58–93; Lucian, *Somn.* 2; Alciphron, *ep.* 3.7.3–5; and, more generally, Plutarch, *De recta rat. aud.* 37D. Again, though, for balance, see the recommendations for leniency of Quintilian (*Inst.* 1.3.6–7 and 2.2.5–7).

9. The endeavor (ἡ πειρᾷ) is presumably the attempt to do the assigned homework. For the paedagogus and homework, see Bonner, *Education in Ancient Rome*, 39.

10. On the responsibility of fathers in their boys' education, see the advice in ps.-Plutarch, *De lib. educ.* 9D, advice that some at least took seriously, such as Aulus Gellius (see *N. A. praef.* 23). On parents' strictness, see Dio, *Orat.* 15.19–19. Note also the testing of Kottalos by his father (so Herodas, 3.22–26 and 30–36).

11. For an example of parents ignoring human nature, see esp. Herodas, 3.56–81. For a plea for leniency, see ps.-Plutarch, *De lib. educ.* 13D.

12. The general meaning of this sentence is fairly obvious. The trouble lies in determining what words Aphthonius used to express the thought. As the apparatus indicates, some copyists had difficulty understanding the construction of the Greek and, in an attempt to make sense of the passage, changed some of the forms. The changes seem deliberate, not the result of an inability to decipher the handwriting.

Three words in particular seem to have troubled the copyists (and some editors). First is the verb introduced by εἰ δέ τις: most mss have φύγῃ, but some copyists were seemingly unaware of the fact that εἰ could be used with the subjunctive and changed it to either the indicative or the optative. Yet the construction with the subjunctive occurs in classical Greek and is not at all uncommon in later times. See, e.g., Rev. 11.5b and cf. BAGD s.v. εἰ I 2, and many authors and passages could be added to their list. Further, φύγῃ seems to fit better with the two indicatives in lines 56–57.

The second troublesome word is ἀποδράσει. Some copyists, apparently thinking that this form was a verb in the future indicative (which is impossible), tried to make some sort of parallel construction with φύγῃ (or φεύγει). They thus converted the noun into a verb and destroyed Aphthonius' own parallelism.

The third problem concerns ἀποστροφείη which, in one way or another, all the MSS have. Yet the optative is surely out of place unless, with Walz and Spengel, we also change φύγῃ (or φεύγει) and ἀποδράσει to the protasis of a condition whose apodosis has the indicative (cf. lines 56-57) is extremely awkward. In fact, any verb at this point upsets the structure of the sentence. The most logical word is a noun in the dative case in parallel with ἀποδράσει.

If, therefore, we read φύγῃ . . . ἀποδράσει . . . ἀποστροφῇ, the pattern becomes clear. First the protasis:

εἰ δέ τις ταῦτα φοβούμενος φύγῃ μὲν
    a) τοὺς διδασκάλους
    b) ἀποδράσει δὲ τοὺς πατέρας
    c) τοὺς δὲ παιδαγωγοὺς ἀποστροφῇ

The noun in each subordinate phrase (a-c) is the direct object of φύγῃ (the key to the whole sentence). The use of μέν . . . δέ serves to point up the parallelism of the three nouns. In b) ἀποδράσει is added because obviously a son can avoid his parents only by running away from home (cf. Herodas, 3.36-39). In c) ἀποστροφῇ, although parallel to ἀποδράσει in the Greek, cannot be rendered the same way in English. It indicates the boy's reason for avoiding the paedagogi: his aversion to them. The use of ἀποστροφή may also be part of the erotic vocabulary associated with the language of education (see Comment 6 above), for Plotinus (*Enn.* 1.1.1), in a series of contrasting pairs, balances ἀποστροφή with ἐπιθυμία.

Finally, consider the apodosis of this condition. It contains two verbs in the perfect (=present) indicative to indicate a present general condition as vividly and distinctly as possible. Thus Aphthonius says that if the boy runs away, he is completely deprived of the teachings and advice of those whom he avoids. Everything seems to fit together rather effectively and in the manner of Aphthonius, who was a more careful writer than many of his fellow rhetoricians.

13. Aphthonius refers to Demosthenes' practice of withdrawing to an underground chamber in order to prepare his speech. During this time he would shave half his head so as to be too ashamed to leave. See Plutarch, *Demosth.* 849B-C. Cf. also Quintilian, *Inst.* 10.3.25, and ps.-Plutarch, *Vit. dec. orat.* 844D.

14. Aphthonius is alluding to Hesiod, *Op.* 287-91. Note that Hermogenes (see line 57) also refers to Hesiod in his much briefer elaboration of this chreia, although he explicitly quotes line 289.

15. Aphthonius' use of θαυμάζειν (to admire) is apt, since he thereby recalls the opening lines of the elaboration (so line 26; cf. also 37).

THE CHREIA DISCUSSION OF

NICOLAUS OF MYRA

Introduction, Translation and Comments

by

LESTER L. GRABBE
RONALD F. HOCK

INTRODUCTION

I

Life and Writings. The *Suda* distinguishes two rhetoricians with the name Nicolaus,[1] but scholars have long suspected that they are one and the same person. They not only share the same name and profession but both also lived at the same time, studied at Athens, and composed various rhetorical writings.[2] Joseph Felten explains the confusion by arguing that the *Suda* keeps separate two sources about Nicolaus, one philosophical and one lexical.[3]

Accordingly, if we assume that only one Nicolaus is involved and combine the two *Suda* articles into one, we can say the following about Nicolaus: He was born in Myra in Lycia, probably about A.D. 430, as Kurt Orinsky estimates,[4] rather than about 410, as Felten claims.[5] As a youth he went to Athens, where he studied under the rhetor Lachares,[6] and later taught rhetoric in Constantinople. He died during the period of Anastasius (491–518), having achieved a considerable reputation as a rhetorician.[7]

Nicolaus is thus the latest of the rhetoricians whose *Progymnasmata* are extant, and his very lateness has led Felten to ask whether this handbook was not also written by a Christian. But apart from circumstantial evidence, such as the fact that a bishop of Myra at this time was named Nicolaus and so might suggest that the parents of our Nicolaus were Christian,[8] there is, as Willy Stegemann rightly notes, nothing in the *Progymnasmata* of Nicolaus that betrays any Christian influence.[9] Thus, the question, however the evidence is interpreted, has no bearing on our concerns.

The *Suda* articles attribute several writings to Nicolaus. Besides the *Progymnasmata*, the lists contain an advanced rhetorical treatise (τέχνη ῥητορική), rhetorical declamations (μελέται ῥητορικαί), and "some other writings" (ἄλλα τινά),[10] a phrase which, if vague, at least suggests a considerable literary activity on the part of Nicolaus.

The τέχνη is no longer extant, although there is a

reference to it in the *Progymnasmata*.[11] The μελέται have likewise not survived. To be sure, some scholars, such as Felten,[12] have assumed the identity of the μελέται with the model exercises (προγυμνάσματα) which are preserved in several MSS and edited by Christian Walz under the name of Nicolaus,[13] but there are weighty objections against this identification. On the one hand, the term μελέται more likely refers to actual rhetorical declamations than to pre-rhetorical exercies, that is, to γυμνάσματα rather than to προγυμνάσματα.[14]

On the other hand, even if this term is not always used so precisely,[15] it is extremely doubtful that these model exercises are correctly attributed to Nicolaus. As Stegemann demonstrates, the MS tradition raises considerable doubt, for only two (of four) MSS ascribe the exercises to Nicolaus and many of these exercises are also handed down in other MSS under the name of Libanius.[16] Stegemann also shows that these exercises, when analyzed for their style, content, and underlying rhetorical theory, are closer to Aphthonius than to Nicolaus.[17] Indeed, the similarities are so close and numerous that Stegemann is led to propose Aphthonius as the author of these model exercises.[18]

Whether Stegemann is right about Aphthonian authorship is a question that must await the treatment of the four model chreia exercises, or elaborations, in volume II. Still, at present it is safe to say that at least Nicolaus did not compse these model exercies, and hence we are left with only the *Progymnasmata* from the many writings of Nicolaus.

The Discovery of the Progymnasmata of Nicolaus. Even the *Progymnasmata* was merely a title in the list of Nicolaus' writings provided by the *Suda* until the mid-nineteenth century when Eberhard Finckh realized that the *Progymnasmata* lay hidden in the anonymous Aphthonius scholia edited by Walz in the second volume of his *Rhetores Graeci*.[19] Finckh's discovery came from a careful and perceptive reading of Doxapatres' *Homiliae* on Aphthonius. He noticed that Doxapatres cited as his sources Nicolaus and an unnamed commentator on Aphthonius when discussing differences between διήγημα and διήγησις.[20] He also noted that this very discussion appears in the Aphthonius scholia.[21] Finckh further identified several passages in Doxapatres which cite Nicolaus as their source and which also appear in the scholia.[22] He concluded that the Aphthonius scholia were Doxapatres' unnamed source and that the scholiast himself had made tacit use of Nicolaus' *Progymnasmata*.[23] Finckh then tried to reconstruct Nicolaus' *Progymnasmata* from the scholia, the results of which are now in Leonard Spengel's third volume of the *Rhetores Graeci*.[24]

That Finckh was largely correct in his reconstruction was proved in 1895 when Heinrich Graeven discovered a MS in the British Museum that contained the *Progymnasmata* of Nicolaus, or at least a large part of it.[25] This fifteenth century MS, numbered 11889 and given the siglum O, prints the *Progymnasmata* along with that of Aphthonius, with the latter in larger script and the former fitted alongside and under the Aphthonius text.[26] Graeven is no doubt right in explaining this format as suggesting that Nicolaus' *Progymnasmata* had little independent value and thus served merely as a commentary on Aphthonius.[27] At any rate, in 1913 Joseph Felten based his Teubner edition of Nicolaus on this MS,[28] although from p. 58, 18 on, where O ends, he had to use the Aphthonius scholia as had Finckh.[29] Thus, while much progress has been made recovering the *Progymnasmata* of Nicolaus, it is still not completely recovered. Nicolaus' chapter on the chreia, however, is preserved in O.

II

Nicolaus' Discussion of the Chreia. Nicolaus, like the others, includes the now familiar topics of defining, classifying, and manipulating the chreia. But while Nicolaus thus has much that is familiar, he is not for that reason undeserving of a careful reading. For, on the one hand, even the familiar topics contain new or differently nuanced positions regarding the chreia. And, on the other hand, the sizeable parts of the chapter that remain introduce subjects not otherwise encountered

in the extant *Progymnasmata*. This mixture of the familiar
and the new — which, incidentally, demonstrates the continuity
and the richness of the rhetorical tradition regarding the
chreia — will become apparent as we survey the contents
of Nicolaus' discussion of the chreia.

Nicolaus has divided his treatment of the chreia into five
parts: 1) the proper place of the chreia in the sequence
of *progymnasmata* (lines 2-44); 2) the definition of the chreia
and related matters, such as etymology (45-64); 3) the
different ways of classifying chreiai (65-137); 4) the usefulness
of the chreia for rhetorical training (138-61); and 5) the
manipulation of the chreia by means of elaboration (162-81).
A few lines close out the chapter (182-84). In addition, in the
second part (cf. 57-58), Nicolaus promises a discussion of how
the chreia differs from the maxim and reminiscence, but he
does not fulfill that promise until he reaches the chapter
on the maxim. For that reason we have included this part
of the latter chapter here (185-214).

The various parts of Nicolaus' chapter on the chreia
conform to his usual treatment of all the *progymnasmata*,
with only comments on the style appropriate to the chreia
being left out.[30] This overall conception of Nicolaus' task for
his *Progymnasmata* thus explains why he shares only the
second, third, and fifth parts with his predecessors.

The first of Nicolaus' five parts treats the placement
(τάξις) of the chreia chapter in the overall sequence of the
progymnasmata (2-44). Theon[31] and Hermogenes[32] had shown
some interest in this subject, but only Nicolaus does so in
the chreia chapter itself and only he does so at such length.
Herein lies his distinctiveness and importance.

Nicolaus identifies two groups (cf. 3: τινες, and 12: ἕτεροι)
whose *Progymnasmata* have the chreia chapter *before* those
on the fable and narrative. One group put the chreia first
because of its moral content (cf. 3-8). The other group,
however, argued pedagogically, saying that the inflection of
the chreia through its cases and numbers was an especially
appropriate exercise for youths who had just left literary

studies and were now beginning the study of rhetoric (cf. 13-18).

Nicolaus does not so much refute these arguments as consider them irrelevant, given the status in his day of the elaboration (his word is διαίρεσις, not ἐργασία) as *the* exercise involving the chreia. Consequently, Nicolaus argues that the very difficulty of the elaboration exercise makes first position untenable; rather, the "best position" (ἀρίστη τάξις) for the chreia is third, that is, *after the fable and narrative* (*cf. 2-3, 8-11, and 39-44*).

Felten and Stegemann regard Nicolaus' remarks on τάξις as directed especially against Theon, whose original sequence had the chreia in first position.[33] They do not, however, assign Theon to either of Nicolaus' groups, though Stegemann seems to suggest the second group, since he is particulary impressed by Nicolaus' use of Chreia 49 to illustrate inflection (cf. 20-35), the same chreia Theon had used in this manipulation.[34] Still, it should be pointed out that Theon also appreciated the moral value of chreia[35] and so might belong to the first group as well.

And yet, Nicolaus hardly seems to have Theon in mind at all. His quotation of the moral argument does not come from Theon but from some other *Progymnasmata* (cf. 7-8). Moreover, Theon's discussion of inflection cites more chreiai than simply Chreia 49 and does not include the nominative case.[36] Finally, whereas Theon makes inflection the second of eight manipulations of the chreia,[37] Nicolaus is thinking of one or several *Progymnasmata* whose writers consider inflection as alone sufficient for new students of rhetoric (cf. 13-18). In short, Nicolaus' remarks on τάξις seem directed against *Progymnasmata* which are no longer extant.

The second of Nicolaus' five parts to his chreia discussion provides his definition of the chreia as well as its differentiation from the maxim and the reminiscence and its etymology (45-64 & 185-214). Generally speaking, Nicolaus is close to what the others say on these matters, although he is more complete than any one of them. Thus, Nicolaus'

difinition of the chreia (cf. 45-48) adds nothing new, except
that he alone has provided it with a phrase by phrase
commentary (cf. 48-58). The various differences between the
maxim, on the one hand, and the reminiscence, on the other
(cf. 52, 53, 57-58, and esp. 185-214), are similar to what we
find in Theon.[38] And Nicolaus' etymology largely follows Theon
(cf. 59-62),[39] although Nicolaus has added a second etymology
to the one he shares with Theon (cf. 63-64). In sum, Nicolaus'
treatment of definition and related matters is a similar, if
expanded, version of what we are used to from Theon and
the others.

In the third part Nicolaus treats the familiar subject of
the chreia's classification (65-137). Indeed, he begins with the
familiar three-fold classification into sayings, action, and
mixed chreiai, complete with familiar examples (cf. 65-79). But
there the familiarity ends. For Nicolaus is neither satisfied
with this principal classification, as Hermogenes and
Aphthonius were,[40] nor does he go on to sub-divide the chreia
into ever more subtle classifications, as Theon did.[41] Rather,
Nicolaus provides three new classifications, or "differentiations" (διαφοραί), as he terms them. Presumably, he
took them from other *Progymnasmata*. At any rate, he says
that some people (cf. 80: φασι) differentiate between chreiai
that are useful and those that are merely witty (cf. 80-115),
between chreiai that are descriptive and those that are
prescriptive (cf. 116-30), and between chreiai that are simple
in formulation and those that are more complex (cf. 131-37).[42]

Nicolaus considers the first differentiation to be vacuous,
for even witty chreiai — he cites Chreiai 48 and 16, doubtlessly
those from his source — appear useful to him in that they
contain good moral advice (cf. 97-99). With the second
differentiation, however, Nicolaus agrees and even considers
it helpful, since knowing whether a chreia is descriptive or
prescriptive determines whether the elaboration of it is to
include an argument from truth or from probability (cf. 125-30
and 169). Finally, Nicolaus makes no judgment on the
differentiation between simple and complex chreiai.

Stegemann once again sees Nicolaus being dependent on Theon, at least for the first and third differentiations, and on Hermogenes for the third.[43] To be sure, there are some similarities in terminology and in examples between Theon and Nicolaus. Nevertheless, it is difficult to see why Nicolaus, if he were dependent on Theon, should have selected only the "witty" chreia among the twelve ways that Theon has classified the saying. With respect to the third differentiation not even the terminology — ἁπλαῖ and πρός τι — is close enough to suggest anything but the vaguest connection. In other words, not only in the second differentiation, but also in the first and third, Nicolaus is probably once again drawing directly on discussions in *Progymnasmata* which are no longer extant.

In the fourth part of Nicolaus' discussion of the chreia (138-61) we find something that may well be original with him. At least, there is no trace in Theon and the others of how the chreia or, more precisely, the elaboration of the chreia is useful in learning rhetoric. Nor in this instance does Nicolaus refer to others as speaking of the rhetorical utility of the *progymnasmata* in this fashion.

At any rate, Nicolaus distinguishes between *progymnasmata* whose very form can be considered a complete speech or merely a part of a speech (138-41).[44] To the former he assigns, for example, the encomium and the comparison,[45] whereas the narrative[46] and chreia (cf. 139-41) are deemed only partial speeches.

In the remainder of this section Nicolaus straightforwardly points out how the chreia and its elaboration teach the skills necessary for rhetoric, whether one is thinking of the three kinds of public speech or the five parts of a speech (142-61). Thus the chreia can be viewed as advisory, "for surely it urges us to something good or restrains us from something evil" (146-47) — precisely the function of the advisory speech.[47] In addition, the elaboration of the chreia has something of the encomium and the judicial speech in it (cf. 147-51). Furthermore, the elaboration prepares the student to write each part of the speech. For example, the first part of the elaboration, the praise of the speaker or actor in the chreia, approximates writing an introduction, the first part of a speech (cf. 152–61). In this way Nicolaus makes explicit the rhetorical utility of the chreia and its elaboration.

The fifth, and last, section of Nicolaus' discussion of the chreia is the elaboration (162–81), a section he shares with Hermogenes and Aphthonius. What is of interest here is Nicolaus' terminology. First of all, he prefers the term διαίρεσις (162: διήρηται; cf. 10 and 14: διαίρεσις) to the more usual ἐργασία.[48] Moreover, his terms for the various parts of the elaboration reveal differences with Aphthonius' terminology (cf. 166–72). Thus Nicolaus prefers the term ἔπαινος ("praise") to Aphthonius' corresponding heading, the ἐγκωμιαστικόν ("encomiastic"). The latter term, Nicolaus says, conjures up the many topoi of the ἐγκώμιον proper and so would lead to an introduction in an elaboration that is longer than the rest of the speech (cf. 162–66).

Further terminological differences occur in the argumentative headings of the elaboration. Aphthonius had used five such headings: the rationale, its opposite, an analogy, an example, and a testimony from ancient writers.[49] Nicolaus, however, names only three: an argument from probability (if the chreia is prescriptive) or from truth (if it is descriptive), an example, and an opinion from others (cf. 169–72).

In other words, the only heading Nicolaus shares with Aphthonius is the example (παράδειγμα). Elsewhere, however, the terminological differences have little significance, as when Nicolaus says "the opinion of others" (ἡ ἀφ' ἑτέρων κρίσις) and Aphthonius "the testimony of ancient writers" (μαρτυρία παλαιῶν). Moreover, Nicolaus admits that the "analogy" (παραβολή), while not explicitly included, could still be used as part of an argument from probability (cf. 174–80). But if Nicolaus' argumentative headings are finally not as different from Aphthonius' as at first glance, still it is clear that

Nicolaus' different terminology betrays some differences in substance as well. These differences would be clearer, however, if Nicolaus had provided a model elaboration to exemplify his formal discussion.

The last heading in Nicolaus' elaboration is also different, but the difference is merely terminological. He prefers "exhortation" (παράκλησις) (172) to Aphthonius' "epilogue" (ἐπίλογος). Interestingly, Nicolaus regards this heading as not essential (cf. 171; ἂν δέη). Still, Nicolaus, like Aphthonius, says that this heading is to be brief (cf. 171).

To sum up: it should now be apparent that Nicolaus' discussion of the chreia, while sharing much with Theon, Hermogenes, and Aphthonius, nevertheless contains more that is different. At times these differences are the result of Nicolaus taking up discussions from *Progymnasmata* which are no longer extant. Here belong Nicolaus' treatments of the sequence of the chreia, the alternative differentiations of the chreia, and perhaps the differences in terminology for the elaboration headings. At other times, however, the differences may be due to Nicolaus' own contributions, such as the demonstration of the rhetorical utility of the chreia and its elaboration. Consequently, Nicolaus' chapter on the chreia not only attests to the continuity of the educational theory regarding the chreia, but also gives ample proof of the diversity and even development of that theory.

The Text of Nicolaus. For the reasons given above in regard to the discovery of the *Progymnasmata* of Nicolaus in a MS of the British Museum,[50] the text of Nicolaus used here is that of Joseph Felten which was published in 1913 as volume 11 in the Teubner *Rhetores Graeci* series.[51]

And yet, while Felten's text is clearly the best text available, it must also be said the text is far from certain in many places (so, for example, 104-08 and especially 182-87). Even where individual sentences or whole sections appear to be sound, the lack of any logical connection or progression raises doubts (see, for example, 116-37). Finally, some sections are still very reminiscent of the scholia and commentaries from which our knowledge of Nicolaus comes (see, for example, 45-57). Consequently, we must be grateful for Felten's pioneering work on the text of Nicolaus, even if we cannot be completely satisfied with it.

No translation of Nicolaus is available.

NOTES

1. See the *Suda* (3.469 Adler): 1) Νικόλαος, ῥήτωρ, γνώριμος Πλουτάρχου καὶ Πρόκλου (Πλουτάρχου δὲ λέγω τοῦ ἐπίκλην Νεστορίου). ἔγραψε προγυμνάσματα καὶ μελέτας ῥητορικὰς καὶ ἄλλα τινά. ἤκμαζεν ἐπὶ Λέοντος βασιλέως τοῦ πρεσβύτου καὶ ἕως Ζήνωνος καὶ Ἀναστασίου. 2) Νικόλαος, Μύρων τῆς Λυκίας, ἀδελφὸς Διοσκορίδου γραμματικοῦ καὶ ὑπάρχου καὶ ὑπάτου καὶ πατρίκου. σοφιστεύσας καὶ αὐτὸς ἐν Κωνσταντινουπόλει, μαθητὴς γεγονὼς Λαχάρους. ἔγραψε τέχνην ῥητορικὴν καὶ μελέτας.

2. See W. Stegemann, "Nikolaos (21)," *RE* 17 (1936) 424-57, esp. 425. Stegemann's *Pauly* article remains the authoritative treatment of Nicolaus.

3. J. Felten (ed.), *Nicolai Progymnasmata* (Rhetores Graeci 11; Leipzig: Teubner, 1913) xxi-xxii.

4. See K. Orinsky, *De Nicolai Myrensis et Libanii quae feruntur progymnasmatis* (Diss. Breslau, 1920) 2. This dissertation, of which only four copies were printed, was not available to us. Fortunately, there is a detailed summary of it in the review by E. Richtsteig in *PhW* 41 (1921) 697-701. References to Orinsky are thus based on Richtsteig's summary.

5. See Felten, *Progymnasmata*, xxiii.

6. On Lachares, see O. Seeck, "Lachares (3)," *RE* 12 (1924) 332.

7. See Stegemann, "Nikolaos," 425.

8. Felten, *Progymnasmata*, xxiii.

9. Stegemann, "Nikolaos," 425. If Nicolaus betrays no Christian influence, he certainly does his neo-Platonist leanings, on which see the detailed comments of Stegemann ("Nikolaos," 425-26).

10. The *Suda* s.v. Νικόλαος (3.469, 2-3 and 7-8 Adler).

11. See Nicolaus, *Progymn.* 1 (p. 1, 1 Felten), and Stegemann, "Nikolaos," 426.

12. Felten, *Progymnasmata*, xxvii.

13. See Walz, *Rhetores Graeci*, 1.266-420, esp. 272-78 which contain elaborations of four chreiai (#26, 64, 6 and 45). Text and translation of these elaborations will appear in volume II of *The Chreia in Ancient Rhetoric*.

14. So Stegemann, "Nikolaos," 426.

15. Note how readily Doxapatres can call Aphthonius' elaborations of a chreia or a maxim a μελέτη (see, e.g., *Hom* [2.267, 16 and 268, 16 Walz]).

16. See Stegemann, "Nikolaos," 451-57.

17. See Stegemann, "Nikolaos," 452-55, esp. 452-53, which treat the chreia. Stegemann points out that the chreiai being

elaborated are classified closer to the system of Aphthonius than to that of Nicolaus. Stegemann could have added that the headings of the elaborations follow Aphthonius rather than Nicolaus.

18. See Stegemann, "Nikolaos," 455–57.

19. See Walz, *Rhetores Graeci*, 2.565–684, esp. 585–91 which contain the scholia on the chreia.

20. See Doxapatres, *Hom.* (2.198, 17–199, 3 Walz).

21. Anonymous scholia (2. 578, 10–17 Walz).

22. See, e.g., Doxapatres, *Hom.* (2.539, 14–18 Walz), with the scholion at 2.657, 22–24 Walz; and Doxapatres, *Hom.* (2.548, 14–17) with the scholion at 2.659, 12–15.

23. Cf. further Felten, *Progymnasmata*, iii.

24. See Spengel, *Rhetores Graeci*, 3.449–98.

25. See H. Graeven, "Die *Progymnasmata* des Nicolaus," *Hermes* 30 (1895) 471–73.

26. See Graeven, "*Progymnasmata* des Nicolaus," 472.

27. See Graeven, "*Progymnasmata* des Nicolaus," 472.

28. See above n. 3.

29. See further Felten, *Progymnasmata*, xx, and Stegemann, "Nikolaos," 426.

30. On Nicolaus' general procedure for each *progymnasma*, see Stegemann, "Nikolaos," 428.

31. See Theon, *Progymn.* 1 (1.157, 3–5 Walz).

32. See Hermogenes, *Progymn.* 2 (p. 4, 7–8 Rabe).

33. See Felten, *Progymnasmata*, xxviii–xxix, and Stegemann, "Nikolaos," 431.

34. See Stegemann, "Nikolaos," 431.

35. See Theon, *Progymn.* 1 (1.148, 12–15 Walz).

36. See Theon 199–275, where, in addition to Chreia 49, he uses Chreiai 21, 23, 25, and 40.

37. See Theon 190–94.

38. See Theon 9–24.

39. See Theon 25–28.

40. Hermogenes, while he is aware of other ways to differentiate chreiai (cf. 27–30), provides only this principal classification (5–15), as does Aphthonius (5–17).

41. See Theon 36–189.

42. Hermogenes (27–28) speaks of older writers discussing the differentiations of the chreia.

43. See Stegemann, "Nikolaos," 431–32.

44. See Stegemann, "Nikolaos," 429. Stegemann may well be right in seeing this distinctioin arising from the problem of the encomium being both a *progymnasma* and a speech in its own right, as well as from the fact that rhetorical teachers published their model exercises, which then laid claim to being considered independent "wholes."

45. See Nicolaus, *Progymn*. 8 (p. 48, 4-10 Felten) and *Progymn* 9 (p. 60, 16-20).

46. See Nicolaus, *Progymn*. 3 (p. 17, 4-13 Felten).

47. See Nicolaus, *Progymn*. 1 (p. 4, 2-3 Felten).

48. On ἐργασία as the technical term for the elaboration, see Hermogenes 32. Cf. also Aphthonius 18.

49. See Aphthonius 20-21: τὸ τῆς αἰτίας, τὸ ἐκ ἐναντίου, παραβολή, παράδιεγμα, μαρτυρία παλαιῶν.

50. See above pp. 238-39.

51. For bibliographical information, see above n. 3.

TEXT
AND
TRANSLATION

Μετὰ τὸ διήγημα τακτέον τὴν χρείαν· αὕτη
γὰρ ἂν ἀρίστη τάξις γένοιτο· εἰσὶ γάρ τινες,
οἳ καὶ πρὸ τοῦ μύθου καὶ πρὸ τοῦ διηγήματος
αὐτὴν ἔταξαν καὶ λέγουσι διὰ τοῦτο δεῖν αὐτὴν　　　　5
προτάττειν, ἐπειδὴ καὶ αὐτὴ χρηστοῦ καθήγησιν

(17,20)　　ἔχει ἢ πονηροῦ φυγήν· " δεῖ δὲ " φασι " τοὺς νέους
περὶ τούτων πρῶτον διδάσκεσθαι. " πρὸς οὓς
λεκτέον· τοῦτο μὲν οὐκ ἔξω λόγου, διὰ ⟨δὲ⟩ τὸ
διαιρέσεως δεῖσθαι πλείονος ἢ κατὰ τὸν μῦθον καὶ　　　10

(18,1)　　τὸ διήγημα μετὰ ταῦτα δεῖ αὐτὴν τάττεσθαι.
Ἕτεροι δὲ τάξαντες αὐτὴν πρώτην οὐ τὴν νῦν
ταύτην αὐτῇ διαίρεσιν ἀποδεδώκασιν, ἀλλὰ τὴν κατὰ
πάσας τὰς πτώσεις καὶ πάντας τοὺς ἀριθμοὺς προ-
φορὰν μόνην ἐνόμισαν τοῖς νέοις ⟨ἄρτι⟩ τῶν　　　15

(18,5)　　ποιητῶν ἀφισταμένοις καὶ ἐπὶ τὴν ῥητορικὴν ἰοῦσιν
ἀρκεῖν πρὸς τὴν τοῦ πολιτικοῦ λόγου μελέτην καὶ
ἐχρῶντο αὐτῇ οὕτως· οἷον (Chreia 49) " Πιττακὸς
ὁ Μιτυληναῖος ἐρωτηθεὶς εἰ λανθάνει τις τοὺς
θεοὺς φαῦλόν τι ποιῶν, ἔφη· 'ἀλλ' οὐδὲ διανο-　　　20
ούμενος.'" καὶ πρῶτον μὲν κατ' εὐθεῖαν προέφερον,

(18,10)　　τὸ δ' ἐντεῦθεν καὶ κατὰ τὰς ἐφεξῆς. οἷον ⟨κατὰ⟩
γενικήν· " Πιττακοῦ⟨τοῦ⟩ Μιτυληναίου ἐρωτηθέντος,
εἰ λανθάνει τις τοὺς θεοὺς φαῦλόν τι ποιῶν, λόγος
ἀπομνημονεύεται· 'ἀλλ' οὐδὲ διανοούμενος.'" κατὰ　　25
δοτικήν· " Πιττακῷ τῷ Μιτυληναίῳ ἐρωτηθέντι, εἰ

(18,15)　　λανθάνει τις τοὺς θεοὺς φαῦλόν τι ποιῶν, ἐπῆλθεν
εἰπεῖν· 'ἀλλ' οὐ⟨δὲ⟩ διανοούμενος.'" κατὰ αἰτια-
τικήν· " Πιττακὸν τὸν Μιτυληναῖον ἐρωτηθέντα, εἰ
τοὺς θεοὺς λανθάνει τις φαῦλόν τι ποιῶν, εἰρηκέναι
φασίν· 'ἀλλ' οὐδὲ διανοούμενος.'" ἡ δὲ κλητικὴ　　　31
σαφής ἐστιν αὐτόθι· πρὸς γὰρ αὐτὸν τὸν εἰπόντα

(18,20)　　⟨τὸν⟩ λόγον ποιησόμεθα· "σύ, ὦ Πιττακὲ Μιτυληναῖε,

On the Chreia

The chreia should be placed after the narrative, for this would be the best position.[1] There are some, indeed, who have placed it even before the fable and the narrative and say that it should have first position because it has inducement for good or avoidance of evil. "Young men," they say, "should be taught about these things first." To these people one can say that this view is not unreasonable, but because of the need for a more advanced division[2] than in the fable and the narrative, the chreia should be placed after these exercises.

Others, however, who placed it first have not assigned it this present-day division. Instead, they considered the declension[3] of the chreia in all the cases and all the numbers alone to be sufficient training for the public speech for the youths who have just left the poets and are moving on to rhetoric. And so they used it as follows. For example (Chreia 49) *Pittacus of Mitylene, on being asked if anyone excapes the notice of the gods in committing some sinful act, said, "Why, not even in contemplating it."* First, they presented it in the nominative case, and then in succession in the other cases as well. For example, in the genitive case: *Pittacus of Mitylene's statement, on being asked if anyone escapes the notice of the gods in committing some sinful act, is remembered, "Why, not even in contemplating it."* In the dative case: *To Pittacus of Mitylene, on being asked if anyone escapes the notice of the gods in committing some sinful act, it occurred to say "Why, not even in contemplating it."* In the accusative case: *They say that Pittacus of Mitylene, on being asked if anyone escapes the notice of the gods in committing some sinful act, said, "Why, not even in contemplating it."* The vocative case is immediately clear, for we are to address the one who utters the statement: *You, Pittacus of Mitylene,*

ἐρωτηθεὶς εἰ λανθάνει τις τοὺς θεοὺς φαῦλόν τι
ποιῶν, εἶπας· 'ἀλλ' οὐδὲ διανοούμενος.'" καὶ   35
οὕτω κατὰ τὸν δυικὸν ἀριθμὸν καὶ πληθυντικόν,
εἰ ἐνδέχοιτο τυχὸν διὰ μελέτην δευτέρῳ Πιττακῷ
(19,1) ἢ καὶ πλείοσιν ἀνατιθέναι τὸν λόγον.
      Ἀλλὰ νῦν διὰ ταύτην τὴν αἰτίαν οὐ τακτέον
πρώτην τὴν χρείαν· ἕως μὲν γὰρ οὐ διῄρητό   40
τισι κεφαλαίοις, καλῶς εἶχεν ἐγγυμνάζεσθαι τῷ
λόγῳ διὰ τὴν ἐξαλλαγὴν τὴν κατὰ τὰς πτώσεις·
(19,5) ἐπειδὴ δὲ ἤδη κεφαλαίοις πῃ διῄρηται, καλῶς
ἂν ἔχοι τάττειν αὐτὴν μετὰ τὸ διήγημα.
      Χρεία δέ ἐστι λόγος ἢ πρᾶξις εὔστοχος   45
καὶ σύντομος, εἴς τι πρόσωπον ὡρισμένον ἔχουσα
τὴν ἀναφοράν, πρὸς ἐπανόρθωσίν τινος τῶν ἐν τῷ
(19,10) βίῳ παραλαμβανομένη. λόγος δὲ ἢ πρᾶξις, ἐπειδὴ
καὶ ἐν λόγοις εὑρίσκεται καὶ ἐν πράξεσιν.
εὔστοχος δέ, ἐπειδὴ ἐν τούτῳ ἐστὶν ἡ ἰσχὺς τῆς   50
χρείας ἐν τῷ εὐστόχως εἰρῆσθαι. σύντομος δέ,
ὡς διὰ τὰ ἀπομνημονεύματα. εἴς τι δὲ πρόσωπον
ἔχουσα τὴν ἀναφοράν, ὡς διὰ τὴν γνώμην· ἐκείνη
(19,15) γὰρ οὐκ εἰς πρόσωπον πάντως ἀναφέρεται. τὸ δὲ
πρὸς ἐπανόρθωσίν τινος τῶν ἐν τῷ βίῳ παρα-   55
λαμβανομένη, ἐπειδὴ ὡς ἐπὶ τὸ πλεῖστον ἀγαθή
τις παραίνεσις ἔπεται. ἀλλὰ περὶ μὲν τῆς
διαφορᾶς αὐτῶν ἐν τῷ περὶ γνώμης λεχθήσεται.
(20,1)   Εἴρηται δὲ χρεία, οὐχ ὅτι καὶ τἆλλα προγυμνάσματα οὐκ ἐκπληροῖ τινα χρείαν, ἀλλ' ὅτι   60
ἢ τῷ κοινῷ ὀνόματι κατ' ἐξοχὴν ὡς ἰδίῳ τετίμηται
ὥσπερ Ὅμηρος ὁ ποιητὴς καὶ Δημοσθένης ὁ ῥήτωρ,
(20,5) ἢ ὡς ἐπὶ τὸ πλεῖστον ἐκ περιστάσεώς τινος καὶ
χρείας τὴν ἀρχὴν αὐτῇ τις ἐχρήσατο.
      Τῶν δὲ χρειῶν αἱ ἀνωτάτω διαφοραὶ τρεῖς·   65
αἱ μὲν γὰρ αὐτῶν εἰσι λογικαί, αἱ δὲ πρακτικαί,
αἱ δὲ μικταί. πρόσκειται τὸ ἀνωτάτω, ἐπειδὴ
καὶ αὗται πολλὰς διαφορὰς πρὸς ἀλλήλας ἔχουσιν,
(20,10) ἃς δεῖ μανθάνειν ἐκ παρασκευῆς τῆς περὶ τὴν
τέχνην ἢ ὕλην πλείονος. λογικαὶ μὲν ⟨οὖν⟩   70
εἰσιν αἱ διὰ λόγων μόνων, οἷον (Chreia 43)

on being asked if anyone escapes the notice of the gods in committing some sinful act, said, "Why, not even in contemplating it." And so on in the dual and plural numbers, if perhaps it should be possible for the sake of practice to attribute the saying to a second Pittacus or even several.

But at present the chreia should not be placed first for this reason: so long as it was not divided into any headings, training with the saying in the declension through the cases was satisfactory. But since the chreia has now been divided into headings at all, it would be appropriate to place it after the narrative.

A chreia is a saying or action which is apt and concise, attributed to some specified character and employed for the purpose of correcting some aspect of life. It is a "saying or action" since it is found with both sayings and actions. It is "apt" since the effectiveness of the chreia lies in its being aptly spoken. It is "concise" as distinct from the reminiscences. It is "attributed to some character" as distinct from the maxim, since the maxim is never attributed to a character. It is "employed for the purpose of improving some aspect of life" since some good advice usually accompanies it. Their differences, however, will be discussed in the section on the maxim.[4]

It is called "chreia," not because the other progymnasmata do not satisfy some need (χρεία), but either because the chreia has been singled out with a common noun as through it were a proper noun because of its excellence, just as Homer is referred to as Poet and Demosthenes as Orator; or because in the beginning someone used (χράομαι) it especially in response to some situation and need.

The main differentiations of the chreia are three: sayings-chreiai, action-chreiai, and mixed chreiai. The word "main" is added because these differentiations also have many minor differences from one another. These differences one must learn from a more advanced study on technique and subject matter.[5] Sayings-chreiai, then, are those which consist only of sayings. For example (Chreia 43)

        " Ἰσοκράτης ἔφη τῆς παιδείας τὴν ῥίζαν εἶναι
        πικράν, τοὺς δὲ καρποὺς γλυκεῖς." πρακτικαὶ
        δὲ αἱ διὰ ἔργων μόνων, οἷον (Chreia 26) " Διο-
        γένης ἰδὼν μειράκιον ἀκοσμοῦν κατὰ τὴν ἀγορὰν   75
(20,15) τῇ βακτηρίᾳ τὸν παιδαγωγὸν ἔτυψε." μικταὶ δὲ
        ⟨αἱ⟩ ἐξ ἀμφοτέρων, οἷον (Chreia 45) " Λάκων
        ἐρωτηθεὶς, ποῦ τὰ τείχη τῆς Σπάρτης, ἀνατείνας
        τὸ δόρυ ἔφη· ' ἐνταῦθα.' "
(21,1)   Ἔτι τῶν χρειῶν φασι τὰς μὲν χρησίμου   80
        τινὸς ἕνεκα παραλαμβάνεσθαι, ⟨τὰς δὲ⟩ χαριεν-
        τισμοῦ μόνου· χρησίμου μὲν ἕνεκα ὡς ἐνταῦθα
        (Chreia 43) " Ἰσοκράτης ἔφη τῆς παιδείας τὴν
        ῥίζαν εἶναι πικράν, τὸν δὲ καρπὸν γλυκύν."
(21,5)   συμβάλλεται γὰρ πρὸς τὸ δεῖν καρτερεῖν τὰ   85
        δυσχερῆ διὰ τὴν ἡδονὴν τὴν μετὰ ταῦτα.
        χαριεντισμοῦ δὲ ἕνεκα μόνου ὡς ἐπ' ἐκείνης
        (Chreia 48) " Ὀλυμπιὰς ἡ μήτηρ Ἀλεξάνδρου
        ἀκούσασα ὅτι ὁ παῖς αὐτῆς υἱὸν αὐτὸν Διὸς
        εἶναι λέγει, ' οὐ παύσεται,' ἔφη, ' τὸ   90
(21,10) μειράκιον διαβάλλον με πρὸς τὴν Ἥραν; ' "
        δοκεῖ γὰρ χαριεντισμὸν ⟨μόνον⟩ ἔχειν. καὶ
        πάλιν (Chreia 16) " Δάμων ὁ παιδοτρίβης, φασί,
        στρεβλοὺς ἔχων τοὺς πόδας καὶ τὰ ὑποδήματα
        ⟨ἐν⟩ τῷ βαλανείῳ ἀπολέσας ηὔχετο ταῦτα τοῖς   95
        ποσὶ τοῦ κλέψαντος ἁρμόσαι." δοκεῖ γὰρ ⟨καὶ⟩
        αὕτη τὸ χάριεν ἔχειν μόνον. ἐμοὶ δὲ μετὰ
(21,15) τοῦ χαριεντισμοῦ φαίνονται καὶ ἀγαθὴν παραίνε-
        σιν ἔχουσαι· ἡ μὲν γὰρ ἀποτρέπει τὸν παῖδα
        τοῦ ἑαυτὸν ὀνομάζειν Διὸς υἱόν, ὁ δὲ φεύγειν   100
        εἰσηγεῖται τὴν κλοπὴν ὡς πρᾶγμα ἀτοπώτατον.
        διὸ οὐ⟨δὲ⟩ πιστέον τοῖς ἀνασκευάζουσι τὰς
        χρείας· εἰσὶ γάρ τινες, οἳ καὶ ταύτας καὶ τοὺς
(21,20) μύθους ἀνασκευάζουσι. πρὸς οὓς λεκτέον ὅτι
        δεῖ μήτε τὰ ὁμολογούμενα ἀγαθὰ ἀνασκευάζειν   105

92: addimus μόνον quod subiecit Brinkmann.

Isocrates said that education's root is bitter, its fruits sweet. Action-chreiai are those which consist only of deeds. For example (Chreia 26) *Diogenes, on seeing a youth misbehaving in the market-place, struck the paedagogus with his staff.* Mixed chreiai are those which are composed of both. For example (Chreia 45) *A Laconian, on being asked where the walls of Sparta were, extended his spear and said, "Here."*

Next, they say that some chreiai are employed because of some usefulness, but others because of wit alone. Because of usefulness, as here (Chreia 43) *Isocrates said that education's root is bitter, its fruits sweet.* For it stresses the need to endure difficulties for the sake of the pleasures which follow them.[6] Because of wit alone, as with this one (Chreia 48) *Olympias, the mother of Alexander, on hearing that her son was saying he was a son of Zeus, said, "Won't this fellow stop slandering me to Hera?"* For the chreia seems to contain only wit. And again (Chreia 16) *Damon the gymnastics teacher,* they say, *whose feet were lame, after he lost his shoes in the bath prayed that they would fit the feet of the thief.* This one, too, seems to contain only wit. But in my opinion these chreiai also appear to contain good advice along with the wit. For Olympias is dissuading her son from calling himself a son of Zeus, while Damon teaches us to avoid theft as a very wicked act. Therefore, one should not trust those who refute chreiai; indeed, there are some who refute both chreiai and fables. To them it should be said that it is not right to refute generally accepted values

διὰ τὸ μηδένα ἔχειν τὸν πειθόμενον μήτε τὰ
ὁμολογούμενα ψευδῆ διὰ τὸ πρόδηλον εἶναι
τὸ ψεῦδος. οὔτε οὖν τοὺς μύθους οὔτε τὰς
χρείας ἀνασκευαστέον· οὔτε γάρ, ὅτι συν-
(22,5)   επλάσθησαν οἱ μῦθοι, νοῦν ἔχων τις ἀγνοεῖ   110
οὔτε πεισθήσεταί τις τῷ ἀποτρέποντι τῆς
ἀγαθῆς παραινέσεως τῆς κατὰ τὴν χρείαν, καὶ
μὴν καὶ ἐν αὐτοῖς τοῖς μύθοις τὸ ἀγαθόν,
πρὸς ὃ βλέποντες πλάττομεν τοὺς μύθους, οὐκ
ἐᾷ πιθανοὺς εἶναι δοκεῖν τοὺς ἀντιλέγοντας.   115
(22,10)   Τῶν χρειῶν ἔτι αἱ μὲν δηλοῦσιν, ὁποῖά
εἰσι τὰ πράγματα, αἱ δὲ ὁποῖα δεῖ εἶναι.
ὁποῖα μέν ἐστιν, ὡς ἐκεῖνο (Chreia 2) " Αἴσωπος
ὁ μυθοποιὸς ἐρωτηθεὶς τί ἐστιν ἰσχυρότατον
⟨τῶν⟩ ἐν ἀνθρώποις εἶπεν· ‘⟨ὁ⟩ λόγος.’" τοῦτο   120
γάρ ἐστιν ἰσχυρότατον. ὁποῖα δὲ δεῖ εἶναι,
(22,15)   ⟨ὡς⟩ ἐκεῖνο (Chreia 8) " ’Αριστείδης ἐρωτηθεὶς
τί ἐστι τὸ δίκαιον, εἶπε· ‘τὸ μὴ ἐπιθυμεῖν
τῶν ἀλλοτρίων.’" τοιαῦτα γὰρ δεῖ εἶναι.
τοῦτο δὲ ἡμῖν συμβάλλεται πρὸς τὸ εἰδέναι   125
τὴν διαίρεσιν· ἐὰν μὲν γὰρ ⟨ᾖ⟩ ἡ χρεία δηλοῦσα
ὁποῖά ἐστι τὰ πράγματα, μετὰ τὸ προοίμιον καὶ
(22,20)   τὴν παράφρασιν ἐπαινεσόμεθα αὐτὴν ὡς ἀληθῶς
ἔχουσαν, ἐὰν δὲ ὁποῖα δεῖ εἶναι, ὡς εἰκότως
ἔχουσαν.   130
       Ἔτι τῶν χρειῶν αἱ μέν εἰσιν ἁπλαῖ, αἱ
δὲ πρός τι· ἁπλαῖ μέν, οἷον (Chreia 43)
" ’Ισοκράτης ἔφη τῆς παιδείας τὴν ῥίζαν εἶναι
πικράν, γλυκεῖς δὲ τοὺς καρπούς." πρός τι
⟨δὲ⟩ αἱ πρὸς τὴν ἐρώτησιν, οἷον (Chreia 52)   135
" Πλάτων ἐρωτηθεὶς ποῦ οἰκοῦσιν αἱ Μοῦσαι,
(23,5)   ‘ἐν ταῖς τῶν παιδευομένων,’ ἔφη, ‘ψυχαῖς.’"
       Τῶν δὲ προγυμνασμάτων τῶν μὲν ὄντων

125-26: πρὸς τὸ εἰδέναι τὴν διαίρεσιν dubite offert Felten: εἰδέναι
πρὸς τὴν διαίρεσιν mss; εἰδέναι sec1. Finckh.

on the grounds that the person who is the object of
the persuasion has none of them, nor generally accepted
fiction on the grounds that the fiction is obvious.[7] Thus
one should refute neither fables nor chreiai. For no
sensible person is ignorant of the fact that fables are
fabricated, nor will anyone be persuaded to heed the
person who is trying to turn him from the good advice
that is in the chreia. And besides, even in the fables
themselves, the good we have in view when composing
fables keeps the critics from appearing plausible.

Next, some chreiai demonstrate the way things are,
while others demonstrate the way they should be. The
way things are, as this one (Chreia 2) *Aesop the fable-
writer, on being asked what the most potent thing among
men is, said, "Speech."* For this remark is most certainly
true.[8] The way things should be, as this one (Chreia 8)
*Aristeides, on being asked what justice is, said, "Not
desiring the possessions of others."* For such is the
way things should be. This distinction contributes to our
understanding of the division of the chreia. For if the
chreia is domonstrating the way things are, we will
commend it after the introduction and the paraphrase
as being true; but if it demonstrates the way they
should be, we will commend it as being probable.

Next, some chreiai are simple,[9] while others are a
response to something. The simple, as (Chreia 43)
*Isocrates said that education's root is bitter, its fruits
sweet.* Chreiai in response to something are those in
response to a question. For example (Chreia 52) *Plato,
on being asked where the Muses dwell, said, "In the souls
of the educated."*

Since some progymnasmata are partial speeches and
others are both partial and whole speeches, the chreia

μερῶν, τῶν δὲ μερῶν καὶ ὅλων, ἡ χρεία τῶν
μερῶν ἂν εἴη· αὐτὴ γὰρ ἐφ'ἑαυτῆς οὐκ ἂν   **140**
πληροίη μόνη ὑπόθεσιν.

(23,10)   Ἔτι τῶν προγυμνασμάτων τῶν μὲν συν-
τελούντων εἰς τὴν τοῦ δικανικοῦ μελέτην. τῶν
δὲ εἰς τὴν τοῦ πανηγυρικοῦ, τῶν δὲ εἰς τὴν
τοῦ συμβουλευτικοῦ, ⟨ἡ χρεία προδήλως ἂν εἴη   **145**
τοῦ συμβουλευτικοῦ·⟩ πάντως γὰρ ⟨ἢ⟩ ἐπί τι
ἀγαθὸν προτρέπει ἢ πονηροῦ τινος εἴργει. συν-
τελέσειε δ'⟨ἂν⟩ καὶ εἰς τὰ ἄλλα· ἐν οἷς μὲν
(23,15)   γὰρ ἐπαινοῦμεν, τοῦ ἐγκωμιαστικοῦ φροντίδα
ποιούμεθα, ἐν οἷς δὲ τὸ εἰκὸς καὶ ⟨τὸ⟩ ἀπὸ   **150**
παραδειγμάτων κατασκευάζομεν, τοῦ δικανικοῦ.

Ἔτι πέντε μερῶν ὄντων τοῦ πολιτικοῦ
λόγου, τουτέστι προοιμίου, διηγήσεως, ἀντι-
(23,20)   θέσεως, λύσεως καὶ ἐπιλόγου, πρὸς τὴν πάντων
μελέτην ἀρκέσει ἡ χρεία· καὶ γὰρ προοιμαζό-   **155**
μεθα, ἔνθα ἐπαινοῦμεν τὸν εἰρηκότα ἢ πράξαντα,
καὶ διηγούμεθα ἐν μέρει, ἔνθα τὴν παράφρασιν
τῆς χρείας ποιούμεθα, καὶ ἀγωνιζόμεθα, κἂν μὴ
(24,1)   ἀντιθέσεως ἁπτώμεθα, ἔνθα κατασκευάζομεν τὸ
εἰρῆσθαι καλῶς ἢ πεπρᾶχθαι, καὶ ἐπιλογιζόμεθα,   **160**
ἐν οἷς παραινοῦμεν ζηλοῦν τὸ λεχθέν.

Διῄρηται ⟨δὲ⟩ κεφαλαίοις τούτοις· ἐπαίνῳ
(24,5)   τοῦ εἰρηκότος βραχεῖ καὶ οὐκ εἰς μῆκος ἐκτειν-
ομένῳ οὐδὲ διὰ πάντων τῶν ἐγκωμιαστικῶν κεφαλαίων γινομένῳ, ἵνα μὴ μεῖζον ᾖ τὸ προοίμιον   **165**
τῆς ὑποθέσεως. πρῶτον οὖν (1) τούτῳ τῷ ἐπαίνῳ
τοῦ εἰρηκότος ἢ τοῦ πράξαντος, ἔπειτα μετ'
αὐτὸν (2) τῇ παραφράσει τῆς χρείας, ἐπὶ ταύτῃ
(24,10)   (3) τῷ εἰκότι καὶ τῷ ἀληθεῖ, εἶτα (4) τῷ ἀπὸ
παραδειγμάτων, καὶ ἐπὶ πᾶσι (5) τῇ ἀφ'ἑτέρων   **170**
κρίσει, μεθ'ἥν, ἂν δέῃ, καὶ (6) ἐπὶ βραχεῖάν
τινα παράκλησιν ἐρχόμεθα.

Ἰστέον δὲ ὅτι τινὲς μετὰ τὸ εἰκὸς τὸ
ἀπὸ παραβολῆς τάττουσιν, ὅπερ ἐστὶ μέρος τοῦ

would belong to the partial progymnasmata.[10] For by itself it cannot fulfill the purpose of a complete speech
alone.

Next, since some progymnasmata contribute to the
practice of the forensic speech, others to that of the
panegyric and still others to that of the deliberative,
the chreia can obviously belong to the deliberative. For
it always urges us to something good or restrains us
from something evil; but it can also contribute to the
others. For in those headings where we praise, we are
concerned with the encomiastic speech; and in those
where we confirm by means of the argument for the
probable and from examples, we are concerned with the
forensic.[11]

Next, even though there are five parts to the public
speech, i.e. introduction, statement of the facts, anti-
thesis, resolution, and epilogue, the chreia will suffice
for the practice of all five. Indeed, we write an introduction where we praise the one who has spoken or
acted. We partially write a statement of the facts where
we paraphrase the chreia. We argue the case, even if
we do not attack a counter proposition, where we
confirm what has been said or done well. And we write
an epilogue where we give advice to emulate what was
said.

The chreia is divided into these headings: (1) The
praise of the speaker which is short and not expanded
at length nor carried through all the encomiastic headings to keep the introduction from being longer than
the main discussion. So first this praise of the one who
has spoken or acted; then after it (2) the paraphrase
of the chreia. In additon to this (3) the Probable and
the True, then (4) From Examples, and in addition to all
these (5) the Opinion of Others; after this, should it
be necessary,[12] we move on to (6) some brief exhortation.

It should be realized, however, that some people
place the proof "From Analogy" after that of "The
Probable" in as much as the former is actually a part
of "The Probable,"

(24,15)   εἰκότος, [ὡς] ἐμπῖπτον ἐν αὐτῷ ὡς ἐνθύμημα.   175
            τῶν γὰρ ἀποδείξεων ⟨πασῶν⟩ τῶν μὲν οὐσῶν
            ἐνθυμηματικῶν, τῶν δὲ παραδειγματικῶν, ἐν
            μὲν τῷ εἰκότι ταῖς ἐνθυμηματικαῖς χρησόμεθα,
            ἐν δὲ τῷ ἀπὸ παραδειγμάτων ταῖς παραδειγματι-
            καῖς. ὡς μὲν οὖν ἐν βραχεῖ προγυμνάσματι,   180
(24,20)   οὕτως καὶ πῶς δεῖ χρῆσθαι ταῖς ἀποδείξεσιν
            ἐν ταῖς τελειοτέραις ὑποθέσεσι μαθησόμεθα.
            δεῖ⟨δὲ⟩ καὶ ταῦτα τὸν διδάσκαλον ἐπ'αὐτῆς
            δεικνύναι τῆς διαιρέσεως.

(25,1)   ⟨Περὶ γνώμης⟩   185

            Γνώμη ἐστὶν ἀπόφανσις καθολική, συμβούλην
            τινα καὶ παραίνεσιν ἔχουσα πρός τι τῶν ἐν τῷ
            βίῳ χρησίμων.
            Διαφέρει δὲ τῆς χρείας, κοινωνοῦσα κατὰ
(25,5)   τὴν πᾶσαν διαίρεσιν, πρῶτον μὲν ἐκείνῳ, (1)   190
            ὅτι ἡ μὲν χρεία καὶ ἐν λόγοις ἐστὶ καὶ ἐν
            πράξεσιν, ἡ δὲ γνώμη ἐν λόγοις μόνοις· εἶτα
            (2) ὅτι ἡ μὲν γνώμη ἀπόφανσίς ἐστι καθολικὴ
            καὶ οὐ πάντως εἰς πρόσωπον ἀναφέρεται, ἡ δὲ
            τὴν ἀναφορὰν πάντως εἰς πρόσωπον ἔχει· πρὸς   195
(25,10)   τούτοις, (3) ὅτι ἡ μὲν χρεία ἐκ περιστάσεώς
            τινος σύγκειται, ἡ δὲ γνώμη ἐν πλήθει λόγων·
            ἐνθυμηματικὴν ⟨γὰρ⟩ ἀπόδειξιν ἔχουσα τοῦ
            ⟨προ⟩κειμένου [καὶ] καθολικὴν ἅμα ποιεῖται
            παραίνεσιν· ἐφ'ἅπασιν [ἢ] (4) ὅτι ἡ μὲν γνώμη   200
            πάντως ἢ αἵρεσιν ἀγαθοῦ ἢ φυγὴν κακοῦ εἰσ-

---

180 ὡς μὲν οὖν P] καὶ οὕτω O; καὶ οὕτω μὲν ὡς Felten. ἐν βραχεῖ
προγυμνάσματι P] ἐν β. τῷ πρ. O, unde Felten.   181 οὕτως καὶ πῶς
scripsimus] οὕτως πῶς δὲ P; καὶ πῶς O; πῶς δὲ Felten. χρῆσθαι O]
κεχρῆσθαι P, fortasse recte.   194 ἡ δὲ ⟨χρεία⟩ scholia quaedam, unde
Felten.

falling as it does within it since it is a proposition. Taking them as a whole, some proofs make use of propositions and others of examples. We will use propositions in "The Probable" and examples in "From examples." So, one should use the proofs like this in the short progymnasma, and we will also learn how one should use them in the more advanced speeches. Yet the teacher must also point out these matters in the course of the division itself.[13]

On the Maxim[14]

A maxim is a general statement containing some counsel and advice for something useful in life.

It differs from the chreia while sharing in the whole division. First (1) because the chreia appears with both sayings and actions, while the maxim appears with sayings alone. Then (2) because the maxim is a general statement and is never attributed to any character, while the chreia always has the attribution to a character. In addition (3) because the chreia is composed on the basis of some circumstance, while the maxim is composed wholly[15] of words. For although it has a propositional proof of the subject matter, the maxim offers at the same time general advice. Finally (4) because the maxim always teaches either the attainment of virtue or the avoidance of evil,

(25,15) ἡγεῖται, ἡ δὲ χρεία καὶ χαριεντισμοῦ ἕνεκα
μόνου παραλαμβάνεται· εὕροι <δ'>ἄν τις οὐκ
ὀλίγας διαφορὰς <καὶ ἄλλας>.

(26,1)   Ἐπεὶ δὲ κοινωνεῖ καὶ τὸ ἀπομνημόνευμα   205
τῇ χρείᾳ καὶ τῇ γνώμῃ κατὰ τὴν παραίνεσιν,
δεῖ καὶ τούτου πρὸς ταύτας τὰς διαφορὰς εἰπεν.
διαφέρει οὖν τῆς μὲν σχεδὸν πᾶσιν. οἷς <καὶ>
ἡ χρεία, τῆς δὲ χρείας τῷ μήκει τῶν λόγων· ἃ

(26,5)   γὰρ εἰσηγεῖται δι'ὀλίγων ἡ χρεία, ταῦτα διὰ   210
πλειόνων τὸ ἀπομνημόνευμα. καὶ μάρτυς τούτου
Ξενοφῶν ἐν τοῖς οὕτω λεγομένοις Ἀπομνημονεύ-
μασιν.

---

208 τῆς μὲν <γνώμης> scholia quaedam, unde Felten.

while the chreia is also employed for the sake of wit alone. One can discover quite a few other differences as well.[16]

Since, however, the reminiscence also shares with the chreia and the maxim in their advice, it is also necessary to discuss the differences from this form. The reminiscence, then, differs from the maxim in nearly all the ways the chreia does, although it differs from the chreia in the length of its sayings. For what the chreia teaches with a few words, the reminiscence teaches with more. And an example of this fact is Xenophon in his work entitled *Reminiscences*.

COMMENTS

1. The references to the chreia and narrative are to the chapters on these forms, and the subject of this section (2-44) is the proper sequence of these chapters within the overall sequence of exercises in Nicolaus' *Progymnasmata*.

2. Nicolaus' use of the word διαίρεσις is not like that of the others (so, e.g., Aphthonius 16). Hence it does not mean "classification." What he does mean by it is the "elaboration" of the chreia, a manipulation usually denoted by the word ἐργασία (so, e.g., Hermogenes 31). Nicolaus' choice of the word διαίρεσις is unfortunate; note, e.g., the confusion of Maximus Planudes (2.19, 10-11 Walz). It seems that Nicolaus uses διαίρεσις in the sense that "division" refers to the dividing up of the elaboration into its various headings (κεφάλαια), such as the praise, paraphrase, etc. (cf. 162-81). Hence our rendering of this word by "division" (or "is divided," when the word is in a verbal form) (so also 13, 40, 43, 126, 162, 184, and 190).

3. Nicolaus again does not use standard terminology. Thus for the "declension" of the chreia he uses προφορά instead of κλίσις (as, e.g., we find in Theon 199).

4. Since Nicolaus' discussion of the differences between the chreia and maxim is so long, we have included it at the end of the chreia chapter (so 185-214).

5. This sentence is not at all clear. Moreover, even if we have rendered it correctly, it is still not clear to what Nicolaus refers.

6. Nicolaus is saying that the utility of Chreia 43 lies in its contributing, along with other maxims, stories, etc., to the general proposition or truism that toil must precede pleasure. Thus, Hermogenes, in his elaboration of this same chreia, finds similar sentiments in Hesiod and Epicharmus (see Hermogenes 55-59); see also, e.g., Musonius, *frag.* 51 (p. 144 Lutz).

7. This sentence, but particularly the clause διὰ τὸ μηδένα ἔχειν τὸν πειθόμενον, is not at all clear. The phrase τὸν πειθόμενον is presumably the person whom the one doing a refutation is trying to persuade. If so, then the διὰ τό c. inf. clause expresses the grounds on which one might make refutation. Accordingly, the second διά- clause also expresses the grounds on which one might refute a fable. At any rate, a textual variant listed by Felten, which replaces τὸν πειθόμενον by τὴν χρείαν understands the sentence in the same say: "on the grounds that the chreia contains no values."

8. This sentence does not so much pick up on the chreia as it refers back to the clause ὁποῖα μέν ἐστιν in line 118.

Hence ἰσχυρότατον means "most valid," or as we have rendered it; "most certainly true." The same goes for the comment following Chreia 8 in line 124.

9. For Nicolaus' use of the word ἁπλαῖ, see Quintilian 20-21; *in voce simplici.*

10. On the distinction between partial and whole *progymnasmata*, see the "Introduction" to Nicolaus, above, pp. 242-43.

11. Nicolaus is vague here. Presumably he is talking about the various headings of the division (or elaboration) of the chreia. Hence our translation of ἐν οἷς by "in those headings." The chreia itself, with its good advice (cf. 98-99), is thus clearly deliberative. But only in the division of the chreia, with its headings of praise, paraphrase, etc. (cf. 162-84), does the encomiastic or the forensic speech come into view.

12. This last heading, i.e., the brief exhortation, is not fixed. Hence Nicolaus neglects it in the following discussion of all the headings (so 173-84). Recall that Hermogenes also considered his heading "statement by an authority" to be optional (see Hermogenes 55).

13. This last section, with its various textual problems (see the apparatus), is obscure at points. Nicolaus is still discussing the argumentative headings of the division of the chreia. Hence the "short progymnasma" seemingly refers to the division itself (cf. 183-84). Nicolaus is thus saying that full treatment of the arguments awaits advanced study. For now, though, the teacher is only to point out various arguments in an inductive fashion in the course of treating the division of the chreia.

14. Nicolaus had referred to his discussion of the several differences between the chreia and maxim in the chreia chapter (cf. 58) but reserved it for the chapter on the maxim. Because of its length we have appended it here, along with his brief definition of a maxim.

15. This sentence is not entirely clear. Given the position of σύγκειται in the first clause, it is probably also to be regarded as governing the second clause as well. If so, then the phrase ἐν πλήθει must be adverbial. Hence our rendering "wholly." In any case, the meaning is clear.

16. Nicolaus would probably be hard pressed to name any more differences than he already has. At any rate, the parallel discussions in Theon (9-18), Hermogenes (19-26), and Aphthonius (see *Progymn.* 4 [p. 8, 7-10 Rabe] and n. 43 to the "Introduction" to Aphthonius) provide no other differences between these two forms. Note, moreover, that Nicolaus allows here the possibility of a merely witty chreia (cf. 202-03), whereas earlier he found good advice in chreiai

usually considered only witty (cf. 98-100).

THE CHREIA DISCUSSION OF

THE VATICAN GRAMMARIAN

Introduction, Translation and Comments

by

EDWARD N. O'NEIL

INTRODUCTION

I

The Manuscript. Codex Vaticanus 5216 (15th-16th cent.)[1] contains a fragment which has five brief excerpts on grammatical subjects: *De Positura, De Chria, De Poemate, De Versu, De Accentibus.* Of these the *De Chria* is the longest and most interesting.

The problems which this excerpt presents are complicated and varied, but in general they are concerned with three main topics: 1) authorship, 2) content and how it relates to other treatments of the chreia,[2] and 3) the Latin text itself.

II

Authorship. Despite some confusion which has arisen in the twentieth century, the author of this excerpt remains unknown. Heinrich Keil indicated as much when he printed the text of the fragment, yet Keil himself inadvertently set in motion a series of misunderstandings which has since led to the erroneous assumption that the author is Flavius Charisius, the 4th century African grammarian whose only surviving work is the *Ars grammatica.*

In his introductory remarks to the fragment, Keil says[3] that these five excerpts "can be traced to that part of the *Art* of Charisius which has disappeared from the Codex Neapolitanus under the section entitled 'On Reading and its Divisions'." Keil's reasoning was that the subject matter of the five excerpts is handled in much the same way by Diomedes, Dostheos and Victorinus, and that these grammarians followed the same source used by Charisius, with whom they usually agree.

Yet Keil nowhere claims that Charisius himself is the author of the fragment,[4] nor indeed would such an attribution have been correct. Even his suggestion that the contents of the fragment probably resembles that of the lost section of Charisius'grammar seems wrong. In the first place, of the three writers whom Keil names, only Diomedes has a section on the chreia.[5] Secondly, even Diomedes does not define and classify the form as the author of this excerpt attempts to do. His section bears the title *De Declinatione Exercitationis Chriarum*, and he limits his treatment of the chreia to just that, the declension of several chreiai through their cases and numbers.[6] Finally, neither Dostheos nor Victorinus mentions the chreia — at least not in an extant passage.

Thus even Keil's analysis and almost casual remark about some affinity between this fragment and the *Ars Grammatica* of Charisius seem incorrect. Karl Barwick understood the situation, and in his edition of Charisius[7] he takes no notice of the fragment. Even in his discussion of the lost section of Charisius' work to which Keil referred,[8] Barwick is silent both about the fragment and about Keil's remark.[9] The connection between the fragment and Charisisu' work, always tenuous at best, was now severed.

Here the matter should have rested, and the five excerpts should have retained their anonymity, but unfortunately such was not the case. Even before Barwick's edition mistaken ideas had already found their way into the scholarly literature. Paul Lejay had used the excerpt *De Chria* in his edition of Horace's *Satires*.[10] Apparently misunderstanding Keil's Latin, he attributed the passaage to Charisius with no reservation or *caveat*.

A few years later George C. Fiske[11] repeated the erroneous attribution, apparently following Lejay whom he quotes very frequently, and added a few mistakes of his own.[12] Despite numerous errors of fact and judgment, Fiske's book, along with that of Lejay, served twenty years later as a major source for Elizabeth Hazelton Haight. Her own book is much too dependent on the work of her two predecessors, and as a result she repeats many of their errors, including the attibution of the *De Chria* to Charisius.[13]

Now it is bad enough that Lejay and Fiske misunderstood Keil's reference to Charisius, but there can be no excuse for Haight's repeating the error. Shortly after the publication of Fiske's work, Barwick's edition of Charisius appeared. It was available to Haight, though she seems to have been unaware of its existence. Had she made a practice of consulting the most recent texts instead of taking her information from secondary works, she would have learned that no editor of Charisius, including Keil, had ever attributed this excerpt, or any part of the fragment, to that author.

Such errors are dangerous, especially when they are repeated in volume after volume over a number of years. The books of Lejay, Fiske and Haight have, in varying degrees, become standard references, and many people have consulted them. Their mistaken notion about the author of the *De Chria*, as well as other errors, has undoubtedly led many an unwary reader astray,[14] for not everyone can — or indeed be forced to — check every reference in every book he reads.

So much, then, for the authorship of this excerpt — or at least so much for Charisius. The author of the *De Chria* remains unknown, but in order to facilitate references he has been arbitrarily assigned the name Vatican Grammarian[15] because he was obviously a grammarian and because the excerpt is a part of Codex Vaticanus 5216.

For our purposes his name is less important than what he has to say about the chreia. His treatment of the subject is not nearly so important as some have supposed, and more to the point it is not entirely representative of ancient discussions. Yet the very differences are perhaps the best justification for including the *De Chria* in the present volume. It clearly has some new, or at least different, things to say about the chreia, and part of the information comes from a tradition which appears nowhere else.

The Vatican Grammarian's Discussion of the Chreia. A brief outline of the *De Chria* shows the main topics which it treats (numbers refer to lines in this text):

A. Definition (2-3)
B. Classification (3-24)

1. Action-chreia and example (3-6)
2. Sayings-chreiai (7-12)
   a. Declarative and example (8-10)
   b. Response to a question and example (11-14)
   c. With a rebuttal and example (15-22)
3. Mixed chreia and example (23-28)
4. With a demonstration and example (29-34)

The definition consists of just seven words and is brief to the point of being almost non-existent:[16] *Chria est dicti vel facti praecipua memoratio.* These words, in fact, seem to serve only as an introduction to the classification which follows. Yet even in this role they are deficient, for they omit any reference to the mixed chreia (*chria conjunctiva*) or to the so-called fourth class (*demonstrativum*), both of which appear in the Vatican Grammarian's classification.

More important, by omitting the six standard elements found in the other versions, these words fail almost completely to define the form which is called chreia.[17] There is no reference here to a chreia's 1) conciseness, 2) aptness, 3) attibution to, 4) a specified, 5) character, or to 6) its usefulness. Without these characteristics, the Vatican Grammarian's definition can refer to almost any apophthegm.

The most interesting and striking feature of the Vatican Grammarian's definition occurs in the last two words: *praecipua memoratio.* In view of the fact that both Hermogenes and Aphthonius define the chreia in terms of the reminiscence (ἀπομνημόνευμα) and that Priscian translates Hermogenes' noun with *commemoratio,* it is reasonable and indeed inevitable that we understand the Vatican Grammarian's *memoroatio* as a translation of ἀπομνημόνευμα.

What about *praecipua*? In the opinion of both Hermogenes and Aphthonius, the chreia is a kind of reminiscence. Hermogenes qualifies by adding a subordinate clause includes the elements of consiseness and usefulness, and Aphthonius uses modifiers to limit reminiscence: "A chreia is a concise reminiscence aptly attributed to some character." The

Vatican Grammarian, or his source, seems to have summarized all of these subordinate ideas in the one word *praecipua*, i.e., "special." Therefore, the Vatican Grammarian seems to have used a definition of the chreia which is somehow related, if only distantly, to that of the two Greek rhetoricians.

In the final analysis, however, the Vatican Grammarian's definition that a chreia is "a special reminiscence of a saying or action" is very unsatisfactory.[18] His attention is clearly focused on the classification, and this section, while fuller and more complex than some, is much less detailed than that of Theon or Nicolaus.

Before we turn, however, to the Vatican Grammarian's actual classification of the chreia, two features of the section merit attention because they help to set this treatment of the form apart from all others. The two are the Vatican Grammarian's choice of chreiai which he uses as examples and the technical vocabulary which he uses to designate the various classes and species of the chreia.

The Vatican Grammarian quotes six chreiai in this brief passage. Of the six, only the first (Chreia 25) appears in other discussions of the chreia, and even it shows a rather different wording here. Two more examples (Chreiai 9 and 29) appear in Diogenes Laertius and elsewhere, but the remaining three (Chreiai 1, 11, 15) seem to occur nowhere else. So even the choice of examples indicates that the Vatican Grammarian has used a source which belongs to a tradition that is different from those we know.

The same observation is true in respect to the technical vocabulary in both the definition and the classification. The terms *praecipua* and *memoratio* have already been discussed. Both occur only here. The Vatican Grammarian's division of the chreia into three classes (although he seems to add a fourth) is the standard one, i.e. sayings-chreiai, action-chreiai and mixed chreiai, yet only his term *facti* appears elsewhere (in Quintilian and Priscian). Its companion, *dicti*, is apt and obvious, but it is not used elsewhere, for Priscian uses *orationis*, and Quintilian employs circumlocution and says *positum in voce.* For the third class, which is elsewhere called *mixti*, the Vatican Grammarian uses *coniunctiva*, a term not attested elsewhere.[19]

When the Vatican Grammarian divides the sayings-chreiai into three species, he continues to use words which appear nowhere else.[20] He calls his first species *praepositiva*, i.e. ἀποφαντικόν which Priscian translates with *indicativi* (sc. *usus*). His second species is *percunctativa*, i.e. ἀποκριτικόν which Priscian translates with *interrogativi*. The Vatican Grammarian's third species, *refutativa*, is one of the most interesting points in the passage. Theon considers this type a "double chreia," and Priscian omits it entirely because Hermogenes omitted it. The opinion of the Vatican Grammarian is discussed below.

One interesting feature of the Vatican Grammarian's names for the three species of sayings-chreiai is that they resemble each other in form. That is, each ends in *-tiva*, and the same ending is used with the third class, i.e. *coniunctiva*. Even the fourth class, although it has a neuter form (sc. *genus*) ends with *-tivum*. Apparently the Vatican Grammarian or his source made a deliberate attempt to achieve some uniformity in the technical terms, and this attempt itself sets the *De Chria* apart from the other treatments of the chreia.

In his actual classification, however, the Vatican Grammarian shows a fairly close resemblance to Hermogenes, Aphthonius and even Nicolaus. Moreover, if we ignore for the moment Theon's detailed analysis, the Vatican Grammarian divides the chreia in much the same way as that Greek rhetorician does.

The Vatican Grammarian gives more detail than Aphthonius, who limits his division to the three classes before turning rather abruptly to the ἐργασία. He gives more detail than Nicolaus, who, despite the length of his chapter on the chreia, simply identifies the three classes and then lists two species of the sayings-chreia: ἀποφαντικόν and ἀποκριτικόν. And in a sense he gives more detail than Hermogenes, who begins with the three classes and is content to divide the sayings-chreiai into three species: ἀποφαντικαί, ἐρωτηματικαί and πυσματικαί, with the last two being in effect sub-species of the ἀποκριτικαί.

The major differences between the Vatican Grammarian's classification and those of the Greek rhetoricians are to be found in two places. One is his designation of a species of sayings-chreiai which he calls *refutativa*, but as we have seen, Theon included this type and called it a double chreia. Still, the Vatican Grammarian's designation is signularly apt, for in the two examples we have (cf. Chreiai 9 and 24) the retort of the second speaker serves as a rebuttal to the remark of the first.[21] Either the Vatican Grammarian himself or his source showed enough independent judgment to give this species of chreia a more appropriate name than the one it had before.

The second major difference is that the Vatican Grammarian has shown more innovation by adding a fourth class of chreia which he calls *demonstrativum* ("with a demonstration"). This addition raises some interesting points. First, the Greek rhetorical tradition is consistent in identifying only three classes of chreiai. The Vatican Grammarian's fourth class is unique in extant writings.

Secondly, the Vatican Grammarian's different approach here may be a further indication of some controversy among the rhetoricians. It is no coincidence that the very type of chreia which he calls *demonstrativum* seems to have been a point of disagreement. Both Theon and Nicolaus use it as an example of a mixed chreia, but they do so for different reasons. Yet the Vatican Grammarian says that "some people assign it to a species of action-chreia."[22] This observation indicates not only more controversy but also a tradition different from any we know.

As a matter of fact, this type of chreia, whether we consider it as an example of a species or follow the Vatican Grammarian and assign it the status of a separate class, does indeed show special characteristics. It can appear as a species of action-chreia if we consider only those versions where the πρόσωπον limits his response to a physical act, i.e.

brandishing a weapon, pointing his hand, etc. On the other hand, if we use those versions which make the πρόσωπον add some remark to his action, the example becomes a mixed chreia according to the definitions of Hermogenes, Aphthonius and Nicolaus.

In every version, however, the action of the πρόσωπον is symbolic. When the Laconian (Chreia 45) silently raises his weapon in response to some such question as "How far do the boundaries of Sparta extend?" his action speaks volumes about the Spartan state. Even if he adds some such brief remark as "Here" or "As far as this reaches," the symbolism and significance of his action remain.[23]

In this respect, then, the Vatican Grammarian's assigning this type of chreia a special and more important role as a class of chreia is reasonable and understandable. His failure, however, to use proper terms, especially *genus*, in key places of the classification seems to have confused the scribe who copied Vaticanus 5216 — or at least some scribe. The result of this confusion is some apparent tampering with the text in one place. So, to this and to one other textual problem of a different type we can now turn.

The Latin Text. The text of the Vatican Grammarian's *De Chria* in Vaticanus 5216, as printed by Keil, seems surprisingly free of errors in view of the fact that the MS is so late. A few minor mistakes in spelling occur here and there, but they are obvious, and Keil has easily corrected them. There are, in fact, only two serious problems, one of which Keil recognized but could not solve and one which he failed to see.

The first problem appears in line 9 with the name which the MS gives as Titus Genetivus Cyrus. No person with this name, or any resembling it, appears elsewhere, and we have followed Keil in placing a dagger here. The unusual name may result from confused spelling or it may be correct and simply belong to someone unknown to us. Keil prints the third name with a small letter, thus implying that it is not a cognomen, but, unless the corruption extends beyond the one word, it is difficult to see what else could have stood here.

The message of the chreia is no less unsatisfactory in helping us identify the man. He could have been a philosopher or a rhetorician or, in the case of a Roman, a grammarian.[24] The general idea of the chreia may go back ultimately to the Platonic and Aristotelian[25] discussions about whether or not virtue can be taught, yet the statement seems somehow to have a Stoic ring to it.[26]

Whatever its source, a less than thorough search of the literature has failed to find the specific statement which this unknown πρόσωπον makes in Chreia 15. Consequently, we must for the moment be resigned to the dagger of despair, but in any case the matter is not important for an understanding of the *De Chria* as a whole.

Such, however, is not the case with the second problem, for it involves the very structure of the Vatican Grammarian's classification of the chreia. As we find this section in the MS, the classification appears in the following order (the numbers in parentheses refer to lines of the text in this volume):

> Genus 1 facti (3-6)
> Genus 2 dicti (7-12)
>> Species 1 praepositiva (8-10)
>> Species 2 percunctativa (11-14)
>> Species 3 refutativa (15-22)
> Genus 4 demonstrativum (29-34)
> Genus 3 coniunctiva (23-28)

Thus he begins by identifying two of the three traditional classes without using the term *genus*. Yet, although the genitives *facti* and *dicti* depend grammatically on *memoratio* (at least indirectly), the Vatican Grammarian could have clarified matters by adding at least one *generis*. Ellipsis, however, seems the rule rather than the exception in many rhetoricians and grammarians.

To continue the analysis: the Vatican Grammarian next clearly divides *dicti* into its three species: *in tres species dividitur* (6), and the following lines (7-22) present the three species of chreia, each with an example. Then the MS (29, which immediately follows 22 in Vaticanus 5216) suddenly has the Vatican Grammarian say *adicitur his quartum genus*, and these words introduce the type of chreia which he calls *demonstrativum* and which his Greek source has called δεικτικόν.

After the example which is provided, the MS has the Vatican Grammarian conclude (23) with the section which begins *est item et coniunctiva*. The last word here refers unmistakably to a mixed chreia, for the example is one which we recognize as everywhere conforming to this type. Furthermore, the mixed chreia is universally assigned the status of a class of chreia, not a species, and in every other classification it is the third class listed.

It must be the third class here as well, although the Vatican Grammarian has once again failed to use the term *genus*. As such, it clearly belongs earlier than the *quartum genus*, and a single reversing of the last two sections restores order to the Vatican Grammarian's classification. This transposition puts the mixed chreia in its regular third position after saying-chreia and action-chreia, and it gives the correct meaning to *quartum genus*.

Why did the displacement happen? No reason for an accidental confusion is apparent, i.e. no occasion for haplography or dittography, but grounds for suspecting a deliberate, though innocent, change certainly exist.

The fault lies partly with the scribe, partly with the author. The Vatican Grammarian (or his source) has created some obscurity by failing to use the appropriate form of *genus* in lines 2 and 7, although this is clearly what he must mean. Then, after dividing the *chria dicti* into its three species, he reaches the third class, i.e. *chria coniunctiva*. Yet even here he fails to identify this type of chreia as a *genus*. Only when he reaches the fourth class, the one which he is adding to the standard classification, does he emphasize the fact by using the words *quartum genus*. In the usual elliptical manner of these writers, he has assumed that the reader can easily recognize the first three *genera*. Because the additional one will be a surprise, he identifies it as a fourth class.

This assumption on the part of the Vatican Grammarian, with its attendant lack of precision and clarity in the wording, confused the scribe. Although he has made a reasonably accurate copy of the excerpt, he seems not to have understood fully the material which he was copying. He reads the words *in tres species dividitur* and saw the three terms which follow. Then his eye caught the phrase *adicitur his quartum quoque genus* and, without realizing the difference between *species* and *genus*, he assumed that the sentence was out of place and moved it so that the *quartum genus* followed immediately after the list of the three *species*.

Such an explanation is, of course, speculative, but it is also reasonable. Whatever the real cause may have been, the fact remains that the last two sentences of the excerpt have been reversed, and the change mars an otherwise simple arrangement of the Vatican Grammarian's classification of the chreia. That his addition of a fourth class is inconsistent with the classifications of other writers is beside the point. The Vatican Grammarian included a fourth class, and our purpose here is to present the text as he intended it to be.

NOTES

1. For a description of this ms and its contents, see H. Keil (ed.), *Grammatici Latini* (8 vols.; Leipzig: Teubner, 1855-78) 6.246-47.

2. In discussions of Latin passages the spelling of "chria-chriae" and "chreia-chreiai" is consistently inconsistent. Where the word is the author's, "chria-chriae" are used because that is his spelling. Discussions of the term itself use "chreia-chreiai" to conform with the practice in other sections of this volume.

3. See Keil, *Grammatici Latini*, 6.254. G. Fiske, *Lucilius and Horace* (Studies in Language and Literature 5; Madison: University of Wisconsin, 1920) 158, erroneously refers to 6.251 and repeats the error in the index (s.v. Charisius, p. 502), so it is not a printing error.

4. Even in his comments on the last section of Charisius Keil (*Grammatici Latini*, 1.287) makes no reference to this fragment or to Vaticanus 5216. Of course, the idea which he discusses in Vol. 6 may not yet have occurred to him when he was preparing Vol. 1.

5. See Diomedes (1.310 Keil). On the relationship between Diomedes and Charisius, see Keil, *Grammatici Latini*, 1.xlix-lvii.

6. Since declension is a topic for our second volume, this exercise of Diomedes will appear there.

7. See K. Barwick (ed.), *Charisii artis grammaticae libri V* (Leipzig: Teubner, 1925; repr. 1964).

8. Cf. p. 375, 10 and apparatus. Yet Barwick himself may have been remiss. Keil's *Grammatici Latini* was an important contribution to scholarship and even now continues to be the standard text for many of the writers whose works appear in his eight volumes. Consequently, Barwick should, at the very least, have discussed Keil's remark that the contents of this fragment were somehow related to Charisius' treatment of the same subjects. Furthermore, even a critical edition which has no full commentary should have found space to refute the erroneous attribution of the fragment to Charisius by Lejay and Fiske.

9. That Barwick did indeed disagree with Keil on numerous points is clear from his discussion on pp. xii-xxvi *passim*.

10. See P. Lejay (ed.), *OEuvres d' Horace, Satires* (Paris: Hachette, 1911).

11. See Fiske, *Lucilius and Horace*, 158.

12. See note 16 below.

13. See E. Haight, *The Roman Use of Anecdotes in Cicero, Livy and the Satirists* (New York: Longmans, 1940) 3. This book,

badly conceived and badly executed, is shallow to a shocking degree and contains very little that is useful.

14. Cf. M. Hammond, "A Famous EXEMPLUM of Spartan Toughness," *CJ* 75 (1979/80) 97-109, esp. 101 n. 15 and 103 n. 26. One scholar has avoided the pitfall: Bonner (*Education in Ancient Rome*) omits any reference to Lejay, Fiske, or Haight.

15. On the analogy of the Vatican Mythographers, three unknown compilers of mythological stories whose MS was found in the Vatican Library.

16. Yet Fiske (*Lucilius and Horace*, 158) goes so far as to say "our fullest definition of the χρεία is found in Charisius," and he then quotes the first seven words of VG. That his statement is meant to include Greek definitions seems clear from his use of χρεία rather than the Latin *chria*.

17. A glance at the definitions of Theon, Hermogenes, Aphthonius and Nicolaus of Myra reveals the importance and persistence of these elements. "Consciseness, character and usefulness" appear in all four definitions, "aptness and attribution" are missing only in Hermogenes, "specified" is found in Theon and Nicolaus but missing in Hermogenes and Aphthonius, though even here it is readily understood.

18. Haight (*Roman Use of Anecdotes*, 3) completely misunderstands this phrase and, indeed, the whole definition of VG. She translates it with "The chria is a clear account of something that has been said or something that has been done." Her unnecessarily verbose — and technically incorrect — translation of *dicti vel facti* shows that she does not really understand the language of such definitions. This lack of understanding is even more apparent in her translation of *praecipua memoratio* with "clear account." She has completely missed the point because she has not taken the trouble to read other definitions. Consequently, despite her assertion, this definition of the chreia is not really clear to her.

19. Nor does the *Oxford Latin Dictionary* include the term, though the omission is not surprising. The errors of omission and commission in this work could fill a good-sized volume.

20. These terms are discussed more fully in the notes to the translation.

21. For this reason the Catalogue of Chreiai lists each chreia which has two speakers under the name of the second. He is, in effect, the chief πρόσωπον.

22. See VG 29-30.

23. In view of the excellence of Chreia 45, one can only wonder why VG did not use it here at the very place where he was elevating this type of chreia to the status of class

(*genus*). It would seem to be a perfect choice. Was Chreia 45 unknown to him? Then he was not familiar with at least a part of the Greek rhetorical tradition or with Plutarch. Was he unaware of it except in the form of a mixed chreia? Whatever the case, his choice of example (Chreia 1) is undoubtedly the most inept chreia we have. It seems to be modeled on Chreia 45, but it has none of the symbolism, none of the aptness that is characteristic of the Laconian's action.

24. Two men by the name of Cyrus are worthy of mention. One is an Ephesian sophist to whom Philostratus refers in a disparaging way (cf. Philostratus, *V. Soph.* 605). He seems to have been a contemmporary of Philostratus and thus late 2nd-early 3rd c. A.D. THE OTHER MAN WROTE A GRAMMATICAL WORK ENTITLED Περὶ διαφορᾶς στάσεως WHICH C. WALZ EDITED (*Rhetores Graeci*, 8.387-99). SOME OF THE SECTIONS IN THIS BRIEF WORK DISCUSS ETHICAL SUBJECTS: E.G., περὶ κακοῦ βίου, περὶ κακοῦ ἔθους, BUT NO SUCH SENTIMENT AS THAT EXPRESSED IN CHREIA 15 APPEARS HERE.

According to Walz (*Rhetores Graeci*, 8.386) Fabricius raised the possibilty that this Cyrus is the same man as the sophist, yet both men seem to be Greek, and our πρόσωπον appears to have a Roman name. The subject deserves more study, for a correct identification of the man to whom VG refers could help us date VG himself, whose *aetas* remains unknown.

25. Cf., e.g., Plato, *Protag.* 345D-E, 352B-C, 375D, and Aristotle, *EN* 7.1145b 22ff, 1146a 7ff, and EE 2.1228a 5ff.

26. For similar and opposite sentiments, see Chreia 15 in the Catalogue of Chreiai.

TEXT
AND
TRANSLATION

De Chria

	Chria est dicti vel facti praecipua	
	memoratio: facti, ut (Chreia 25) "Diogenes,	
	cynicus philosophus, cum animadvertisset	
(273,10)	pueros nobiles inhumane cibum appetentes,	5
	paedagogum eorum scipione percussit."	

(273,10)

Chria est dicti vel facti praecipua
memoratio: facti, ut (Chreia 25) "Diogenes,
cynicus philosophus, cum animadvertisset
pueros nobiles inhumane cibum appetentes,   5
paedagogum eorum scipione percussit."
Dicti autem chria in tres species dividitur est enim (1) praepositiva, ut (Chreia 15)
"Titus + Genetivus Cyrus dixit viros bonos
scire oportere male agere, sed non agere."   10
(2) Percunctativa, ut (Chreia 11) "M. Porcius
Cato interrogatus quid ita post quadragesimum
annum litteras graecas disceret, dixit, 'non

(273,15) ut doctus, sed ut ne indoctus moriar.'" (3)
Refutativa, ut (Chreia 9) "Antisthenes,   15
cynicus philosophus, cum oluscula lavaret et
animadvertisset Aristippum, cyrenaeum philosophum, cum Dionysio, tyranno Siculorum, ingredientem, dixit, 'Aristippe, si his contentus
esses, non regis pedes sequereris.' cui   20
respondit Aristippus, 'at tu si posses commode cum rege loqui, non his contentus esses.'"

(273,22) Est item et coniunctiva, ut (Chreia 29)
"Diogenes, cynicus philosophus, cum manu
haurientem rusticum ad potandum aquam   25

(273,25) vidisset, poculum, quod in pera gerebat, abiecit et dixit, 'hoc ego levior esse iam
possum.'"

(273,20) Adicitur his quartum quoque genus, quod
graece δεικτικόν dicitur, latine demonstra-   30
tivum dici potest, ut (Chreia 1) "Achilles
interrogatus quem ad modum vicisset Hectorem,
arma ostendit." Quam quidam in facti speciem
redegerunt.

9: De nomine vide proemii adn. 23.
23: Ordinem versuum 23-28 et 29-34 retroegi.

On the Chreia[1]

A chreia is a special kind of reminiscence of a saying or action.[2] Of an action, as (Chreia 25): *Diogenes, the Cynic philosopher, when he noticed some well-born boys attacking their food in an ill-mannered way, struck their paedagogus with a staff.*

The sayings-chreia, however, is divided into three species: (1) Declarative,[3] as (Chreia 15): *Titus + Genetivus Cyrus*[4] *said that good men should know how to behave badly but should not do so.* (2) In response to a question,[5] as (Chreia 11): *Marcus Porcius Cato, on being asked why he was learning Greek past the age of forty, said, "Not that I may die learned, but that I may not die unlearned."* (3) With a rebuttal,[6] as (Chreia 9): *Antisthenes, the Cynic philosopher, when he was washing greens and noticed Aristippus, the Cyrenaic philosopher, walking with Dionysius, the Sicilian tyrant, said, "Aristippus, if you were content with these greens, you would not be dogging the footsteps of a king." To him Aristippus replied, "Well, if you could converse profitably with a king, you would not be content with them."*

There is likewise[7] the mixed chreia,[8] as (Chreia 29): *Diogenes, the Cynic philosopher, when he saw a rustic taking up water with his hand in order to drink, threw away the cup which he was carrying in his knapsack and said, "Now I can be this much lighter."*

In addition to these, there is also a fourth class which in Greek is called δεικτικόν, in Latin can be called *demonstrativum*,[9] as (Chreia 1): *Achilles, on being asked how he had defeated Hector, showed his weapons.* But some people[10] have assigned this chreia to a species of action-chreia.

COMMENTS

1. Since the introduction has dealt with most of the problems of structure and content, the few comments here are concerned with isolated points.

2. Although VG later (24-28) takes up the mixed chreia, he omits it here. In this regard he departs from the definition of Hermogenes, but follows Theon, Aphthonius, and Nicolaus.

3. The term *praepositiva*, like several other terms in this section, seems not to appear elsewhere, but it obviously identifies the species called ἀποφαντικόν. Priscian (line 28) uses *indicativi* (sc. *usus*) to translate Hermogenes' ἀποφαντικαί (sc. χρεῖαι). This species resembles a maxim, for the only difference is that when an unattributed maxim is attributed to a character it becomes a chreia, specifically a gnomic chreia (cf. Theon 124). Cf. also Quintilian 20-21.

4. On the problems in this name, see the "Introduction," pp. 280-281 above.

5. The term *percunctativa*, unattested elsewhere, translates ἀποκριτικόν. As observed in the chapter on Priscian (see Comment 18 to the translation), no Roman treatment of the subject makes a distinction between the types of questions to which the character responds. Thus *percunctativa* includes both κατ' ἐρώτησιν and κατὰ πύσμα, though actually the chreia of Cato is an example of the latter.

6. On the meaning and appropriateness of *refutativa*, see the "Introduction," p. 278 above. For another example of this kind of chreia, see Chreia 24.

7. On the position of these two sections, see the "Introduction," pp. 280-282 above.

8. The term *coniunctiva* occurs only here (cf. "Introduction," p. 278 above). The usual word is some form of *mixtus*.

9. On *demonstrativum*, see the "Introduction," pp. 279-280 above. The Greek term δεικτικόν is not used by the Greek rhetoricians in their discussions of the chreia, but in some versions of Chreia 45 the action of the character is indicated by ἔδειξεν.

10. These "some people" must remain unknown. As we pointed out in the Introduction, this type of chreia can reasonably be considered a species of action-chreia, but none of the classifications which we have places it in this category.

CATALOGUE OF CHREIAI

by

RONALD F. HOCK
EDWARD N. O'NEIL

INTRODUCTION

In the bulk of Greek and Latin writings which have come down to us hundreds, perhaps even thousands, of chreiai appear. It would be a worthwhile — and monumental — task to collect and analyze them all, but that is not our intention in this Catalogue of Chreiai.

Here we have assembled only the 68 different chreiai which the writers whom we are studying in these volumes saw fit to use in one way or another. We have arranged these chreiai alphabetically according to the name of the chief πρόσωπον. Where the same πρόσωπον appears in more than one chreia, each chreia has its own number, and the order follows the sequence of appearance in the texts. A good example is Diogenes in Chreiai 22-36. Moreover, this chreia-number appears not only in the Catalogue but also at the appropriate place in both the text and the translation of each author, usually just before the quotation of the chreia.

Some chreiai appear only once, some two or three times, while a few seem to have been especially popular or useful among Greek rhetoricians and Latin grammarians and are consequently found in numerous passages.

For a variety of reasons, many chreiai differ from text to text. Some of these differences are slight, some are significant. Among the latter are such matters as ἀναφορά (attribution to a πρόσωπον), διαίρεσις (classification as sayings-chreia, action-chreia or mixed chreia), and ἀπαγγελία (expression or wording).

In the Catalogue, however, the text and translation of each chreia are the same as those in its first appearance in the corpus of rhetorical compositions which constitute the basic texts of this study. Minor verbal differences in the various appearances of the same chreia have usually not been noted. For these differences readers must check for themselves by using the citations which immediately follow the text and translation.

These citations are arranged in a deliberate sequence.

First come those writers whose treatment of the chreia appears in Volume I, and they are listed in the order in which they appear (for the abbreviations see the list given below): Theon, Quint, Hermog, Prisc, Aphth, NicMyra, Vat Gram. After these seven appear the eleven authors who deal primarily with exercises involving the chreia, the subject of Volume II. These are PSI, BritMus, Diom, PBour, Nic, Lib, Greg, NicephCall, NicephBas, Georg, ProgAnon. Finally, in immediate sequence, come the seven authors whose primary function is to provide commentary on the passages contained in Volume I, the subject of Volume III. These authors are: JohnSard, Dox, Planud, Matt, Darm, EpitAnon, and ScholAnon.

After the citations to the authors of the rhetorical tradition come references to authors who alluded to, quoted or otherwise used chreiai. Here appear the names of such writers as Plutarch, Diogenes Laertius, Athenaeus, Cicero, Seneca, Aulus Gellius and the various collections of *gnomologiae*, although we have made no special attempt to find every such reference in ancient literature. For each of these writers we have identified the edition used (if they are not available in the Loeb edition). Thus references, say, to Stobaeus include the volume and page of the edition by C. Wachsmuth and O. Hense.

The same procedure is used for the eighteen rhetorical texts which will appear in our two subsequent volumes. Since we have not yet established our own texts, we have found it necessary to cite the currently standard edition. Thus references to JohnSard include page and line from H. Rabe's edition.

ABBREVIATIONS

In the following list, the standard text is provided for each author who does not appear in Volume I. For the seven authors in Volume I the name of the editor(s) and "Chreia I" are added.

Aphth	=	Aphthonius of Antioch (Butts-Hock, Chreia I)
BritMus	=	British Museum Add. ms 37516 (F. G. Kenyon, *JHS* 29 [1909] 29-31)
Darm	=	Darmstadt Fragment (1.141-43 Walz)
Diom	=	Diomedes (1.310 Keil)
Dox	=	Doxapatres (2.247-86 Walz)
EpitAnon	=	Anonymous Epitome (1.129-30 Walz)
Georg	=	Georgius (1.553-55 Walz)
GregCyp	=	Gregorius (or Georgius) of Cyprus (J. Fr. Boissonade, ΑΝΕΚΔΟΤΑ: *Anecdota Graeca e Codicibus Regiis* [5 vols.; Paris, 1829-33; repr. Hildesheim: Olms, 1962] 2.269-73)
Hermog	=	Hermogenes of Tarsus (Mack-O'Neil, Chreia I)
JohnSard	=	Ioannis Sardianus (pp. 34-55 Rabe)
Lib	=	Libanius (8.63-102 Foerster)
Matt	=	Matthaeus Cameriota (1.122-23 Walz)
Nic	=	Nicolaus (1.272-78 Walz)
NicephBas	=	Nicepherus Basilicus (1.442-49 Walz)
NicephCall	=	Nicepherus Callistus Xanthopulus (J. Glettner, *BZ* 33 [1933] 9-10)
NicMyra	=	Nicolaus of Myra (Grabbe-Hock, Chreia I)

PBour	=	Papyrus Bouriant (P. Collart, *Les papyrus Bouriant* [Paris; Champion, 1926] 23-24)
Planud	=	Maximus Planudes (2.ix-x; 15-21 Walz)
Prisc	=	Priscian (O'Neil, Chreia I)
ProgAnon	=	Anonymous Progymnasmata (1.602-05 Walz)
PSI	=	*Papiri greci e latini* (Publicazioni della Societa italiana per la ricerca dei papiri greci e latini in Egitto [Firenze, 1912] Vol. 1, no. 85)
Quint	=	Marcus Fabius Quintilianus, *Inst. Orat.* 1.9,1-10,1 (O'Neil, Chreia I)
ScholAnon	=	Anonymous Scholia (2.585-91 Walz)
Theon	=	Aelius Theon of Alexandria (Hock-O'Neil, Chreia I)
VatGram	=	Vatican Grammarian (O'Neil, Chreia I)

CATALOGUE

1. Achilles

Achilles interrogatus quem ad modum
vicisset Hectorem arma ostendit.

Achilles, on being asked how he had defeated
Hector, showed his weapons.

VatGram 31-33

This chreia technically belongs to the same species as
Chreia 45 (Laconian), but its sense is puerile and fails to
provide the same insight into the character of either the
situation or the πρόσωπον which the other chreia does.

2. Aesop

Αἴσωπος ὁ μυθοποιὸς ἐρωτηθεὶς τί
ἐστιν ἰσχυρότατον ⟨τῶν⟩ ἐν ἀνθρώποις
εἶπεν· "⟨ὁ⟩ λόγος."

Aesop the fable writer, on being asked what the
most potent thing among men's possessions is,
said: "Speech."

NicMyra 118-20; Planud 2.19, 6-7; Darm 1.143, 15-16; ScholAnon 2.587, 26-28

Although this chreia appears four times in the rhetorical
tradition, there are no significant differences, which is not
surprising, given the literary dependence (direct or indirect)
of Planud, Darm, and ScholAnon on NicMyra. Hence Aesop
remains the πρόσωπον throughout, and the form of the chreia
is always ἀποκριτικὸν κατὰ πύσμα. Indeed, even the ἀπαγγελία
of the chreia is in virtually the same words (cf. Theon 195-98).

We have not found this chreia outside the rhetorical
tradition, although several passages are reminiscent of it and
deserve attention here. Thus the same sentiment appears
in ps.-Menander, *Mon.* 361 (p. 53 Jaekel): "There is nothing more
potent than speech." Similarly, in a chreia attributed to
Demosthenes, the question is not the same but the answer
is: Demosthenes, on being asked what the greatest weapon
is, said: "Speech" (*Gnom. Vat.* 219 [p. 87 Sternbach]). For the
same question but different response, see Athenaeus, 10.451b-
c.

For a chreia similar to this one, see Chreia 63.

3. Alexander

Ἀλέξανδρος ὁ τῶν Μακεδόνων βασιλεύς,
παρακαλούμενος ὑπὸ τῶν φίλων συναγαγεῖν
χρήματα, εἶπεν· "Ἀλλὰ ταῦτα οὐκ
ὤνησεν οὐδὲ Κροῖσον."

Alexander the Macedonian king, on being urged
by his friends to amass money, said: "But it didn't
help even Croesus."

Theon 151-53; Dox 2.258, 11-13

Gnom. Vat. 90 (p. 42 Sternbach)

Croesus, of course, is a proverbial figure of a ruler who
possessed both the enormous wealth and attendant pride
that precede disaster (cf. Herodotus, 1.30-35, 85-90 *et passim*).
This chreia employs both themes (wealth and pride) and
therefore conveys a different lesson from the chreia which
Plutarch cites (*Reg. et imp. apoph.* 181E) in which Alexander
makes a similar remark about Darius.

4. Alexander

Ἀλέξανδρος ὁ τῶν Μακεδόνων βασιλεὺς
ἐρωτηθεὶς ὑπό τινος ποῦ ἔχει τοὺς
θησαυρούς, " Ἐν τούτοις, " ἔφη δείξας
τοὺς φίλους.

Alexander the Macedonian king, on being asked
by someone where he had his treasures, pointed
to his friends and said: "In these."

Theon 158-61; Lib 8.63, 3-4; JohnSard 42, 20-21; Dox 2.259, 10-12; 283,
22-23; ScholAnon 2.586, 33-587, 2.

Ammianus Marcellinus, 25.4.15. See *Gnom. Vat.* 86 (p. 39 Sternbach) and
Gnom. Par. 110 (p. 14 Sternbach) where the remark is attributed to Antigonus.

Although the different versions of this chreia use a
variety of expressions to convey the same idea, the most
interesting difference results from the fact that this is one
of the few chreiai in our collection which appear in all three
classes of the form (Chreia 45 is another): sayings-chreia
(Ammianus Marcellinus), action-chreia (Lib, Dox, ScholAnon),
mixed chreia (Theon, JohnSard).

The central idea of the chreia, i.e., that friends are
treasures, was a commonplace. See, e.g., ps.-Menander, *Mon.*
810 (p. 79 Jaekel) and PBour 1 (p. 25 Collart).

5. Alexander

'Αλέξανδρος ἐρωτηθεὶς πόθεν ἐκτήσατο
ταυσαύτην δυναστείαν, ἔφη, " Μηδὲν εἰς
αὔριον ἀναβαλλόμενος."

Alexander, on being asked from what source he had acquired such great power, said: "By putting nothing off until tomorrow."

JohnSard 40, 6-8

This chreia occurs only the one time in the rhetorical texts, but similar chreiai appear elsewhere. See *Gnom. Vat.* 74 (p. 34 Sternbach) where several examples appear with a number of variations in both the question and in the reply. To this list we may add Stobaeus, 4.13.48 (p. 364 Hense) where Alexander makes a characteristic reply to a similar question by quoting Homer, although the line which he quotes does not appear in any Homeric text (cf. Hense's note). On Alexander's fondness for quoting Homer, see Dio, *Orat.* 2.3ff. For an example of this fondness, see Chreia 24.

6. Antisthenes

Μὴ εἰκος ἐστιν
'Αντισθένην ('Αττικόν γε ὄντα) παραγενόμενον
'Αθήνηθεν εἰς Λακεδαίμονα, ἐκ τῆς
γυναικωνίτιδος λέγειν εἰς τὴν
ἀνδρωνῖτιν ἐπιέναι.

It is unlikely that
Antisthenes (who was of course an Athenian) said on coming from Athens to Lacedaemon that he was coming from the men's quarters to the women's.

Theon 363-66; Nic 1.275, 17-19

Diogenes Laertius, 6.59; Aulus Gellius, *N.A.* 17.21.33

This chreia appears only three times, twice in the rhetorical traditioin and once elsewhere, but the differences in these passages are significant in three respects: ἀναφορά, ἀπαγγελία, and ὑποδιαίρεσις. (This chreia is also the subject of an ἐργασία in Nic [see 1.275, 20-276, 32] and hence will receive treatment in that respect in Volume II of *The Chreia in Ancient Rhetoric.*)

Variations in attribution are frequent among the chreiai of this collection and elsewhere, but in this instance we also find explicit reflection on the chreia's attribution. In his discussion of ἀνασκευή Theon (cf. 334-83) illustrates the criticism from implausibility by using this chreia (362-66). He knew of this chreia as one attributed to the Cynic Antisthenes. For Theon, however, it was implausible that an Athenian philosopher would speak so disparagingly of Athens.

Theon does not go on to name a more plausible πρόσωπον but Nic and Diogenes Laertius (aware of Theon's criticism?) attribute this chreia to another Cynic, Diogenes of Sinope. Aulus Gellius attributes this saying to Alexander Molossus, king of Epirus and uncle of Alexander, although in this case the metaphor of men's and women's quarters refers to Rome and Persia. Indeed, the use of this metaphor is no doubt proverbial (see, e.g., Plutarch, *De cohib. ira.* 457C).

Variations in recitation are numerous. Theon, e.g., has Antisthenes go from Athens to Lacedaemon, but Nic and Diogenes Laertius have Diogenes going from Lacedaemon to Athens.

The most significant change in recitation, however, is better discussed in terms of classification. In Theon Antisthenes makes his saying simply on arriving in Lacedaemon, thereby making this chreia ἀποφαντικὸν καθ' ἑκούσιον. In Nic and Diogenes Laertius, however, Diogenes makes his saying in response to the standard question ποῖ καὶ πόθεν, thus turning the chreia into one called ἀποκριτικὸν κατὰ πύσμα. In other words, the change in recitation amounts to a change in form.

7. Aphthonius

'Αφθονίου τοῦ ῥήτορος τὸ εἰς πεῖραν
ἧκον ἀνιαρὸν εἰς ἀφαίρεσιν εἶναι
εἰπόντος, τὸ ῥηθὲν ἀπομνημονεύεται.

Aphthonius the rhetor's statement, when he said that what we've come to possess is distressing at its loss, is remembered.

Dox 2.282, 12-14

This chreia, which appears only here, is the subject of an ἐργασία in Dox (see 2.282, 14-283, 21) and hence will receive treatment again in Volume II of *The Chreia in Ancient Rhetoric*.

At this point, however, the κλίσις of this chreia deserves comment. For it is the only chreia outside the context of discussions of κλίσις (see Theon 199-275 and NicMyra 14-38) that is recited with the πρόσωπον in the genitive case: 'Αφθονίου τοῦ ῥήτορος. Accordingly, we also have a complementary formula: ⟨εἰπόντος⟩ τὸ ῥηθὲν ἀπομνημονεύεται.

Surprisingly, though, Dox has not declined this chreia according to the rules as set forth by Theon, nor does he follow the practice of this manipulation as we find it in school texts. Thus Theon (226-42) gives two formulae for sayings-chreiai in the genitive case. If, as in Chreia 7, it is ἀποφαντικὸν καθ' ἑκούσιον, the formula is τὸ ῥηθὲν μνήμης ἔτυχε. But if it is any other species of sayings-chreia, the formula is λόγος ἀπομνημονεύεται. In the school text (BritMus) the formula is λόγος ἀπομνημονεύεται, as it is in NicMyra 24-27. Dox, however, has thus used a hybrid form: τὸ ῥηθὲν ἀπομνημονεύεται. And yet, elsewhere (see, e.g., 2.264, 20) he uses the correct formula.

8. Aristeides

'Αριστείδης ἐρωτηθεὶς τί ἐστι τὸ
δίκαιον, εἶπε· " Τὸ μὴ ἐπιθυμεῖν
τῶν ἀλλοτρίων. "

Aristeides, on being asked what justice is, said:
"Not desiring the possessions of others."

NicMyra 122-24; Planud 2.19, 8-9; Darm 1.143, 17-18; ScholAnon 2.587, 29-31

Stobaeus, 3.9.32 (p. 357 Hense)

This chreia is always paired in the rhetorical texts with Chreia 2 and thus appears in the same four sources as that chreia. Moreover, like Chreia 2, this chreia appears with no significant changes. Even the ἀπαγγελία of it is virtually identical, not to mention attribution and form. (Incidentally, Darm breaks off mid-way in this chreia, but what is preserved suggests no changes in what has been lost.)

The appearance of this chreia in Stobaeus also shows no significant changes. Still, Stobaeus' inclusion of this chreia in his section entitled Περὶ δικαιοσύνης and his identification of Aristeides as ὁ δίκαιος only underscore how εὐστόχως the attribution is. For Aristeides came to be regarded as pre-eminently the just man (see, e.g., Dio, *Orat.* 64.27, and Philostratus, *V. Apoll.* 6.21). What better πρόσωπον could be asked about the essence of justice?

9. Aristippus-Antisthenes

Antisthenes, cynicus philosophus, cum
oluscula lavaret et animadvertisset
Aristippum, Cyrenaeum philosophum, cum
Dionysio, tyranno Siculorum, ingredientem,
dixit, "Aristippe, si his contentus esses,
non regis pedes sequereris." cui respondit
Aristippus, "at tu si posses commode cum
rege, non his contentus esses."

Antisthenes, the Cynic philosopher, when he was
washing greens and noticed Aristippus, the
Cyrenaic philosopher, walking with Dionysius, the
Sicilian tyrant, said, "Aristippus, if you were
content with these greens, you would not be
dogging the footsteps of a king." To him
Aristippus replied, "Well, if you could converse
profitably with a king, you would not be content
with them."

VatGram 15-22

Diogenes Laertius, 2.68, 102; 6.58; Horace, *Epist.* 1.17.13-32; Valerius Maximus,
4.3.4; ps.-Diogenes, *ep.* 32.3 (p. 138 Malherbe); *Gnom. Vat.* 192 (p. 78 Sternbach).
Cf. also E. Mannebach, *Aristippi et Cyrenaicorum Fragmenta* (Leiden: Brill, 1961)
frags. 52A-C and 53A-B.

This chreia is an example of a double chreia (cf. Theon
84-95), but even for this species it is long. Perhaps its very
length is the reason that it appears only the one time in
rhetorical texts although it if found numerous times and in
a variety of forms in literary texts and commentaries.

The most important variations involve the identity of the
two speakers, yet in most cases one (usually the first)
represents the ascetic side of Cynicism, the other (usually
the second) is spokesman for hedonistic Cynicism. Since the
second speaker delivers the "punch line" in every case, he
is to be considered the chief πρόσωπον and is consequently
listed first in any reference to the chreia.

Thus in Diogenes Laertius, 2.68, we have Diogenes-
Aristippus, while in Valerius Maximus the order is the reverse,
as it is also implied in the ps.-Diogenean letter. In Diogenes
Laertius, 2.102, the speakers are Metrodorus and Theodorus,
and in 6.58 they are Plato and Diogenes. It is interesting
to notice that Antisthenes appears in this chreia nowhere
except in VatGram.

The earliest and most interesting use of Chreia 9 appears
in Horace's epistle, where the speakers are *mordax
cynicus*-Aristippus. Since the name Diogenes cannot fit the
dactylic hexameter, we may reasonably suppose that Horace's
"biting Cynic" is actually Diogenes. In any case, the
conversation between this unnamed Cynic and Aristippus
provides the very basis for the whole poem.

Finally, in *Gnom. Vat.* 350 (p. 135 Sternbach) we may have
an example of this chreia reduced to a simple sayings-chreia
where Theocritus of Chios is the πρόσωπον.

10. Bion

Βίων ὁ σοφιστὴς τὴν φιλαργυρίαν
μητρόπολιν ἔλεγε πάσης κακίας εἶναι.

Bion the sophist used to say that love of money
is the mother-city of every evil.

Theon 125-26, 368-69; Dox 2.257, 29-30; Darm 1.142,18-19; Planud 2.17,
25-18,1

Diogenes Laertius, 6.50; Stobaeus, 3.10.37 (p. 147 Hense); *Gnom. Vat.* 265
(p. 102 Sternbach)

Most noteworthy of the many occurrences of this chreia,
both within and without the rhetorical tradition, is the
variation in ἀναφορά. Theon of course attributes this chreia
to Bion, but elsewhere in the rhetorical tradition the
attribution is always to Bias. Outside the tradtion the
attribution is more varied. Stobaeus once again has Bion, but
Diogenes Laertius attributes this saying to Diogenes, the
Gnom. Vat. to Democritus, and the *florilegium Monacense* to
Demetrius of Phalerum (as cited in Sternbach, *Gnomologium
Vaticanum*, p. 102).

This variation in attribution is hardly surprising, given the
gnomic character of the saying. The sentiment is very
widespread, appearing, e.g., albeit with a different metaphor,
in 1 Tim 6.10. Likewise, the metaphor of the μητρόπολις occurs
elsewhere—e.g., in Athenaeus (10.443c) where it is wine that
is the μητρόπολις of every evil. Consequently, with nothing
distinctive in sentiment or in expression, it would be difficult,
if not impossible, to identify the historically correct πρόσωπον.

Nevertheless, rhetorically speaking, Bias is perhaps the
most defensible. For as one of the wise men Bias is a εὔστοχος
attribution since gnomic wisdom is especially characteristic
of the wise men (see Diogenes Laertius, 1.35 [Thales], 60, 63
[Solon], 69-70 [Chilon], 76-78 [Pittacus], 87-88 [Bias], 91-93
[Cleobulus], etc.).

11. Cato, Marcus Porcius

M. Porcius Cato interrogatus quid ita
post quadragesimum annum litteras graecas
disceret, dixit, "non ut doctus, sed ut
ne indoctus moriar."

M. Porcius Cato, on being asked why he was
learning Greek literature after the age of forty,
said, "Not that I may die learned, but that I
may not die unlearned."

VatGram 11-14

This chreia which occurs only the one time may have been composed on the basis of Cicero, *De sen.* 8.26. The same subject is mentioned by Quint *(Inst.* 12.11.23) and by Plutarch *(Cato,* ch. 2 [337D]). Elsewhere Cato is said to have begun his study of Greek literature at age 80, but the author of this chreia may have read the Ciceronian Cato's words *qui litteras Graecas senex didici* literally and altered *senex* to *post quadragesimum annum.*

12. Cato, Marcus Porcius

Marcus Porcius Cato dixit leges
nervos esse civitatium

Marcus Porcius Cato said that laws are the
sinews of states.

Diom 1.310, 20

This chreia, which appears in Latin form only the one time, may be an example of a chreia which has been translated from Greek with its πρόσωπον changed to an apt Roman figure. *Gnom. Vat.* 211 (p. 85 Sternbach) gives the Greek form and attributes the saying to Demosthenes: ὁ αὐτὸς ἔφησε τοὺς νόμους δημοκρατίας νεῦρα. The Greek version, in turn, may have been composed on the basis of Demosthenes' *De fals. leg.* 283.

13. Chaeremon

Χαιρήμων ἔφη, " Πάντα τὰ ἀγαθὰ ἐν
μόνῳ τῷ φρονεῖν ἐστιν."

Chaeremon said, "Every good exists in reasoning
alone."

Georg 1.553, 21-22

The language of this chreia suggests that the πρόσωπον is a Stoic or at least influenced by Stoicism. Yet he cannot be Chaeremon of Alexandria *(RE* 7), who was a teacher of the young Nero and the subject of Martial's *Epigr.* 11.56 or at least called to mind by the epigrammatist in that poem. The ἐργασία which Georg composed on Chreia 13 says that Chaeremon was, among other things, a successful general, and we have no such information about the Stoic.

The same statement holds true for the 4th cent. BC poet named Chaeremon *(RE* 5), whose style and themes alone would seem to rule him out as the πρόσωπον. In fact, none of the

men named Chaeremon known to us seems to be a candidate
for the πρόσωπον of Chreia 13. We must therefore assume that
he is otherwise unknown.

14. Crates

Crates, cum indoctum puerum vidisset,
paedagogum eius percussit.

Crates, when he saw an uneducated boy, struck
his paedagogus.

Quint 26-27

This chreia is very similar to Chreiai 25-26 and might
arguably be included under either of them. Certainly the
action of striking the paedagogus is the same. Nevertheless,
this chreia is distinctive in two respects and so seems to
merit separate treatment. On the one hand, the πρόσωπον here
is Crates, not his more famous teacher, Diogenes, as it always
is in Chreiai 25-26. On the other hand, the περίστασις which
prompts Crates' action is his seeing an uneducated boy, not
a youth who was a gourmand (so Chreia 25) nor a youth who
was misbehaving (so Chreia 26). In other words, the
Traditionsgeschichte of this chreia appears to be
independent of the others, even though the chreia is
obviously similar.

On the action of striking a paedagogus, see the discussion
of Chreia 25.

15. Cyrus, Titus Genetius (?)

Titus + Genetius Cyrus + dixit viros
bonos scire oportere male agere, sed
non agere.

Titus + Genetius Cyrus + said that good men
should know how to act badly but should not do
so.

VatGram 9-10

This chreia may be ultimately based on some such Platonic
passages as *Resp.* 3.396A or *Leg.* 7.816D-E. A similar idea
appears in Publilius Syrus 532, but in 721 the reverse is found:
Viri boni est nescire facere iniuriam ("It is the mark of a
good man not to know how to commit a wrong").

The name, and consequently the identity, of the πρόσωπον
is uncertain. No one with a name even remotely similar seems
to occur elsewhere, and the *nomen* is hardly Roman.

16. Damon

Δάμων ὁ παιδοτρίβης χωλοὺς ἔχων
τοὺς πόδας κλαπέντων αὐτοῦ τῶν
ὑποδημάτων ἔφη, " Εἴθε ἐναρμόσειε
τῷ κλέπτῃ."

Damon the gymnastic teacher whose feet were
deformed, when his shoes had been stolen, said:
"May they fit the thief."

Theon 154-57; NicMyra 93-96; JohnSard 51, 2-4; Dox 2.258, 14-16; Planud
2.18, 8-10; Darm 1.142, 27-29; Schol Anon 2.587, 12-14

Plutarch, *De aud. poet.* 18D; Athenaeus, 8.338a; *Gnom. Vat.* 284 (p. 110
Sternbach)

Within the rhetorical texts this chreia is always
attributed to Damon, but elsewhere the attribution varies,
although obviously the chreia requires a πρόσωπον who is lame.
Thus Plutarch knows of this chreia as attributed to a certain
cripple named Damonidas; Athenaeus to Dorion, the crippled
musician at the court of Philip; and *Gnom. Vat.* to a crippled
Theban named Eumonidas.

Not unexpectedly, the ἀπαγγελία varies considerably.
Athenaeus shows the most variation. Otherwise, only two
changes deserve comment. In Theon and Dox this chreia
illustrates an ἀπόφασις expressed εὐκτικῶς (cf. Theon 154);
hence the εἴθε c. opt. Elsewhere, however, the chreia is used
to illustrate the wit of chreiai and hence the tendency to
drop this grammatical construction (so NicMyra, JohnSard, and
ScholAnon). Also, the scene of the chreia sometimes is explicit,
but varies depending on the πρόσωπον; a bath for Damon (so
NicMyra and JohnSard) and a symposium for Dorion (so
Athenaeus).

17. Demosthenes

⟨ὅταν δείκνυμεν μὴ καλῶς φάμενον
τὸν Δημοσθένην⟩ ὑπόκρισιν εἶναι τὴν
ῥητορικήν.

⟨whenever we show that Demosthenes did not
speak properly in saying that⟩ rhetoric is simply
delivery.

Theon 356-57

This reference to Demosthenes' well-known analysis of
rhetoric may in fact not really be a chreia so much as an
allusion to one. Generally, the statement of Demosthenes is

longer and more detailed than Theon's simple version, for in response to a series of questions he says that in importance "delivery is first," then "second," then "third," etc. The obvious implication, as Theon puts it, is that "delivery is rhetoric" and hence "rhetoric is delivery." The version which includes all these details while retaining the form and flavor of a chreia is ps.-Plutarch, *Vit. dec. orat.* 845B.

Demosthenes' remark is, however, well-attested in non-chreia form. See, e.g., Cicero, *Brutus* 142; *Orat.* 17.56; *De Orat.* 3.56.213; Valerius Maximus, 8.10.1; Quint, *Inst.* 11.3.6; cf. also Dionysius of Halicarnassus, *Dem.* 53. *Gnom. Vat.* 217 (pp. 86-87 Sternbach) lists several other passages which refer in one way or another to Demosthenes' view of ὑπόκρισις.

If we consider Theon's version as a chreia, it is an instance of one appearing in the accusative case and thus an example of κλίσις which Theon discusses earlier (216-75, esp. 264-69 on the accusative case). Such a chreia in the nominative would undoubtedly be: ὁ Δημοσθένης ἔφη, "'Υπόκρισις ἐστιν ἡ ῥητορική."

18. Demosthenes

Demosthenes Atheniensis interrogatus
quo modo orator factus sit, respondit,
"Plus vino impendens olei."

Demosthenes the Athenian, on being asked how
an orator is made, replied: "By spending more on
oil than wine."

Diom 1.310, 21-22

Stobaeus, 3.29.90 (p. 655 Hense)

There are many references in ancient texts to Demosthenes' hard work, to his "burning the mid-night oil" and to his practice of drinking water instead of wine. For an extensive list of these references, see Sternbach, *Gnomologium Vaticanum*, pp. 82-83. This chreia, therefore, concisely summarizes this tradition in one brief remark and aptly attributes it to Demosthenes as the πρόσωπον. For a similar version of this chreia, see also *Gnom. Vat.* 204 (p. 82 Sternbach).

19. Demosthenes

Δημοσθένης ὁ ῥήτωρ ἐρωτηθεὶς ὑπό
τινος τί ῥητορικὴ περιποιεῖ τοῖς
μανθάνουσιν, εἶπεν (*Il.* 24.369, etc.),
"Ἄνδρ' ἐπαμύνασθαι ὅτε τις πρότερος χαλεπήνῃ"

Demosthenes the orator, on being asked by
someone what advantage rhetoric gives to those
who learn it, said (*Il.* 24.369) "Defense against a
man when he is angry first."

JohnSard 40, 20-23

This chreia is an example of the technique of quoting
Homer as the answer to almost any question. The verse here
appears three times in the Homeric poems: *Il.* 24.369; *Od.* 16.72;
21.133. Standard editions read ἀπαμύνασθαι, but in the first
and third passages here some MSS have ἐπαμύνασθαι, and
JohnSard (or his source) seems to have used a MS belonging
to the same class. Cf. *Gnom. Vat.* 360 (p. 139 Sternbach) where
the saying is attributed to Isocrates.

20. Demosthenes

Δημοσθένης ὁ ῥήτωρ ἰδὼν πεδήτην ἐπὶ
πολὺν χρόνον λουόμενον εἶπε, " Θάρσει·
οὐ μὴ ἐκλυθῆς. "

Demosthenes the orator, on seeing a prisoner
bathing for a long time, said, "Don't worry, you
won't get free."

JohnSard 43, 10-11.

This chreia is cited as one of two examples (Chreia 65
is the other) of chreiai which contain only wit, and JohnSard
says, "The phrase οὐ μὴ ἐκλυθῆς is spoken by the orator in
a witty fashion but also politely." The "witty" sense must
be "you won't get free," while the "polite" sense must be
"you aren't discouraged." There may be an additional pun
which JohnSard failed to mention: a play on the sound of
λουόμενον and ἐκλυθῆς (i.e. ἐκλουθῆς: "you won't get clean," i.e.,
"clear of the chains").
The aptness of Demosthenes as the πρόσωπον of such a
chreia is questionable. Tthere is no tradition of Demosthenes
as a man fond of jesting like this. Rather the reverse seems
true. Cf., e.g., Plutarch's *Comparison* of Demosthenes and
Cicero, ch. 1 (886D-F). The life of Demosthenes in ps.-Plutarch,
Vit. dec. orat. 844A-848D, fails to mention wit even once.

21. Didymon

Διδύμων ὁ αὐλητὴς ἁλοὺς ἐπὶ μοιχείᾳ
ἐκ τοῦ ὀνόματος ἐκρεμάσθη.

Didymon the flute-player, on being convicted of
adultery, was hanged by his namesake.

Theon 103-104, 248-50, 262-63, cf. 343-44; JohnSard 42, 14-15; Dox 2.257, 20-21; Planud 2.17, 21-23

Diogenes Laertius, 6.51

The pun in ἐκ τοῦ ὀνόματος (=ἐκ τῶν διδύμων) results from the (slang?) meaning of δίδυμος as "testicles." See, e.g., Philodemus in the *Greek Anthology* 5.126, 6 (Loeb) and LXX Deut 25.11.

Diogenes Laertius includes this chreia among those attributed to Diogenes, but has recited it as a sayings-chreia in which Diogenes is the πρόσωπον who comments on the plight of Didymon, using, of course, the same pun. In 6.68 Didymon appears in a Diogenes chreia, but now the "pair" involved is the eyes.

22. Diogenes

Διογένης ὁ φιλόσοφος ἐρωτηθεὶς ὑπό
τινος πῶς ἂν ἔνδοξος γένοιτο ἀπεκρίνατο,
"῝Οτι ἥκιστα δόξης φροντίζων. "

Diogenes the philosopher, on being asked by someone how he could become famous, responded: "By worrying about fame as little as possible."

Theon 33-35; JohnSard 40, 11-13; Dox 2.192, 21-193, 4

Lucian, *Pr. Im.* 17

In this and the next fourteen chreiai (Chreiai 23-36) Diogenes is the chief πρόσωπον (cf. also Chreia 50), thereby making him the most popular πρόσωπον in this collection (a popularity that is also true of ancient literature as a whole).

This chreia is recited in virtually the same words in all four passages. The aptness of Diogenes as the πρόσωπον to answer this question may be argued on the tradition that is preserved about Diogenes in Diogenes Laertius, 6.21.

23. Diogenes

Διογένης ὁ Κυνικὸς φιλόσοφος ἰδὼν
μειράκιον πλούσιον ἀπαίδευτον εἶπεν,
" Οὗτός ἐστι ῥύπος περιηργυρωμένος. "

Diogenes the Cynic philosopher, on seeing a rich young man who was uneducated, said: "This man is silverplated filth."

Theon 41-44, 257-60, 266-69, 272-75; Dox 2.256, 16-17; Planud 2.16, 19-21; Darm 1.141, 8-9

Gnom. Vat. 546 (p. 196 Sternbach)

Within the rhetorical tradition this chreia is always attributed to Diogenes and recited in the form ἀποφαντικὸν κατὰ περίστασιν. Even the wording is the same, except for vacillation between ῥύπος and ἵππος. Outside it, however, the chreia is attributed to Philip and recited in the form ἀποφαντικὸν καθ' ἑκούσιον (so *Gnom. Vat.*).

Similar chreiai abound, especially those comparing the same rich but uneducated person to golden sheep or golden slaves. Among these chreiai Socrates is usually the πρόσωπον (see, e.g., Stobaeus, 2.31.46 [p. 209 Wachsmuth]; 3.4.84 [p. 238 Hense]; *Gnom. Vat.* 484 [p. 180 Sternbach]; and *Gnom. Par.* 154 [p. 18 Sternbach]). Diogenes is the πρόσωπον, however, in the occurrence of this chreia in Diogenes Laertius, 6.47.

24. Diogenes-Alexander

᾿Αλέξανδρος ὁ τῶν Μακεδόνων βασιλεὺς
ἐπιστὰς Διογένει κοιμωμένῳ εἶπεν (*Il.* 2.24),
　"οὐ χρὴ παννύχιον εὕδειν βουληφόρον ἄνδρα."
καὶ ὁ Διογένης ἀπεκρίνατο (*Il.* 2.25),
　"ᾧ λαοί τ' ἐπιτετράφαται καὶ τόσσα μέμηλεν."

Alexander the Macedonian king stood over Diogenes as he slept and said (*Il.* 2.24),
　"To sleep all night ill-suits a counsellor."
And Diogenes responded (*Il.* 2.25),
　"On whom the folk rely, whose cares are many."

Theon 88-93; JohnSard 39, 7-9; 41, 4-11; Dox 2.254, 5-12

Epictetus, *Diss.* 3.22.92

In the rhetorical tradition this chreia is recited in various forms, depending on the use to which it is put. In its most familiar form, the one cited above, it is used to illustrate what Theon and JohnSard call a double chreia, i.e., a chreia with the sayings of two πρόσωπα (see Theon 86-88), the second of which refutes the first (see John Sard 41, 7-8; cf. VatGram 15; *refutativa*). Epictetus also recites this chreia as a double chreia.

When, however, JohnSard and Dox merely want to use this chreia to illustrate one etymology of the word χρεία as deriving from the "need" (χρεία) or a "circumstance" (περίστασις) that requires some saying or action, they can use it as a simple chreia, i.e., the saying of one πρόσωπον, because Alexander's saying was prompted by the περίστασις of seeing Diogenes asleep. Accordingly, they recite this chreia in the form ἀποφαντικὸν κατὰ περίστασιν: Alexander the

Macedonian King stood over Diogenes as he slept and said (*Il.* 2.24):

"To sleep all night ill-suits a counsellor."

Finally, when not even the περίστασις is necessary, it can be recited in the form ἀποφαντικὸν καθ' ἑκούσιον, as NicephCall does, when the two Homeric lines, attributed to the poet himself, become the subject of an ἐργασία (see NicephCall [p. 9, 69-71 Glettner]).

To return, however, to the double form of this chreia, it should be noted that the practice of quoting two consecutive lines of a poem where one person quotes the first and another quotes the second in order to top the first appears elsewhere. See, e.g., Diogenes Laertius, 4.29, and ps.-Seneca, *Apocol.* 5. Indeed, Athenaeus (10.457e) refers to this practice as one of several literary games which were played at symposia. He calls such games γαστρολογίαι (or γαστρονομίαι). One need think only of the στιχομυθίαι in tragedy, the ἀγών-section of Old Comedy, the pastoral contests in the *Idylls* of Theocritus (and Vergil), and such playful contests as those alluded to in, e.g., Catullus, 50, and Horace, *Odes* 3.9.

25. Diogenes

Διογένης ὁ Κυνικὸς φιλόσοφος ἰδὼν
ὀψοφάγον παῖδα τὸν παιδαγωγὸν τῇ
βακτηρίᾳ ἔπαισε.

Diogenes the Cynic philosopher, on seeing a boy who was a gourmand, struck the paedagogus with his staff.

Theon 100-102, 251-53; VatGram 2-6; JohnSard 42, 12-13; Dox 2.257, 18-19; Planud 2.17, 19-20; Darm 1.142, 11-12

Plutarch, *An virt. doc. poss.* 439D

This chreia is very similar to Chreia 26. They both have the same πρόσωπον (Diogenes) and the same πρᾶξις (striking the paedagogus) (cf. also Chreia 14). Nevertheless, Chreia 25 has a different περίστασις that prompts the action and hence a different setting. Thus in Chreia 25 Diogenes' action is prompted by his seeing a boy who was a gourmand and so suggests a meal setting, as indeed VatGram's recitation of the περίστασις makes clear. In Chreia 26, however, Diogenes' action results from his seeing a youth misbehaving and so suggests a setting in the marketplace, as NicMyra 75 makes explicit. Add the fact that Chreia 25 is always an action chreia (even in Plutarch), whereas Chreia 26 is sometimes an action chreia, sometimes a mixed one (see comment on Chreia 26), and it thus appears that these chreiai are distinct in the minds of the ancient writers and so are treated as distinct here.

In any case, the recitation of Chreia 25 is remarkably concise, although VatGram is somewhat more expansive in presenting the circumstance. And Plutarch adds an explanation, saying that Diogenes acted rightly in punishing the one who failed to teach rather than the one who failed to learn.

That the attribution to Diogenes is εὔστοχος is easily demonstrated. On his own role as a strict paedagogus, see Diogenes Laertius, 6.30-31. Furthermore, on Diogenes as one to use his staff to chastise, see Lucian, *Bis acc.* 24, and ps.-Diogenes, *ep.* 38.2 (p. 160 Malherbe). More generally, on paedagogi using their staffs on their charges, see, e.g., Alciphron, *ep.* 3.7.3-4. Conversely, on their failing to keep boys or youths out of trouble, see, e.g., Athenaeus, 3.103c-e.

26. Diogenes

Διογένης ἰδὼν μειράκιον ἀτακτοῦν
τὸν παιδαγωγὸν ἐτύπτησε.

Diogenes, on seeing a youth misbehaving, beat the paedagogus.

Hermog 10-11, 13-15; Prisc 12-13; 14-15; Aphth 14-16; NicMyra 74-76; Nic 1.272, 21-23; Lib 8.74, 2-4; JohnSard 39, 12-14; 42, 6-7, 12-13; Dox 2.261, 13-15; 284, 33-285, 2; EpitAnon 1.129, 27-28

This chreia is the most popular in our collection, appearing fourteen times in nine authors, although, surprisingly, it seems not to occur outside the rhetorical tradition. Its recitation varies little with one exception. In the form cited above it is an action chreia, but in eight instances it is used to illustrate a mixed chreia and so has this saying added: "Why do you teach such things?" (so Hermog 13-15; Prisc 14-15; Aphth; Nic; Lib; Dox; EpitAnon). In this latter form it is the subject of an ἐργασία (so Nic, Lib, and Dox) and hence will receive further discussion in volume II of *The Chreia in Ancient Rhetoric*.

For further discussion, see the comments on Chreia 25.

27. Diogenes

Διογένης ὁ φιλόσοφος ἰδὼν μειράκιον
περισσῶς καλλωπιζόμενον, εἶπεν· " Εἰ
μὲν πρὸς ἄνδρας, ἀτυχεῖς, εἰ δὲ πρὸς

γυναῖκας, ἀδικεῖς."

Diogenes the philosopher, on seeing a youth dressed foppishly, said: "If you are doing this for husbands, you are accursed; if for wives, you are unjust."

Theon 139-41; JohnSard 40, 9-11

Diogenes Laertius, 6.54; Stobaeus, 3.6.38 (p. 294 Hense); *Gnom. Vat.* 171 (p. 70 Sternbach)

This chreia, whose saying is expressed in the form of a syllogism (cf. Theon 115-17), appears in the rhetoricians and outside without changes in πρόσωπον or even in ἀπαγγελία.

The similar sound of ἀτυχεῖς and ἀδικεῖς is an example of παρομοίωσις (cf. *Rhet. ad Alex.* 1436a 5ff) and is lost in translation.

28. Diogenes

Διογένης ὁ Κυνικὸς φιλόσοφος ἰδὼν
μειράκιον ἐκ μοιχοῦ λίθους βάλλον,
" Παῦσαι, " ἔφη, " παιδίον, μὴ ἀγνοοῦν
παίσῃς τὸν πατέρα. "

Diogenes the Cynic philosopher, on seeing a youth who was the son of an adulterer throwing stones, said: "Stop, boy! You may unwittingly hit your father."

Theon 186-88; Dox 2.258, 18-20; Planud 2.18, 11-13; Darm 1.142, 30-32

Diogenes Laertius, 6.62; *Gnom. Vat.* 178 (p. 73 Sternbach)

This chreia is not only witty, as Theon says (cf. 188-89) (the wit residing in the pun παιδίον/παίσῃς). It is also poignant, suggesting a street urchin who is on his own and who takes to throwing stones much like Kottalos in Herodas, 3.44. In any case, the recitation varies, though usually in order to clarify the circumstance. Thus the μειράκιον ἐκ μοιχοῦ becomes ἑταιρίδος υἱόν (so *Gnom. Vat.*; cf. Diogenes Laertius). Also for clarification is the addition of εἰς ὄχλον (so Diogenes Laertius) or of εἰς πλῆθος (so Dox and Planud).

29. Diogenes

Diogenes Cynicus philosophus, cum manu haurientem rusticum ad potandum aquam vidisset, poculum, quod in pera gerebat, abiecit et dixit, "Hoc ego levior esse iam possum."

Diogenes the Cynic philosopher, when he saw a
rustic taking up water with his hand in order
to drink, threw away the cup which he was
carrying in his knapsack and said; "Now I can
be this much lighter."

VatGram 24-28

Seneca, *ep.* 90.14; Plutarch, *De prof. in virt.* 79E; *A.P.* 16.333 (Antiphilus
of Byzantium); Diogenes Laertius, 6.37; *Gnom. Vat.* 185 (p. 75 Sternbach); cf.
ps.-Diogenes, *ep.* 6.1-2 (p. 96 Malherbe)

Except for attribution (which is always to Diogenes) this
popular   chreia   shows   considerable   variations — in
classification, in recitation, and in manipulation. Thus all three
γένη appear. It is a sayings-chreia in Antiphilus of Byzantium,
an action-chreia in Plutarch, and a mixed chreia in VatGram,
Seneca, Diogenes Laertius, and *Gnom. Vat.*
ʾΑπαγγελία also changes considerably. Plutarch writes it
most concisely: Diogenes, on seeing someone drinking with his
hands, threw away the cup from his knapsack. In the
Diogenean letter, however, the recitation is so long that it
constitutes an expanded chreia (cf. Theon 309-12). The others
fall between these two, but even where length is fairly
constant, variation in the saying is especially apparent. Thus
Diogenes Laertius has "A child has vanquished me in living
simply," while Seneca has "O how long, fool that I am, have
I had this excess baggage!"
The Diogenean letter, besides expanding the chreia, also
demonstrates how a chreia can be taken up into an epistolary
setting (see also ps.-Crates, *ep.* 20 [p. 70 Malherbe] and
Diogenes Laertius, 6.89). Likewise, Antiphilus shows how a
chreia can also be taken up into an epigram (cf. also Ausonius,
epit. 29).

30. Diogenes

ʾΙδὼν μυῖαν ἐπάνω τῆς τραπέζης αὐτοῦ
εἶπεν· " Καὶ Διογένης παρασίτους τρέφει. "

On seeing a mouse on his table, he said; "Even
Diogenes keeps parasites."

PBour (p. 23 Collart)

Diogenes Laertius, 6.40

Chreiai 30-34 all appear on a papyrus text from the third
or fourth century A.D. (=Pack[2] 2643). Besides the chreiai, which
take up two of the eleven pages of this text, there are
various lists of words, proper names, and maxims — all in

alphabetical order. This other material suggests an educational setting for the papyrus and hence our inclusion of these chreiai in Volume II of *The Chreia in Ancient Rhetoric.*

Formally speaking, the chreiai are all the same, specifically in the form ἀποφαντικὸν κατὰ περίστασιν (N.B. ἰδὼν . . . εἶπεν). What is unusual is the lack of an explicit πρόσωπον, although Diogenes is named in the saying of Chreia 30. Moreover, these chreiai are elsewhere attributed to Diogenes or are otherwise apt. Finally, a formally similar group of five chreiai, as A. Packmohr (*De Diogenis Sinopensis apophthegmatis quaestiones selectae* [Diss. Guestfala, 1913] 33) has rightly observed, is clearly attributed to Diogenes since it appears in Diogenes Laertius, 6.51-52. Accordingly, Diogenes is surely the πρόσωπον of Chreiai 30-34.

Chreia 30 is attributed elsewhere to Diogenes and in much the same language (so Diogenes Laertius). Expanded versions of this chreia appear in Plutarch, *Quom. quis suos in virt. sent. prof.* 77F-78A, and in Aelian, *V.H.* 13.26, although these expansions seem to develop also the tradition preserved in Diogenes Laertius, 6.22.

31. Diogenes

Ἰδὼν γ[υν]αῖκα διδα[σκ]ομένην
γράμματα, εἶπεν· " οἷον ξίφος
ἀκονᾶται."

On seeing a woman being taught letters, he said: "Wow! A sword is being sharpened."

PBour 1 (p. 23 Collart)

For discussion, see comment on Chreia 32.

32. Diogenes

Ἰδὼν γυν[αῖ]κα γυ[ν]αικὶ συμ-
βουλεύουσαν, εἶπεν· "Ἀσπὶς παρ'
ἐχίδνης φάρμακον πορίζεται."

On seeing a woman giving advice to a woman, he said: "As asp is being supplied venom from a viper."

PBour 1 (p. 23 Collart)

Antonius and Maximus, *Serm. de mulieribus improbis,* p. 609 (as cited in F. Mullach, *Fragmenta* 3.304)

This chreia is elsewhere attributed explicitly to Diogenes (Antonius and Maximus), although the sentiment of the saying also finds a parallel in Menander (*frag.* 702 Koch):

γυναῖχ' ὁ διδάσκων γράμματ' οὐ καλῶς ποιεῖ
ἀσπίδι δὲ φοβερᾷ προσποτίζει φάρμακον

who teaches woman how to write acts wrongly,
gives fearful asp more venom to imbibe.

Interestingly, this Menandrian fragment is related to both Chreiai 31 and 32. The first line parallels the circumstance of Chreia 31, but the second parallels the saying of Chreia 32.

Moreover, that these chreiai, which are so negative toward women, should appear in an educational setting is distressing to us but not unprecedented, given the similar classroom use of Menander's *Monostichoi*, many of which are equally misogynist (see, e.g., *Mon.* 342 [p. 52 Jaekel], 371 [p. 54], 502 [p. 62], 591 [p. 67], and 700 [p. 73]).

Presumably, what men feared about an educated woman is humorously illustrated by a chreia which, incidentally, makes use of a line from Homer (*Il.* 2.24) that is used in Chreia 24. In any case, Packmohr (*De Diogenis Sinopensis apophthegmatis*, 68–69) quotes from a Viennese ms which has this chreia: A Samian woman who had a husband fond of drinking said:

"To drink all night ill-suits a counsellor."

He said: "Damned be the one who taught you letters," but she responded: "No, the one who didn't teach you."

See also Juvenal, *Sat.* 6.434–56.

33. Diogenes

Ἰδὼν Ἀιθίοπα καθαρὸν τρωγόντα,
⟨εἶπεν⟩· "Ἰδοὺ ἡ νὺξ τὴν ἡμέραν
πνίγει."

On seeing an Ethiopian eating white bread, ⟨he said⟩: "Look! Night is swallowing day."

PBour 1 (p. 23–24 Collart)

This chreia, unlike the others on this papyrus, does not even have εἶπεν, much less explicit reference to the πρόσωπον. The omission, however, is probably an oversight.

This chreia seems not to appear elsewhere, although chreiai attributed to Diogenes involving "white" bread do occur (see Diogenes Laertius, 6.64) as do those focusing on the blackness of Ethiopians (see Antonius and Maximus, *Serm. de hominibus malis*, p. 64 [as cited in Mullach, *Fragmenta*, 3.300]).

For the proverbial nature of Diogenes' remark, see Lucian, *Ind.* 28. Hence the attribution is clearly apt.

Incidentally, the choice of τρώγειν for "eating" is probably deliberate. For it is not only attested elsewhere in Diogenes chreiai (see Diogenes Laertius, 6.61) but also recalls the name of an Ethiopian people (i.e., Τρωγοδύται) (so, e.g., Herodotus, 4.183).

34. Diogenes

Ἰδὼν Αἰθίοπα δὲ χέζοντα, εἶπεν·
" Οἷος λέβης τέτρηται."

On seeing an Ethiopian shiting, he said: "Wow! A kettle with holes in it."

PBour (p. 24 Collart)

Theon (cf. 373-74) was seemingly unable to cite one useless chreia. here is an obvious candidate!

35. Diogenes

Diogenes Cynicus philosophus in die
accensa lucerna quaerebat hominem.

Diogenes the Cynic philosopher used to seek a
man with a lighted lamp by day.

Diom 1.310, 22-23 and 24-30

Diogenes Laertius, 6.41; Antonius and Maximus, *Serm. malitiam esse facilem*, p. 39 (as cited in Mullach, *Fragmenta*, 3.300)

This well-known story about Diogenes looking for an "honest man" is preserved for us in chreiai of all three γένη: as a sayings-chreia in Antonius and Maximus, an action-chreia in Diom, and a mixed chreia in Diogenes Laertius.

While an attribution to Diogenes is certainly apt, as is clear from similar chreiai (see, e.g., Diogenes Laertius, 6.40) as well as from a well-known tendency to characterize Diogenes as pessimistic (see esp. G. A. Gerhard, "Zur Legende vom Kyniker Diogenes," *ARW* 15 [1912] 388-408), it is nevertheless the case that this chreia is also attributed to Aesop (so Phaedrus, 3.19).

36. Diogenes

ὁ αὐτὸς ἰδών τινα αἰσχρῶς βιοῦντα
εἶτ᾽ ἄλλῳ τινὶ ταὐτὸ τοῦτο ὀνειδίσαντα,
" ἔοικας," φησί, " τέφραν φυσᾶν ἀνέμου
κατεναντίον."

ἄλλος δέ φησι " Τί κόνιν φυσᾷς εἰς
τὸ σὸν ἀναστρέφεται πρόσωπον. "

The same man, on seeing someone living shamefully
and then rebuking someone else for the very
same thing, said: "You are like a man who blows
ash against the wind."

Another man, however, said: "Why are you blowing
dust? It is being carried back into your face."

JohnSard 40, 13-16

What is of interest here is that JohnSard is not reciting
a double chreia (see Chreia 24) but is, it seems, merely
appending an alternative saying to that of Diogenes. It is
clearly not Diogenes' (N.B. ἄλλος), but the other πρόσωπον is
not further identified.

37. Epameinondas

Ἐπαμεινώνδας ἄτεκνος ἀποφνήσκων
ἔλεγε τοῖς φίλοις, " Δύο θυγατέρας
ἀπέλιπον, τήν τε περὶ Λεύκτραν
νίκην καὶ τὴν περὶ Μαντίνειαν. "

Epameinondas, as he was dying childless, said to
his friends: "I have left two daughters, the
victory at Leuctra and the one at Mantineia."

Theon 314-17, cf. 318-33; JohnSard 38, 12-15

Diodorus Siculus, 15.87.6; Valerius Maximus, 3.2.5. Cf. also Nepos,
Epameinondas 10.2, for a similar remark, and *Gnom. Vat.* 76 (p. 35 Sternbach)
for further references.

In both Theon and JohnSard this chreia is used as an
example of the way in which a chreia can be expanded. With
a little thought, of course, most chreiai can be expanded
into a fairly extensive passage, and such exercises seem
to have been a regular part of the young student's training.

38. Euripides

Εὐριπίδης ὁ ποιητὴς τὸν νοῦν ἡμῶν
ἑκάστου ἔφησεν εἶναι θεόν.

The poet Euripides has said that the mind of each
of us is a god.

Theon 281-82

This saying of Euripides appears as *frag.* 1018 in Nauck's
Trag. Gr. Frag. in the nominative form:

ὁ νοῦς γὰρ ἡμῶν ἐστιν ἐν ἑκάστῳ θεός.

This line, or one very similar to it, is quoted numerous times, attributed sometimes to Euripides, sometimes to Menander (cf. *Mon.* 588 (p. 67 Jaekel), sometimes to still other poets. It is alluded to, without the author's name, in the *Catonis Disticha* 1.1-2:

Si deus est animus, nobis ut carmina dicunt,
Hic tibi praecipue sit pura mente colendus.

This chreia shows how a quotable remark of a writer, of prose or poetry, could be lifted from the context, attributed to the author and thus made into a chreia. Such chreiai as 60-61 (Socphocles) and 67-68 (Vergil) show the same technique. In the case of ps.-Menander's *Monostichoi* we have the same situation except that the whole collection, rather than each individual line or couplet, is attributed to the comic poet.

39. Gregory

εὐεργετῶν νόμιζε μιμεῖσθαι θεόν.

Practise imitating God by showing kindness.

NicephBas 1.442, 12

This saying, in one form or another, is very common in antiquity (see *Gnom. Vat.* 53 [pp. 25-27] for an extensive list, yet one which omits this passage in NicephBas). Sometimes the thought appears in the form of a maxim, but more frequently it has been attributed to some apt philosopher, e.g., Aristotle, Pythagoras, Praxagoras, Democritus, or even to an orator such as Demosthenes or Isocrates. Occasionally we find the saying attributed to a Christian, e.g., the fifth century ascetic Neilus of Constantinople and, as here, to Gregory of Nazianzus (St. Gregory).

Although the saying itself does not incorporate the attribution to Gregory, the ἐργασία which NicephBas has composed (see 1.442, 13ff) names him in the encomium and refers to several of his writings. Thus here we have an example of a chreia which deals with one of humanity's common concepts of the divine. Among the Greeks and Romans the idea was expressed either as a general maxim or was attributed to some individual likely to have discussed such matters. When Christianity adopted some of the forms used by Greek rhetoricians, it was logical to attribute the same idea to various church fathers.

40. Isocrates

'Ισοκράτης ὁ σοφιστὴς τοὺς εὐφυεῖς
τῶν μαθητῶν θεῶν παῖδας ἔλεγεν εἶναι.

Isocrates the sophist used to say that gifted
students are children of gods.

Theon 39-40, 206-208, 209-10, 211-12, 213-15, 231-33; cf 360-61; JohnSard
40, 8-9; 41, 23-24; Dox 2.256, 11-12; 264, 19-20; Planud 2.16, 16-17; Darm
1.141, 5

This chreia shows no variations throughout its many
occurrences in the rhetorical tradition—in attribution, in
classification, even in recitation.
For a similar sentiment, see Chreia 52.

41. Isocrates

'Ισοκράτης ὁ ῥήτωρ παρῄνει τοῖς
γνωρίμοις προτιμᾶν τῶν γονέων
τοὺς διδασκάλους ὅτι οἱ μὲν τοῦ
ζῆν μόνον, οἱ δὲ διδάσκαλοι καὶ
τοῦ καλῶς ζῆν αἴτιοι γεγόνασιν.

Isocrates the rhetor used to advise his students
to honor their teachers above their parents,
because the latter are the cause only of living,
while teachers are the cause of living nobly.

Theon 128-31, 299-302; Dox 2.258,2-5; Planud 2.18,3-5; Darm 1.142,21-23

Diogenes Laertius 5.19

In the rhetorical tradition this chreia is consistently
attributed to Isocrates, while non-rhetorical texts (so
Diogenes Laertius) attribute it to Aristotle. Moreover, Theon's
dislike of this chreia for its slighting of parents (cf. Theon
302-304) seems reflected in a more balanced and individualized
version of this chreia, again attributed to Alexander, in which
he said that he admired Aristotle but he loved Philip no less,
because the latter had given him life while the former had
taught him to live well (cf. Plutarch, *Alex.* 8, and *Gnom. Vat.*
87 [p. 40 Sternbach]). Indeed, the contrast between τὸ ζῆν
and τὸ καλῶς ζῆν is a commonplace (see e.g. Diogenes Laertius
6.65; ps.-Crates, *ep.* 6 [p. 56 Malherbe]; and Stobaeus 3.4.85
[p. 239 Hense]). What is meant by τὸ καλῶς ζῆν is clear in
Stobaeus (3.1.140 [p. 101 Hense]), where the phrase is clarified
with the virtues of σωφροσύνη, αὐτάρκεια, εὐταξία, and κοσμιότης.

42. Isocrates

Ἰσοκράτης ὁ ῥήτωρ συνισταμένου
αὐτῷ παιδίου καὶ ἐρωτῶντος τοῦ
συνιστάντος τίνος αὐτῷ δεῖ, εἶπε,
" Πινακιδίου ΚΑΙΝΟΥ καὶ γραφειδίου
ΚΑΙΝΟΥ. "

Isocrates the rhetor, when a boy was being
enrolled with him and when the one who was
enrolling him asked what the boy needed, said,
"A new tablet and a new stylus."

Theon 166-69; Dox 2.258,26-28; Planud 2.18,18-21; Darm 1.143,4-7

Cf. Diogenes Laertius 6.3.

In the rhetorical tradition this chreia is repeated without
significant changes and always with an eye to the ambiguity
of ΚΑΙΝΟΥ (on which see Comment 15 to the translation of
Theon). This chreia also appears outside the rhetorical
tradition, but now attributed to Antisthenes with a
corresponding change in the περίστασις: To the youth from
Pontus (presumably Diogenes) who was about to begin study
with him and had asked what he needed, Antisthenes said,
"A small roll ΚΑΙΝΟΥ, a stylus ΚΑΙΝΟΥ, and a tablet ΚΑΙΝΟΥ"
(Diogenes Laertius 6.3). The ambiguous ΚΑΙΝΟΥ also appears
in a chreia attributed to Stilpo (see Diogenes Laertius 2.118).

43. Isocrates

Ἰσοκράτης ἔφησε τῆς παιδείας τὴν
μὲν ῥίζαν εἶναι πικράν, τὸν δὲ
καρπὸν γλυκύν.

Isocrates said that education's root is bitter,
its fruit is sweet.

Hermog 35-37; Prisc 36-38; Aphth 24-25; NicMyra 72-73, 83-84, 133-34;
Diom 1.310,2-17; Lib 8.82,13-14; JohnSard 50,20-21; Dox 2.254,13-15; 272,14-15;
ScholAnon 2.587,5-6; 588,4-5

Diogenes Laertius 5.18; Stobaeus 2.31.29 (p. 207 Wachsmuth); *Gnom. Vat.*
59 (p. 28 Sternbach); Julius Rufinianus, *De fig. sent. et eloc.* 19 (1.43 Halm).

Dox (2.274,24-25) classifies this chreia as λογική, καθ'ἑκούσιον,
ἀποφαντική, and τροπική, and so it remains throughout the
rhetorical tradition and outside it. Recitation is also constant,
except for indecision about whether καρπός should be singular
or plural. Attribution, however, varies. In the rhetorical
tradition, it is nearly always to Isocrates—and quite aptly
in light of a similar sentiment of ps.-Isocrates, *Ad Demon.*

47. But Diom attributes this chreia to Cato, again with aptness (see *Catonis distich.* 4.27 and *Catonis monostich.* 53). Elsewhere the attribution is to Aristotle (Diogenes Laertius and *Gnom. Vat.*), to Demosthenes (Stobaeus), or to Cicero (Julius Rufinianus). And others, of course, use the "bitter-sweet" contrast of other subjects (so, e.g., Aulus Gellius 13.2.5 and Athenaeus 2.55f.).

44. Lacedaemonians

Φιλίππου πρὸς Λακεδαιμονίους γράψ-
οντος πολλὰ καὶ δεινά, αὐτοὶ πρὸς
αὐτὸν ἀντέγραψαν, " Λακεδαιμόνιοι
Φιλίππῳ· Διονύσιος ἐν Κορίνθῳ·
γράμματα. "

When Philip wrote many threatening letters to the Lacedaemonians, they wrote back to him. "Lacedaemonians to Philip: Dionysius in Corinth; alphbet."

Dox 2.258,6-9, cf. 9-11

A shorter version of this chreia, consisting of an even more terse reply of the Lacedaemonians, is found several times in ancient compositions. From the comments of the authors who quote or allude to it, the reply itself seems to have become a commonplace as well as an example of both Laconic brevity and of allegory. See, for example, the discussion in Demetrius, *Eloc.* 8 and 102; Quint. *Inst. Orat.* 8.6,52; Plutarch, *De garr.* 511A; ps.-Dio Chrysostom 64.18; Diogenes Laertius 3.34. None of these passages, however, includes a reference to Dionysius' activity at Corinth as Chreia 44 does with the single word γράμματα. In each passage the saying is simply "Lacedaemonians to Philip: Dionysius at Corinth" or even more briefly "Dionysius at Corinth."

In Demetrius, *Eloc.* 241, however, a passage not unlike the discussion in sect. 8, the author expands the meaning of the Lacedaemonians' reply like this: "Dionysius has been deposed from power and πτωχεύει ἐν Κορίνθῳ γράμματα διδάσκων." Demetrius concludes with the observation that if the Lacedaemonians had expressed all these details, the result would have been a διήγημα (narrative) instead of a λοιδορία (taunt).

This passage adds two pieces of information. First it supplies the word γράμματα which the chreia contains and even clarifies its meaning by adding διδάσκων. Secondly, with the word πτωχεύει it adds the idea that Dionysius was at best eeking out a bare livelihood as a teacher at Corinth. This

additional idea provides another dimension to the
Lacedaemonians' taunting reply to Philip.
What type of teacher was Dionysius? Cicero's statement
(*Tusc.Disp.* 3.12,27) that he *Corinthi pueros docebat* could mean
that he was a *grammaticus*, but such passages as Lucian,
Gall. 23 (cf. *Pseudol.* 25; *Menipp.* 17; Plutarch, *Prin. phil. diss.*
776B) show that he was teaching at a more elementary level;
ἐν Κορίνθῳ γραμματιστὴς βλέπηται . . . παιδία συλλαβίζειν διδάσκων
("seen in Corinth as a schoolmaster teaching children how
to make syllables out of letters"). For a contemporary picture
of such a teacher's duties see first Demosthenes, *De cor.*
265 where the orator says to Aeschines ἐδίδασκες γράμματα
and then *De cor.* 258 where he describes exactly what it
is that his opponent did:

With your father at the school you served as menial, grinding the ink,
sponging off the benches, and sweeping out the waiting room of the paedagogi,
holding the position of a slave, not that of a free-born boy.

So apparently we—or rather the Philip in the chreia—must
think of the once-powerful tyrant of Syracuse who had
received Plato and other philosophers in his palace (as Philip
had received Aristotle), who had written poetry and
philosophic treatises, as now earning a bare subsistence in
exile by teaching at the very lowest level.
    And though this point may have nothing to do with the
meaning of the chreia, we hear from ps.-Diogenes, *ep.* 8, that
Dionysius was a bad teacher even at this level. We also hear
from Plutarch, *seni resp. ger.* 783D, that the Cynic Diogenes
conversed with the ex-tyrant in Corinth and berated him
for living ἐλευθέρως καὶ ἀδεῶς ("free and unafraid"), all a part
of the Cynic's sarcastic taunt. On the other hand, Dio
Chrysostom, 37.19, paints an almost glowing picture of
Dionysius' days at Corinth; a θέαμα κάλλιστον ("a glorious
spectacle") whom no one tried to wrong or to deprive of
the possessions which he had brought from Sicily. Yet, more
to the point intended by Chreia 44, Stobaeus, 4.47,13 (p. 1006
Hense), gives us a different picture and quotes Dionysius as
saying ὡς μακάριοι οἱ ἐκ παίδων δυστυχεῖς ("how blessed are
those who are from childhood unfortunate"). With this
sentiment cf. Chreia 7.
    There is, of course, no proof—or indeed much proability
—that the Lacedaemonians actually made such a reply to Philip
as Chreia 44 suggests. Yet the author of the chreia was
careful to keep the content not only apt to its characters
but appropriate to historical reality.
    The situation to which the chreia alludes was real, or
at least could have been real. Dionysius II, driven from power

at Syracuse, surrendered to Timoleon, whom the Corinthians supported, and sometime late in 343 BC went to Corinth where he remained for the rest of his life. He arrived in Greece at the time when Philip of Macedon was in the process of tightening his grip on the states of Greece. At least as early as 344 BC (*CAH* Vol. 6, Ch. 9, p. 245), and undoubtedly on later occasions, Philip wrote threatening letters to the Lacedaemonians. Certainly in 338 BC Philip convened a congress of Greek states and chose Corinth as the meeting-place (so Dionysius was not the only "tyrant" in Corinth). Sparta refused to attend the congress, and it may be this situation that the author had in mind when he composed the original saying which appears here as Chreia 44.

45. Laconian

Λάκων ἐρομένου τινὸς αὐτὸν ποῦ
τοὺς ὅρους τῆς γῆς ἔχουσι Λακεδαιμόνιοι, ἔδειξε τὸ δόρυ.

A Laconian, when someone asked him where the Lacedaemonians consider the boundaries of their land to be, showed his spear.

Theon 111-113; NicMyra 77-79; Nic 1.277,2-278,3; JohnSard 42, 18-19, cf. 49,9; Dox 2.251,30-252,2; 261,10-11; ScholAnon 2.587,2-4.

Plutarch, *Reg. et imper. apoth.* 190E; *Apoth. lac.* 210E, 217E, 218F, 229C; *Quaest. rom.* 267C; *Lysander*, ch. 22,1 (445D); cf. Cicero, *De resp.* 3.9,15; cf. also *Gnom. Vat.* 396 (pp. 149-150 Sternbach); *Gnom. Par.* 88 (p. 12 Sternbach) *Append. Vat.* 73 (p. 76 Sternbach). Chreia 1 (Achilles) seems to have been modelled on Chreia 45.

In addition to resembling several other chreiai which involve Spartan kings (cf., for example, Plutarch, *Apoth. lac.* 210E [#28 with #29] and 217E [#7 with #8], Chreia 45 appears with more variations, both major and minor, than any other chreia in this collection. Even Plutarch never uses exactly the same version twice. The following elements represent the most obvious variations, but there are still others.

Attribution (ἀναφορά): The πρόσωπον is always an unnamed Laconian in the rhetorical texts as well as in Plutarch's *Quaest. rom.* 267C. See also *Gnom. Vat.* 396; *Gnom. Par.* 88; *Append. Vat.* 73. Elsewhere in Plutarch, however, the πρόσωπον is a specified Spartan king, i.e. Agesilaus (*Apoth. lac.* 210E, 217E); Archidemus (*Apoth. lac.* 218F); Lysander (*Reg. et imper. apoth.* 190E; *Apoth. lac.* 229C; *Lysander*, ch. 22,1). See also Cicero, *De resp.* 3.9,15.

Classification (διαίρεσις): The examples fall into all three γένη of the chreia: Sayings-chreia (λογική) in Plutarch, *Apoth.*

Iac. 217E, 218F; *Quaest. rom.* 267C; Cicero *De resp.*; *Gnom. Vat.*; *Gnom. Par.*; *Append. Vat.* Action-chreia (πρακτική) in Theon and Nic. Mixed chreia (μικτή) in NicMyra; JohnSard; Dox; ScholAnon; Plutarch, *Reg. et imper. apoth.* 190E; *Apoth. Iac.* 210E, 229C, *Lysander.*

Wording (ἀπαγγελία): (1) The type of weapon varies. In most cases it is δόρυ, but in Plutarch, *Apoth. Iac.* 217E it is ἐπιδορατίς (spear-point), and in *Reg. et imper. apoth.* 190E, *Apoth. Iac.* 229C and *Lysander* it is μάχαιρα. (2) Different verbs are used to indicate how the πρόσωπον uses the weapon: some form of δείκνυμι in Theon; Nic; Plutarch, *Lysander*; ἀνατείνω in NicMyra; ScholAnon; and δείκνυμι καὶ ἀνατείνω in JohnSard; Dox; σπάω in Plutarch, *Reg. et imper. apoth.* 190E; *Apoth. Iac.* 229C; κραδαίνω in Plutarch, *Apoth. Iac.* 210E. (3) Even the question concerns τείχη rather than ὅροι in NicMyra; ScholAnon; cf. *Gnom. Par.* 88.

The very variety of form and expression in which Chreia 45 is found points to its popularity in antiquity. Such popularity undoubtedly resulted from the special aptness of the chreia, for by its question and pointed reply it manages to bring out one of the salient chracteristics of the whole Spartan state.

46. Laconian

Λάκων τις κατὰ πόλεμον αἰχμάλωτος
γενόμενος καὶ πωλούμενος ἐρωτηθεὶς
ὑπότινος τί δύναται, ἔφη, " ἐλεύθερος
εἶναι. "

A Laconian, who had become a prisoner of war
and was being sold, on being asked by someone
what he could do, said, "Be free."

JohnSard 40,17-19.

We have several chreiai in which a Laconian (Spartan, Lacedaemonian) man or woman is sold into slavery and is asked a similar question. The response varies, but it is always appropriate to some Spartan characteristic and most often depicts him or her as still defiant in servitude. See, for example, Plutarch, *Apoth. Iac.* 233C (#21), 234B-C (#37-40) and *Lac. apoth.* 242C-D (#27-30); cf. also *Gnom. Vat. 570 (p. 202 Sternbach).*

Diogenes Laertius, 6.29, cites a chreia about the Cynic Diogenes, who is asked the same question when he is put up for sale. His response is ἀνδρῶν ἄρχειν. Indeed, the sale of Diogenes seems to have become something of a *cause célèbre*, for Diogenes Laertius quotes from two works entitled

Διογένους Πρᾶξις, one by either Menippus or Hermippus, one by Eubulus. Strangely enough, we have found no chreia about Plato and his reaction to being sold by the tyrant Dionysius II.

47. Milo

Milo, quem vitulum adsueverat ferre,
taurum ferebat.

Milo used to carry the bull which he had grown accustomed to carry as a calf.

Quint 29-30

On the form of this chreia see the discussion in the "Introduction to Quintilian" (above, pp. 133-34).

Milo of Crotona (6th cent. BC) was a famous Olympian athlete (see, for example, David C. Young, *The Olympic Myth of Greek Amateur Athletics* [Chicago: Ares Publ., 1984] p. 134 *et passim*). He was also famed for his extraordinary physical strength and enormous appetite, as we see in such passages as Herodotus 3.137; Diodorus Siculus 12.9; Pausanias 6,14,5-8; Athenaeus 10.412F.

In fact, Milo's strength became proverbial, and some form of the proverb is probably the source of Quintilian's version. The same proverb seems to lie behind the humorous passage in Petronius *Satyr.* 25 where the prostitute Quartilla explains that as a girl she lay with boys and as she grew older gradually worked up to fully grown men. She then adds *Hinc etiam puto proverbium natum illud, ut dicatur posse taurum tollere, qui vitulum sustulerit* ("I think that this is the origin of that proverb 'It is said that he lifts a bull who has lifted a calf'."). Stobaeus 3.29.69 (p. 641 Hense) quotes a similar remark about an old woman.

48. Olympias

Ὀλυμπίας πυθομένη τὸν υἱὸν Ἀλέξανδρον Διὸς αὐτὸν ἀποφαίνειν, " Οὐ
παύσεται οὗτος, " ἔφη, " διαβάλλων
με πρὸς τὴν Ἥραν; "

Olympias, on hearing that her son Alexander was proclaiming himself the offspring of Zeus, said, "Won't this fellow stop slandering me to Hera?"

Theon 135-37; NicMyra 88-91, cf. 97-100; ProgAnon 1.18,5-8; Darm 1.142,24-27; ScholAnon 2.587.9-11.

CATALOGUE OF CHREIAI   331

A similar remark of Olympias is found in Plutarch, *Alex.* ch. 3,2 (665E), and Aulus Gellius, 13.4, quotes from a letter of Olympias to Alexander which he found in Marcus Varro's *Orestes vel De Insania.* Gellius then not only briefly expands the remark much in the way that Theon does the chreia about Epameinondas (lines 317-33), he also explains its lesson. In doing so, Gellius agrees with the analysis of NicMyra (97-100) that Olympias' reply serves as a gentle warning to her son and does not constitute merely a witty remark. For a humorous reference to the same subject see the conversation betwen Alexander and Diogenes in Dio Chrysostom 4.19 where the Cynic calls the king ὑποβολιμαῖος ("bastard") and then defends his remark by referring to a statement of Olympias that Zeus or some god was Alexander's father.

49. Pittacus

Πιττακὸς ὁ Μιτυληναῖος ἐρωτηθεὶς
εἰ λανθάνει τις τοὺς θεοὺς φαῦλον
τι ποιῶν, εἶπεν, " Οὐδὲ διανοούμενος."

Pittacus of Mitylene, on being asked if anyone escapes the notice of the gods in committing some sinful act, said, "Not even in contemplating it."

Theon 56-58; 235-38; NicMyra 18-21, cf. 22-38; ProgAnon 1.216,24-217,4; Dox 2.256,25-27; 264,16-18; 264,30-265,2; 265,8-10; Planud 2.16,24-17,1, cf. 21,8-13; Darm 1.141,13-15, cf. 15-16; ScholAnon 2.585,19-23.

Theon quotes this chreia (lines 56-58) for a special purpose: i.e. to exemplify his definition of the sub-species of a responsive chreia (κατ'ἐρώτησιν). His understanding of this category is that it requires only a simple ναί or οὔ, or even just a nod or shake of the head (lines 50-54). Since he apparently had no such chreia available, he adapted the one about Pittacus and added an οὔ before the standard οὐδὲ διανοούμενος. Then (lines 58-60) he explains that the οὔ (which he himself has added!) is a sufficient response to the simple question and that anything else that is said is superfluous.

Theon's own use of this chreia later (235-238) shows clearly that the simple οὔ itself is the intrusion. In the later passage, he gives the chreia in the genitive case, but if we convert it to the nominative, we have a version that is identical with the one printed here in the Catalogue — and with that of Theon in lines 56-58 with the οὔ removed.

Chreia 49 was a popular one in antiquity and appears in numerous collections and discussions. See *Append. Vat.* 22 (p.

70 Sternbach) and esp. *Gnom. Vat.* 316 (pp. 121-122 Sternbach). In addition, the same sentiment appears frequently in non-chreia form; e.g. *Rhet. ad Alex.* 1432a35-40; ps.-Menander, *Mon.* 626 (p. 69 Jaekel) and cf. 347, 432, 841; Epictetus, *Diss.* 2.14.11; Lucian, *Anth.Pal.* 10.27; Sextus, *Ench.* 57a (Chadwick); Stobaeus 1.3,11 (p. 54 Wachsmuth) = *Trag. Frag. Adesp.* 487 (p. 934 Nauck-Snell).

Similar remarks abound; e.g. Juvenal, *Sat.* 13.209-10; Aelian, *V.H.* 14.28; Marcus Aurelius i.3; Aulus Gellius 12.11,2; Apuleius, *Flor.* 4.20; Xenophon, *Mem.* 1.4,19; and Critias, Frag. 1 (p. 771 Nauck-Snell), esp. vv. 22-23. For additional references see J. E. B. Mayor's *Juvenal*, comment to *Sat.* 13,209-10 (vol. 2,pp. 281-82).

The popularity of the sentiment in general and of the chreia in particular has caused some differences to develop in the wording of Chreia 49; (1) The πρόσωπον is always Pittacus in the rhetorical texts, but in other writers we find Thales in Diogenes Laertius 1.36; Valerius Maximus 7.2,8; Clement of Alexandria, *Strom.* 5.14; and we find Zeno in Maximus of Tyre 5 (p. 545,21ff. [Combéfis]); Arsenius, p. 265,18f. (2) The question in the chreia is introduced sometimes by ἐρωτηθείς, sometimes by πυθομένου ἐτέρου, etc. The question itself has ποιῶν τι, φαῦλα ποιῶν, φαῦλον τι ποιῶν or τι πράσσων, κακὰ πράσσων. (3) The response, in addition to the regular οὐδέ and the οὐ οὐδέ of Theon (58) sometimes has ἀλλ'οὐδέ, ὅτι μηδέ, and in Clement we find καὶ πῶς . . . ὅς γε οὐδέ. Valerius Maximus has *ne cogitata quidem* which is probably a translation of the usual οὐδὲ διανοούμενος.

Many other minor variations in the wording could be listed, but none of them affects the basic sense of the chreia in any important way. They are merely what one expects to find in a chreia, or in any type of saying, that was as popular and as widely-used in a variety of ways as Chreia 49 seems to have been.

50. Plato

Πλάτων ποτὲ Διογένους ἀπιστῶντος
ἐν ἀγοπᾷ καὶ καλοῦντος αὐτὸν ἐπὶ
τὸ ἄπιστον, "Ꙧ Διόγενες." εἶπεν,
"ὡς χαρίεν ἂν ἦν σου τὸ ἄπλαστον
εἰ μὴ πλαστὸν ἦν."

Once when Diogenes was having lunch in the marketplace and invited him to lunch, Plato said, "Diogenes, how charming your unpretentiousness would be, if it were not so pretentious."

Theon 77-80; Dox 2.257,10-13; Planud 2.17,14-17; Darm 1.142,6-10; *Gnom.*
lat. 445 (p. 167 Sternbach).

In each occurrence of this chreia, the form and wording
remain virtually constant. On Diogenes eating in the marketplace, see, e.g. Diogenes
Laertius 6.22,58 and 69. On the numerous instances of enmity
between Diogenes and Plato, see Diogenes Laertius 6.24-26,
40-41, and 53.

51. Plato

Πλάτων ὁ φιλόσοφος τοὺς τῆς ἀρετῆς
κλῶνας ἔφη ἱδρῶτι καὶ πόνοις φύεσθαι.

Plato the philosopher used to say that the off-
shoots of virtue grow by sweat and toil.

Theon 161-63; Aphth 8-9; Dox 2.254,12-13; 256,12-13; 258,23-24; 260,10-11;
264,14-15; Planud 2.18,16-17; Matt 1.122,26-27; Darm 1.143,2-3; EpitAnon
1.129,22-23.

This chreia, although it is rather popular in the rhetorical
tradition, seems not to appear outside it, nor does it appear
to be derived from a Platonic passage. At any rate, it is
missing even from the collection of passages in A. Riginos
(*Platonica: The Anecdotes concerning the Life and Writings of
Plato* [Leiden: Brill, 1976]).

52. Plato

Πλάτων ἔφησεν τὰς Μούσας ἐν ταῖς
ψυχαῖς τῶν εὐφυῶν οἰκεῖν.

Plato said that the Muses dwell in the souls of
the gifted.

Hermog 7-8; Prisc 9-10; NicMyra 136-37; ScholAnon 2.588,5-6.

This chreia, which seems not to occur outside the
rhetorical tradition, appears in two forms within it. The simpler
form, as shown above, belongs to Hermog (and, of course,
Prisc). In this form the chreia is, to use Theon's more precise
terminology (cf. Theon, lines 36-40), ἀποφαντικὸν καθ' ἑκούσιον (cf.
Hermog 28-29: ἀποφαντικαί; NicMyra 131-34: ἀπλαῖ). NicMyra (cf.
also ScholAnon), however, not only recites the chreia
differently (changing εὐφυῶν to παιδευομένων) but alters its
form. He adds a question—"on being asked where the Muses
dwell"—and hence turns the chreia into one which Theon would
call ἀποκριτικὸν κατὰ πύσμα (Theon 46-49; cf. Hermog 29: πυσματική,
and NicMyra 135: αἱ [sc. χρεῖαι] πρὸς τὴν ἐρώτησιν). In sentiment

the chreia is similar to Chreia 40.

53. Pyrrhus

Πύρρος ὁ τῶν Ἠπειρωτῶν βασιλεύς,
ζητούντων τινῶν παρὰ πότον πότερος
κρείττων αὐλητὴς Ἀντιγεννίδας ἢ
Σάτυρος, "Ἐμοὶ μέν," εἶπε, "στρα-
τηγὸς Πολυσπέρχων."

Pyrrhus, the king of Epirus, when some people
were debating over wine whether Antigennidas or
Satyrus was the better flute-player, said, "In
my opinion, Polysperchon is the better general."

Theon 174-78; Dox 2.259,4-7; Planud 2.18,25-19,2; Darm 1.143,9-12.

Plutarch, *Reg. et imp. apoth.* 184C; *Pyrrhus*, ch. 8 (387D); Stobaeus 4.13,57
(p. 367 Hense).

In addition to numerous minor variations in the wording
of the different versions of this chreia, we find two πρόσωπα:
Pyrrhus in Theon, Plutarch, and Stobaeus; it is Epameinondas
in Dox, Planud, and Darm.

The rhetoricians cite this chreia as an example of one
which contains a change of subject. To make such a change
more feasible and effective, the chreia mentions a discussion
which takes place over wine and concerns two flute-players
(Antigennidas of Thebes was the son of Satyrus). Flute-
players often appear as objects of ridicule (cf., for example,
Plutarch, *Reg. et imp. apoth.* 193F; 200C), and so Pyrrhus (or
Epameinondas) changes the discussion to a more serious
subject, i.e. to Polysperchon (or, more commonly, Polyperchon),
one of Alexander's famous generals. As Stobaeus says, he
makes the change διδάσκων ὅτι ἀναγκαῖα δεῖ ζητεῖν καὶ μὴ ἄχρηστα.
For a discussion of the technique used here as well as an
example of a change of subject from music to military matters
and other serious matters, see Plutarch, *Non posse suaviter
vivi* 1095C-1096C.

54. Pythagoras

Πυθαγόρας ὁ φιλόσοφος ἐρωτηθεὶς
πόσος ἐστιν ὁ τῶν ἀνθρώπων βίος,
ἀναβὰς ἐπὶ τὸ δωμάτιον παρέκυψεν
ὀλίγον, δηλῶν διὰ τούτου τὴν
βραχύτητα.

Pythagoras the philosopher, on being asked how
long human life is, went up to his bedroom and

peeked in for a short time, showing thereby its
brevity.

Theon 107-11; Aphth 10-12; JohnSard 43,1-3; Dox 2.251,28-29; 257,16-18;
260,20-21; 261,6-7; 264,25-26; 265,5-7,11-12; EpitAnon 1.129,24-26.

Theon uses this chreia to illustrate a mixed chreia (cf.
Theon, lines 105-7), but his definition is idiosyncratic (see
"General Introduction," above p. 24). Usually a mixed chreia
contains both a saying and an action. On this understanding
the chreia is clearly an action-chreia, as indeed Aphth
classifies it without changing its form (see Aphth 9-12).

Nevertheless, Aphth's recitation differs from Theon's in
having Pythagoras merely stay a short time and then
disappear. In either case, though, by having Pythagoras make
no remark, Theon and Aphth make their attribution εὔστοχος,
since silence was characteristic of Pythagoreans (see, e.g.
Lucian, *Demonax* 14 and Athenaeus 7.308d). Moreover,
Pythagoras' action is rightly classified by Dox as συμβολική
(cf. 2.260,28-29) and thus recalls the oft-cited Pythagorean
σύμβολα (see Diogenes Laertius 8.17-18; Athenaeus 10.452d-e,
Plutarch(?), *De lib. educ.* 12D-F).

But whether Pythagoras went up to his room for a quick
peek or merely remained for a short time, both Theon and
Aphth understand the action in the same way: as indicating
the shortness of life, a common enough notion (see e.g. Dio
Chrysostom, *Orat.* 29.19 and Diogenes Laertius 9.51) but
perhaps too common. At any rate, Dox, who recites this chreia
seven times, never once gives it this interpretation and at
one point (2.251,30) says that Pythagoras' action σοφίαν ἐλέγχει.

55. Pythagoras

Ὁ Πυθαγόρας φιλόσοφος ἀποβὰς καὶ
γράμματα διδάσκων συνεβούλευεν τοῖς
ἑαυτοῦ μαθηταῖς ἐναιμόνων ἀπέχεσθαι.

Pythagoras the philosopher, once he had
disembarked and was teaching writings, used to
counsel his students to abstain from red meat.

BritMus Add ms 37516

This chreia which appears only here in our collection and
seemingly nowhere else nevertheless contains a well-known
Pythagorean tenet and hence is attributed εὐστόχως. For
Pythagorean prohibitions on the eating of meat, see e.g.
Diogenes Laertius 8.33; Philostratus, *V. Apoll.* 1.1,8,21, 32; and
esp. Athenaeus 2.60d and 4.161a-b where πυθαγορίζειν means
"not to eat meat."

336

THE CHREIA IN ANCIENT RHETORIC

Two statements in the chreia require some comment. For two reaons ἀποβάς is clearly intended to refer to Pythagoras' arrival in Italy. First, Italy is the place with which he is most closely associated. Secondly, although he had "disembarked" in many places before reaching Italy and Crotona, it had been as one who was acquiring knowledge, not imparting it. He began to teach only after his arrival in Italy. The other expression here which requires comment is γράμματα διδάσκων which does not have the same meaning that it does in Chreia 44. It may be that γράμματα here refers to Pythagoras' own writings (which in some traditions he is supposed to have composed). See, for example, Diogenes Laertius 8.9 where Diogenes makes a connection between Pythagoras' writings and his teaching.

56. Simonides

(βλαβερῶς) παραινεῖ Σιμωνίδης παίζειν
ἐν τῷ βίῳ καὶ περὶ μηδὲν ἁπλῶς σπουδάζειν.

Simonides' advice to play in life and to be entirely serious about nothing (is harmful).

Theon 371-72.

Although this chreia resembles several others in the collection (cf. 38, 60-61, 67-68) by being a quotation from a poet, it is the only example of this technique in Theon — except of course the double quotation of Homer in Chreia 24, where the purpose of the quotation is more than merely the basis for an analysis of the verses.

This passage in Theon has been accepted as a fragment of Simonides by Bergk (*Poetae Lyrici Graeci*, p. 522) as Frag. 192 and by Page (*Poetae Melici Graeci*, p. 320) as Frag. 646. Theon is our only witness to the passage, but the quotation cannot be exact because it is expressed indirectly, and it does not scan properly. We have no way of knowing how close to the original Theon's version is or what the context or even the nature of Simonides' poem was. The rhetorician seems to have deliberately sought out a quotation around which he could construct a chreia to fit his category of "unsuitability" (see Theon, line 370).

57. Socrates

Σωκράτης ἐρωτηθεὶς εἰ εὐδαίμων
αὐτῷ ὁ Περσῶν βασιλεύς, " Οὐκ ἔχω
λέγειν," εἶπε, " μηδὲ γὰρ εἰδέναι

πῶς ἔχει παιδείας."

Socrates, on being asked whether the Persian
king seemed happy to him, said, "I can't say, for
I can't know where he stands on education."

Theon 70-73; 347-50, cf. 350-54; Dox 2.257, 4-6; Planud 2.17,9-11; Darm
1.142,1-3

The origin of this chreia is Plato, *Gorgias* 470E, and this
fact renders Theon's criticism of Socrates' reply (cf. lines
350-54) unfair unless the rhetorician was unaware of the
original setting of the conversation. Such a lack of knowledge
seems unlikely.

This Platonic passage is used by several writers. Among
them are Cicero, *Tusc. Disp.* 5.12,35; Plutarch(?) *De lib. educ.*
6A; and Dio Chrysostom, *Orat.* 3.1 (cf. 3.29-32). See also *Gnom.
Vat.* 496 (pp. 183-84 Sternbach) for additional references.

58. Socrates

Σωκράτης ὁ φιλόσοφος, 'Απολλοδώρου
τινὸς γνωρίμου λέγοντος αὐτῷ, " 'Α-
δικῶς σου θάνατον κατέγνωσαν 'Αθη-
ναῖοι," γελάσας ἔφη, " Σὺ δὲ ἐβούλου
δικαίως; "

Socrates the philosopher, when a certain student
named Apollodorus said to him, "The Athenians
have unjustly condemned you to death," said with
a laugh, "But did you want them to do it justly?"

Theon 143-46; Dox 2.265,16-20.

Despite the apt and witty reply of Socrates, this chreia
appears, with some variations, in only a few other places:
Xenophon, *Apol.* 28 (an even more wordy version than Chreia
58); Seneca, *De Constan.* 7.3; Diogenes Laertius 2.35 (where
Socrates makes his remark to Xanthippe). See also *Gnom. Vat.*
478 (p. 177 Sternbach) and 487 (p. 181), where similar passages
are listed, and add perhaps Teles 3.93-96 (p. 26 O'Neil) and
Aulus Gellius 12.9,6.

59. Socrates

ἄλλοις μὲν ἄλλα κοσμεῖται· ψυχῆς
δὲ κοσμήτωρ οἰκεῖος μόνος ὁ λόγος.

Some things are adorned by one thing, some by
another, but only reason is the proper adorner
of the soul.

GregCyp 2.269,1-273,14; see esp. 270,9-10.

The passage which GregCyp has written is an ἐργασία of some saying attributed to Socrates, as Hunger (*Die hochsprachliche profane Literatur*, p. 100) has correctly observed. Yet, although the word Χρεία appears as the title, GregCyp has neither quoted the saying nor made an attribution to Socrates except, as NicephBas does in Chreiai 39 and 60, in the ἐργασία itself.

Consequently, it is far from certain what the precise wording of the chreia is, although its general sense is reasonably clear. We have therefore resorted to quoting the words which GregCyp introduces in the Paraphrase of the chreia (270,9-10) with the question Καὶ τί φησι (sc. ὁ Σωκράτης).

The confusion over the identity of the chreia is further complicated by the fact that nothing in the writings on Socrates in Plato and Xenophon seems close enough to GregCyp's discussion for us to make a firm identification (cf. N. G. Wilson, *Scholars of Byzantium* [Baltimore: Johns Hopkins Press, 1983], p. 224). Oddly enough, however, Lucian, *Imag.* 11, uses much of the same vocabulary and imagery which we find in GregCyp's ἐργασία, but uncertainty about Lucian's own sources renders such similarity useless for the purpose of identifying GregCyp's source.

This passage will be dealt with more fully in the second volume of *The Chreia in Ancient Rhetoric*.

60. Sophocles

Χάρις χάριν γάρ ἐστιν ἡ τίκτουσ'ἀεί.

(*Ajax* 522)

For tis kindness that ere begets kindness.

NicephBas 1.445,1.

Like Chreia 38 (cf. also 61, 67-68), this chreia consists merely of a line of verse which has been lifted from its context. Unlike the other examples, the attribution to the author is not a part of the chreia; instead, NicephBas has identified him, as he does Gregory in Chreia 39, in the ἐργασία composed on the verse.

61. Sophocles

"Οἱ φροῦντες εὖ," φησιν Σοφοκλῆς
(Ajax 1252) "κρατοῦσι πανταχοῦ."

"Those who are wise," says Sophocles, "do everywhere prevail."

ProgAnon 1.602,2-3.

Although Walz fails to identify this verse, it is *Ajax* 1252, with only an initial ἀλλ' omitted. Richard Jebb, in his edition of *Ajax* (p. 237), shows that this Sophoclean verse was coupled with a verse of the dramatist Chaeremon (*Trag. Gr. Frag.*, p. 788 Nauck-Snell, Frag. 23) in several collections of "commonplaces and proverbs" (so Jebb), notably those of Maximus Confessor (6th cent.) and Michael Apostolius (15th cent.). See also *Paroemiographi Graeci*, ed. Leutsch and Schneidewin, vol. 2, p. 765.

Like Chreia 60, this Sophoclean verse is also the subject of a fully-developed ἐργασία. For the significance of this chreia and the technique employed see the comment on Chreia 38 (Euripides).

62. Sybarite

Ἀνὴρ Συβαρίτης ἰδὼν Λακεδαιμονίους
ἐπιπόνως ζῶντας οὐ θαυμάζειν ἔφησεν
ὅτι ἐν τοῖς πολέμοις οὐκ ὀκνοῦσιν
ἀποθνήσκειν, ἄμεινον γὰρ εἶναι τὸν
θάνατον τοῦ τοιούτου βίου.

A Sybarite, on seeing the Lacedaemonians living a life of toil, said he did not wonder that in their wars they do not hesitate to die, for death is better than such a life.

Theon 377-81.

Athenaeus 4.138d; 12.518e; Stobaeus 3.29.96 (p. 658 Hense).

Although this chreia appears only once in the rhetorical tradition, its occurrences outside it make this chreia a good example of the variations permissible in recitation. To be sure, the form is always ἀποφαντικὸν κατὰ περίστασιν—note the ἰδών ... ἔφησεν above. The variations, however, occur in the wording. Thus while the Sybarite in Theon's version speaks after having observed the overall toilsome life of the Lacedaemonians, he speaks in the other versions on the basis of more specific observations: the simple diet of their common mess (so Athenaeus) or the ritual beatings with which they were reared from childhood (so Stobaeus).

These variations in the περίστασις are matched by those in the ἀπόφασις. The two versions of Athenaeus differ from those in Theon and Stobaeus in not referring specifically to the readiness of Lacedaemonians to die in war, but even they differ from one another in length, with the second (12.518e) perhaps qualifying as the ἀπόφασις of an expanded chreia (cf. Theon 316-17 and 328-33); A Sybarite said . . . that previously he had been astounded on hearing about the courage of the Lacedaemonians, but now after seeing them he considered them to be no different from other people, for even the most cowardly person would prefer to die rather than endure living such a life.

On the Lacedaemonians' preference for toil, see, e.g. Dio Chrysostom, *Orat.* 32.92-93; on the Sybarites' rejection of toil, see, e.g., Dio Chrysostom, *Orat.* 64.14; and for their notorious luxury, see Athenaeus 6.273b-c; 12.511c; 518c-521f; and 541a-c.

63. Thales

Θαλῆς ὁ Μιλήσιος ἐρωτηθεὶς ὑπό
τινος τί ἐστιν ἀγαθὸν καὶ κακόν,
εἶπεν, " ἡ γλῶττα. "

Thales of Miletus, on being asked by someone
what is good and bad, said, "The tongue."

JohnSard 40,19-20.

This chreia occurs, in one form or another, many times and is attributed to several πρόσωπα besides Thales: For example, Anacharsis (Diogenes Laertius 1.105, etc.), Bias (Plutarch, *De aud.* 38B, etc.), Pittacus (Plutarch, *De garr.* 506C; Frag. 89, etc.), Aesop (*Vit. Aesop.* 1.13). In addition, in Plutarch's *Sept. sapient. conv.* 146F Thales is made to say that Bias once answered the Egyptian king's question by sending him the tongue of a sacrificial victim (cf. Plutarch, *De aud.* 38B). In this way, perhaps, Thales became associated with the saying or perhaps Plutarch is taking advantage of the association to introduce this piece of by-play into the conversation.

In any case, all the men who serve as πρόσωπα in this chreia have one thing in common: each appears on some list of the Seven Wise Men, with the exception of Aesop. Yet he, too, appears at the banquet in Plutarch's *Sept. sapient. conv.* (146B-164D). It may be no mere coincidence, then, that Aesop is the πρόσωπον of Chreia 2 which is similar to Chreia 63.

For an extensive list of occurrences of this chreia see *Gnom. Vat.* 131 (pp. 57-58 Sternbach).

64. Theano

Θεανὼ ἡ Πυθαγορικὴ φιλόσοφος
ἐρωτηθεῖσα ὑπό τινος ποσταία

γυνὴ ἀπ'ἀνδρὸς καθαρὰ εἰς τὸ
Θεσμοφορεῖον κάτεισιν, εἶπεν,
" Ἀπὸ μὲν τοῦ ἰδίου παραχρῆμα,
ἀπὸ δὲ τοῦ ἀλλοτρίου οὐδέποτε."

Theano the Pythagorean philosopher, on being
asked by someone how long after intercourse
with a man does a woman go in purity to the
Thesmophorion, said, "With your own, immediately;
with another's, never."

Theon 62-66; Nic 1.274,8-11; Dox 2.256,28-257,1; Planud 2.17,4-8; Darm
1.141,18-22.

Diogenes Laertius 8.43; Stobaeus 4.23.55 (pp. 586-87 Hense); *Gnom. Par.*
77 (p. 11 Sternbach).

This chreia, despite its popularity within the rhetorical
tradition and without, varies little in its recitation. Thus the
form is always ἀποκριτικὸν κατὰ πύσμα. But even the wording
varies little. The question sometimes refers to the temple
(τὸ Θεσμοφορεῖον in Theon), sometimes to the festival (τὰ
Θεσμοφόρια in Nic, Dox, Planud, and Darm), and sometimes to
no special place or occasion (in Diogenes Laertius, Stobaeus,
and *Gnom Par.*). In addition, the saying is always the same,
except in Nic where it is expressed κατὰ συλλογισμόν (cf. Theon
138); εἰ μὲν ... εἰ δέ.

65. Theocritus

Θεόκριτον ἐξίοντα ἐκ τῆς Ἀντιγόνου
οἰκίας οὐδὲν παρὰ τοῦ βασιλέως δεξ-
άμενον ἤρετό τις, τί ποιεῖ ὁ βασι-
λεύς· ὁ δὲ εἶπε, " Πτωχεύει."

As Theocritus was leaving Antigonus' house
without having received anything from the king,
someone asked him how the king was faring; and
he said, "He's faring poorly."

JohnSard 43,8-10.

This chreia is an example of one in the accusative case
(cf. Chreia 17). JohnSard cites it, along with Chreia 20, as
an example of a witty chreia. Unlike Demosthenes in Chreia
20, however, Theocritus of Chios is an apt πρόσωπον. He appears
frequently as almost a court jester; cf., for example, *Gnom.
Vat.* 338-351 (pp. 132-135 Sternbach) for several such witty
chreiai. Plutarch, too, cites a number of examples, e.g. *Symp.*
2.1 (631E and esp. 633C). One may say of Theocritus that he
lived by his wits and died because of his wit.

66. Theophrastus

Θεόφραστος ἐρωτηθεὶς τί ἐστιν
ἔρως ἔφησε " Πάθος ψυχῆς σχολα-
ζούσης. "

Theophrastus, on being asked what love is, said,
"Passion of an idle soul."

Lib 8.97.11-12

Stobaeus 4.20.66 (p. 468 Hense); *Gnom. Vat.* 332 (p. 130 Sternbach).

This chreia is usually attributed to Theophrastus, and
perhaps aptly, given a similar sentiment in another chreia
attributed to him: Ἔρως δέ ἐστιν ἀλογίστου τινὸς ἐπιθυμίας
ὑπερβολὴ ταχεῖον μὲν ἔχουσα τὴν πρόσοδον, βραδεῖαν δὲ τὴν ἀπόλυσιν
("Love is an excess of some illogical desire with a quick onset
and a slow release"); cf. Stobaeus 4.20.64 (p. 468 Hense). Still,
Packmohr (*De Diogenis apophthegmatis*, 31) knows of MSS that
attribute this chreia to Theano, and the sentiment itself is
not uncommon (see, e.g., Diogenes Laertius 6.51 and Publilius
Syrus 34).

67. Vergil

Publius Vergilius Maro dixit
(*Aen.* 3.57)
　　　　　　　Auri sacra fames.

Publius Vergilius Maro said: "Accursed (is) the
hunger for gold."

Diom 1.310,18

This chreia and the following one, like several others in
this collection, consist of a brief quotation from a poet who
thus becomes the πρόσωπον. Sometimes, as in Chreiai 60-61, the
quotation becomes the subject of an ἐργασία; at other times,
it is used in a κλίσις, as Diom suggests can be done with
Chreiai 67-68, or it can even be the subject of a κατασκευή,
as Theon (280-297) uses Chreia 38, or of an ἀνασκευή, as Theon
(370-372) uses Chreia 56.

68. Vergil

Publius Vergilius Maro dixit
(*Aen.* 4.13),
Degeneres animos timor arguit.

Publius Vergilius Maro said: "Fear reveals base-
born souls."

Diom 1.310,19

See the comment on Chreia 67 for the significance of this chreia and the techniques that may be employed in its use.

INDEX OF ALTERNATE ΠΡΟΣΩΠΑ

Occasionally one of the 68 chreiai in the Catalogue appears with a different πρόσωπον. The list which follows identifies these alternate πρόσωπα together with the one used in the Catalogue. These variants are treated where necessary in the comments to the chreiai.

Aesop, *pro* Diogenes (Chreia 35).

Agesilaus, *pro* Laconian (Chreia 45).

Alexander Molossus, *pro* Antisthenes (Chreia 6).

Anacharsis, *pro* Thales (Chreia 63).

Antigonus, *pro* Alexander (Chreia 4).

Antisthenes, *pro* Isocrates (Chreia 42).

Archidemus, *pro* Laconian (Chreia 45).

Aristotle, *pro* Gregory (Chreia 39); *pro* Isocrates (Chreiai 41 and 43).

Bias, *pro* Bion (Chreia 10); *pro* Thales (Chreia 63).

Cato, *pro* Isocrates (Chreia 43).

Cicero, *pro* Isocrates (Chreia 43).

"Cynicus mordax," *pro* Antisthenes (Chreia 9).

Damonidas, *pro* Damon (Chreia 16).

Demetrius of Phalerum, *pro* Bion (Chreia 10).

Democritus, *pro* Bion (Chreia 10); *pro* Gregory (Chreia 39).

Demosthenes, *pro* Cato (Chreia 12); *pro* Gregory (Chreia 39); *pro* Isocrates (Chreia 43).

Diogenes, *pro* Antisthenes (Chreia 6); *pro* Aristippus *vel etiam pro* Antisthenes (Chreia 9); *pro* Bion (Chreia 10).

Dorion, *pro* Damon (Chreia 16).

Epameinondas, *pro* Pyrrhus (Chreia 53).

Eumonidas, *pro* Damon (Chreia 16).

Homer, see discussion of Chreia 24.

Isocrates, *pro* Gregory (Chreia 39).

Lysander, *pro* Laconian (Chreia 45).

Menander, see discussion of Chreia 38.

Metrodorus, *pro* Aristippus (Chreia 9).

Neilus of Constantinople, *pro* Gregory (Chreia 39).

Philip of Macedon, *pro* Diogenes (Chreia 23).

Pittacus, *pro* Thales (Chreia 63).

Plato, *pro* Aristippus (Chreia 9).

Praxagoras, *pro* Gregory (Chreia 39).

Pythagoras, *pro* Gregory (Chreia 39).

Thales, *pro* Pittacus (Chreia 49).

Theano, *pro* Theophrastus (Chreia 66).

Theocritus of Chios, see discussion of Chreia 9.

Theodorus, *pro* Antisthenes (Chreia 9).

Zeno, *pro* Pittacus (Chreia 49).

INDEX NOMINUM

by

EDWARD N. O'NEIL

Abbreviations:

Aphth	=	Aphthonius of Antioch
Hermog	=	Hermogenes of Tarsus
NicMyra	=	Nicolaus of Myra
Prisc	=	Priscian of Caesarea
Quint	=	Marcus Fabius Quintilianus
Theon	=	Aelius Theon of Alexandria
VatGram	=	Vatican Grammarian

The order of citations follows the sequence in which the authors appear in Volume I: Theon, quint, Hermog, Prisc, Aphth, NicMyra, VatGram.

* = Chief πρόσωπον of a chreia.

Achilles, VatGram 31*. Hero of the *Iliad*.
Aesop, Quint 6; NicMyra 118*. Writer of fables.
Alexander, Theon 88*, 135*, 151*, 158*; NicMyra 88, cf. 99. The Macedonian king.
Antigennidas, Theon 176. Theban flute-player.
Apollodorus, Theon 143. Follower of Socrates.
Aristeides, NicMyra 122*. Athenian statesman.
Aristippus, VatGram 17*, 19*, 21*. Cyrenaic philosopher.
Athenian(s), Theon 145, [318]. See also Attic.
Athens, Theon 364.
Attic, Theon 363. See also Athenian(s).

Bion, Theon 125*, 368*. Cynic philosopher.

Cato, M. Porcius, VatGram 12*. Cato the Elder; Roman statesman.
Crates, Quint 26*. Cynic philosopher.
Croesus, Theon 153. Lydian king.
cynic, (=Antisthenes) VatGram

16; (=Diogenes) Theon 42, 100, 186, 251, 258, 267, 272; VatGram 4, 24.
Cyrenaic, (=Aristippus) VatGram 17.
Cyrus, Titus Genetivus(?), VatGram 9*. Unknown.

Damon, Theon 154*; NicMyra 93*, cf. 100. Gymnastic teacher.
Demosthenes, Theon 356*; Hermog 51; Prisc 54; Aphth 64; NicMyra 62. Athenian orator.
Didymon, Theon 103*, 248*, 262*, 343. Flute-player.
Diogenes, Theon 33*, 41*, 44, 77*, 78*, 80, 89*, 92*, 100*, 139*, 186*, 251*, 257*, 266, 272*; Hermog 10*, 13*; Prisc 12*; Aphth 14*; NicMyra 74*; VatGram 3*, 24*. Cynic philosopher.
Dionysius, VatGram 18. The elder, tyrant of Syracuse.

Epameinondas, Theon 314*, 318*. Theban general.
Epicharmus, quoted: Frag. 287 (Kaibel), Hermog 59; Prisc

SELECT BIBLIOGRAPHY

by

RONALD F. HOCK

Baldwin, C. S. *Medieval Rhetoric and Poetic*. New York: Macmillan, 1928.

Bolognesi, G. "Nuovi contributi allo studio del testo dei *Progymnasmata* di Elio Teone." *Athenaeum* 47 (1969) 32–38.

Bonner, S. F. *Education in Ancient Rome from the elder Cato to the younger Pliny*. Berkeley: University of California, 1977.

Brzoska, J. "Aphthonios (1)." *RE* 1 (1884) 2797–2800.

Cameron, A. "The Date of Priscian's *De laude Anastasii*." *GRBS* 15 (1974) 313–16.

Christ, W. v., Schmid, W., Stählin, O. *Geschichte der griechischen Literatur* (Handbuch der Altertumswissenschaft; 6th edition; Munich: Beck, 1924).

Clark, D. L. "Rhetoric and the Literature of the English Middle Ages." *QJS* 45 (1959) 19–28.

_____. "The Rise and Fall of *Progymnasmata* in Sixteenth and Seventeenth Century Grammar Schools." *SM* 19 (1952) 259–63.

Colson, F. H. "Phaedrus and Quintilian, 1.9.2." *CR* 33 (1919) 59–61.

_____. "Quintilian 1.9 and the 'Chria' in Ancient Education." *CR* 35 (1921) 150–54.

Dibelius, M. *From Tradition to Gospel*. New York: Scribner's, 1935.

Duff, J. *A Literary History of Rome in the Silver Age*. London: Benn, 1960.

Fischel, H. A. "Studies in Cynicism and the Ancient Near East: The Transformation of a Chria." In J. Neusner (ed.), *Religions in Antiquity: Essays in Memory of E. R. Goodenough*. Leiden: Brill, 1968, 372–411.

Gerhard, G. A. *Phoinix von Kolophon*. Leipzig: Teubner, 1909.

Glöckner, S. "Sopatros (10)." *RE* 2nd reihe 5 (1927) 1002–1006.

Gow, A. S. F. "Introduction" to *Machon: The Fragments*. Cambridge: Cambridge University, 1965; esp. 12–15.

Graeven, H. "Die *Progymnasmata* des Nicolaus." *Hermes* 30 (1895) 471–73.

Gronewald, M. "Ein Fragment aus Theon, *Progymnasmata*." *ZPE* 24 (1977) 23–24.

Helm, R. "Priscianus (1)." *RE* 22 (1954) 2327–46.

Hollerbach, H. R. *Zur Bedeutung des Worts* XPEIA. Diss. Köln, 1964.

Hopplicher, O. *De Theone, Hermogene Aphthonioque Progymnasmatum scriptoribus.* Diss. Virceburg, 1884.

Horna, K. "Gnome, Gnomendichtung, Gnomologie." *RE* Suppl. 6 (1935) 74-87 (with additional acomments by K. v. Fritz, 87-90).

Hunger, H. *Die hochsprachliche profane Literatur der Byzantiner* (Handbuch der Altertumswissenschaft; 2 vols.; Munich: Beck, 1978).

Jullien, E. *Les Professeurs de Littérature dans l'ancienne Rome.* Paris: Leroux, 1895.

Kennedy, G. *The Art of Rhetoric in the Roman World.* Princeton: Princeton University, 1972.

_____. *Classical Rhetoric and its Christian and Secular Tradition from Ancient to Modern Times.* Chapel Hill: University of North Carolina, 1980.

_____. *Greek Rhetoric under Christian Emperors.* Princeton: Princeton University, 1983.

_____. *Quintilian.* New York: Twayne, 1969.

Kustas, G. L. "The Function and Evolution of Byzantine Rhetoric." *Viator* 1 (1970) 55-73.

_____. *Studies in Byzantine Rhetoric* (Analecta Vlatadon 17; Thessaloniki: Patriarchal Institute for Patristic Studies, 1973).

Lana, I. *I Progimnasmi di Elio Teone.* Turin: Università di Torino, 1959.

Luscher, A. *De Prisciani studiis Graecis.* Diss. Breslau, 1912.

Marrou, H. I. *A History of Educatioin in Antiquity.* New York: Sheed & Ward, 1956.

Montfasani, J. *George of Trebizond: A Biography and a Study of his Rhetoric and Logic.* Leiden: Brill, 1976.

Morison, S. E. *Harvard College in the Seventeenth Century.* Cambridge: Harvard University, 1936.

Nadeau, R. "The *Progymnasmata* of Aphthonius in Translation." *SM* 19 (1952) 264-85.

Norton, A. O. "Harvard Textbooks and Reference Books of the Seventeenth Century." *CSM* 28 (1933) 361-438.

Orinsky, K. *De Nicolai Myrensis et Libanii quae feruntur progymnasmatis*. Diss. Breslau, 1920 (see review by E. Richssteig in *PhW* 41 [1921] 697-701).

Patterson, A. *Hermogenes and the Renaissance: Seven Ideas of Style*. Princeton: Princeton University, 1970.

Postgate, J. P. "Phaedrus and Seneca." *CR* 33 (1919) 19-24.

_____. "Quintilian, 1.9.2." *CR* 33 (1919) 108.

Rabe, H. "Aus Rhetoren-Handscriften. 1. Nachrichten über das Leben des Hermogenes." *RhM* 62 (1907) 247-62.

Reichel, G. *Quaestiones progymnasmaticae*. Diss. Leipzig, 1909.

Robinson, R. P. "Ethologia or Aetiologia in Suetonius' *De Grammaticis* 4 and Quintilian, 1.9." *CPh* 15 (1920) 370-79.

Radermacher, L. "Hermogenes (22)." *RE* 8 (1912) 865-77.

Robbins, V. K. "Pronouncement Stories and Jesus' Blessing of the Children: A Rhetorical Approach." *Semeia* 29 (1984) 43-74 (with additional comments by R. F. Hock, 97-101).

Russell, D. A. *Greek Declamation*. New York: Cambridge, 1983.

Salaman, M. "Priscianus und seine Schülerkreis in Konstantinopel." *Philologus* 123 (1979) 91-96.

Saller, R. "Anecdotes as Historical Evidence for the Principate." *G & R* 27 (1980) 69-83.

Schissel von Fleschenberg, O. "Die Einteilung der Chrie bei Quintilian." *Hermes* 68 (1933) 245-48.

_____. "Die Familie des Minukianos." *Klio* 21 (1926) 361-73.

_____. *Novellendränze Lukians*. Halle: Neumeyer, 1912.

Smith, R. W. *The Art of Rhetoric in Alexandria*. The Hague: Nijhoff, 1974.

Stegemann, W. "Minukianos (1)." *RE* 15 (1932) 1975-86.

_____. "Nikolaos (21)." *RE* 17 (1936) 424-57.

_____. "Onasimos." *RE* 35 (1939) 406-408.

_____. "Theon (5)." *RE* 5A (1934) 2037-54.

Susemihl, F. *Geschichte der griechischen Litteratur in der Alexandrinerzeit*. 2 vols.; Leipzig: Teubner, 1891-92.

Wartensleben, G. v. *Begriff der griechischen Chreia und Beiträge ihrer Form*. Heidelberg: Winter, 1901.

Wilson, N. G. *Scholars of Byzantium*. Baltimore: Johns Hopkins University, 1983.

Winter, J. G. "Some Literary Papyri in the University of Michigan Collection." *TAPA* 53 (1922) 128–41.

Winterbottom, M. *Problems in Quintilian* (BICS Suppl. 25; London: Institute of Classical Studies, 1970).

Wolf, E. 2nd. *The Library of James Logan of Philadelphia*. Philadelphia: Library Company of Philadelphia, 1974.

Wright, F. A. and T. A. Sinclair. *A History of Later Latin Literature*. London: Dawson, 1969.